The Advaitika and Tāntrika
Philosophy of Śaṅkara

Rajesh Kumar Jha

BlueRose ONE .com
Stories Matter

BLUEROSE PUBLISHERS
India | U.K.

For permissions requests or inquiries regarding this publication,
please contact:

BLUEROSE PUBLISHERS
www.BlueRoseONE.com
info@bluerosepublishers.com
+91 8882 898 898
+4407342408967

ISBN: 978-93-5668-112-5

Cover design: Muskan Sachdeva
Typesetting: Pooja Sharma

First Edition: July 2023

Dedication

I reverently dedicate this work to the divine feet of Lord Sadāśiva and Goddess Tripurasundarī, whose love, intelligence and bliss permeate each and every corner of this cosmos and also the infinite transcendent sphere.

Acknowledgement

This volume represents the materialization of the blessings and well wishes of so many people who have influenced and uplifted my understanding of Indian philosophy and religious-cultural tradition. At the outset, I would like to express my gratitude to the Department of Philosophy, Delhi University, for giving me the opportunity to learn the basics of Philosophy and nurture my philosophical skills at the research levels of M.Phil. and Ph.D. The present volume is largely based on my Doctoral thesis, completed and awarded at Delhi University. I shall forever be grateful to my alma mater for enhancing my academic skills and granting me my primary academic identity. In this connection, I cannot sufficiently express my gratitude to Prof. H. S. Prasad, who supervised my Doctoral thesis. I am especially indebted to him for the full faith he reposed in me by giving me complete freedom to pursue and shape my doctoral research project. His vast research experience and expertise have always been a constant source of inspiration for me. Nonetheless, despite his erudite knowledge and expertise, he was always accessible as a friend, philosopher and guide. In addition to his academic support, he was always ready to give me a personal helping hand in times of crisis. I shall be forever indebted to him for all that I have received from him and I feel privileged to have been his research scholar in Delhi University.

Next, I would like to express my gratitude to late Prof. R.C. Pandeya, who was instrumental in encouraging my philosophical curiosity during my Post Graduation and M.Phil. stages. He introduced me to the wonders of Indian philosophical tradition and also supervised my M. Phil. dissertation on "Advaitism as Revealed in the Saundarya-Laharī". I still recall his fatherly affection with wet eyes. My solemn salutations to his departed soul. I take this opportunity to express my heartfelt thanks to Prof. G. L. Pandit also, who showered great affection on me and showed enormous faith in my academic potential, especially in the field of Kāśmīra Śaivism. His encouragement and guidance definitely helped in shaping my academic direction and ambition.

I would also like to express my heartfelt thanks to Prof. V.N. Jha, late Prof. N.S.S. Raman and Prof. Jodh Singh for appreciating my doctoral research and encouraging me to go further in the field of this research. Words of appreciation from these eminent academic figures surely meant a lot to me. My research period was quite long and three institutions sustained my research during this period. Firstly, I would like to thank University Grants Commission for awarding me UGC-JRF and SRF, which sustained my research for approximately three years. Next, I would like to thank Jawahar Lal Nehru Memorial Fund, Teen Murti House, New Delhi, for awarding me Jawahar Lal Nehru Memorial Fund Scholarship for Doctoral Studies, which sustained my doctoral research for two years. In this connection, I would like to especially express my gratitude to veteran academician and politician, erstwhile Crown Prince of Jammu & Kashmir, former Union Cabinet Minister and Indian Ambassador to U.S.A., Dr. Karan Singh, who showed keen interest in my doctoral research and granted me the J.L. Nehru Memorial Scholarship, as the Chairman of the selection committee. Even after the award of the scholarship, he provided me with the opportunity to personally interact with him on multiple occasions in I.I.C., New Delhi, wherein he posed many queries regarding my research and also gave me riddles to resolve in the course of my doctoral research. Once again, he has been so kind and gracious to bless me with his Foreword for this volume. I shall be forever indebted to him for his affection, support and encouragement. Next, I would like to express my gratitude to Dr. Ashwini Kumar, Department of Philosophy, Zakir Husain College, Delhi University and the erstwhile college Principal, late Dr. S.G. Hashmi, for giving me the opportunity to teach in the Department of Philosophy,

Zakir Husain College, which helped me sustain my research activity for approximately five years. I humbly accept that without the support of these three great institutions my doctoral research could not have materialized the way it did. Also, I humbly pay my obeisance at the feet of Gauḍapādācārya, Ādi Śaṅkarācārya, Toṭakācārya (Ānandagiri) and Karapātrī ji (Swāmī Hariharānanda Saraswatī), without whose blessings and guidance it would have been absolutely impossible to get any worthwhile insight into the difficult and mystical subject matter of this research project. Whatever is there in this work, is nothing but a reiteration of the teachings of these great spiritual masters. A thousand salutations to them!

I would also like to thank my college time dearest buddy Pramod Kumar (I.A.A.S.), who always stood by me like a rock in times of crises when I felt abandoned by almost everyone around me. Words fail to express my love and gratitude towards my dearest friend. I cannot forget to express my respect and obeisance towards my late uncle (Foofa ji) Ācārya Shri Munnilal Jha, who was a great scholar of Sanskrit grammar, Vedic astrology and Tāntrika philosophy. It was he who introduced me to the wonderous world of philosophy, religion and Indian mysticism at a very early age. He was a scholar and sage simultaneously and I feel myself blessed to have received his blessings and guidance as a young boy. He truly moulded my worldview forever. I also express my love and deep gratitude to my parents who have been my source of constant inspiration and guides in the tumultuous journey of life. I am whatever I am, because of them only. I would also like to express my love and gratitude to my better half, Dr. Manju, for giving me her unconditional support and guidance in both academic and extra-academic spheres. Her presence itself is a constant source of inspiration for me. I cannot forget to lovingly thank my sweet daughters, Nitya and Sadhyaa, for unconditionally coming to my help whenever I needed them. Last but not the least, I bow down to the omnipresent love, intelligence and inspiration of Lord Śiva and Goddess

Tripurasundarī, without whose love and blessings I could not have done anything whatsoever. I reverently pay my obeisance at their divine lotus feet.

Foreword

It is a matter of pleasure for me to see this book entitled "The Advaitika and Tāntrika Philosophy of Śaṅkara" address some of the core issues related to Advaitika metaphysics and spiritual disciplines. I am glad that this research project was sponsored by the Jawahar Lal Nehru Memorial Fund, Teen Murti House, and I was instrumental in making this decision. The Advaitika philosophy expounded by Śaṅkara represents one of the most important philosophical schools blossoming in the Indian subcontinent. Despite the fact that the contribution of Gauḍapāda to Śaṅkara's philosophy is indisputable, Śaṅkara's own effort towards the systematic exposition of the Advaitika philosophy has been gigantic. However, the contemporary understanding of Śaṅkara's Advaitika philosophy is largely based on his commentaries on the prasthānatraya, consisting of the principal Upaniṣads, the Bhagavadgītā and the Brahma sūtras. Apart from these, Śaṅkara had also authored generally acclaimed tāntrika texts like the Saundarya-laharī and Prapañcasāra Tantra. The contents of these texts have unfortunately remained mostly untouched while trying to understand the philosophical ideas of Śaṅkara.

A holistic comprehension of Śaṅkara's philosophy should not ignore his independent works because they have great potential to reflect his ideas in totality. This academic lapse is sought to be addressed in this work where the Advaitika philosophy of Śaṅkara, as reflected in his commentary works, has been juxtaposed with the contents of Saundarya-laharī and Prapañcasāra Tantra. This juxtaposition has led to some interesting implications for the philosophical contours of Śaṅkara. The logical riddles pertaining to the nature and relationship of Saguṇa and Nirguṇa Brahman, the status and process of jīvanamukti, the significance of actions and devotion are some of the vulnerable points in the contemporary understanding of Śaṅkara's Advaitism. The present work seeks to suggest coherent solutions to these riddles in the light of the holistic understanding of Śaṅkara's philosophy which takes note of both his commentaries and independent works, which are largely complementary. This holistic philosophical framework incorporates the salient features of both Advaitika and Tāntrika philosophies, which has led the author to suggest a new term for it, namely 'Tantrādvaita.' The author finds the philosophical framework of Tantrādvaita consistent and in harmony with the primary tenets of Advaitika and Tāntrika philosophies.

Interestingly, the author has also traced Gauḍapāda's involvement with the philosophical framework of Tantrādvaita, with reference to his Subhagodaya-stotram and Śrīvidyāratna-sūtram. The author has also discussed the concept and desirability of Advaitika devotion (advaita-bhakti) in the context of Tantrādvaita and sought to validate his point by highlighting the historical fact that Śaṅkara had established the sacred seats at Badrikāśrama, Dwārkā, Purī and Śriṅgerī, dedicated to Lord Viṣṇu and Goddess Saraswatī. In addition to these, he had also enshrined Goddess Tripurasundarī, the deity praised in Saundarya-laharī, in the Kāñcī Kāmakoṭi Pīṭham. Thus, with the help of philosophical, hermeneutic and historical arguments the author seeks to present a holistic and consistent framework of Śaṅkara's philosophy. I hope this work will facilitate a more comprehensive understanding of Śaṅkara's philosophy and I commend the author for his valuable contribution.

Karan Singh

Nov. 11, 2022

Prologue

It is a matter of immense happiness to go through the present scholarly book "*The Advaitika and Tāntrika Philosophy of Śaṅkara*" which is an outgrowth of Ph.D. thesis *(The Concept of Devotion in the Prasthānatraya Bhāṣya-s of Śaṅkara in the Light of his Saundarya-Laharī)*, written by my erstwhile outstanding student, Rajesh Kumar Jha, whose relation with me goes back to around thirty years and who is now a Senior Professor of Philosophy in the Department of Philosophy and Religion, Banaras Hindu University. This book is an integration of philosophy and religious devotion (i.e., Advaitism and Tāntrism) within Śaṅkara's Advaitika conceptual framework. He has gone deep into Śaṅkara's primary sources, such as three sets of commentaries on the principal Upaniṣads, Bādarāyaṇa's *Brahmasūtra* and the *Bhagavadgītā* (i.e., the *Prasthānatraya-bhāṣya*) and numerous independent texts like *Saundarya-laharī*, apart from many more relevant texts like (1) Gauḍapāda's *Subhagodaya-stotram*, *Śrīvidyāratna-sūtram* (with the commentary of Śaṅkarāraṇya) and the *Māṇḍūkya-kārikā*; (2) Śaṅkara's *Prapañcasāra-tantra,* along with the commentary of Śaṅkara's brilliant disciple Padmapāda on it (3) Śaṅkara's *Vyāsabhāṣya-vivaraṇa*, a commentary on the *Vyāsa-bhāṣya* on Patañjali's *Yogasūtra*; (4) Śaṅkara's *Pañcīkaraṇam*; (5) the *Vivekacūḍāmani*; (6) *Lalitāsahasranāma* (a part of *Brahmāṇḍa-purāṇa*); and (7) some of the principal commentaries on *Saundarya-laharī*, such as the *Lakṣmīdharā*, the *Saubhāgya-vardhinī*, the *Aruṇāmodinī* and *Ānandagirīyā*. Note that the book has rich bibliographical references of both original and secondary sources, lucid expression, advaitika methodology, and textual grounding, which are requirements not easy to execute in an appropriate manner. This book shows authentic approach to the structure and contents of the text, which marks the author's deep textual and semantic understanding, exposition, and interpretation of Śaṅkara's philosophical Advaitism and devotional Tāntrism.

Moreover, the author has tried to show the consistency and compatibility of Advaitism with the Tāntrika literature composed by both Śaṅkara and Gauḍapāda. In addition to these historical and textual indicators, the author has discussed the unique features associated with the concepts of *Śiva*, *Śakti*, *Paramaśiva*, *Parāśakti*, *Nāda*, *Bindu*, etc., as presented in the *Saundarya-laharī* and has tried to show their basic consistency with the Advaitika framework. In fact, this work even points out the imperativeness of looking into these works of Śaṅkara and Gauḍapāda for developing a comprehensive understanding of the religious, philosophical and mystical aspects of Advaitism to such an extent that the author coins and suggests the term *'Tantrādvaita'* for the holistic philosophical framework of Śaṅkara. Many enigmatic philosophical issues related with the concepts of Saguṇa Brahman, Nirguṇa Brahman, Māyā, Jīvanmukti, creation and dissolution of the cosmos etc. may be approached in a more consistent manner from this holistic perspective. The oft repeated charge of other-worldliness levelled against Advaitism too can be contested more effectively from the holistic perspective of Tantrādvaita.

In his research pursuit, the author has given central importance to Śaṅkara's *Saundarya-laharī*, which is a text that is usually associated with the Tāntrika tradition and as a consequence of that, scholars are hesitant in regarding it as a work of Śaṅkara. There is a general perception among the scholars of Advaitism that the content of Saundarya-laharī is incompatible with the basic philosophical framework of Śaṅkara's Advaitism. This perception has been contested thoroughly by the author in this work. Firstly, it has been pointed out that there are presently thirty-five extant commentaries on the *Saundarya-laharī* available in the Indian subcontinent, out of which thirty-four commentaries clearly attribute its authorship to Śaṅkara, while only one attributes its authorship to *'draviḍa-śiśu'*, which too has been interpreted by many scholars as pointing towards Śaṅkara. Secondly, Śaṅkara is widely believed to be associated with the establishment of the four Pīṭha-s, situated in the four directions of the Indian peninsula, which have Lord Viṣṇu and Goddess Śārdā as their presiding deities. As such, the different forms of Saguṇa Brahman had been consecrated as the presiding deities in these four Pīṭha-s by Śaṅkara, which is sufficient to highlight the significance of Saguṇa Brahman and the importance of practising devotion towards the Saguṇa Brahman, in the philosophical framework of Śaṅkara. Thirdly, Śaṅkara has also been traditionally associated with the establishment of the Kāñcī Kāmakoṭi Pīṭham at Kanchipuram, where Devī Kāmākṣī is the presiding deity, who also happens to be the primary deity being addressed and eulogized in the *Saundaryalaharī*.

The present volume is undoubtedly a work that had taken its foundational shape under my formal research supervision. As such, I had the first opportunity to notice the novelty associated with this work. It goes without saying that Advaitism is one of the most well-known philosophical schools in the Indian context. Therefore, the basic philosophical framework of this school is usually understood in a clear manner. Despite that, the author has focused on raising new questions and possibilities related to the metaphysical framework of Advaitism.

In view of the above-mentioned points of discussion and examination presented in this volume, it may be safely presumed that this work will offer the scholars of Advaitism and Indian philosophy an opportunity to take a fresh look at the thoughts of Śaṅkara and Gauḍapāda and notice the linkages existing between their Advaitika and Tāntrika concepts.

Hari Shankar Prasad

Former Professor, Head & Dean

Department of Philosophy

Faculty of Arts

University of Delhi

Preface

Advaitism is one of the leading philosophical schools of Indian origin and it has fascinated me since my childhood. During my high school days, I had the first opportunity to come across the Saundarya-laharī of Śaṅkara and the first impression of that work left me bedazzled with its philosophical depth, even though I did not have any philosophical training at that stage. Much later, at the research level I decided to study Advaitism from the perspective of Śaṅkara's Saundarya-laharī in both my M.Phil. and Ph.D. My respected teacher, late Prof. R. C. Pandeya, played a crucial role in encouraging me to do research in the light of Saundarya-laharī. He was also my research Supervisor at my M.Phil. level. After studying Advaitism formally at my P.G. level I felt confused about the status and significance of Saguṇa Brahman or Īśvara in the metaphysical framework of Advaitism, especially when I noticed that all the four Pīṭha-s or religious-spiritual centres established by Śaṅkara had the different forms of Saguṇa Brahman installed there as the presiding deities. In the meantime, I also came across Śaṅkara's Śivānanda-laharī, his commentary on Viṣṇu-sahasranāma, Prapañcasāra-tantra, as well as many other hymns addressed to various deities. All these circumstantial evidences prompted me to wonder whether the academic understanding of Advaitism truly reflects the original religious and philosophical outlook of Śaṅkara.

With this backdrop, I ventured into formal research at my M.Phil. level and my research work was later published as "Advaitism as revealed in the Saundarya-Lahari " (in *Philosophy, Grammar and Indology,* Sri Satguru Publications, New Delhi, 1992). After completing this panoramic study of Saundarya-laharī from the viewpoint of Advaitism, I decided to study this field more deeply at my doctoral research level and my respected teachers in the Department of Philosophy, Delhi University, graciously helped me in deciding the exact focus and topic of my doctoral research as "The Concept of Devotion in the Prasthānatraya-Bhāṣyas of Śaṅkara in the Light of his Saundarya-Laharī ". In the initial stages of my doctoral research itself I came across the Subhagodaya-stotram and Śrīvidyāratna-sūtram of Gauḍapāda, which convinced me to a great extent about the plausibility of my research hypothesis. It also indicated that what I was noticing in the case of Śaṅkara with reference to his Saundarya-laharī, was actually very much there even at the level of Gauḍapāda. After that it was just a matter of patient study and analysis for understanding the intricate details of the philosophical and religious framework of Śaṅkara's Advaitism.

Saundarya-laharī is usually regarded as a Tāntrika text by contemporary scholars due to its elaborate discussion about the various *cakra-s* and the mystical *Śrī-yantra*. The primary deity addressed in this work is *Devī Tripurasundarī*. The first forty-one stanzas of this work constitute the Ānanda-laharī, which is immensely rich in terms of philosophical significance and calls for a patient study. The explicitly Tāntrika orientation of this work has persuaded most contemporary scholars to treat it as a work that is not associated with Śaṅkara because prima facie the metaphysical framework of Advaitism seems incompatible with the metaphysical framework of Saundarya-laharī. This conclusion seems to be arising more out of academic convenience, rather than academic research. Presently, there are thirty-five commentaries on Saundarya-laharī available throughout the expanse of India and Nepal. Out of these thirty-five commentaries, thirty-four commentaries attribute its authorship to Śaṅkara, whereas only one commentary attributes its authorship to *'draviḍa-śiśu'*, which too has been interpreted by many scholars as pointing towards Śaṅkara. Moreover, this is not the only ground for accepting Saundarya-laharī as a genuine work of Śaṅkara. One also needs to take into account Śaṅkara's other independent works like Prapañcasāra-tantra, Śivānanda-laharī, his commentary on Viṣṇusahasranāma, apart from many other hymn works attributed to him, wherein he has praised various forms of Saguṇa Brahman elaborately. In all these works, apart from the significance of true intuitive knowledge of the Self/Brahman, the emphasis on the desirability of devotion to Saguṇa Brahman cannot be overlooked. This is further corroborated by the forms of Saguṇa Brahman installed as the presiding deities in the four sacred *Pīṭha-s* established by Śaṅkara. In addition to these four *Pīṭha-s,* the fifth *Pīṭha* of Kāñcī Kāmakoṭi, situated at Kanchipuram, Tamil Nadu, is also traditionally believed to be established by Śaṅkara and here the presiding deity is the same as the primary deity of Saundarya-laharī, namely *Devī Kāmākṣī,* also known as *Devī Tripurasundarī.* It is also fascinating to note that the primary deity of Gauḍapāda's Subhagodaya-stotram too is *Devī Tripurasundarī.*

All these facts are sufficient to clearly indicate the importance of Saguṇa Brahman and the desirability of practising devotion towards Saguṇa Brahman in the context of Śaṅkara's philosophical framework. However, the obvious logical objection facing the desirability of devotion in an Advaitika metaphysical framework would be regarding the inevitable requirement of the distinction between the deity and the devotee, for the possibility of devotion. At this juncture, it is worth recalling a basic premise of Śaṅkara that as long as the intuitive knowledge of the identity of the Self with Brahman has not been realized, one ought to treat the world of duality as real and relevant and act accordingly. Thus, as long as the supreme intuitive realization of non-duality has not taken place, there is no logical inconsistency in the plausibility of devotion. After this, the question about the desirability of devotion in an Advaitika framework arises. In order to understand the need for devotion, it is worth noting that the ordinary human mind is inherently incapable of discursively imagining and grasping the transcendental non-dual Brahman. This means the ordinary human mind cannot effectively meditate on the non-dual Para Brahman and this is further corroborated by the negative and indicative Upaniṣadika suggestions regarding the nature of Para Brahman. Due to the phenomenal moulding of the ordinary human mind in terms of space, time, causality, plurality, etc., even if one tries to meditate on the transcendental non-dual Brahman, one will only be successful in meditating on the Saguṇa Brahman. Further, all phenomenal beings are considered bound by the karmic chains and their fructifying or Prārabdha karmas determine their important life conditions and experiences to a large extent. At the same time, it is Īśvara or Saguṇa Brahman who is considered the bestower of the fruits of karmas. That is, out of the plethora of past karmas waiting to fructify, which karmas will actually fructify first, is a matter to be decided ultimately by the sweet will of God. Hence, unless and until God facilitates the cleansing of the mind and heart of a phenomenal being by permitting the fructification of spiritually uplifting karmas, it is impossible for anyone to move towards spiritual enlightenment. However, if one wins the grace of God by acknowledging one's utter helplessness and surrendering to God's will, as well as acknowledging the supreme authority and control of God over the entire dualistic cosmos, God bestows grace upon that phenomenal being by permitting the early fructification of spiritually uplifting karmas, which in turn facilitates the removal of spiritual ignorance and takes one towards the supreme liberating non-dual intuitive realization. Acknowledging the supreme authority and control of God and surrendering to His will is but the essence of devotion or *bhakti*. The cultivation and perfection of such devotion facilitates the supreme non-dual realization through the grace of God. Without the helping hand of God all phenomenal beings are but puppets in hands of their Prārabdha karmas, which is impossible for them to overcome through their egoistic actions. Therefore, it makes great practical sense to cultivate devotion to

God for facilitating one's evolution towards the supreme liberating non-dual intuitive realization.

The Tāntrika tradition elaborately discussed in the Saundarya-laharī is known as the *Samaya* tradition of Tantra, in contrast with the *Miśra* and *Kaula* traditions of Tantra. The Subhagodaya-stotram too is an illustration in the discussion of the *Samaya Tantra*. Saundarya-laharī clearly states that the *Samaya Tantra* is in complete conformity with the Vedas. The *Samaya Tantra* focuses on the metaphysics and spiritual disciplines related to the *Śrī-vidyā* tradition. According to this tradition, the various *āvaraṇa-s* of the *Śrī-cakra* represent the various levels of epistemic manifestations of the non-dual transcendent reality (Parama tattva). This sequential representation pertains to both the microcosm *(Piṇḍa)* and the macrososm *(Brahmāṇḍa)*. That is to say, the non-dual transcendent consciousness of Para Brahman *or Śiva-Śakti sāmarasya* epistemically manifests sequentially through the nine levels represented by the nine *āvaraṇa-s* of the *Śrī-cakra*. These nine levels are shown as having a corresponding identity with the various *cakra-s* and nodes lying in the pathway of the *Kuṇḍalinī* in the individual human body or the microcosm *(Piṇḍa)*. The entire pathway of the *Kuṇḍalinī,* starting from the *Kula-sahasrāra* and going up to the *Akula-sahasrāra,* represents the evolutionary pathway of consciousness from the level of gross elements up to the non-dual transcendent Para Brahman. This entire evolutionary pathway of consciousness may also be compared with the seven constitutive levels of Praṇava (A, U, M, Bindu, Nāda, Śakti and Śānta), as indicated by Śaṅkara in his *Prapañcasāra-tantra*. It can also be seen in the light of the *Catuṣpāda Praṇava* discussion of Gauḍapāda's *Māṇḍūkya-kārikā*.

The *Bindu* and *Nāda* levels have a very special significance in the evolutionary pathway of the *Kuṇḍalinī*. They are situated between the *Ājñā cakra* and the *Sahasrāra*. The *Sahasrāra cakra* has a corresponding identity with the non-dual transcendent Brahman, whereas the *Nāda* level represents the level of *Sadāśiva* and *Śuddhavidyā* which is the first epistemic projection of duality, although it is totally beyond the realm of ignorance or *avidyā*. The next level of epistemic manifestation is *Bindu* which represents the level of *Navātman Śiva* and *Nava-prakṛtyātmaka Śakti,* who are jointly responsible for the epistemic projections of the *jīva-s, deśa, kāla* etc. which lead to the projection of the phenomenal cosmos, starting from the causal state to the gross material state. Thus, the level representing the initiation of the *jīva-bhāva* is Bindu, which is certainly down the ladder in comparison with the non-dual level of the *Sahasrāra.* During the evolutionary course of consciousness through the *Kuṇḍalinī* pathway, its rise up to the *Bindu* level shows the attainment of the *jīvanmukti* state, while the merger of *jīva-cidābhāsa* in the consciousness represented by the *Nāda* or *Sahasrāra* levels depicts the complete sublation of *jīvabhāva* i.e., the *videhamukti* state. The state of *jīva-cidābhāsa* at the *Bindu* level is a dormant, passive seed-like state, where the *jīva* cannot act as a limited subject, but while evolving up to the *Bindu* level it becomes aware of its identity with the *Navātman Śiva,* which in turn is constantly aware of its basic ontological identity with the non-dual transcendent Brahman. This intuitive awareness of the *jīva* regarding its basic identity with the non-dual Brahman is the highest *Brahma-jñāna* accessible to a *jivanmukta* person. This scheme of epistemic manifestation levels goes a long way in resolving the puzzle of *jīvanmukti, Brahma-jñāna* and *prārabdha karma-s.*

The concept of the transcendent non-dual consciousness has been represented as the *Sāmarasya* state of *Paramaśiva* and *Parāśakti,* which is identical with the highest Brahman. It is the same transcendent absolute that is referred to as both *Paramaśiva* and *Parāśakti,* where *Paramaśiva* highlights the substantive metaphysical aspect of that absolute and *Parāśakti* highlights the epistemically active aspect of that absolute. This conception has been strongly emphasized in the very first stanza of the Saundarya-laharī by Śaṅkara and this idea is very significant in resolving the Nirguṇa Saguṇa Brahman puzzle in the advaitika metaphysical framework. Moreover, Saundarya-laharī represents the concepts of *Śiva* and *Śakti* in terms of *Prakāśa* and *Vimarśa* respectively, which denote the subjectivity and objectivity aspects involved in any knowledge situation. Thus, the *Śiva-Śakti* duality being projected in the non-dual consciousness does not compromise its ontological non-duality. On the other hand, this projected epistemic duality is the hallmark of the epistemically projected cosmos. All the varied levels of the cosmos thus represent the various levels of the manifestation of *Śiva-Śakti*. These various levels are represented by the various stations in the *Kuṇḍalinī* pathway and also by the various *āvaraṇa-s* of the *Śrī-cakra*.

Thus, in the light of the ensuing discussion in this book, it is my humble opinion that a serious study of the Tāntrika literature of Śaṅkara and Gauḍapāda not only shows it to be compatible with the advaitika framework but perhaps it even shows the great desirability of the study since many finer points duly emphasized in these works are greatly helpful in resolving many puzzling conceptions of the advaitika framework. The usually accepted advaitika literature of Śaṅkara viz. the *prasthānatraya-bhāṣya-s* and his Tāntrika literature seem to be complementary to the extent that a consistent comprehension of Śaṅkara's philosophy calls for treating them holistically. Therefore, I have suggested the term *'Tantrādvaita'* for this holistic approach to Śaṅkara's philosophy. I do not have any hesitation in confessing that whatever has been discussed in this volume is already very much there in Śaṅkara's works. I have not said anything new at all but only tried to understand his philosophy in the light of his very own works. Also, I am not ashamed to confess that I am not fit enough to properly comprehend the depth and details of Śaṅkara's works, yet I have tried to present whatever little I was capable of understanding in his works. I beseech pardon in advance from all those learned scholars who may not find anything worthwhile in this volume.

Rajesh Kumar Jha

February 15, 2023

Chart of Diacritical Marks

a	ā	i	ī	u	ū	ṛ	e	ai	o	au	ṁ	ḥ
अ	आ	इ	ई	उ	ऊ	ऋ	ए	ऐ	ओ	औ	अं	अः

ka	kha	ga	gha	ṅa
क	ख	ग	घ	ङ
ca	cha	ja	jha	ña
च	छ	ज	झ	ञ
ṭa	ṭha	ḍa	ḍha	ṇa
ट	ठ	ड	ढ	ण
ta	tha	da	dha	na
त	थ	द	ध	न
pa	pha	ba	bha	ma
प	फ	ब	भ	म
ya	ra	la	va	
य	र	ल	व	
śa	ṣa	sa	ha	
श	ष	स	ह	
kṣa	tra	jña		
क्ष	त्र	ज्ञ		

Abbreviations

Ai.Up.Bh. (Eight Up.-II)	Aitareya Upaniṣad Bhāṣya of Śaṅkara (Eight Upaniṣads, vol II)
Ai.Up.Bh. (Īśādi. Bh.)	Aitareya Upaniṣad Bhāṣya of Śaṅkara (Īśādinavopaniṣadaḥ)
Bh.G.	Bhagavadgītā (tr. Swāmī Gambhīrānanda)
Bh.G.Bh.	Bhagavadgītā Bhāṣya of Śaṅkara (ed. Pt. Gaṇeśaśāstrī Jośī)
Bh.G.Bh. (tr.)	Bhagavadgītā Bhāṣya of Śaṅkara (tr. Swāmī Gambhīrānanda)
Bṛ.Up.	Bṛhadāraṇyaka Upaniṣad (tr. Swāmī Mādhavānanda)
Bṛ.Up.Bh of Shastri)	Bṛhadāraṇyaka Upaniṣad Bhāṣya Śaṅkara (ed. S. Subrahmanya
Bṛ.Up.Bh. (tr.)	Bṛhadāraṇyaka Upaniṣad Bhāṣya of Śaṅkara (tr. Swāmī Mādhavānanda)
B.S.Bh.	Brahma-Sūtra Bhāṣya of Śaṅkara (ed. Śrī Anantakrishna Śāstrī)
B.S.Bh. (tr.)	Brahma-Sūtra Bhāṣya of Śaṅkara

	(tr. Swāmī Gambhīrānanda)
Ch.Up.Bh. (Īśādi. Bh.)	Chāndogya Upaniṣad Bhāṣya of Śaṅkara (Īśādinavopaniṣadaḥ)
Ch.Up.Bh.(tr.)	Chāndogya Upaniṣad Bhāṣya of Śaṅkara (tr. Swāmī Gambhīrānanda)
Īśā Up.Bh. (Eight Up.-I)Īśā	Upaniṣad Bhāṣya of Śaṅkara (Eight Upaniṣads, vol I)
Īśā Up.Bh. (Īśādi. Bh.)	Īśā Upaniṣad Bhāṣya of Śaṅkara (Īśādinavopaniṣadaḥ)
Ka.Up.Bh. (Eight Up.-I)	Kaṭha Upaniṣad Bhāṣya of Śaṅkara (Eight Upaniṣads, vol I)
Ka.Up.Bh. (Īśādi. Bh.)	Kaṭha Upaniṣad Bhāṣya of Śaṅkara (Īśādinavopaniṣadaḥ)
Ke.Up.Bh. (Eight Up.-I)	Kena Upaniṣad Bhāṣya of Śaṅkara (Eight Upaniṣads, vol I)
Ke.Up.Bh. (Īśādi. Bh.)	Kena Upaniṣad Bhāṣya of Śaṅkara (Īśādinavopaniṣadaḥ)
L.S.	Lalitā Sahasranāma (Śrī Rājarājeśvarī-Tripurasundarī Nityārādhana-Stotrāṇi)

Mā.Kā.	Māṇḍūkya Kārikā
	(Eight Upaniṣads, vol II)
Mā.Up. (tr.)	Māṇḍūkya Upaniṣad
	(Eight Upaniṣads, vol II)
Mā.Up.Bh.(Eight Up.-II)	Māṇḍūkya Upaniṣad Bhāṣya of Śaṅkara
	(Eight Upaniṣads, vol II)
Mā.Up.Bh. (Īśādi. Bh.)	Māṇḍūkya Upaniṣad Bhāṣya of Śaṅkara
	(Īśādinavopaniṣadaḥ)
Mu.Up.Bh.(Eight Up.-II)	Muṇḍaka Upaniṣad Bhāṣya of Śaṅkara
	(Eight Upaniṣads, vol II)
Mu.Up.Bh. (Īśādi. Bh.)	Muṇḍaka Upaniṣad Bhāṣya of Śaṅkara
	(Īśādinavopaniṣadaḥ)
Pañcī.	Pañcīkaraṇam
Pr.Up.Bh. (Eight Up.-II)	Praśna Upaniṣad Bhāṣya of Śaṅkara
	(Eight Upaniṣads, vol II)
Pr.Up.Bh. (Īśādi. Bh.)	Praśna Upaniṣad Bhāṣya of Śaṅkara
	(Īśādinavopaniṣadaḥ)
S. laharī	Saundarya-laharī
	(tr. S.S. Sastri and T.R.S. Ayyangar)
S.L.	Saundarya-laharī

	(ed. A. Kuppuswami)
S.L. (tr.)	Saundarya-laharī
	(ed. A. Kuppuswami)
S.L.Bh. (Aruṇāmodinī)	Saundarya-laharī
	(ed. A. Kuppuswami)
S.L.Bh. (Ānandagirīyā)	Saundarya-laharī
	(ed. A. Kuppuswami)
S.L.Bh. (Ḍiṇḍimabhāṣyam)	Saundarya-laharī
	(ed. A. Kuppuswami)
S.L.Bh. (Lakṣmīdharā)	Saundarya-laharī
	(ed. A. Kuppuswami)
S.L.Bh. (Saubhāgyavardhanī)	Saundarya-laharī
	(ed. A. Kuppuswami)
S.L.Bh. (Tātparyadīpinī)	Saundarya-laharī
	(ed. A. Kuppuswami)
Subh.	Subhagodaya-stotram
Subh. Bh.	Subhagodaya-stotram Bhāṣya
S.V.R.	Śrīvidyā-Ratnākaraḥ
SVRS.	Śrīvidyāratna-Sūtram
SVRS. Bh.	Śrīvidyāratna-Sūtram
	(bhāṣya of Śaṅkarāraṇya)
Śv.Up.Bh.	Śvetāśvatara Upaniṣad Bhāṣya of Śaṅkara
Śv.Up.Bh. (tr.)	Śvetāśvatara Upaniṣad Bhāṣya of Śaṅkara

	(tr. Swāmī Gambhīrānanda)
Tai.Up.Bh. (Eight Up.-I)	Taittirīya Upaniṣad Bhāṣya of Śaṅkara (Eight Upaniṣads, vol I)
Tai.Up.Bh. (Īśādi. Bh.)	Taittirīya Upaniṣad Bhāṣya of Śaṅkara (Īśādinavopaniṣadaḥ)
U. Sā. (tr.)	Upadeśasāhasrī (tr. Sengaku Mayeda)
V.P.	Vedānta Paribhāṣā
Viv.Cd.	Vivekacūḍāmaṇi
Y.S.V.	Yoga-Sūtra-Vivaraṇa of Śaṅkara (Śaṅkara on the Yoga-Sūtras)

Contents

Chapter I: Reflections Over Devotion in Śaṅkara's Philosophy **1**

The Fundamentals of Advaitism 2

The Fundamentals of Devotion (Bhakti) 5

Compatibility of Devotion (Bhakti) with Advaitism 6

Twin Aspects of Advaitika Devotion (Advaita bhakti) 8

The Need of Devotion (Bhakti) in Śaṅkara's Advaitism 9

Possibility of Devotion (Bhakti) in Śaṅkara's Advaitism 12

Chapter II: Gauḍapāda's Heritage to Śaṅkara **16**

Śrīvidyāratna-sūtram 16

Subhagodaya-stotram 20

Māṇḍūkya Kārikā 27

An Overview of Gauḍapāda's Contribution 36

Chapter III: Nature and Significance of Devotion in Saundarya-Laharī **38**

Parameters for the Study of Devotion (Bhakti) 39

The Analysis of Saundarya-laharī 40

Devotion (Bhakti) as Depicted in Saundarya-laharī 121

Chapter IV: Depiction of Devotion in Prasthānatraya-Bhāṣya-s **127**

Devotion (Bhakti) in the Brahma-sūtra-bhāṣya of Śaṅkara... 128

Devotion (Bhakti) in the Upaniṣad-bhāṣya-s of Śaṅkara 145

Devotion (Bhakti) in the Gītā-bhāṣya of Śaṅkara 166

Chapter V: Advaitika Devotion as the Essence of Tantrādvaita **178**

Illustration of Corresponding Identities in Tantrādvaita **191**

Notes and References **192**

Bibliography **285**

Chapter I

Reflections Over Devotion in Śaṅkara's Philosophy

For studying the various dimensions of devotion (*bhakti*) as revealed in the *Prasthāntraya-bhāṣya-s* of Śaṅkara in the light of his *Saundarya-laharī,* it is necessary to keep the study focused on the different emergent issues. The first stage of the study will be dealing with the philosophical requirement for the concept of devotion (*bhakti*) in advaitism. It will also examine the possibility of devotion within the framework of advaita philosophy, as depicted in the *Prasthānatraya-bhāṣya-s* of Śaṅkara. The second stage will be dealing with the philosophical backdrop to the concept of advaitika devotion (*advaita-bhakti*), especially in the context of Gauḍāpada's contribution to Śaṅkara's philosophy. Here the term '*advaitika devotion*' is being used to signify the type of devotion that is possible within the framework of advaitism. The third stage of the study will be making a detailed analysis of the explicit and implicit significance of the philosophically important sections of *Saundarya-laharī*, so that the outline of advaitika devotion as depicted therein may become clear. The next stage will be making a selective and representative study of the *Prasthānatraya-bhāṣya-s* of Śaṅkara with the aim of showing their relationship with the idea of advaitika devotion, as depicted in the *Saundarya-laharī*. The fifth and last stage of the study will be attempting to summarize and conclude about the overall importance of advaitika devotion, thereby showing the comprehensive framework of advaita philosophy.

Before discussing the need of devotion (*bhakti*) in Śaṅkara's advaitism, it would be useful to have before us a preliminary outline of the concept of devotion itself. At this stage of study the conceptual outline of devotion can only be a preliminary one because the exact sense of devotion (*bhakti*) that is to be analyzed and discovered in the present project would be emerging out of a detailed examination of the *Saundarya-laharī* of Śaṅkara. Succeeding chapters would take up the study of the *Saundarya-laharī*. Till then, it would suffice to comprehend that there is no fundamental conflict of devotion (*bhakti*), as depicted in the *Saundarya-laharī*, with the basic tenets of Śaṅkara's advaitism. Also, a brief statement about the general sense of devotion (*bhakti*) may be quite useful. But even prior to this, it is necessary to take an overview of the fundamentals of advaitism so that the general compatibility of advaitism with devotion may be understood in a preliminary manner.

The Fundamentals of Advaitism

A brief overview of the philosophy of advaitism in the context of advaitika devotion (*bhakti*) would be very helpful in identifying the parameters for a study of such devotion. Firstly, ontological absolutism is the very core of advaitism and it upholds absolute and immutable ontological unity, i.e., non-duality, of the entire cosmos (as also all that is ever possible).[1] T.R.V. Murti points out the essential nature of this absolutism despite worldly appearances.[2] That is to say, all types of dualities are only epistemically manifested as separate entities, but basically, they are all ontologically identified with the highest reality.

Secondly, the principle of epistemic relativism in advaitika philosophy is as important as that of ontological absolutism. In fact, the principle of epistemic relativism is the logical corollary to the principle of ontological absolutism, in the light of all perceived duality. Bina Gupta has pointed out the necessary element of duality involved in all worldly cognitions.[3] According to this principle, all cognition of duality whatsoever has a mere epistemic status and thus they jointly constitute a network of epistemic relativities.[4] Thus, all perceptions of duality are unreal ontologically, when viewed from the ultimate standpoint.[5] This amounts to saying that the whole spatio-temporal cosmos is a network of epistemic relativities. Hiriyanna points out that the world is a *vivarta* or appearance of *Brahman.*[6] Further, advaitism also talks of the different levels of ontological reality (*sattā*) corresponding to different levels of epistemic relativity. Broadly speaking, there are four levels of reality -- 1. transcendental (*pāramārthika*), 2. phenomenal (*vyāvahārika*), 3. apparitional (*prātibhāsika*) and 4. imaginary (*tuccha*).[7] Further, the phenomenal level of reality itself consists of three levels of cognition corresponding to the degree of epistemic superimposition (*adhyāsa*) involved therein. N.V. Bannerjee says that these levels of phenomenal reality are all ultimately appearances only with respect to the *Para Brahman.*[8] These three levels have been variously depicted as the three worlds -- causal, subtle and gross (*kāraṇa, sūkṣhma* and *sthūla jagat*), as the first three quarters of *Praṇava* -- *a, u* and *m*, as the three levels of epistemic manifestation of *śabda* --- *paśyantī, madhyamā* and *vaikharī,* and even as three duality-ridden epistemic states of *jīva* --- the *Prājña* in deep sleep, *Taijasa* in dream and *Viśva* in waking states.[9] It may be noted that the basic mechanism of all the instances of epistemic relativism is the process of *adhyāsa*, which is nothing but the process of epistemic superimposition.[10] Thus , all the cases of *adhyāsa* are epistemically valid at their own levels of reality or *sattā*. However, from the standpoint of the highest ontological reality, all cases of *adhyāsa* turn out to be non-existent as separate ontological entities. K.C. Bhattacharya highlights this sense of reality and unreality of the phenomenal world.[11] Thus, the principle of epistemic relativism, applying itself through the process of *adhyāsa,* is one of the most important features of advaitism.

Thirdly, the final aim of realizing the ontologically absolute non-duality of *Brahman* is also a fundamental feature of advaitism.[12] Ramakant Tripathi has brought out the necessity of the absolute *Brahman* being the content of the highest spiritual realization.[13] This realization of absolute non-duality must be an ontological realization and not a mere epistemic one.

Fourthly, as a consequence of such ontological realization being taken as the final aim of advaitism, the means adopted for achieving it cannot be a mere rational and intellectual exercise; rather, it depends crucially on meditation (*nididhyāsana*) and the supplementary use of the great Upaniṣadika dictums (*mahā vākyas*). Such specific reliance on meditation and the great dictums for attaining the final realization is also a fundamental principle of advaitism.[14]

Fifthly, the possibility of the 'liberated-while-alive' state (*jīvanmukti*), in addition to the 'bodiless liberation' (*videhamukti*), is also a fundamental aspect of advaitism. While *videhamukti* is the state of irreversible ontological realization of the absolute non-duality of *Brahman*, achievable only after the annihilation of all bodies (gross, subtle and causal), the state of *jīvanmukti* does not requisition the end of all bodies. The *jīvanmukti* state begins with the realization of *Brahman* and continues until the end of all the three bodies, as and when required by the fructifying karmas (*prārabdha karma*) of the *jīva*.[15] In the state of *jīvanmukti*, the *jīva* continually apprehends the ontological absoluteness of *Brahman*. He is always aware of the sole and ultimate reality of *Brahman*, as also of the ontological hollowness of the spatio-temporal world (except in the sense of it being ontologically grounded in *Brahman* itself in the final analysis). These, then, are the five most important features of advaitism, so far as the study of advaitika devotion is concerned. However, this list of the fundamental principles of advaitism is not an exhaustive one. The principles enumerated above have been selected only in the light of their relevance to the matter under study.

The Fundamentals of Devotion (Bhakti)

The task of enumerating the fundamentals of devotion (*bhakti*) is a very difficult one because the particular sense of devotion that is to be discussed in this section is not defined by the connotations given to it by some particular philosophical and/or religious traditions. As such, this section would strive to point out such features of devotion which hold true for almost all philosophical and religious traditions.

Firstly, the most fundamental element of devotion (*bhakti*) is that there must be a devotee (*bhakta*), as also an object of his devotion, namely the deity (*iṣṭa*). That is to say, there must be a distinction between the deity and the devotee. Although the nature of such distinction may vary from case to case, the fact remains that this distinction as such is a *sine-qua-non* of devotion (*bhakti*).

Secondly, the concept of devotion being studied here requires that the deity must have some sort of divinity (*aiśvarya*) associated with it. Thus, the concept of devotion becomes relevant only when it is directed towards some divine entity. However, it is obvious that the sense of divinity attached with the deity may vary from case to case. Yet, there will be some sense of divinity in each and every case, otherwise devotion itself would become quite meaningless.

Thirdly, all devotees resort to the use of words and meditation, either directly or indirectly, to achieve perfection in their devotions. The varieties of the usage of words and meditational techniques towards this end are endless. Their importance lies in the fact that they are the most prevalent means of perfecting one's devotion.

Fourthly, the surrender of one's ego (*ahaṅkāra*) and its attendant features before the deity may very well be treated as both a means and an objective of devotion (*bhakti*). The repeated effort of perfecting such surrender is a very important means of perfecting one's devotion. The justifications given for such surrender may vary from case to case, but it is almost indisputable that such a surrender is an inalienable feature of devotion (*bhakti*).

Fifthly, it is generally true for all types of devotion (*bhakti*) that the final aim of the devotee is to win the deity's unceasing love and mercy, as also endless communion with the deity. The form of communion with the deity, as desired by the devotee, may vary from tradition to tradition. It may be the constant proximity of the devotee to his deity, or the devotee acquiring the deity's form, or the devotee acquiring the deity's nature, or even the complete and irreversible merger of the devotee's being in the deity and so on.

Last, but not the least, is the yearning of all devotees to propitiate their deities by singing their praise and glory and enjoying the bliss thereof. Such yearning springs from the inherent wish of all sincere devotees to share their joy and enlightenment with one and all.

The fundamentals of devotion (*bhakti*) as enumerated above do not constitute an exhaustive list. N.S.S. Raman has given a detailed discussion of the core elements of *bhakti* on the basis of traditional Hindu texts.[16] However, the above enumeration has been done only to facilitate the study of advaitika devotion by highlighting the relevant features of devotion.

Compatibility of Devotion (Bhakti) with Advaitism

In this section it would be seen whether and to what extent the fundamentals of devotion are compatible with the fundamentals of advaitism. Firstly, let us take up the deity-devotee distinction which is a *sine-qua-non* of devotion. It is quite clear that the ontological absolutism of *Brahman* in advaitism cannot tolerate any real ontological distinction between the deity and the devotee. But, advaitism also propounds the principle of epistemic relativism, which permits the cognition of all sorts of duality, but only at the epistemic level. Obviously, this epistemic relativism also holds key to the deity-devotee distinction in the advaitika context. This epistemic distinction persists as long as the individual identity of the devotee persists. That is, this distinction dissolves only after the ontological realization of *Brahman* by the devotee, which at once manifests the absolute ontological identity of the devotee and *Brahman*. So, for all the practical purposes of devotion, this element of devotion (*bhakti*) is quite compatible with advaitism.

Secondly, the concept of devotion requires that the deity must have some sort of divinity. In the case of advaitism, *saguṇa Brahman* in its various immanent aspects holds the position of the deity for the devotee. In advaitism, *saguṇa Brahman* has been described as the power (*śakti*) of the transcendent or *Para Brahman*.[17] The immanent aspect of *saguṇa Brahman*, namely *Īśvara,* is the omniscient and omnipotent Lord of the spatio-temporal world. As such, *Īśvara* is the overlord of all matters concerning the devotees, including the ontological realization of the transcendent or *Para Brahman*. This means that for all the beings enmeshed in the world of duality, *Īśvara* is all in all. Therefore, the requirement of devotion (*bhakti*) pertaining to the presence of divinity in the deity is well-fulfilled in advaitism.

Thirdly, an important aspect of devotion is the explicit reliance on the use of words and meditation for achieving perfection in devotion. This requirement of devotion is well-fulfilled by the advaitika emphasis on the constant practice of meditation, i.e., *nididhyāsana*, on the true import of the great dictums *(mahā vākyas)*[18] of advaita vedānta. Further, the use of words is forcefully illustrated in the hymns (*stuti* or *stotra*) of Śaṅkara and Gauḍapāda, e.g., *Subhagodayastotram, Śrīvidyāratnasūtram, Saundarya-laharī, Śivānanda-laharī, Śrīdakṣiṇāmūrtistotram,* etc. Thus, there is sufficient emphasis on the use of words and meditation in advaitism for the perfection of devotion.

Fourthly, devotion (*bhakti*) requires the devotee to surrender his ego (*ahaṅkāra*) before his deity (*iṣṭa*). In the case of advaitism, this particular requirement of devotion is fulfilled to an incredible extent. Advaitism strives for the absolute sublimation of the devotee's ego in the infinite being of the deity.[19] This, in turn, results in the direct ontological realization of the *Para Brahman*. Thus, this feature of devotion is also compatible with advaitism.

Fifthly, there is the aspect of the final objective of the devotee. In the context of advaitism, it may be observed that the devotee's thirst for his deity's love and benediction can find ample satisfaction. Apart from the other levels of communion with his deity, the devotee, in the case of advaitism, may even win the highest communion with his deity by the absolute sublimation of his ego in the being of his deity.[20] Thus, this requirement of devotion is fulfilled in the case of advaitism.

Lastly, it is a very special feature of devotion that the devotee yearns to sing the glories of his deity. Although in advaitism the culmination of perfect devotion results in the sublimation of the devotee's ego in his deity, yet so long as the deity-devotee distinction persists, there is no contradiction in the fulfillment of the devotee's desire to this end. In advaitism, the perfected devotee continues to live in his physical body until the complete exhaustion of his fructifying (*prārabdha*) karmas. This is the state of 'liberated-while-alive' or *jīvanmukti*. Such devotees unceasingly spread the message of true devotion, knowledge and love. The sermons and texts of all the sages of the advaitika tradition are a living testimony to the fulfillment of this requirement of devotion. Thus, it is clear that there is a definite inner harmony between the fundamentals of devotion and those of advaitism.

Twin Aspects of Advaitika Devotion (Advaita bhakti)

The very term 'advaitika devotion' or '*advaita bhakti*' connotes the twin aspects of advaitism and devotion. The two aspects of advaitika devotion together determine its parameters through a process of mutual modulation. As a result of this process, the two aspects get intertwined in such a fashion that it becomes almost impossible to classify the various features of advaitika devotion into one of these two aspects. Most of the features of advaitika devotion bear a tinge of both the aspects. As such, it is but appropriate to call them the 'twin aspects' of advaitika devotion, instead of its 'two aspects'. Yet, the fact remains that in the case of any particular feature of advaitika devotion one of these twin aspects is seen to dominate over the other. At the same time, it should be noted that the primary connotation of 'advaitika devotion' is devotion (*bhakti*). Advaitism provides the backdrop to this devotion and constitutes its secondary connotation. However, this secondary connotation, i.e., advaitism, is crucial in determining the contours of advaitika devotion. Thus, we may call devotion (*bhakti*) and advaitism the explicit and implicit aspects of advaitika devotion respectively.

The Need of Devotion (Bhakti) in Śaṅkara's Advaitism

Thus, broadly speaking, devotion (*bhakti*) may be taken as a broad set of intensely positive feelings entertained by a person towards some being or beings. Mostly, the feelings constitutive of devotion (*bhakti*) are those of impeccable love, faith, affection and a willing surrender before the wishes of the object of one's devotion. Further, the concept of devotion (*bhakti*) generally requires that the object of devotion be a divine being or personality, a *Deity*.

Coming back to the central topic of discussion, it may be recalled that the spiritual practices required for the attainment of *Brahma jñāna*, that is, the realization of one's identity with *Brahman*, are *śravaṇa*, *manana* and *nididhyāsana*.[21] As far as the steps of *śravaṇa* and *manana* are concerned, there is no philosophical problem or dilemma concerning the basic tenets of Śaṅkara's advaitism. But the last step of *nididhyāsana* raises some pertinent philosophical issues that demand an adequate answer, if the logical and philosophical consistency of Śaṅkara's advaitism has to remain intact. What is *nididhyāsana*? It is defined as constant meditation upon the conclusions derived through *śravaṇa* and *manana*, especially regarding the import of the *mahā vākyas*.[22] With the perfection of *nididhyāsana*, such constant meditation is believed to lead to the realization of the true ontological import of the *mahā vākyas*, namely, the ontological absoluteness of *Brahman*.[23] Now, *nididhyāsana* is a special kind of meditation and as such, it also presupposes the duality of the subject and the object of meditation. Now, the subject of meditation is the ego (*ahaṅkāra*) of the *jīva*, who is the spiritual aspirant; while the object of meditation refers to the whole array of concepts being taken as the true import of the *mahā vākya-s,* as well as the conclusions of advaitism. Both of them, the ego (*ahaṅkāra*) and the concepts, are riddled with duality *(dvaita)* and limited by space and time. As such, they are parts of the spatio-temporal causal world, namely, *jagat*. But this *jagat* itself is a product of cosmic superimposition (*adhyāsa*), according to the doctrines of Śaṅkara's advaitism.[24] Thus, *nididhyāsana* being a part of *jagat*, is also a product of the cosmic superimposition (*adhyāsa*). It follows that *nididhyāsana* itself is also limited by space, time, causality etc. Such being the case, how can a spatio-temporal-causal *nididhyāsana* by itself lead to the sublimation of the (epistemic) duality of *jagat*, along with *jagat* itself, and thus bring about the realization of the ontological absoluteness of *Brahman*? If it is held that *nididhyāsana* by itself is capable of bringing about the sublimation of cosmic superimposition (*adhyāsa*), then a strange conclusion follows -- that an effect of cosmic superimposition can also become the cause of the sublimation of its very own cause. Thus, it follows that *nididhyāsana*, being itself delimited by space, time and causality, cannot by itself become the cause of the sublimation of space, time and causality. H.S. Prasad has noted the logical inconsistency in supposing that the *jīva* may, through his own efforts, transcend the phenomenal realm to get the non-dual realization.[25] From this discussion, it is clear that if *nididhyāsana* has to be somehow instrumental in bringing about the transcendental realization of *Brahman* (*Brahma jñāna*) without violating the fundamentals of advaitism, then some very crucial elements seem amiss in the traditional exposition of *nididhyāsana*.

To find out these missing links in the exposition of *nididhyāsana* it would be helpful to examine the possibility and nature of the point of deliverance from the world (*jagat*) of duality, in agreement with the basics of Śaṅkara's advaitism. It is quite clear that no such being, entity or fact can become a point of deliverance from the spatio-temporal-causal world of cosmic superimposition, which itself is its result or product. As such, all the spatio-temporal-causal entities and beings of the world are ruled out, except the cosmic superimposition (*adhyāsa*) itself. Now, this cosmic superimposition, being the cause of the epistemic relativism of the appearance (*vivarta*) of the world, is never exhausted ontologically in its effect, that is, the world. Therefore, this cosmic superimposition (*adhyāsa*) is also transcendent to the spatio-temporal-causal world (*jagat*).[26] At the same time, one must not overlook that this transcendence of cosmic superimposition (*adhyāsa*), with respect to the world (*jagat*), is of an epistemically relativistic nature only. This means that if there be a scale of epistemic relativism (or epistemic superimpositions), then the degree of epistemic relativism of the cosmic superimposition (*adhyāsa*) would immediately precede that of the world (*jagat*). In this sense the cosmic superimposition, while being the epistemic cause of the spatio-temporal-causal world, also transcends it simultaneously. At the same time, this cosmic superimposition is also immanent in the world (*jagat*), as it is itself the (epistemically) constitutive cause of the spatio-temporal-causal world.[27] Thus, the cosmic superimposition (*adhyāsa*) is clearly both immanent and transcendent to the world (*jagat*) in the epistemic sense.

The simultaneous epistemic immanence and transcendence of cosmic superimposition (*adhyāsa*) with respect to the world, provides us the point of deliverance being searched in Śaṅkara's advaitism. This cosmic superimposition is not totally unrelated to and beyond the reach of the *jīvas* of the world, since they are capable of referring to it while being confined within the spatio-temporal-causal world (*jagat*).[28] Being the hub of the epistemic relativism of the world, while also remaining epistemically transcendent to it, emphatically reveals this cosmic superimposition as the controlling authority, the master of the world of duality.[29] Now, such a nature of the cosmic superimposition *(adhyāsa)* exactly fits the criteria required for the point of absolute deliverance from the world. Having seen that this cosmic superimposition alone is the point of deliverance from the world, it may be noted that this very principle of cosmic superimposition (*adhyāsa*) is none other than *Īśvara.*[30] *Īśvara* is the power (*śakti*) of *Brahman.*[31] *Īśvara* is the master of *māyā*, the master of cosmic superimposition (*adhyāsa*).[32] It is the wish of *Īśvara* and *Īśvara* alone that can cause the cessation of *māyā*, the epistemic sublimation of the spatio-temporal-causal world (*jagat*).[33] It is the wish of *Īśvara* alone that can grant the realization of *Brahman* (*Brahma jñāna*). Now, what is the means of obtaining the benediction of *Īśvara* regarding this matter? It is devotion (*bhakti*) to *Īśvara*. This devotion propitiates *Īśvara* to grant the realization of *Brahman* (*Brahma jñāna*). N.S.S. Raman points out that *bhakti* paves the way for the highest knowledge.[34] Thus, considering the basic framework of Śaṅkara's advaitism, there is a conclusive and inevitable need of devotion (*bhakti*) to *Īśvara*.

Possibility of Devotion (Bhakti) in Śaṅkara's Advaitism

According to advaitism, the transcendent *Brahman* (*Para Brahman*), variously known as the *nirākāra*, the *nirguṇa*, or the *niṣkala Brahman*, is absolutely beyond the realm of all duality, names and forms.[35] T. M. P. Mahadevan points out that the description of *Brahman* as *sat-cit-ānanda* refers to its essential nature, *svarūpa-lakṣaṇa.*[36] Obviously, the concept of *Para Brahman* cannot possibly accommodate even the subject-object duality. Now, since *nididhyāsana* is by definition a special kind of meditation (*dhyāna*), it presupposes the duality of the subject and the object of meditation. This leads to the conclusion that, strictly speaking, *nididhyāsana* can never be meditation (*dhyāna*) upon the *Para Brahman*. D.M. Dutta highlights this logical inevitability.[37] But, if it be so, then what could be the object of *nididhyāsana*? In order to answer this question, it may be recalled that *nididhyāsana* is the continuous meditation upon the considered conclusions, derived through the preceding stages of *śravaṇa* and *manana*, regarding the true import of the *mahā vākyas* and the philosophy of advaitism.[38] But the philosophy of advaitism clearly states that *Īśvara* is both the fundamental principle of epistemic relativism, as well as the primordial evolute of epistemic relativism.[39] Brian Carr says there is no incompatibility between the transcendent absoluteness of *Brahman* and the role of God as the creator.[40] As such, the status of *Īśvara* depicts the very limits of the duality infested spatio-temporal-causal world (*jagat*). This shows us that *nididhyāsana* is nothing but meditation (*dhyāna*) upon the fundamental principle of epistemic relativism, i.e., *Īśvara*. This conclusion also follows from the following two arguments. First, since *jīva* itself is a part of the spatio-temporal causal world (*jagat*), it is incapable of stretching its conceptual limits beyond the worldly parameters. Therefore, the effort of *jīva* to go back in the evolutionary cycle of epistemic relativism comes to a halt after touching the level of *Īśvara*. This means that *Īśvara* alone is the befitting object of *nididhyāsana*, emerging out of the stages of *śravaṇa* and *manana*. Furthermore, the philosophy of advaitism, according to Śaṅkara, declares that *nididhyāsana* is the last stage of spiritual disciplines required for the realization of *Brahma jñāna*. As such, it is instrumental in causing the realization of *Brahma jñāna*.[41] But from the preceding discussion it is quite clear that *Īśvara* alone is capable of granting *Brahma jñāna*. Therefore, the wish of *Īśvara* alone is the true and immediate cause of the realization of *Brahma jñāna*. From this also, it follows that *nididhyāsana* is instrumental in obtaining the benediction of *Īśvara* for the attainment of *Brahma jñāna*. The propitiation of *Īśvara* through meditation (*dhyāna*) upon his divine qualities alone can win the blessings of *Īśvara*. This is nothing but devotion (*bhakti*) to *Īśvara*. Therefore, the object of *nididhyāsana* is *Īśvara* and the nature of *nididhyāsana* is devotion (*bhakti*) to *Īśvara*.

Now, if the *jīva* practising *nididhyāsana* believes that the object of his *nididhyāsana* is the transcendent (*Para*) *Brahman*, then he definitely commits a conceptual error. Even then, the *nididhyāsana* turns out to be functionally effective in due course of time. This means it becomes successful in obtaining the grace of *Īśvara* for the realization of *Brahma jñāna*. K.C. Bhattacharya says that duality based knowledge ultimately gives way to the non-dual realization.[42] As such, despite being conceptually erroneous to some degree, such *nididhyāsana* also is nothing but a form of devotion (*bhakti*) to *Īśvara*. Such devotion (*bhakti*) towards *Īśvara* may be termed as *implicit devotion*. Although being effective in obtaining the grace of *Īśvara*, such implicit devotion is also, in a significant sense, at loggerheads with the conceptual framework of advaita philosophy.

In contrast to such implicit devotion, there is also the possibility of an *explicit devotion* to *Īśvara*, which maintains its total attunement with the fundamentals of advaitism. The important elements of such an explicit devotion to *Īśvara* are as follows. *First*, such devotion consists of a sincere recognition and realization of the omnipotence and omnipresence of *Īśvara* in the spatio-temporal-causal world (*jagat*).[43] This belief has to be a living one, and not a mere theoretical one. *Second*, a proper cultivation of unflinching love and affection for *Īśvara*[44] is essential. *Third*, there must be a living faith in the benevolence of *Īśvara*.[45] *Fourth*, there must be a willing surrender of one's ego (*ahaṅkāra*) before *Īśvara* and his wishes.[46] *Fifth*, there should be a sincere appeal to *Īśvara* to end the dualistic appearances and grant *Brahma jñāna*.[47] These constitutive elements give the outlines of explicit devotion to *Īśvara*, as practised through *nididhyāsana*, in the context of Śaṅkara's advaitism. In a way, these elements also reflect the true parameters of *nididhyāsana*, showing perfect harmony with the general framework of advaiti

Clearly, *nididhyāsana* can be practised either through implicit or explicit devotion (*bhakti*) to *Īśvara*. Although both types of devotion are functionally effective in obtaining the grace of *Īśvara* for the realization of *Brahma jñāna*, the implicit one betrays a conceptual error with respect to the framework of advaitism. As against this, the explicit devotion to *Īśvara* is in total agreement with advaitism. Due to this total conceptual harmony, the explicit devotion to *Īśvara* is able to appreciate the true nature, limits and object of *nididhyāsana*. This in turn lends a certain degree of excellence to the explicit devotion as compared with the implicit devotion. This fact is also proved by Śaṅkara's advocacy of explicit devotion to *Īśvara* in the *Saundarya-laharī*. K.H. Potter has noted the devotional element in Śaṅkara's *bhāṣya-s* but he has not identified its philosophical importance.[48] Such an explicit devotion to *Īśvara*, within the framework of advaitism, may be rightly termed *non-dualistic devotion* or *advaitika devotion* (*advaita bhakti*). Thus, the philosophy of *Saundarya-laharī* and the type of devotion depicted therein, has a definite and very important place in advaitism. This in turn indicates the need, possibility and even inevitability of devotion (*bhakti*) in Śaṅkara's advaitism.

Chapter II

Gauḍapāda's Heritage to Śaṅkara

The previous chapter highlighted the necessity and possibility of devotion in advaitism. The special type of devotion discussed there is an essential and inevitable aspect of Śaṅkara's advaitism, as its omission would lead to glaring philosophical and logical inconsistencies in the conceptual framework of advaitism. The present work aims to highlight the role and nature of this special devotion (*bhakti*) by examining the *Saundarya-laharī* and the *Prasthānatraya bhāṣya-s* of Śaṅkara. Before doing this, it would be quite illuminating to see whether and to what extent Gauḍapāda has given importance to this special kind of devotion in his works. Towards this end, this chapter would seek to examine three texts of Gauḍapāda ṣ *Śrīvidyāratna-sūtram*, *Subhagodaya stotram* and *Māṇḍūkya Kārikā*. These texts would be studied to highlight the explicit and implicit elements of the above-mentioned devotion (*bhakti*). The relevant and representative passages would be briefly discussed to bring out their significance in this context. Such a study of these three texts would clearly indicate the philosophical heritage of Gauḍapāda to Śaṅkara.

Śrīvidyāratna-sūtram

The very first *sūtra*[49] of this text, which may be roughly translated as,

> "(Hence) the beginning of inquiry into the *tantra* literature related to *śakti mantra-s,"*

makes it clear that the objective of the text is to satisfy the yearning for knowledge of the *āgama*[50] concerning the *śākta*[51] *mantras*[52]. As such, it makes it clear that the philosophical and mystical aspects of *śakti mantra-s* would form the corpus of the text. Śaṅkarāraṇya, the commentator of this text, explains that a *mantra* is that which is capable of causing the realization of the unity of *jīva* and *ātman* through the process of reflective deliberations.[53] Therefore, the choice of Gauḍapāda to elaborate on the *śakti mantras* points to the fact that the place of *Śakti* is quite significant in his philosophical scheme, so far as the realization of *Brahman* or *ātman* is concerned.

The second *sūtra*[54], which may be roughly translated as,

> "*Ātman* alone has an (undivided) immutable nature",

states the immutability of *ātman* or *Brahman*. Thus, it also declares the essential inseparability, rather identity, of *jīva* and *Paramātman*. Śaṅkarāraṇya states that whatever is mutable is limited by space and time.[55] Thus, he declares the immutability of *ātman*, as *ātman* is beyond space and time. Further, *Paramātman* himself pervades the epistemically created *jīvas*. This also shows the inseparability of *jīva* and *ātman*. Juxtaposed to this inseparability and essential unity of *jīva* and *ātman*, is the illusion of the ontological distinction of *jīva* and *ātman*, which is the cause of the spatio-temporal *vyāvahārika sattā* [56] of the *jīva-s*.

The third *sūtra*[57], which may be roughly put as,

> "The power of cognition is of a conscious nature"

states that *citśakti* is essentially of the form of consciousness. This *citśakti*, or simply *Śakti*, is the power of *Brahman*, *Saccidānanda*. Thus, while *Brahman* is pure *cit* and *ānanda*, *śakti* is the capacity to cognize the bliss of *Brahman*. The unity and distinction of *Brahman* and its *Śakti* can be compared with an object and its image, or with the moon and its beams. Though they may be talked of as if they were different from each other, the reality is that they are one and the same. Such apparent distinctions are made only for the purpose of easy understanding.

The fourth aphorism[58] may be roughly put as,

> "That unnameable (*citśakti,* the potency to cognize) alone is known as *Śrīvidyā,*"

It makes it clear that this condensed illuminative energy, *Śakti*, is known as *Śrīvidyā*. But, this *Śrīvidyā* can be referred to only as '*anāmā*', that which is beyond all names. Thus, the term '*Śrīvidyā*' is used only for indicative reference, as its real nature is beyond the realm of language and deliberative rationality. This *anāmā śakti Śrīvidyā* is also the '*prathamā vidyā*',[59] which means it is the highest (and ultimately sole) existent and hence, also the highest (and ultimately the only one) to be realized. This *Śrīvidyā Śakti* is not the product of *māyā*. Rather, *māyā* exists and operates within this *Śakti*. This *Śrīvidyā* alone is the pervader of *cidākāśa* and all causal, subtle and gross bodies. Thus, this *Śrīvidyā Śakti* is the final and immutable cause and pervader of all (epistemically created) spatio-temporal entities.

The fifth aphorism[60] may be roughly translated as,

> "(She becomes) manifold due to (Her) triple (aspected) categories."

Thus, it refers to *Śakti* in its intertwined triple aspects and shows that this is the cause of the epistemic creation of all triple-aspected things. Thus, this *Śrīvidyā Śakti* generates the triplet of the subject of knowledge, the object of knowledge and knowledge itself. Similar is the genesis of the triplet of *jñāna*, *icchā* and *kriyā*, that is, cognition, volition and action. Similar is the case of *paśyantī*, *madhyamā* and *vaikharī* in the realm of vibration (*śabda*). It is the same case with the three *caraṇas* or *pādas* of *Praṇava*, as also with the causal, subtle and gross worlds. This *Śrīvidyā* is also the origin of the moon-region (*candra khaṇḍa*), the sun-region (*sūrya khaṇḍa*) and the fire-region (*agni khaṇḍa*).[61] Thus, everything emerging (although epistemically) out of *Śrīvidyā Śakti* has a three-fold nature. This secret of the three-fold nature of *Śakti* as well as the varied three-fold aspects of the cosmos forms the basis of different kinds of meditations (*dhyāna-s*) and spiritual practices (*sādhanā-s*).

The sixth aphorism[62] refers to the group of angles and leaves (*koṇas* and *patras*) constituting the *cakra*. This *cakra* stands for the *Śrīcakra* as well as the six *cakra-s* in the *suṣumṇā* nerve. With reference to the previous aphorism, it also shows that both the *cakra-s* indicated here are triple-aspected, that is, they have the three regions of moon, sun and fire. The next aphorism[63] shows that out of the triple-aspected Primordial *Śakti*, *Śrīvidyā*, emerge three epistemically distinct manifestations of *Śakti*, namely *Śāmbhavī*, *Vidyā* and *Śyāmā*, which are the *śaktis* of *sattva*, *rajas* and *tamas* respectively. Therefore, these three *śaktis* are also known as the spouses of *Brahmā, Viṣṇu* and *Rudra,* the divinities responsible for the creation, sustenance and dissolution of the universe. The eighth aphorism[64] states that these manifestations of the *Śrīvidyā Śakti* cause the emergence of the various deities, belonging to the fivefold traditions (*āmnāyas*), as well as their *mantra-s* and *yantra-s*. But it must not be overlooked that the emergence of these deities is an epistemic one only. The fifteenth aphorism[65] provides information about the transcendental aspect of *Śrīvidyā*, the Goddess *Tripurasundarī*, and it may be roughly translated as,

> "The unsurpassable (Goddess) *Tripurasundarī*, the ultimate Knowledge - Existent, resides in the house of *cintāmaṇi* jewels (the *bindu cakra* or the sahasrāra cakra)."

The dynamic feminine aspect of *Paramaśiva*, i.e., His *śakti* and spouse, is also known as *Mahāvidyā*, *Parāvidyā*, *Parāśāmbhavī*, *Kameśvarī*, *Rājarājeśvarī*, *Ṣoḍaśī*, etc. She is none other than the *Śrīvidyā*, the Primordial *Śakti*. Since the entire cosmos, consisting of the three worlds (*pura-s*) is but the manifestation of the beauty and grace of this Primordial *Śakti*, *Śrīvidyā*, She is also known as *'Tri-pura-sundarī.'* [66] Vinoba Bhave says that for the devotee having realizational knowledge of the highest Reality everything is but a manifestation of that Reality alone.[67] There is nothing beyond or prior to this *Mahāvidyā Tripurasundarī*. The *Sāmarasya* state[68] of *Paramaśiva* and *Śrīvidyā Tripurasundarī* is the same as the *nirākāra*, *niṣkala Brahman*. The sixteenth aphorism[69] points out that this Primordial *Śakti*, the *citśakti Śrīvidyā*, despite its immutability, manifests Herself in different forms. The next aphorism[70] may be put as,

> "Hence, from them, the (origination of) various mantra-s, yantra-s and tantra-s."

It emphasizes that due to various reasons on different occasions, this *citśakti* manifested Herself in various forms. This has brought about the various *tantras*, comprising of numerous *mantra-s* and *yantra-s*. The eighteenth aphorism[71] may be put as,

> "(Therefore) the various kinds of devotions and propitiations,"

and it shows that the different devotional traditions (*upāsanā-s*) have developed due to the peculiarities of different devotees (*bhakta-s*). The next aphorism[72] points out the fact that the different kinds of devotions and propitiations (*upāsanā-s*) bring their own particular results (*phala*), which may be either phenomenal or transcendental. Accordingly, various types of devotions may be categorized as either *parā bhakti* or *aparā bhakti*.

Subhagodaya-stotram

The very first stanza (*śloka*)[73] of this text brings out many features of the Primordial *Śakti*. The different names addressed to Her, the *Ṣoḍaśī Tripurasundarī*, indicate the intense significance attached to the status of the Primordial *Śakti* by Gauḍapāda in his philosophy. The use of the terms '*Bhavānī*' and '*Bhava-mahiṣī*' to address *Tripurasundarī* shows that She is the supreme controller of the universe, as also the spouse (the dynamic feminine counterpart) of *Paramaśiva*. She has also been referred to as '*sac-cit-sukha-vapuḥ,*' which shows Her essential form as *sat-cit-ānanda*, the same as that of *Para Brahman*. The address '*parākārā*' highlights the point that

She is beyond the spatio-temporal realm of phenomena. The term '*devī*', as explained in the *Lalitopākhyāna,* shows that She is the final cause of the epistemic projection of the phenomenal world (*līlā*).[74] The term '*amṛta laharī*' has a double significance. First, it shows that She is the same as the immortal and immutable (*amṛta*). Thus, ontologically, She is devoid of any origin or end. Further, She may be understood as one of the two waves (the other being *Śiva*) arising out of the immutable ocean of *Śiva-Śakti sāmarasya.*[75] Her address as '*baindava kalā*' shows that She is identical with the *baindava kalā* in the microcosm (*piṇḍa*).[76] As such, She is the same as the immutable *saccidānanda*. Her reference as '*mahākālātītā*' reveals that She is beyond even the *Mahākāla Śiva*, and so the concept (and epistemic appearance) of time both originates and vanishes in the Primordial *Śakti*. Further, She is addressed as '*kalita saraṇī kalpita tanu,*' which shows that She alone is the aim and objective of the three traditions (*saraṇī-s*) of *tantra*. That is to say, She alone is the objective of the *sāttvika*, *rājasika* and *tāmasika* traditions of tantra, viz., the *samaya*, *miśra* and *kaula mārgas* respectively. Also, in accordance with the nuances of each tradition, it is She alone who assumes different forms for the votaries of different traditions. Her next reference as '*sudhā-sindhor-antaravasatim*' shows that She is the very essence of the Ocean of Immortality, that is, the immutable state of *Śiva-Śakti sāmarasya* (*Para Brahman*). The last term '*vāsaramayī*' reveals that She, being the ultimate cause, the ontological ground of (the darkness of) the epistemic creation of duality, is the only one capable of saving one from the darkness of duality. Thus, five addresses for the Primordial *Śakti* in this stanza indicate Her transcendent form. These are - *bhavāni*, *sac-cit-sukha-vapuḥ*, *parākārā*, *baindava kalā*, and *mahākālātītā*. Also, the five other references of *Śakti* highlight Her immanent aspect. These are -- *bhava mahiṣi*, *amṛta laharī*, *kalpita tanu*, *antarvasatim*, and *vāsaramayī*. The term '*devī*' depicts both the aspects of the Primordial *Śakti*.[77]

The second stanza[78] states that by the practice of yogic disciplines (*sādhanā*), consisting of mastering the five subtle elements as also the subtle mind-element (*manas*), followed by meditation upon the transcendental *Śakti*, the spiritual aspirant witnesses the direct manifestation of the transcendental bliss-form of the *Śakti*, both within and without himself. This is the actual state of a *jīvanmukta*, a 'liberated-while-alive' person. N.K. Devaraja says that freedom consists in feeling one's identity with the pure and blissful consciousness.[79] The remarkable point is that a *jīvanmukta* is not restricted to the internal and mental realization of the *Devī*, but he is also privileged enough to actually witness Her direct manifestation in the external world as well. The third stanza[80] briefly sketches the outline of the spiritual disciplines (*sādhanā*) prescribed by the *samaya-mārga*. It mainly consists of the practice of vital-energy control (*prāṇāyāma*), controlling the subtle nerves *iḍā* and *piṅgalā*, using the resultant energy to make the microcosmic *Śakti,* the *kuṇḍalinī,* enter the path of the *suṣ-umṇā* nerve and then surpass the subtle moon-centre, the *ājñā cakra*, to reach the *sahasrāra*; thus causing the subtle shower of the immortal Bliss of the *sāmarasya* state of *Śiva* and *Śakti*.

The fifth stanza[81] enumerates the basic principles (*tattva*) of the spatio-temporal world. These twenty-five principles are - the five subtle elements (*pañca tattva*), their five corresponding subtle essences (*tanmātrā*), the ten organs of knowledge (*jñānendriya*) and action (*karmendriya*), the mind (*manas*), *Māyā*, *Vidyā*, *Maheśvara* and *Śiva*. Beyond these principles lies the *Sāmarasya* state of *Śiva* and *Śakti*. This *Sāmarasya* state is the same as the *Ṣoḍaśī kalā* of the moon, the *Devī Tripurasundarī*. The seventh stanza[82] shows that the final residing place of *Śakti* is the *bindu,* the innermost *āvaraṇa* of *Śrīcakra*, as well as the *sahasrāra cakra* of the microcosmic subtle body. In this place, the *Devī Ṣoḍaśī* joyfully communes with *Paramaśiva* in the *Sāmarasya* state. The eighth stanza[83] brings out the basic identity of the *śrīcakra* with the microcosmic subtle body (*piṇḍa*) containing the six *cakra-s*. This identity derives from the fact that both of them possess the three regions of fire, sun and moon (*agni*, *sūrya* and *candra*). Both of them also have distinct regions dominated by the five subtle elements and the sixth element *manas*.

The ninth stanza[84] says that all the 360 rays emanating from the *Devī's* feet are categorizable as the rays of fire (108 rays), sun (116 rays) and moon (136 rays). These 360 rays together become the *Mahākāla* and thus constitute the transcendent Time. Therefore, the *Devī* is not restricted even by the *Mahākāla*, as *Mahākāla* Himself originates from Her feet. The next stanza[85] gives the correspondence of the various *śiva cakras* and *śakti cakras* of the *Śrīcakra* with the various plexuses (*cakra-s*) of the microcosmic *piṇḍa*.

The eleventh stanza,[86] makes the significant revelation that even the *śakti cakras* and the *śiva cakra-s* of *Śrīcakra* are fundamentally inseparable, as the four *śiva cakra-s* of *Śrīcakra* are inherently assimilated in the form of the *Devī* as the five *śakti cakra-s* of *Śrīcakra*.

The next stanza[87] enumerates six types of identities existing between the *kalā*, *bindu* and *nāda*, and says that constant meditation upon these identities is the crux of the *samaya* tradition. The thirteenth stanza[88] gives us the technical meaning of *kalā*, *nāda* and *bindu* as the fifty letters of the sanskrit alphabet, the *Śrīcakra* and the six *cakra-s* of the microcosmic *piṇḍa* respectively, according to the *samaya* tradition. The worship of the four-fold identity, existing between *kalā*, *bindu*, *nāda* and *mantra*, is said to be accomplished by only such followers of this tradition who have successfully meditated upon the six-fold identity of *kalā*, *nāda* and *bindu*.

The seventeenth stanza[89] brings out the sequence of origination of the various *āvaraṇa-s* of the *Śrīcakra* from the *bindu* and says that the *Śrīcakra* thus formed is verily the residence of *Ṣoḍaśī Tripurasundarī*. The next stanza[90] says that the sixty-four *tantra-s* of the *kaula mārga* have been criticized by the wise persons. So is the case with the *miśra mārga*. But the *samaya mārga*, which consists of the five *tantra-s* based on the *śubhāgama pañcaka,*[91] is in true harmony with the Vedas and therefore, can be rightfully treated as a higher form of spiritual knowledge (*mahāvidyā)*. Thus, it is only in this *samaya* tradition that the name of the Primordial *Śakti* as *'bhagavatī,'* attains and justifies its transcendental connotation.

The nineteenth stanza[92] gives the fifteen-lettered *mantra* of the *samaya* tradition in an indirect manner and says that this *mantra* consists of three parts. The next stanza[93] says that the three parts of the fifteen-lettered *mantra* correspond with the first forty-nine letters of the sanskrit alphabet and the silent eternal *ṣoḍaśī kalā* of the mantra corresponds with the last letter *'kṣa'* of the sanskrit alphabet.

The twenty-third stanza[94] states that the fifteen-lettered *mantra* and the *Śrīcakra* stand in a relation of corresponding identity. Besides, the six *cakra-s* of the microcosmic body (*piṇḍa*) also have a relation of corresponding identity with both the *mantra* and the *Śrīcakra*. The next stanza[95] summarizes by saying that meditation upon the corresponding identities of the *mantra, Śrīcakra*, microcosmic six *cakra-s* and the sanskrit alphabet in the heart brings about the (epistemic) revelation of the (ontological) identity of the votary and the *Sādākhyā kalā* of *Devī Tripurasundarī*.

The twenty-fifth stanza[96] says that the *bindu* of *Śrīcakra* is neither a *śiva cakra* nor a *śakti cakra*. It symbolizes the *Sāmarasya* state of *Śiva* and *Śakti*. It also says that the fifteen *nityā-s* proclaimed by the śrutis are really the fifteen phases of the moon during the bright and the dark lunar fortnights, and they have a relation of corresponding identity with the fifteen letters of the *mantra*.

The next stanza[97] points out that the fifteen *nityā-s* are ontologically identified with the eternal and transcendent *Ṣoḍaśī kalā* of *Devī Tripurasundarī* situated in the *sahasrāra*. This *Ṣoḍaśī kalā*, in its manifest aspect, is symbolized by the *Śrīcakra* and thus the fifteen *nityā-s* stand in a relation of corresponding identity with the *Śrīcakra*.

The twenty-eighth stanza[98] gives the view of the *samaya mārga* about the *maṇipura cakra*. It gives the meaning of *'maṇi'* as the halo of the *Devī* seen in that *cakra* and also says that the *anāhata nāda* becomes subtly audible upon the rise of *vāyu* in that *cakra*. The next stanza[99] states that the *samaya mārga* takes *viśuddhi cakra* to be the *cakra* related with the origin of the element *ākāśa*. The thirtieth stanza[100] says that the *sahasrāra* (or rather, a point very close to it) is the residence of the fifteen *kalā-s*, which are also known as the fifteen *nityā-s*. The next stanza[101] points out that along with the reflection of the *Ṣoḍaśī kalā*, the fifteen *kalā-s* become sixteen in all, and the nectar oozing from that *Ṣoḍaśī kalā* permeates the devotee with its bliss. It further says that the various phases (*tithi*) of the bright and dark lunar fortnights are quite the same, but the followers of *samaya* tradition do not worship in the phase of the new moon (*amāvasyā*).

The thirty-second stanza[102] describes the positions of the *Rudra granthi*, the *Viṣṇu granthi* and the *Brahma granthi* with respect to the *svādhiṣṭhāna*, *anāhata* and the *ājñā cakra-s* respectively. The next stanza[103] describes the new moon phase (*amāvasyā tithi*) as that period when the sun and the moon (running through *iḍā* and *piṅgalā*) get immersed in the darkness of the *mūlādhāra cakra*. It also describes the state of the showering of the immortal nectar (*amṛta sravaṇa*) as that when the moon situated in the *ājñā cakra* becomes sun-like, by virtue of getting engulfed by the sun. The thirty-fourth stanza[104] describes how the *kuṇḍalinī* after reaching up to the *ājñā cakra* and then rising further to penetrate the *Brahma granthi* causes the divine permeation of the whole body and all its *cakra-s* with the blissful nectar oozing out of the *Ṣoḍaśī kalā* located in the *sahasrāra*.

The next stanza[105] continues by saying that penetrating the *Brahma granthi*, the *kuṇḍalinī* enters the *samaya loka*, where it gets united with *Paramaśiva* in the form of *Parāśakti*, the *Sādākhyā Śakti* (and thus enters the *sāmarasya* state of *Śiva* and *Śakti*). The moon or *candra* located in the *sahasrāra* is also known as *śrīcakra, saragha* and *baindava*. The thirty-sixth[106] stanza says that the wise men perfected in the *samaya* tradition know that the forms of both *Śiva* and *Śakti* are immanent in the twenty-five elements or *tattva-s*. The twenty-sixth element, transcending them, is explicitly known as the '*Śiva Śakti Sāmarasya*'. Those who worship the *Devī*, sitting in the lap of *Paramaśiva* in the *Sādākhya Śrīcakra* of *sahasrāra*, by meditating upon the four types of identities (mentioned before), are blessed with the realization of their fundamental identity with the *Śiva Śakti Sāmarasya*. The thirty-ninth stanza[107] clearly states that the *samaya* tradition accepts five types of similarities between *Śiva* and *Śakti*, viz. *kriyā, avasthā, rūpa, prakṛti* and *nāma*. The adepts perceive these similarities in the forms of *Śiva* and *Śakti* residing in the six microcosmic *cakras* as well. The forty-second stanza[108] says that the *kaula-s* worship in the dark regions of the *mūlādhāra* and *svādhiṣṭhāna cakra-s* by making them illuminated with the rays of fire. But the votaries of *samaya* tradition completely reject such worship, as also any other kind of worship in the dark regions of the *mūlādhāra* and *svādhiṣṭhāna cakra-s*.

The forty-fourth stanza[109] says that *Paramaśiva* and *Devī Ṣoḍaśī Tripurasundarī,* who reside in the *bindu sahasrāra,* manifest themselves as *Navātmā* by getting associated with the nine *vyūha-s* and nine *prakṛti-s* respectively. It is with the help of such association that they, becoming the father and mother of the cosmos, create (or rather project) it out of themselves. The forty-sixth stanza[110] hints at the manner of the rise of the *kuṇḍalinī* (from the *kula sahasrāra*) through the various *cakra-s* by the process of assimilative transformation of the lower levels into their immediate higher levels. The forty-ninth stanza[111] emphatically declares that the followers of the *samaya* tradition worship only the *Devī* who, united with the form of *Śiva*, is the ultimate source of all beings and is also the source of immortal blissful nectar as the *Ṣoḍaśī kalā* of the moon.

The next stanza[112] briefly recapitulates the issues discussed in the *samaya* tradition, e.g., the arousal of *kuṇḍaliṇī*, its union with *Śiva*, its re-entry into the *mūlādhāra*; the corresponding identities of six or four types between the letters of the sanskrit alphabet, the six microcosmic *cakra-s*, the triple-regioned *śrīcakra* and the *mantra* (used as the means of arousing the *kuṇḍalinī*); and the five types of similarities between *Śiva* and *Śakti*. The fifty-first stanza[113] says that the successful completion of the *samaya* disciplines raises the *kuṇḍaliṇī* up to the *sahasrāra* and causes (the epistemic realization of) one's absolute identity with the deity, *Devī Ṣoḍaśī Tripurasundarī*. The last stanza[114] concludes by stating that the blessings of a worthy preceptor or *Guru* is essential for the correct practice of the *samaya* disciplines, as only then the realization of the final objective becomes distinctly possible for the votary. Once the ultimate goal is attained by the votary, he wanders in the world as a *jīvanmukta*, free of all the worldly limitations and spiritual ignorance (*avidyā*). Drenched in the immortal nectar of the *Ṣoḍaśī kalā*, beholding the beatitude of the *Devī Tripurasundarī* as manifest in the three worlds, the *jīvanmukta* goes on spreading love, devotion and knowledge among the masses. The masters of the *samaya* and advaita traditions are living testimonies to this fact.

Māṇḍūkya Kārikā

The very beginning of the first section of the text implies the explicit epistemic status of the three distinct manifestations of *jīva*, namely *Viśva, Taijasa* and *Prājña*. It also states that their common ontological ground is the transcendent fourth state of the Self.[115] The objects of enjoyment differ for the various epistemic states of the Self. Thus, while *Viśva* enjoys the gross objects, *Taijasa* enjoys the subtle objects. But for *Prājña*, the sole object is the pure constitutive bliss of the Self.[116] He who understands properly the epistemically divergent forms along with the underlying immutable ontological unity of the three types of enjoyment and the various states of the Self enjoying them, is not adversely affected even while enjoying them.[117] It adequately hints at the possibility of the *jīvanmukta* state, as also the freedom and transcendence associated with it.

The first section of the *Mā. Kā.* further says that the non-dual, transcendent, all-pervasive fourth (*Turīya*) state of the Self alone is capable of completely eradicating the sorrows afflicting the three (epistemic) states of the Self. Such eradication of sorrows results from the realization of the transcendental and non-dual Self.[118] The three phenomenal and epistemically manifested states of the Self are conditioned by causes and effects but the fourth state or *turīya* transcends the realm of causality.[119] Ramakant Tripathi points out that although in deep sleep there is no explicit cognition, yet there is definitely the feeling of deep peace and happiness, along with the usual phenomenal state of being ignorant of *Brahman.*[120] Even *Prājña* is enveloped by ignorance (*avidyā*), but the *Turīya* is the constant witness of all and it is truly everything ontologically.[121]

Bringing out the difference of *Prājña* and *Turīya*, the text goes on to say that *Prājña*, being associated with deep sleep, does not perceive duality. However, since deep sleep itself is of the form of non-perception of (highest) reality, it turns out to be the source of the cognition of all kinds of duality. Deep sleep state, being the causal state (*kāraṇa avasthā*) and the first manifestation of ignorance *(avidyā)* of reality, is truly the source of all sorts of epistemic duality. In contrast to such association with *avidyā*, the *Turīya*, by virtue of being the constant and transcendent witness (*sākṣī*) of all the other states, is always free of any such binding limitations.[122]

The cessation of control of the beginningless *māyā* over the *jīva* brings about the realization of its own identity with the immutable non-dual *Turīya*. Such a realization immediately breaks the bonds of phenomenal limitations.[123] This section also states that the experience of all kinds of duality, taking place due to *māyā*, has a mere epistemic status. As such, all dualities are only epistemically true and lack any independent ontological status. The fundamental ontological ground of all dualistic cognitions is the non-dual *Turīya* alone.[124] Since duality ceases to exist after realizing the *Turīya,* all talks of philosophy, knowledge, ignorance, bondage, liberation, etc. are relevant and purposeful only so long as the *Turīya* has not been realized. All such talks only serve the purpose of making comprehensible the instruction about the nature of highest reality as well as the means of realizing it.[125]

Bringing out the significance of the syllable *'OM,'* as also the significance of its constitutive sounds, the text reveals that a person who has realized the *Turīya* also has a firm conviction regarding the corresponding identities existing between the three states and the three sounds of the syllable *OM,* that is, between the *Viśva, Taijasa, Prājña* and *a, u, m* respectively.[126]

Elaborating upon the meditation of *OM,* the text says[127] that perfection in the meditation on the *'a'* of *OM,* in the context of its corresponding identity with *Viśva*, grants the aspirant the realization of his own identity with *Vaiśvānara* (the macrocosmic divinity at the gross level). Similarly, perfection in meditation upon *'u'* and *'m'* of *OM* leads to the realization of one's own identity with the *Hiraṇyagarbha* (the macrocosmic divinity at the subtle level) and *Īśvara* (the macrocosmic divinity at the causal level) respectively. With the transcendence of even the causal level, perfect meditation on the silent, vibrationless fourth quarter (*pāda*) of *OM* leads the aspirant to the realization of his own identity with the transcendent *Turīya* or *Para Brahman.*

Emphasizing the identity of the syllable *OM* and *Brahman*, the text further says that this *Praṇava* or the syllable *OM,* is verily both the *Para Brahman* and the *Apara Brahman*. It is beyond causality, non-dual, immutable and transcendent.[128] One who really knows that the whole phenomenal universe of duality has its origination, sustenance and dissolution in *OM* alone, automatically realizes his own identity with the highest Self.[129] It is only the fourth quarter *(pāda)* of *OM*, the *Amātra,* the *Turīya,* which absolutely transcends the realm of duality.[130]

The second section of the text focuses on bringing out the epistemic and hence ontologically unreal nature of all kinds of duality vis-à-vis the non-dual transcendent reality of *Brahman*. It begins by giving arguments to prove the merely epistemic nature of all dream objects. This in turn goes to show their lack of separate ontological reality as against the reality of *Brahman*.[131] The unreal does not exist either in the beginning or the end, despite the fact that it may seem to be existing at the intermediate spatio-temporal points. However, the fact is that even in the intervening space and time it is just as non-existent as in the beginning or in the end.[132] Just as the utility of dream objects is restricted to dream state, so is the utility of the objects of waking state limited to the waking state only. As such, since both the waking and the dream states have only a limited realm of (epistemic) reality, often delimiting each another, therefore they are proved to be ultimately unreal. Both the states have only a limited spatio-temporal domain of epistemic reality.[133] Even within the dream state, the sense and perception of reality and unreality persists just as in the waking state.[134]

The text goes on to say that it is the definite conclusion of vedānta that the self-effulgent Self imagines itself through itself, i.e., by the power of its own *māyā*. It is the Self alone that cognizes the objects of the various states. In this manner, the text highlights the mere epistemic character of the realm of duality as also the fact that It is the Lord Himself who is the ultimate ground and cause all such epistemic manifestations.[135] This means that all the *jīva-s*, as well as all their internal and external cognitions of various objects, in the final analysis, are nothing but the epistemic products of the Lord's imagination.[136]

Just like the case of a rope in the dark, the Self is imagined to be all sorts of things so long as its real nature has not been well ascertained.[137] Also, just as in the case of the rope, as soon as the real nature of the Self is realized, all its numerous imagined ascriptions vanish once and for all.[138] However, this cosmic projection (*māyā*) of the self-effulgent *Brahman* is so powerful that He Himself seems to be deluded by It for a while.[139] At the same time, advaitism holds that from the viewpoint of the transcendent non-dual reality of *Brahman*, the whole universe has a mere epistemic status and it is therefore as real and unreal as a dream or magic.[140] The text goes on to boldly declare that, in the ultimate analysis, the highest truth is that there is no (ontologically) real dissolution, no origination, none in bondage, none striving or aspiring for liberation and none getting liberated.[141] Despite this, the fact remains that this whole realm of illusion and projection becomes possible only because it is grounded in the ontology of the non-dual *Brahman*, since even illusions require the real existence of its supporting consciousness.[142]

The third section of the text, i.e., the *advaita prakaraṇa,* seeks to bring out the logical possibility and necessity of the ontological non-dualism of *Brahman*. Highlighting the homogeneity and immutability of *Brahman*, it indicates that all duality is rooted in epistemic relativism only, which itself is grounded in the transcendent non-dual *Brahman*.[143] Just as the same all pervasive space exists in the names and forms of all the spaces confined by the various individual jars, so are all the individual souls (*jīva*) and composite things (ontologically) existent in the Self alone.[144] Furthermore, just as the distinction of names and forms associated with the spaces confined by the different jars gets dissolved with the disintegration of those jars, so also do the *jīva-s* merge completely in the highest Self after the final disintegration of their three bodies.[145] Extending the simile of jars and space makes clear the possibility of the individual feelings and experiences of the different *jīva-s*.[146] It is also clear from this simile that any *jīva* cannot be regarded as a real transformation (*vikāra*) or even a real part (*avayava*) of the supreme Self.[147] Just like a dream, all the composite objects and phenomena are the projections of *māyā* and thus they have no real individual ontological status. They are the products of the epistemic relativity of *māyā*.[148] Referring to the *Taittirīya upaniṣad*, the text says that the *jīva* residing inside the five sheaths (*kośa*) is none other than the supreme Self.[149] The text then goes on to emphasize the significant point that wherever in the Vedas and the Upaniṣads, especially in the context of creation, there is any statement regarding the distinction of individual self and the supreme self, such distinction must be understood to hold in a secondary sense only. The text says it must be so since such statements about distinction are made for the sole purpose of demonstrating the ultimate ontological unity of *Brahman*, later on, in the course of the text.[150] The similes of sparks, gold, earth, space, etc. given in the scriptures are only illustrations to make the process and nature of creation easily understood by the aspirant and thus convey to him the idea of a basic ontological unity. One should not commit the error of stretching these similes too far, since ultimately there is no real multiplicity anyway.[151] The supreme Self can become the ground of all sorts of duality only in an epistemic sense because if it were to be accepted in any real and ontological sense then the immortal, immutable, non-dual Self would become mortal, mutable and full of duality.[152]

Vedic texts are in equal evidence regarding the reality of creation and the subsistence of creation on *māyā* alone. However, only that should be accepted as the real purport of creation related Vedic statements which has the support of both the Vedas and reasoning. But, that which is determined by the Vedas to be the One without a second, birthless and immortal, alone can manage to claim the full support of reasoning as well. As such, only that supreme non-dual Self should be treated as the real purport of the Vedas. In consequence, the world of duality has to be accepted as a projection of epistemic relativism in the final analysis.[153] The birth of an already existing entity can be possible only through *māyā* and never in reality because if it were to be real then there will be the problem of *regressus-ad-infinitum.*[154] On the other hand, the philosophy of nihilism seems to go against logic itself since there cannot be birth of an absolutely non-existent entity either through *māyā* or in reality, as in the case of a barren woman's son.[155]

Elaborating upon the nature of meditation leading to the realization of one's own identity with *Brahman,* the text goes on to say that the birthless supra-rational knowledge attained through such meditation is truly identical with its object, namely *Brahman*. This means that the Self is realized only through the Self itself.[156] The state of such a perfectly controlled mind, which is immersed in the realization of *Brahman*, is very different from the state of mind in deep sleep.[157] The difference lies in the fact that while the mind loses itself in ignorance (*avidyā*) in the deep sleep state, that same mind, when perfectly controlled, reveals itself as the fearless *Brahman*, the supreme Self.[158] Strictly speaking, the realizational state of such a supreme and transcendent *Brahman* does not allow the least logical possibility of any kind of ceremony, worship or meditation.[159] All the ceremonies, worships and meditations are useful only as the means of attaining realization of the supreme transcendent *Brahman*.

The realization of Self, the resultant removal of all kinds of misery, as also attainment of ever lasting peace depend upon the perfection of mind-control achieved.[160] By constantly meditating on the ultimate misery latent in all phenomenal experiences, one should withdraw the mind from the fleeting enjoyments arising out of fulfilled desires. The perfection of such withdrawal should be accompanied by meditation on the all-pervasive, non-dual, transcendent *Brahman*. The perfection of such meditation enables the aspirant to transcend the realm of duality and realize his own identity with the supreme transcendent *Brahman*.[161] Giving further details of such meditative process, the text says that with the help of detachment and diligent practice one should prevent the mind from both merging in deep sleep or getting engrossed in the ideas of phenomenal enjoyments. Neither should the mind be allowed to remain in a state infested with latent desires for phenomenal enjoyments. The mind should be established in a state of equipoise such that it would effortlessly start moving in the desired direction of meditation and then it should not be disturbed with any kind of phenomenal thoughts.[162] Then, one should not get attached even to the inner joy emanating in the equipoised state of mind. One should apply discrimination to remain detached from it and one must ceaselessly meditate on the Self alone.[163] In due course, such a mind which is motionless and not lost or scattered or appearing in the form of objects, becomes or rather reveals itself as the transcendent *Brahman*.[164] The highest Reality is the same as the highest Bliss and it is located in one's own Self.[165] Thus, the highest reality or transcendent *Brahman* is such that there is absolutely no possibility of any real ontological change or birth within it.[166]

The fourth and last section of the *Māṇḍūkya Kārikā*, namely the *alātaśānti prakaraṇa*, seeks to prove the philosophy of non-duality or advaitism by showing the contradictions of both the dualist and nihilist philosophies. Bringing out the epistemic nature of all dualistic limitations and ascriptions suffered by the *jīva-s*, the text says that although the souls are truly free from old age and death, they epistemically digress from their true nature by getting engrossed in the anxieties of senility and death.[167] As far as the reality of causality is concerned, the text says that a plausible sequence of causality has to be provided by those upholding it.[168] The text clearly highlights the point that there can be no birth or causation in any real sense. It demonstrates its impossibility by explicating the contradictions involved in the alternative solutions to the problem of causality.[169] The futility of all possible explanations of causality indicates that the Real is also the beginningless. This beginninglessness implies birthlessness or *ajāti*.[170] The highest truth is that nothing whatsoever can be born that is already existing, or that is absolutely non-existent, or that which is both existent and non-existent simultaneously.[171]

Taking up the problem of cognition of objects, the text says that the pure consciousness does not ever come into a direct and real contact with any object in all the three possible phenomenal states. Since there is no independent object in reality, all the possibilities of its true or false apprehension are equally meaningless in the ultimate analysis.[172] The fact is that it is consciousness itself appearing to itself in the form of various objects. Therefore, neither consciousness nor the objects cognized by it can be attributed any real birth or origination.[173] All the scriptural instructions about world-creation are meant for the sake of those who, although following the path of right behaviour and discrimination, are still fettered to the epistemic illusion of independent substantiality at the phenomenal plane and therefore, are not yet prepared to fully accept the sole reality of the birthless entity.[174] It is consciousness alone - birthless, motionless, non-material, tranquil and non-dual, which acquires the semblance of birth, motion and substantiality, possessing the various qualities.[175] Just as the movement of a firebrand appears to be straight or curved despite the fact that it is never really affected by it, similarly it is the vibration of consciousness alone, occurring due to the presence of ignorance (*avidyā*), that is responsible for the epistemic projection of the subject and object dichotomy in its own non-dual self.[176] As long as the mind is occupied with phenomenal causality and substantiality, the epistemic delusion of the spatio-temporal world continues. Once the mind gets rid of such preoccupations, by diligently practising the necessary spiritual disciplines, the aspirant transcends the worldly state and becomes firmly established in the transcendental reality.[177] Everything seems to be born due to the empirical outlook; therefore, there is nothing that is eternal. From the viewpoint of the highest reality, whatever is, is nothing apart from the birthless Self. R.C. Pandeya and Manju note the non-causal nature of the Self, as given in the *Māṇḍūkya Kārikā*.[178] As such, there can be really no annihilation at all.[179] The appearance of birth of all the things at the phenomenal level does not imply birth in the true ontological sense as well. Such birth is similar to the birth of a magical thing. It is the result of the transcendental *māyā*, which itself has no ontological reality apart from the supreme *Brahman*.[180]

With regard to all the birthless entities, the words 'eternal' and 'non-eternal' cannot be applied meaningfully. Further, it is not possible to make any categorical statement about a realm where no word can apply in a meaningful and significant way.[181] The highest truth is that nothing whatsoever is ever born at all.[182] All the souls are intrinsically ever illumined. Only that person who can rid himself of the very need and desire of the acquisition of some transcendental knowledge and status, in the light of his very own immutable and transcendental non-dual nature, becomes fit for immortality.[183]

An Overview of Gauḍapāda's Contribution

In the light of previous discussions of selective portions of the important works of Gauḍapāda, it is not very difficult to see the magnitude of his contribution to Śaṅkara's philosophical genius. While the *Śrīvidyāratnasūtram* and the *Subhagodayastotram* greatly emphasize the aspects of devotion and devotional meditation, in the case of *Māṇḍūkya Kārikā* the aspects of ontological absolutism and epistemic relativism get the primary attention. B.K. Matilal has noted the importance of *ajātivāda* theory of *Mā.Kā.* in facilitating the epistemic explanation of all phenomena.[184] Thus, all the three texts basically deal with matters concerning advaitika devotion *(advaita bhakti)* only. However, they emphasize different aspects of it.[185] While the *Māṇḍūkya Kārikā* focuses on the implicit aspect of advaitika devotion, the other two works focus on the explicit aspect of it. At the same time, it should not be overlooked that all the three works do give attention to both the aspects of advaitika devotion, despite the fact that one of them may be getting the primary treatment.

The content and philosophical framework of these three works jointly give a definite shape to the concept of advaitika devotion. We have already seen how all the three works bring out the concepts of ontological absolutism, epistemic relativism, the immanence of the transcendent at the phenomenal level, the importance of devotion and devotional meditation towards the divine cosmic manifestations of the transcendent Reality for realizing one's own absolute identity with the transcendent *Brahman*, as also the fact that ultimately the whole game of creation, bondage, devotion, knowledge and liberation is nothing but a sport or *līlā* of the transcendent primordial energy or *Śakti*, which is none other than the transcendent *Brahman* itself.

We will see in the coming chapters how the *Prasthānatraya bhāṣya* of Śaṅkara is a more detailed and continued discussion of *Māṇḍūkya Kārikā*. Just like it, it emphasizes the implicit aspect of advaitika devotion. However, it also takes up the explicit aspect of it in a secondary manner. On the other hand, we will also see how the *Saundarya-laharī* presents itself as a continuation, or rather a complementary text, of *Subhagodayastotram*, both content wise and style wise. The important concepts and nuances of the *Śrīvidyāratnasūtram* are also easily noticeable in the *Saundarya-laharī*. Thus, the *Saundarya-laharī* focuses on the explicit aspect of advaitika devotion. Furthermore, in the case of some other works of Śaṅkara, it may be easily noticed how he brings out the explicit aspect of advaitika devotion with reference to the other divine manifestations of the transcendent *Brahman*, such as *Śivānanda-laharī, Viṣṇusahasranāma bhāṣya, Prapañcasāra tantra*, etc. However, in the present project we will concentrate only on the *Saundarya-laharī* to understand the nature of advaitika devotion.

Chapter III

Nature and Significance of Devotion in Saundarya-Laharī

The *Saundarya-laharī*, which means the 'The Ocean of Beauty', is a text of superlative degree by Śaṅkara[186] as regards its philosophical depth, literary beauty and spiritual significance. It is basically a hymn addressed to the Primordial Energy, *Śakti*, in Her aspect as *Lalitā Mahātripurasundarī*. Being the spouse of *Śakti*, *Śiva* is also addressed along with *Śakti* in this work. As the text is primarily a hymn, it abounds in exquisite expressions of devotion (*bhakti*). The first forty-one stanzas *(śloka)* of the text are also collectively known as the *Ānanda-laharī* (The Ocean of Bliss), while the remaining section of the text is known as *Saundarya-laharī*. The *Ānanda-laharī* and the *Saundarya-laharī* are together also known as the *Saundarya-laharī*. Out of these two sections of the text, the *Ānanda-laharī* has profound philosophical and spiritual depth, besides the explicit expressions of devotion *(bhakti)*. The second section of the text, starting with the forty-second stanza, describes the infinitely exquisite beauty of *Śakti*, in Her form as *Mahātripurasundarī*.

To properly comprehend the characteristics of devotion *(bhakti)*, as illustrated in the *S.L.* (*Saundarya-laharī*), it is necessary to appreciate its philosophical and metaphysical background. This is so because this background defines the nature of relationship and interaction between the deity *(Iṣṭa)* and the devotee *(bhakta)*. Before we start focusing on the various stanzas of the text, it would suffice to point out that there is an exclusive and obvious presence of non-dualistic metaphysical implications throughout the text, especially in the *Ānanda-laharī*. The compatibility of devotion *(bhakti)* with non-dualism or advaitism has already been shown in the second section of the first chapter. In fact, non-dualism or advaitism is not only compatible with devotion *(bhakti)*, rather it requires this special type of devotion for its philosophical consistency. This point has been elaborated in the first chapter under the section *'The Need of Devotion (Bhakti) in Śaṅkara's Advaitism'*.

Parameters for the Study of Devotion (Bhakti)

Making a systematic effort to study the concept and practice of devotion *(bhakti)*, as expounded in the *S.L.*, requires prior delineation of the relevant parameters. These parameters should be able to accommodate all the important features of devotion, while being non-repetitive and minimal in number. As such we may fix up four parameters for the study of the concept and practice of devotion *(bhakti)*. These are (1) the concept of deity *(iṣṭa),* (2) the concept of devotee *(bhakta),* (3) the means of devotion, and (4) the state of perfect devotion and its result.

The first parameter, that is, the concept of deity *(iṣṭa),* would require that we try to comprehend and analyze all aspects of the deity, as given in the *S.L.* These aspects could be the immanence and transcendence of the deity with respect to the phenomenal world, or the nature of its epistemic and metaphysical relationship with the devotee *(bhakta),* or its simultaneously non-dualistic (advaitika) and pluralistic reality and manifestations. It could also be the nature of its grace and the means to obtain it. It would also require the study of the various levels of manifestation of the deity, their mutual relationship and the sequence of epistemic and/or metaphysical evolution and involution. Besides these, anything else concerning the deity and of relevance to the concept and practice of devotion *(bhakti),* has to be discussed under this parameter, subject to the constraints of the present project.

The second parameter, that is, the concept of devotee *(bhakta),* would demand that we focus on the characteristic nature of a devotee, as indicated in the *S.L.* Also, it would require the categorization of the devotees according to the stages of their spiritual evolution. It would also demand a study of the actual and perceived relationship of the devotee *(bhakta)* with his deity *(iṣṭa)*.

The third parameter, namely the means of devotion, would require a detailed study of the mental, verbal and physical actions and dispositions of devotees. It should encompass the whole range of devotees, from the beginner to the perfect. Along with the different expressions of devotion valid for the different levels of devotees, it requires the study of the results of these different devotional practices.

The fourth and last parameter for the study of the concept and practice of devotion *(bhakti)*, namely the state of perfect devotion and its result, focusses on the culminating point of spiritual evolution through devotion *(bhakti)*, as described in the *S.L.* Specifically, it would demand the study of highest possible type of devotion *(bhakti)*, as given in the *S.L.* Also, it would entail the study of the effect or result of such supreme devotion, as indicated in the *S.L.* In the light of these parameters, we would now undertake a detailed analysis of the explicit and implicit meanings of the various stanzas of the *S.L.*, especially those of the *Ānanda-laharī*. During the course of this analysis, references would be made to other works of Śaṅkara and Gauḍapāda, to make matters clear, as and when required.

The Analysis of Saundarya-laharī

The very first stanza of *S.L.* points to the highest Reality and shows the complementarity of *Śiva* and *Śakti*. This stanza may be roughly translated as -

> "Only when being united with *Śakti*, does *Śiva* become able to act as the Lord, otherwise He is not capable of stirring even a vibration (*spanda*). While so, how can one, who has acquired no merit, either praise or salute Thee, (O Goddess

Tripurasundarī!) who art worthy of being adored even by *Hari, Hara, Viriñca* and others?"[187]

To comprehend the full significance of the first half of this stanza, we need to understand the two aspects of *Brahman* - the *nirguṇa nirākāra Brahman* and *saguṇa sākāra Brahman*. These are only two aspects of the absolute non-dual reality, the *Brahman*. They are not in any way two separate ontological realities or even epistemic manifestations. As such, neither is ontologically or epistemically dependent on the other one. In reality, they are one and the same, and transcend all the phenomenal categories of space, time, causality, etc. P.T. Raju has noted the possible contradictions arising from treating the *saguṇa* and *nirguṇa Brahman* as being different in status of their reality.[188] The *nirguṇa nirākāra Brahman* is absolutely beyond all descriptions, and it has been pointed out only through negative indications in the works of advaitism and *tantra*.[189]

The second aspect of *Brahman* as the *saguṇa sākāra Brahman*, is also known as the *Sāmarasya* or *Yugnaddha* or *Ardhnārīśvara* state[190] of *Śiva* and *Śakti*. This is a state of indistinguishable interpenetrative union or conjointness of *Śiva* and *Śakti*, which is absolutely non-dual and transcendent to all the phenomenal categories. But, whereas the *nirguṇa nirākāra Brahman* does not highlight the potentiality of *Brahman* as the basis of possible epistemic projections of duality, the aspect of *saguṇa sākāra Brahman* highlights the potentiality of *Brahman* as the basis of possible epistemic projections of duality *(dvaita)*. This conjoint form of *Śiva* and *Śakti* is the basis of all epistemic vibrations *(spanda)* of duality, and this has been indicated in the first half of the first stanza of the *S.L.*

Although in this *Sāmarasya* or *Ardhanārīśvara* state of *Śiva* and *Śakti*, that is, in the *saguṇa sākāra Brahman*, *Śiva* and *Śakti* form a single non-dual entity, yet this very interpenetrative conjointness also implies that there is an aspect of *Śiva* and an aspect of *Śakti* in it. Now, similar to the case of *saguṇa* and *nirguṇa Brahman*, the aspects of *Śiva* and *Śakti* are merely two aspects of the non-dual *Sāmarasya* or *Ardhanārīśvara* state. They do not depict a distinction of *Śiva* and *Śakti* at this level. Yet, these two aspects provide the very basis of all possible epistemic projections or superimpositions *(adhyāsa)*[191] or vibrations *(spanda)*[192] at the lower manifestational levels of reality.[193] The *Śiva* aspect of the *Sāmarasya* or *Ardhanārīśvara* state signifies the illuminative, subjective *(prakāśa)*[194] and conscious *(cit)*[195] aspects of manifestations, whereas the *Śakti* aspect signifies the illumined, objective *(vimarśa)*[196] and blissful *(ānanda)*[197] aspects of manifestations.

The *saguṇa sākāra Brahman*, which is the same as the *Sāmarasya* or *Ardhanārīśvara* or *Yugnaddha* state of *Śiva* and *Śakti*, cannot be separated from the *nirguṇa nirākāra* aspect of *Brahman*, either ontologically or epistemically. They are only two attempts at indicating the nature of the highest *Brahman*, in a negative and positive manner. The negative indication of the *nirguṇa nirākāra Brahman* highlights the absolute transcendence of *Brahman* to all the phenomenal categories, constituted by the numerous levels of epistemic projections of duality. Advaitism abounds in such negative descriptions of *Brahman*.[198] On the other hand, the positive description or indication of the *saguṇa sākāra Brahman*, that is, the *Sāmarasya* or *Ardhanārīśvara* state of *Śiva* and *Śakti*, highlights *Brahman* as the fundamental ground of all epistemic projections and superimpositions of duality. The texts of *samaya tantra* [199] are replete with such descriptions of the highest Reality, *Brahman*.[200] So, the highest Reality of advaitism is one and the same with the highest Reality of *tantra*.

Viewing from another angle, if we take the *nirguṇa nirākāra Brahman* as the sole, immutable and absolute ontological Reality (as described in advaitika texts), but do not accept the *saguṇa Brahman* or the *Sāmarasya* state as an indistinguishable and inseparable aspect of the same *Brahman*, then we would be left with no option but to accept the *saguṇa Brahman* as an epistemic projection out of the *nirākāra Brahman*. But, on the basis of its negative indication, it would be inconsistent to visualize the presence of any seed or cause of projecting an epistemic duality in the *nirākāra Brahman*. This incoherence can be removed only by accepting the potentiality of the same transcendent *Brahman* to also act as the fundamental ground of all possible epistemic projections and superimpositions. This is precisely the positive description of *Brahman*, as the *saguṇa sākāra Brahman* or the *Sāmarasya* or *Ardhanārīśvara* state of *Śiva* and *Śakti*. Thus, it would be illogical and contradictory to treat *saguṇa Brahman* itself as an epistemic projection, for how can it simultaneously be both the cause and effect of epistemic projections of duality. The solution to this dilemma is that the *saguṇa Brahman* or the *Sāmarasya* state is a non-dual ontologically absolute state, at par and identical with the *nirguṇa nirākāra Brahman*. They are only two aspects of *Brahman*, absolutely non-dual and transcendent to all phenomenal categories of thought, existence and language. They are like the fire and its potency to burn, like the water and its coolness, like the magnet and its nature to attract.[201] In fact, all linguistic descriptions are inherently incapable of fully indicating, the nature of *Brahman*, as It transcends the categories of space, time, language and logic. At best, we can only partially indicate some aspects of *Brahman*.

Thus, the first half of the first stanza of *S.L.* emphatically states that *Śiva* cannot be possibly taken as the Lord of Universe in isolation from *Śakti*. *Śiva* and *Śakti* refer to one another in an essential way. The second half of this stanza then brings out the consequent inevitability of seeking the grace of *Śakti* for obtaining the highest knowledge and liberation. Since all the aspects of the dualistic world are directly under the control of *Śakti*, therefore despite the absolutist framework of advaitism, Śaṅkara has emphatically stated here the need for seeking the grace of *Śakti*. Not only this, Śaṅkara also makes it clear that even the highest placed beings of the universe have to seek the blessings of *Śakti* for transcending the pain and misery of the world. The last line of this stanza is very illuminating and sobering. It says that only when a person has performed righteous deeds for many lifetimes, does he become capable of thinking and accepting the omniscience, omnipresence, omnipotence of *Śakti* and therefore, only then he becomes duly eligible for saluting and praising *Śakti*. Thus, the comprehension of *Śakti*'s role and domain requires immense intellectual, ethical and spiritual purification. Thus, even the preliminary votary of *Śakti* must be highly evolved spiritually. The devotion of *Śakti* thus requires immense spiritual purification on the part of even the beginner devotee *(bhakta)*.

The second stanza of the *S.L.*[202] says that *Brahmā* creates the worlds from the tiniest speck of dust collected from the lotus-feet of the Goddess *Tripurasundarī,* while *Hari* upholds these worlds with great effort, and *Hara* destroys these worlds at the time of *pralaya,* the great dissolution. This stanza points out the infinite power of the Goddess by saying that all the worlds are created out of a mere speck of dust collected from Her feet. Further, it also brings out the fact that the Goddess *Tripurasundarī,* being the fundamental *vimarśa śakti,*[203] alone is the final cause of all objectifications in the worlds. The level of epistemic manifestation of the Goddess *Tripurasundarī* serving as the immediate source of the creation of the worlds, is referred in the *S.L.*[204] and the *Subhagodaya*[205] as the level where She is qualified by the nine *prakṛtis*. Śaṅkara has described this level of manifestation of the Goddess as *'vicikīṣurghanībhūtā'* in his *Prapañcasāra-tantra*.[206] This epistemic manifestational level of the Goddess is also the residing locus for the seeds *(saṁskāras)* of all the worlds during the great dissolution *(pralaya),* besides being the source of the creation of the worlds at the time of creation *(sarga)*. *Śiva*, as qualified by the nine *vyūhas,*[207] is the counterpart epistemic manifestation for this manifestation of *Śakti*. This manifestational level of *Śiva* and *Śakti* is the first level of immanence, because at this level they are qualified with space, time, etc. Above this level of *Śiva* and *Śakti*, in the ladder of epistemic manifestations, lie the transcendent forms of *Śiva* and

Śakti, manifesting themselves as the first level of epistemically projected duality. This is the transcendent level of *Śiva* and *Śakti* because at this level there is no trace of space, time, etc. This primordial epistemically projected duality is grounded in the *saguṇa Brahman* i.e., the *Sāmarasya* state of *Śiva* and *Śakti*. It is beyond all phenomenal categories. This is the primordial epistemic duality and it has been referred to as the *'nāda'* [208] component of the universal vibration '*Aum*' in the *Prapañcasāra-tantra* of Śaṅkara. The first level of immanence of *Śiva* and *Śakti*, which is qualified by the nine *vyūhas* and the nine *prakṛtis* respectively, is referred to as the fourth component of *Aum*, that is, the *'bindu'*,[209] in the *Prapañcasāra-tantra* of Śaṅkara. The first three components of *Aum*, namely *'A'*, *'U'* and *'M'* correspond respectively with the gross *(sthūla),* subtle *(sūkṣma)* and causal *(kāraṇa)* worlds. The last two components of *Aum*, namely *'śakti'* and *'śānta'*, correspond with the *saguṇa sākāra Brahman,* i.e., the *Sāmarasya* state of *Śiva* and *Śakti,*[210] and the *nirguṇa nirākāra Brahman* respectively. Thus, out of the seven components of *Aum - A, U, M, bindu, nāda, śakti* and *śānta* - the first four are immanent and dualistic, while the fifth one is transcendent but dualistic, but the last two are non-dual and transcendent. In fact, the last two are only two aspects of the same supreme reality namely *Brahman*.

The third stanza of *S.L.* describes the Goddess *Tripurasundarī* as the island-city of suns illuminating the internal darkness of the ignorant, and as the tusk of the wild boar incarnation of *Muraripu* for those submerged in the ocean of births (and deaths).[211] Here, the thrust of the stanza is that it is *Śakti* alone who grants knowledge and illumination of the highest Reality to those enmeshed in the phenomenal world. Manju has noted the role of devotion in the purification of *citta* for having the highest realization.[212] *Śakti*, i.e., the *vimarśa śakti,* is the object to be illumined by the *prakāśa śakti* i.e., the illuminative power of *Śiva*. This holds true for all levels of epistemic manifestations of *Śiva* and *Śakti*. Thus, the epistemically projected form of *Śakti* alone determines the level of epistemic identification for *Śiva*. While moving up or down the sequence of epistemic projections, it is *Śakti* who takes the lead and *Śiva* follows Her accordingly. But, there is a slight difference between the upward and downward movement of the manifestations of *Śiva* and *Śakti*, in the sequence of epistemic projections. During the downward movement, it is *Śakti* who takes the exclusive lead and then *Śiva* follows Her. But during the course of upward movement, the epistemic projection of *Śiva (prakāśa-śakti)* has to contemplate and visualize itself as illuminating and being identified with the epistemic projection of *Śakti (vimarśa śakti)* belonging to the next higher level of epistemic projection. But, the epistemic projection of *Śiva*, of a given level, does not really move on to the next higher level just by contemplating and visualizing so. Only when the epistemic projection of *Śakti* of that level moves on to the next higher level, that is, gets Herself sublated into the next higher level of epistemic projection, the epistemic projection of *Śiva* at that level becomes able to sublate Himself into His own next higher level of epistemic projection. However, exactly when that epistemic projection of *Śakti* would sublate Herself into Her own next higher level of epistemic projection, is decided primarily by Her own sweet will. Therefore, it is *Śakti* alone who is both knowledge *(vidyā)* and ignorance *(avidyā)*.[213]

The fourth stanza of the *S.L.* says that the Goddess *Tripurasundarī* does not show either the fear-dispelling gesture *(abhaya mudrā)* or the boon-bestowing gesture *(varada mudrā)* of Her hands, as Her feet, by themselves, are proficient in granting immunity from fear and bestowing boons transcending one's desires.[214] This stanza makes it quite clear that unlike other deities, the Goddess *Tripurasundarī* does not have to make or even show any extra effort in order to grant the desired boons and immunity from fear to Her devotees *(bhakta)*. This is so because Her devotees surrender themselves at Her feet, ever contemplating them, and as a result of it, all their fears are dispelled and they get more than their desired boons. It is the very nature of Her feet that whosoever contemplates them, receives Her grace and mercy. Now, in the *samaya tantra*, the feet of Goddess *Tripurasundarī* also signify the various component parts of *Aum*, either the four components - *A, U, M,* and *Turīya*,[215] or the seven components - *A, U, M, bindu, nāda, śakti* and *śānta*.[216] Here, the component *'A'* stands for the epistemic manifestations of *Śiva* and *Śakti*[217] corresponding to the macrocosmic gross universe[218] *(sthūla jagat),* while the components *'U'* and *'M'* stand for those manifestations of *Śiva* and *Śakti*[219] that correspond to the macrocosmic subtle[220] *(sūkṣma jagat)* and causal universes[221] *(kāraṇa jagat)* respectively. The *'bindu'* component of *Aum* corresponds with the epistemic projections of *Śiva* and *Śakti*, as qualified by the nine *vyūhas* and the nine *prakṛtis* respectively.[222] The epistemic projections of *Śiva* corresponding to the macrocosmic gross, subtle and causal universe are the *Virāṭa (Vaiśvānara), Hiraṇyagarbha (Sūtrātman)* and *Īśvara* respectively.[223] The epistemic projections of *Śakti (vimarśa śakti)* corresponding to the macrocosmic gross, subtle and causal universe are the whole gross universe, the subtle universe and the causal universe respectively. The epistemic manifestations of *Śakti* corresponding to *A, U, M* and *bindu* serve as the objects to be illumined, and thus to be identified with, for the corresponding manifestations of *Śiva* at these levels. These component parts of *Aum* also correspond with different sections of the path to be traversed by the *kuṇḍalinī* [224] in the devotee's subtle body. Thus, *A, U, M* and *bindu* correspond with the *Rudra granthi,* the *Viṣṇu granthi,* the *Brahma granthi* and *bindu* respectively in the path of *kuṇḍalinī*.[225] So, when by way of contemplating the feet of Goddess *Tripurasundarī* the devotee starts meditating on the manifestations of *Śiva* and *Śakti*, corresponding to the different components of *Aum*, at the specified points in the *kuṇḍalinī* pathway, then by the grace of the Goddess the various manifestation of *Śakti* successively sublate into their own next higher epistemic manifestation. As a result of this sublation, the manifestation of *Śiva* also gets sublated into the next higher epistemic manifestation. The manifestational level of *Śiva* determines the level of identification for the consciousness *(cidābhāsa)* of the *jīva,* and the extent of upward movement of the *kuṇḍalinī* specifies the manifestational level of *Śakti*, which serves as the object *(vimarśa)* for the *jīva cidābhāsa*.[226] Thus, by unceasing meditation on the feet of the Goddess the consciousness of the *jīva* is uplifted to higher and higher levels of epistemic projections until it reaches the level of *bindu*, where *Śiva* manifests Himself as qualified by the nine *vyūhas* and identifies Himself with *Śakti*, qualified by the nine *prakṛtis,* as his objective counterpart. As a result of this process the devotee acquires overlordship over the gross, subtle and causal universes one by one, and he has nothing to fear and everything belonging to those realms come under his command. This overlordship of the different worlds comes naturally to the devotees of *Śakti* as they contemplate Her feet and hence there is no need for the Goddess to show either the fear-dispelling gesture *(abhaya mudrā)* or the boon-bestowing gesture *(varada mudrā)*.

The fifth stanza points out that by worshipping the Goddess *Tripurasundarī, Viṣṇu* acquired the body of such a beautiful damsel that even the most renunciant god, *Hara,* got fascinated by it. Also, it is through the worship of the Goddess that *Smara,* the god of passions, is able to rule over the whole world.[227] This stanza highlights the infinite strength of the deluding power *(avidyā śakti)* of the Goddess since even *Hara,* the most reclusive of the gods, could not withstand the onslaught of Her deluding power, when it was so desired by Her. Similarly, with the benediction of the Goddess, *Smara* rules over the whole world through the power of love and passion. This stanza also highlights the point that the Goddess confers material boons as well, when so desired by Her devotees. But the tradition of the *samaya mārga* prohibits its followers from getting entangled in the fulfillment of material desires. It is the *kaula mārga*[228] which advocates the fulfillment of both material and spiritual aspirations simultaneously. Maurice Winternitz says the more one appreciates the bliss of the Highest

Reality, the less attractive would be the phenomenal objects,[229] and so the *samaya mārga* forbids seeking worldly goals. Even though the *samaya mārga* prohibits pursuing material goals for their own sake, it is realistic enough to recognize that there are some minimal material needs necessary for survival in this material world. As far as these needs are concerned, the Goddess takes care of them even though the devotee may not ask for them.

The next stanza again highlights the point that it is due to the grace of the Goddess that *Anaṅga (Smara)* rules over the world.[230] Thus, it is the *avidyā śakti* of the Goddess alone that primarily deludes the world, just like the fact that it is Her will alone that can give spiritual enlightenment to any *jīva*.

The seventh stanza says -

> "May the great Pride (incarnate) of the Vanquisher of the (three) *Pura-s,* with a jingling girdle, (slightly) bent (under the weight of) the breasts resembling the frontal globes of a young elephant, slim in the waist, with a face (bright) like the autumnal fullmoon, and weilding a bow, arrows, a noose and a goad with Her hands, stand forth before us!"[231]

In this stanza the expression *'pura mathitur āho puruṣikā'* is very significant. It stands for the Goddess *Tripurasundarī*. Lakṣmīdhara, the illustrious author of *Lakṣmīdharā* (a famous commentary on the *S.L.*), says that the word *'aho'* stands for 'I-ness' and so the term *'āho puruṣikā'* means *ahaṅkāra* or egoism. Further, he says that the *ahaṅkāra* of *Śiva* consists of the form *(rūpa)* of *Śakti*, the Goddess *Tripurasundarī*.[232] The term *'aho'* also signifies a wondrous exclamation. Here *Śiva* has been referred by the name *'pura mathitṛ'*, one who has churned or vanquished the three worlds. The famous text of *tantra*, *Rudrayāmala*, relates how *Śiva* churned up the three sacred syllables or *mantras* of the Goddess to bring forth the form of the Goddess (i.e., Her *svarūpa*).[233] *'Pura'* also stands for a realm or world. So, the reference to *Śiva* as *'pura mathitṛ'* may also mean that *Śiva*, by churning up and vanquishing the three worlds or realms, came up with the form of the Goddess and realized with wondrous exclamation that His own ego *(ahaṅkāra)* was nothing but the form of the Goddess *(āho puruṣikā)*. Now, it may be recalled that after establishing complete harmony and identity *(tādātmya)* with the first three components of *Aum* - *A, U* and *M* - the spiritual aspirant strives to establish identity with the fourth component, namely *bindu*. This *bindu* is the level of the epistemic manifestation of *Śiva* and *Śakti* as qualified by the nine *vyūhas* and the nine *prakṛtis* respectively. It represents the outer limits of phenomenal categories and immanent dualism. Beyond it lie the realms of transcendent dualism and absolute transcendent non-dualism. This level, the *bindu*, corresponds to a point just above the *Brahma granthi,* in the path of the *kuṇḍalinī*. The spiritual aspirant *(sādhaka)* and devotee *(bhakta)* approaches the level of the *bindu* after conquering the three worlds - gross, subtle, causal - by realizing his own Self as the *Virāṭa,* the *Hiraṇyagarbha* and the *Īśvara* respectively. On attaining the level of *bindu*, by raising his *kuṇḍalinī* up to it, the devotee realizes his own Self as the *Navātmā Śiva*, i.e., *Śiva*, as qualified by the nine *vyūhas,* and then he also realizes the form of the *Nava prakṛtyātmaka Śakti*, i.e., the Goddess *Tripurasundarī,* as qualified by the nine *prakṛtis,* as His own ego *(ahaṅkāra)*. As such, the bewildered and joyous exclamation of *'āho'* by the devotee is but appropriate. Further, such joyous exclamation can be appropriate only for the devotee who has just realized the manifestations of the *bindu* level, and not for the transcendent *Śiva* as He cannot be deluded even for a moment. The transcendent *Śiva* is ever conscious of His inseparable identity with *Śakti*. Apart from realizing His own Self as the *Navātmā Śiva* and *Śakti* as His very own ego *(ahaṅkāra),* the devotee also gets a glimpse of the transcendent forms of *Śiva* and *Śakti* at the level of *nāda,* as also their inseparable identity. Once the devotee reaches the level of *bindu,* he becomes a *jīvanmukta,* a person 'liberated-while-living'. To raise his *kuṇḍalinī* up to the *bindu,* the devotee has to develop mastery over the *nirvikalpa* or *nirbīja* or *dharmamegha samādhi.* [234] Śaṅkara has extensively commented on this supreme *samādhi* in his *Vivaraṇa*[235] (sub-commentary) on the *Vyāsa bhāṣya* (commentary by Vyāsa) of the *Yoga sūtra* of Patañjali. A *jīvanmukta* person is not deluded by the phenomenal categories although living in the world. Manju has noted that realization consists in getting rid of belief in duality, and not an absolute absence of appearances of duality.[236] A *jīvanmukta* person holds on to his body only as long as his *prārabdha karmas* [237] are not exhausted. Thereafter, he relinquishes his body once and forever, and his consciousness gets merged in that of *Śiva*, either at the level of *nāda* [238] or at the level of the *sahasrāra,*[239] depending upon the nature of his devotion *(bhakti).*[240] The merger of his consciousness with that of *Śiva* implies the absolute and irrevocable realization of his own Self either as *Śiva* (at *nāda*), or as *Brahman* i.e., the *Sāmarasya* state of *Śiva* and *Śakti* (at *sahasrāra*). This absolute mergence is known as *'videhamukti'*.[241] This stanza also says that the Goddess holds a (coral) noose *(pāśa),* a goad *(aṅkuśa),* a (red) sugarcane bow *(ikṣu daṇḍa dhanuḥ)* and five flower-arrows *(bāṇāḥ)* in Her four hands. The *Bhāvanopaniṣad* states that the noose symbolizes attachment, the goad aversion, the bow the mind, and the five flower-arrows the five *tanmātrās* - the five subtle essences of the five elements.[242] The *Lalitāsahasranāma* gives the same symbolism, except in case of the goad, which it takes as a symbol of anger *(krodha).*[243] The *Yoginihṛdaya* (VI-53) takes the noose, the goad and the five flower-arrows to signify the powers of volition or desire *(icchā śakti),* cognition or knowledge *(jñāna śakti)* and action *(kriyā śakti)* respectively, while the bow makes them effulgent.[244]

The eighth stanza of *S.L.* says -

> "Blessed are few that serve Thee, the Ocean of Consciousness and Bliss, having, as Thy abode, the lap of *Paramaśiva*, placed on the couch of the form of *Śiva*, in the mansion of *Cintamaṇi*-stones, attached to the pleasure garden of *Nīpa* trees, in the isle

of gems, surrounded by an avenue of *kalpa* trees, and situated amidst the ocean of nectar."[245]

This stanza describes the residing place of the Goddess *Tripurasundarī,* in the form of *'Cid ānanda laharī'*, the Ocean of Consciousness and Bliss. This form of the Goddess signifies the *Sāmarasya* state or the *saguṇa Brahman* (the *śakti* component of *Aum*). The interpretations of this stanza by the *samaya mārga* and the *kaula mārga* differ, as they advocate internal and external worship respectively. So, the *samaya mārga* teaches the internal worship of the *Śrīcakra*[246] through meditation, while the *kaula mārga* teaches external worship of it. The different *āvaraṇas* or *cakras*[247] of the *Śrīcakra* are taken as corresponding with the different *cakras*[248] lying in the *kuṇḍalinī* path through the *suṣumṇā* nerve.[249] The *sṛṣti cakra* (the four *Śiva cakras*) of the *Śrīcakra* is taken to be symbolized by the 'Ocean of nectar', the *caturdaśāra cakra* by the 'avenue of *Kalpa* trees', the *bahirdaśāra* and the *antardaśāra cakras* by the 'isle of gems' and the 'garden of *Nīpa* trees' respectively, the *aṣṭāra cakra* by the 'mansion of *Cintāmaṇi* stones', the *trikoṇa cakra* by the 'couch', and the *bindu cakra* by *Sadāśiva.*[250] The Kulārṇava also takes the *bindu cakra* as representing the transcendental *Brahman*, and it is depicted by the level of the *sahasrāra.*[251]

The next stanza of *S.L.* also says that the Goddess in Her transcendental form as *Parāśakti* sports with Her spouse, the *Paramaśiva,* in the *sahasrāra.*[252] The *Subhagodaya* also testifies to the sporting of the Goddess as *Parāśakti* with *Paramaśiva* in the *sahasrāra.*[253] It also makes it clear that Her form is of the *Sāmarasya* state *(śivayor melan vapuḥ).*[254] The *Lalitāsahasranāma* too testifies to this location of *Parāśakti* by calling Her *'Pañca brahmāsana sthitā'.*[255] The *Paramaśiva,* in whose lap the *Parāśakti* is taken to be sporting, is the same as the *nirguṇa nirākāra Brahman*, the *śānta* component of *Aum*, whereas *Parāśakti* Herself is the *saguṇa Brahman* or the *Sāmarasya* state,[256] as She is the Ocean of both Consciousness and Bliss *(cid ānanda laharī). Parāśakti* or the *Sāmarasya* state is the same as the *śakti* component of *Aum*. Below the level of *śānta* and *śakti,* is that of *nāda* which represents the transcendental dualistic form of *Śiva* (as *Sadāśiva*) and *Śakti*. This *nāda* level is symbolized by the couch of the Goddess in this stanza. The four legs of this couch are *Rudra, Viṣṇu, Brahmā* and *Īśāna (Navātmā Śiva),* which are represented by the first four components of *Aum (A, U, M, bindu)* at the levels of *Rudra granthi, Viṣṇu granthi, Brahma granthi* and the *bindu*.[257] This stanza also says that there are only a few blessed souls who worship the Goddess in Her *Sāmarasya* state as the Ocean of Consciousness *(cit)* and Bliss *(ānanda)*. The significance of this is that only when a devotee rises up to the *bindu* level, he is able to get a glimpse of the transcendental states of *Śiva-Śakti*, namely, the transcendental dualistic form of *Śiva-Śakti* (at the *nāda* level) and the transcendental non-dualistic form of *Paramaśiva* and *Parāśakti* (as *śānta* and *śakti* at the level of *sahasrāra)*. One who goes up to the *bindu* level becomes a *jīvanmukta,* 'liberated-while-living', and only such a *jīvanmukta* can get a glimpse of the *Sāmarasya* state of *Parāśakti Tripurasundarī*.[258] The actual merger of one's own self in this *Sāmarasya* state is possible only for the *videhamukta,* and none else.[259] Therefore, being able to worship the *Cid ānanda laharī,* i.e., *Sāmarasya* state of Goddess *Tripurasundarī,* denotes the highest spiritual excellence possible for any living devotee.

The ninth stanza of *S.L.* says,

> "Thou art diverting Thyself, in secrecy with Thy Lord, in the thousand-petalled lotus, having pierced through the Earth situated in the *mūlādhāra*, the water in the *maṇipūra*, the fire abiding in the *svādhiṣṭhāna*, the air in the Heart (*anāhata*), the ether above (in the *viśuddhi*), and *manas* between the eyebrows (*ājñā*) and thus broken through the entire *kula* path."[260]

This stanza is of great significance as it briefly hints at the whole process of spiritual evolution through the rise of the *kuṇḍalinī* from the *mūlādhāra* to the *sahasrāra*. This whole region is known as the *kula patha,* the path of the *kuṇḍalinī śakti*. This *kuṇḍalinī* is the microcosmic manifestation of Goddess *Tripurasundarī*. Kaivalyāśrama in his commentary on the *S.L.*, namely the *Saubhāgyavardhinī*, says that there are three kinds of meditation *(dhyāna)* upon the Goddess *Tripurasundarī* - the gross, subtle and the transcendental. He also makes it clear that the seventh and the eighth stanzas of *S.L.* give the description of Goddess suitable for the gross and transcendental meditations respectively, while the ninth stanza, describing the rise of *kuṇḍalinī* through the *kula* path, is suitable for the subtle meditation.[261] Regarding the position and elemental aspect of *maṇipūra,* Lakṣmīdhara (in his *Lakṣmīdharā*) says that *'kaṅ'* denotes the water-element,[262] and so the elemental aspect of *maṇipūra* is water. Further, the sequence of *cakras* given in this stanza, as well as the evolutionary sequence of the elements (in advaitism) demand that the water-*cakra maṇipūra* should come right above the *mūlādhāra*. This sequence of *cakra*s is also supported by the *Vāmakeśvara tantra*, according to Bhāskararāya.[263] Gauḍapāda also supports this position and elemental aspect of the *maṇipūra cakra* in his *Subhagodaya*.[264]

Now, to comprehend the full significance of the rise of *kuṇḍalinī* through this *kula* path, we need to be very clear about the significance of various centres and sections of the *kula* path. The lowest end of the *kula* path is the *kula sahasrāra*, also called the *mūlādhāra kulkuṇḍa*. Some views take this to be the lowest part of *mulādhāra* itself. This is the center where the *kuṇḍalinī* rests in three and a half coils, waiting to be awakened. Right above the *kula sahasrāra* lies the *mūlādhāra cakra*. Then come the *maṇipūra*, the *svādhiṣṭhāna*, the *anāhata*, the *viśuddhi* and the *ājñā cakra*s. There are three knots *(granthi-s)* in the *kula* path. The *Rudra granthi* lies between the *maṇipūra* and the *svādhiṣ- ṭhāna*, the *Viṣṇu granthi* between the *anāhata* and *viśuddhi*, while the *Brahma granthi* lies just above the *ājñā cakra*. Just above the *Brahma granthi* is the point representing the level of the *bindu*, which corresponds with the *bindu* component of *Aum*. Next to this is the point depicting the *nāda*, which corresponds with the *nāda* component of *Aum*. Even above the *nāda* is the *sahasrāra* (or the *akula sahasrāra*), the white thousand-petalled lotus-*cakra*, representing the *śakti* and *śānta* components of *Aum*. Now, the section of the *kula* path up to the *Rudra granthi* represents the gross universe (*sthūla jagat*). The section between the *Rudra granthi* and the *Viṣṇu granthi* depicts the subtle universe (*sūkṣma jagat*), while the section between the *Viṣṇu granthi* and the *Brahma granthi* stands for the causal universe (*kāraṇa jagat*). The three knots (*granthi-s*) depict the macrocosmic manifestational levels of *Śiva* and *Śakti* (as *prakāśa* and its *vimarśa*) with respect to the three realms. So, the *Rudra granthi* represents *Virāṭ* or *Vaiśvānara* and the whole gross world. The *Viṣṇu granthi* represents the *Hiraṇyagarbha* and the whole subtle universe, while the *Brahma granthi* stands for *Īśvara* and the whole causal world. The microcosmic aspects of *Virāṭ*, *Hiraṇyagarbha* and *Īśvara* are *Viśva*, *Taijasa* and *Prājña* respectively. The *jīva cidābhāsa* (the *jīva* soul), as conscious of its gross body (*sthūla śarīra*) is called *Viśva*. The *jīva cidābhāsa*, as conscious of its subtle body (*sūkṣma śarīra*) and causal body (*kāraṇa śarīra*), is called *Taijasa* and *Prājña* respectively.[265] From the viewpoint of the five sheaths *(pañca kośas),* the gross body is constituted by the *annamaya kośa*. This *kośa* consists of the material aspect of the body. The subtle body of the *jīva* consists of the *prāṇamaya, manomaya* and *vijñānamaya kośa*s. The *prāṇamaya kośa* is constituted by the five *prāṇas* (vital forces or airs), the five organs of cognition *(jñānendriyas)* and the five organs of action *(karmendriyas)*. The *manomaya kośa* consists of the mind *(manas),* whereas the *vijñānamaya kośa* consists of the intellect *(buddhi)*. The causal body consists of the basic ignorance (*avidyā*), or the *citta*, which is the fundamental cause of *ahaṅkāra* (egoism) of *jīva*.[266] As per the *samaya mārga*, apart from the transcendental non-dual *Brahman*, there are twenty-five eternal categories - the five elements, the five *tanmātrās*, the five organs of perception, the five organs of motor action, the mind (*manasa tattva*, the cause of the five elements and their *tanmātrās*), *Māyā*,

Śuddha vidyā, *Maheśvara* and *Sadāśiva*.[267] Out of these categories, the five elements and their respective five *tanmātrās* are dominantly associated with the five *cakras* (starting with the *mūlādhāra*) as follows - *mūlādhāra* - earth (smell), *maṇipūra* - water (taste), *svādhiṣṭhāna* - fire (form), *anāhata* - air (touch), and *viśuddhi* - ether (sound). The *ājñā cakra* is the center of the *manas tattva* (mind), and this *manas* is the causative element for the other five elements and their *tanmātrās*. The mind associated with the *manomaya kośa* is the mental faculty of mind, and not this causative *manas tattva*. *Māyā* and *Maheśvara* are associated with the *bindu* level, which lies just above the *Brahma granthi*, and they are the same as the *Navātmā Śiva* and *Śakti*. *Śuddha vidyā* and *Sadāśiva* are associated with the *nāda* level, lying just above the *bindu*, and they are the same as the transcendental dualistic forms of *Śiva* and *Śakti*, manifesting the primordial *spanda* (epistemic vibration) of dualistic projection. Even above the *nāda* is the thousand-petalled *sahasrāra*, depicting the level of *Paramaśiva* (*nirguṇa Brahman*) and *Parāśakti* (*saguṇa Brahman* or the *Sāmarasya* state of *Śiva* and *Śakti*), which correspond with the *śānta* and *śakti* components of *Aum* respectively. This *sahasrāra* is also said to be the place of the twenty-sixth (transcendental) element, the *Sādākhya tattva,* representing the *Sāmarasya* state.[268]

Now, having considered the significance of the various centres and sections of the *kula* path, we need to understand the significance of the *mūlādhāra kulkuṇḍa* as the resting place of the *kuṇḍalinī* and also the significance of the (*akula-*) *sahasrāra* as the destination of the *kuṇḍalinī*. The transcendent non-dual *Brahman* or *Sāmarasya* state is the state of perfect equilibrium and interpenetration of *Śiva* (*prakāśa*) and *Śakti* (*vimarśa*), the perfect equilibrium of consciousness (*cit*) and bliss (*ānanda*). The epistemic projection of the most subtle disequilibrium of these forces results in the epistemic projection of duality (*dvaita*). The first such projected duality is the dualism of *Śiva* and *Śakti* (as *Sadāśiva* and *Śuddha vidyā*) at the level of *nāda*. This is the manifestation of the primordial *spanda*. This then leads to the epistemic projections of a series of dualistic manifestations, each projected dualistic manifestation being grounded in its immediately preceding one. This is the gist of the creative process accruing through epistemic superimpositions (*adhyāsa*), leading to the (epistemic) manifestation of all the three realms - the causal, subtle and the gross. The main levels of epistemic projections are depicted by the various components of *Aum*, from *nāda* to *A*. The *śakti* and *śānta* components are not manifestations of epistemic projections. The various levels of epistemic projections correspond with the various sections and points of the *kula* path. Just as the transcendental non-dual *Brahman* has two aspects (*nirguṇa Brahman* or *Paramaśiva* and *saguṇa Brahman* or *Parāśakti* or *sāmarasya* state), and just as the *saguṇa Brahman* or *sāmarasya* state has two aspects (*Śiva* and *Śakti*), similarly all epistemic projections of duality are dual-aspected, although one aspect would always dominate over the other. Where the cognitive or illuminative aspect (*cit* or *prakāśa*) dominates, the epistemic projection is taken as a manifestation of *Śiva*, and where the objective and blissful aspects (*ānanda* or *vimarśa*) dominate, it is taken as a manifestation of *Śakti*. But, all epistemic manifestations of *Śiva* and *Śakti* also possess the secondary aspects of *vimarśa* or *ānanda* and *cit* or *prakāśa* respectively. Even the grossest material particle has an illuminative cognitive (*cit* or *prakāśa*) aspect. The opposite is also true. The state of gross material objects depicts the highest degree of the epistemic manifestation of duality, the state of greatest disequilibrium of *Śiva* and *Śakti*. This is the level of quintuplicated elements[269] (*pañcīkṛta pañca mahābhūta*), and it corresponds with the resting place of *kuṇḍalinī*, that is, the *mūlādhāra kulkuṇḍa*. From this level, the microcosmic *Śakti*, the *kuṇḍalinī*, has to rise up to the *sahasrāra* to sublate all the levels of epistemic projections one by one and thus enter the absolute and irrevocable state of transcendental non-dualism, the *Sāmarasya* state.

Now, we move on to the meditative devotional process, which awakens and uplifts the *kuṇḍalinī* through the *kula* path. This upliftment of *kuṇḍalinī* (*vimarśa śakti*) is essential for uplifting the cognitive level (*cit*) of the *jīva* (*cidābhāsa*), as it is the manifestational level of *vimarśa śakti* that determines the manifestational level of the *prakāśa śakti,* and not vice-versa. When the *kuṇḍalinī* lies sleeping in the *kulkuṇḍa*, the *jīva cit* or *jīva cidābhāsa* identifies with its gross body (*annamaya kośa*), which is made up of the five quintuplicated elements. The *kuṇḍalinī* has to be aroused by the *jīva cidābhāsa* through hymns (*stuti*), repetition of sacred syllables (*mantra japa*), control of vital-forces (*prāṇāyāma*) and meditation (*dhyāna*) upon the *Virāṭ* and his corresponding objective identification. That is, the *jīva* has to meditatively visualize his own *cidābhāsa* as the *Virāṭ*, taking the whole gross world as His own body (objective state or *vimarśa bhāva*). The perfection of this discipline raises the *kuṇḍalinī* up to the *Rudra granthi*, the level corresponding to the *Virāṭ*. But, before reaching this level, it has to cross the *mūlādhāra* and the *maṇipūra cakra*s. When the *kuṇḍalinī* rises up to the *mūlādhāra* level, the *jīva cidābhāsa* actually witnesses the resolution of the quintuplicated five elements into their causal unquintuplicated five elements. During the course of creation of these elements (through epistemic projections), each element is created out of its preceding element. The first of these five elements, *ākāśa* or ether, comes out of the mind or *manas tattva*. From *ākāśa* or ether emerges air or *vāyu*, then fire or *vahni* from the air, then water or *jala* or *āpas* from fire, and lastly *kṣiti* or earth element comes out of water. The creative sequence of these elements is reflected in the *kula* path in such a manner that out of these five elements the earth is the lowest placed, while the ether is the highest place, the other falling in between. So, the *mūlādhāra* is known as the earth-centre (*kṣiti cakra*), as it shows the highest limit of the earth element in the creative scheme. Beyond the *mūlādhāra*, the earth element gets resolved into its causative element, namely the water element.

Therefore, at the *maṇipūra* level of the *kuṇḍalinī*, there are only four elements remaining for objective identification by the *cidābhāsa*, the lowest amongst them being the water element. Hence, *maṇipūra* is the *āpas cakra*. Crossing the *maṇipūra* when the *kuṇḍalinī* reaches the *Rudra granthi*, the *jīva cidābhāsa* (*Viśva*) realizes its identity (*tādātmya*) with the *Virāṭ cit* and cognizes its own gross body (*annamaya kośa*) as the whole gross world. But, he cognizes this gross world as being made up of the unquintiplicated four elements - ether, air, fire and water only.

In a similar fashion, to raise the *kuṇḍalinī* from the *Rudra granthi* to the *Viṣṇu granthi*, the *jīva cidābhāsa* has to meditatively visualize his own Self as the *Hiraṇyagarbha* and the whole subtle world as His own objective counterpart (*vimarśa*). As a result of the perfection of this meditation, the *kuṇḍalinī* reaches the *Viṣṇu granthi* and then the *jīva* actually realizes his own Self, the *Taijasa*, as identical (in *tādātmya*) with the macrocosmic *Hiraṇyagarbha*, and the whole subtle world as his very own subtle body. The whole subtle world as the body of *Hiraṇyagarbha* is constituted by the macrocosmic aspects of infinite vital-sheaths (*prāṇamaya kośa*), mind-sheaths (*manomaya kośa*) and intellect-sheaths (*vijñānamaya kośa*).[270] To reach this *Viṣṇu granthi*, the *kuṇḍalinī* has to pass through the *svādhiṣṭhāna* and *anāhata cakras*. At the *svādhiṣṭhāna* level, the water element resolves into its causative fire element (*vahni tattva*). Thus, the *svādhiṣṭhāna cakra* is the fire centre (*vahni cakra*). At the *anāhata* level the fire element resolves into its causative air element (*vāyu tattva*). So, the *anāhata cakra* is the air-centre (*vāyu cakra*). Consequently, the *jīva cidābhāsa*, as *Hiraṇyagarbha*, cognizes the whole subtle world (his own body) as made up of only the ether (*ākāśa*) and air (*vāyu*) elements. This happens at the level of *Viṣṇu granthi*.

To raise the *kuṇḍalinī* from the *Viṣṇu granthi* to the *Brahma granthi*, meditation on *Īśvara,* as the macrocosmic aspect of all causal selves (*Prājña-s*), and on the whole causal world (the sum of all individual *avidyā-s*, i.e., the *māyā śakti*) as his own body, needs to be perfected. During this process, while passing through the *viśuddhi* and the *ājñā cakra*s, the air element resolves into the ether element (at the *viśuddhi* level) and the ether element resolves into the *manas tattva*, the primary causative element (at the *ājñā cakra*). So, the *viśuddhi* and the *ājñā cakra*s are known as the *ākāśa* and *manas cakra*s respectively. Swāmī Hariharānanda Saraswatī (also famous as Karapātrī Swāmī), a great contemporary exponent of *Śrīvidyā*, has also testified to the sequential sublation of subtle elements during the rise of the *kuṇḍalinī*.[271] When the *kuṇḍalinī* goes up to the *Brahma granthi*, the *jīva cidābhāsa* (as *Prājña*) realizes its own identity with *Īśvara* and cognizes His own body as the whole causal world (*avyakta* or *māyā śakti*). Also, the whole causal world is revealed as being constituted by the mind element (*manas tattva*) alone.[272] The blissful form of *Māyā Śakti* (*ānandamayī Śakti*), as the macrocosmic aspect of all blissful sheaths (*ānandamaya kośa-s*), is also revealed at this stage.[273]

Beyond the *Brahma granthi* is the level of *bindu*, the fourth component of *Aum*. To raise the *kuṇḍalinī* up to the *bindu*, the supreme meditation upon the fundamental aspect of *Īśvara* as *Navātmā Śiva* and *Navātmā Śakti* as his body (*vimarśa bhāva*), has to be perfected. This perfection is the same as that required for attaining the *nirvikalpa samādhi* or *nirbīja samādhi* or *dharmamegha samādhi*.[274] At this level, the *cidābhāsa* realizes its own Self as the *Navātmā Śiva* and cognizes the *Navātmā Śakti* alone as his objective body (*vimarśa*).[275] This heralds the state of *jīvanmukti,* the state of being liberated-while-alive (in the phenomenal world). All the karma seeds (*karma saṁskāras*) are burnt forever, except the *prārabdha karmas*. With the exhaustion of *prārabdha karmas* as well in due course of time, the *jīva cit* realizes irrevocable identity with either the transcendental *Śiva-Śakti* (at the *nāda* level) or the transcendental non-dual *Brahman* i.e., the *Sāmarasya* state of *Śiva-Śakti* (at the *sahasrāra* level), depending upon the chosen ideal of his devotion (*bhakti*).[276] While at the *bindu* level, the *jīva cit* also gets an intuitive glimpse of the transcendental *nāda* and *sahasrāra* levels.[277] This is the limit of spiritual evolution for a phenomenally alive person, a *jīvanmukta*. Only a *videhamukta* can actually reach the *nāda* and *sahasrāra* levels.[278] During the course of this spiritual evolution, depicted by the rise of *kuṇḍalinī* up to *bindu*, the *jīva* acquires special powers (*siddhi-s*) over such phenomenal spheres which correspond with those sections of the *kula patha*, which the *kuṇḍalinī* has already traversed.

The tenth stanza of the *S.L.* says -

> "Having in-filled the pathway of the *Nāḍīs* with the streaming shower of nectar flowing from Thy pair of feet, having resumed Thine own position from out of the resplendent lunar regions, and Thyself assuming the form of a serpent of three-and-a-half coils, sleepest Thou in the hollow of the *kulkuṇḍa*."[279]

The ascent and descent of *kuṇḍalinī* through the *kula* path are called the *unneya bhūmikā* and the *pratyāvṛtti bhūmikā* respectively.[280] While the previous stanza described the ascent of *kuṇḍalinī,* this stanza describes the descent of it. Since the *kuṇḍalinī* of a *jīvanmukta* person rises up to the *bindu* level and then the shower of nectar occurs originating from the two feet of the Goddess, it is clear that the primordial dualism of the transcendent *Śiva-Śakti* at the *nāda* level alone can be understood as the immediate source of that nectar. This is also supported by the fourteenth stanza of *S.L.*, which says that Her feet lie far above the region of the six *cakras*.[281] During the descent, the *kuṇḍalinī śakti* moves down from the lunar region (at the *bindu* level) towards the *kulkuṇḍa*. The *Lakṣmīdharā,* referring to the *Yāmala-tantra,* says that *'rasāmnāya mahasaḥ'* refers to the Moon *(kalānidhau).*[282] This stanza also makes it clear that the resting place for the *kuṇḍalinī,* after completing Her descent, is the *mūlādhāra kulkuṇḍa*. The *Saubhāgyavardhanī* says that during the descent of *kuṇḍalinī* the nectar originating from the feet of the Goddess drenches and thus divinizes the various centres *(cakras* and *granthis)* of the *kula* path.[283] Also, during the descent, the elements, which had sublated into their causative elements during the ascent of the *kuṇḍaliṇī,* start being epistemically reprojected from their causes at their respective elemental *cakra* levels. Karpātrī Swāmī also supports such sequential epistemic reprojection of elements during the descent of the *kuṇḍaliṇī.*[284] Gauḍapāda too, in his *Subhagodayastotra*, mentions this drenching and divinization of all the *naḍīs* by the shower of nectar *(amṛta)* resulting from the rise of *kuṇḍaliṇī* up to the *bindu* level.[285]

What is the real significance of the shower of nectar and the resultant divinization of all the *cakras* and *nāḍīs* of the *kula* path? This shower occurs at the rise of *kuṇḍaliṇī* up to the *bindu* level and the source of it is the *(nāda)* level of the transcendent dualism of *Śiva-Śakti*. It is from the *bindu* level alone that the *cidābhāsa* of a *jīvanmukta* acquires the knowledge of its own transcendental identity with the non-dual reality of the *Sāmarasya* state (at the *sahasrāra* level), as also with the primordial dualistic manifestation of *Śiva-Śakti* at the *nāda* level. This transcendental knowledge itself is the nectar *(amṛta)* as it reveals the immortality and immutability of the *jīva cit* to the *jīvanmukta.*[286] This transcendental knowledge is the highest possible knowledge even for a *jīvanmukta*. This nectar of transcendental knowledge then drenches and divinizes, that is, gets firmly established at all the levels of epistemic manifestations of *cidābhāsa* (along with the corresponding *vimarśa bhāvas)* depicted by the various *cakras* and *granthis* of the *kula* path. As a result of such divinization, the realization of identities of the various microcosmic manifestations of *cidābhāsa* (and its *vimarśa*) with their corresponding macrocosmic manifestations of *Śiva* (and *Śakti*) gets firmly rooted. Then, the *jīvanmukta* person is able to keep his *jīva cit* at the *cakra* level of his choice. Thus, he becomes able to choose the level of his consciousness, starting from the gross material level of the *mūlādhāra kulkuṇḍa* up to the *bindu* level of *Navātman Śiva-Śakti*. Thus, the level of rise of the *kuṇḍaliṇī* at a given point of time reflects the level of epistemic manifestation of the *jīva cidābhāsa*.

The eleventh stanza says -

> "The angles of Thy abode (the *Śrīcakra*) which is made up of the nine mūla-prakṛtis or basic triangles (the nine primary causative forces of the universe), consisting of the four distinct *Śiva* triangles (with apex upwards), and the five distinct *Śakti*-triangles (with apex downwards), kept apart from the former by the *bindu*, with the eight-petalled lotus, the lotus of sixteen petals with the three circles around and the three lines, are counted as forty-three (forty-four)."[287]

This stanza describes the basic features of the external *Śrīcakra*. Since the *samaya mārga* believes in the internal worship of the *Śrīcakra* through meditative devotion, it treats the whole *kula* path, along with the *kuṇḍalinī* and the *jīva cidābhāsa*, as the subtle *Śrīcakra* existing inside the body itself. Consequently, the external and the internal *Śrīcakra*-s are taken to correspond with each other in all their details.

The *Śrīcakra* emerges from the combination of the five downwards pointing triangles (*Śakti cakra*s) and the four upwards pointing triangles (*Śiva cakra*s). This combination of nine triangles (nine basic causative forces of creation) throws up a total of forty-three angles at the ends. These angles are then successively bound by a lotus of eight petals, then a lotus of sixteen petals, then by a girdle of three circular rings, and at last by three quadrangular lines, with entrance like openings in the middle of each side of the quadrangular lines.[288] The *Lakṣmīdharā* clearly opines, referring to the *Yāmala tantra*, that all the three quadrangular lines (*bhūpura traya*) have four openings in the middle of their four sides.[289] The nine basic causative forces (*mūla prakṛtis*), arising from the combination of the five *Śakti cakra*s (triangles) and four *Śiva cakra*s (triangles), are the causes of both the microcosm and the macrocosm.[290] As far as the microcosm (the human body or *piṇḍāṇḍa*) is concerned, these *mūla prakṛtis* are the nine basic components (*dhātus*) of the human frame. Out of these nine, the five corresponding to the *śakti cakras* are - *tvak* (skin), *asṛk* (blood), *māṁsa* (flesh), *medas* (lymph) and *asthi* (bone). The four *śiva cakras* are representative of - *majjā* (marrow), *śuklam* (semen), *prāṇāḥ* (the five vital forces or *prāṇa-s*) and the *jīva* (soul). *Parāśakti* is taken as the tenth *dhātu,* transcending these nine.[291] As far as the macrocosm or the universe *(brahmāṇḍa)* is concerned, out of the nine basic forces the five *śakti cakras* denote the five elements *(pañca tattva),* whereas the four *śiva cakras* depict *Māyā, Śuddha vidyā, Maheśvara* and *Sadāśiva.* The four macrocosmic *śiva cakras* denote the manifestations of *Śiva-Śakti* at the *bindu* and *nāda* levels, while *Parāśakti* (as well as *Paramaśiva* and their *Sāmarasya* state) transcends even the *bindu* and the *nāda.*

There are two readings regarding the total count of the angles of the *śrīcakra,* as shown in the third line of this stanza.[292] While the use of *'trayaś catvāriṁśat'* clearly takes the count of the angles as forty-three (easily verified by observation of *śrīcakra*), the use of *'catuś catvāriṁśat'* seems to be taking count of the *bindu* as well. Now, the *bindu* of *śrīcakra* is representative of *Parāśakti,* which is the same as the *Paramaśiva* or *Sāmarasya* state.[293] If the visible *bindu* of *śrīcakra* is taken as *Parāśakti* then the reading *'trayaś catvāriṁśat'* seems appropriate. But the reading *'catuś catvāriṁśat'* would imply that the visible *bindu* itself lies upon the transcendent non-dual *Parāśakti,* which is the same as *Paramaśiva.* In that case, the *Parāśakti* is taken as being depicted by the invisible (non-dual) *Mahābindu,* lying just behind the visible *bindu.* Then, the *bindu* and the *Mahābindu* are taken as representing the *nāda* (the primordial dualism of *Śiva-Śakti* as *Sadāśiva* and *Śuddha vidyā*) and the *śakti-śānta* levels (the absolute non-dual *Brahman* or the *Sāmarasya* state) respectively. The distinction of the *bindu* and *Mahābindu* is supported by that of the *nāda* and *śakti-śānta* levels, which in turn is supported by the framework of advaitism.[294] Further, this distinction is also corroborated by the mantra tradition of *samaya mārga*.[295] Hence, the reading *'catuś catvāriṁśat'* seems to better reflect the advaitika outlook of Śaṅkara.

The various component parts or *āvaraṇa-s* of the *Śrīcakra* are as follows. The outermost *āvaraṇa* is the *bhūpura*, consisting of three quadrangular lines, with openings (*dvāra*) in the middle of each side. Then comes the *mekhlā traya*, consisting of the three circles or girdles around the sixteen-petalled lotus. Then comes the *ṣoḍaśāra* or *ṣoḍaśa dala padma*, the sixteen-petalled lotus. The next *āvaraṇa* is the *aṣṭa dala padma*, the eight-petalled lotus. Inside it lies the *catur daśāra*, the set of fourteen triangles (or angles). Then comes the *bahir daśāra*, the outer set of ten triangles or angles. The next *āvaraṇa* is the *antar daśāra*, the inner set of ten triangles. Then comes the *aṣṭāra* or *aṣṭa koṇa*, the set of eight triangles. Inside it, is the *trikoṇa*, a small red triangle. Even inside this, is the *bindu*, the visible central point of *Śrīcakra*. Just behind the *bindu*, lies the place of the invisible *Mahābindu*, representing the level of *Parāśakti* and *Paramaśiva* or the *Sāmarasya* state. Among these *āvaraṇa*-s, the *bindu* (and *Mahābindu*), the two lotuses and the *bhūpura-s* are known as the *Śiva cakra*s, while the rest of them are called the *Śakti cakra*s. The different *Śiva cakra*s and *Śakti cakra*s are treated as existing in one another, namely, the *bindu* (and *Mahābindu*) existing in the *trikoṇa*, the eight-petalled lotus in the *aṣṭāra*, the sixteen-petalled lotus in the two *daśāras*, and the *bhūpura* in the *catur daśāra*. The *Subhagodaya* also supports such mutual corresponding presence of the *Śiva cakra*s and *Śakti cakras*.[296] This indicates the invariable co-existence of *Śiva* and *Śakti* with one another; *avinābhāva saṁbandha* of *prakāśa* and *vimarśa*, as also *cit* and *ānanda*. As mentioned before, the various *āvaraṇa*-s of *Śrīcakra* correspond with different points of the *kula* path,[297] such as, the *bhūpura* with the *mūlādhāra kulkuṇḍa*, the *mekhalā traya* and the *ṣoḍaśāra* with the *mūlādhāra*, the *aṣṭa dala padma* with the *maṇipūra*, the *caturdaśāra* with the *svādhiṣṭhāna*, the *bahir daśāra* with the *anāhata*, the *antar daśāra* with the *viśuddhi*, the *aṣṭāra* with the *ājñā cakra*, the *tri koṇa* with the *bindu*, the *bindu* (visible centre of *Śrīcakra*) with the *nāda* level (depicting *Sadāśiva* and *Śuddha vidyā*), and lastly the *Mahābindu* (the invisible non-dual center of *Śrīcakra*) with the transcendental non-dual level of *sahasrāra* (depicting *śakti-śānta* components of *Aum*, or the *Parāśakti - Paramaśiva Sāmarasya* state). Thus, the *Śrīcakra* is taken as an external symbol of the causes and structure of the microcosm and the macrocosm. It may be worshipped devotionally, both externally and internally (through meditation, as in the *samaya mārga*).

The twelfth stanza of *S.L.* says -

> "Oh, Daughter of the snow-clad Mountain (Himālaya) ! The best of thinkers - *Brahmā* and others - are at great pains to find a suitable comparison to Thy beauty. Even the celestial damsels, out of great eagerness to get a glimpse of Thy splendour, mentally attain a condition of absorption into *Śiva*, which is unobtainable even by penance."[298]

This stanza highlights the infinite beauty of *Devī Tripurasundarī*, as also the significance of devotionally meditating upon Her. So, when the celestial damsels continuously meditate upon the form of *Devī* to get a glimpse of Her infinite beauty, they easily acquire absorption into *Śiva* by the grace of *Devī*. Without Her grace, such absorption is unattainable even by great penance and meditation. Further, only *Śiva* can really behold Her infinite beauty. So, by becoming one with *Śiva*, the desire of the celestial damsels to behold the beauty of *Devī* gets fulfilled. That is to say, when anyone, desirous of beholding Her beauty, starts contemplating and meditating upon the form of *Devī*, he easily acquires absorption (*sāyujya*) into *Śiva*. The absorption (*sāyujya*) is temporary for a *jīvanmukta* person, but permanent for a *videhamukta*.[299] While maintaining duality with *Śakti*, i.e., the *Devī Tripurasundarī,* to behold Her beauty, *sāyujya* with *Śiva* is depicted by the level of *bindu* for a *jīvanmukta*, and by the level of *nāda* for a *videhamukta*.[300] The spiritual and philosophical justification of the elaborate description of *Devī*'s beauty by Śaṅkara, in the *S.L.* (starting with the forty-second stanza), may be easily understood in the light of this stanza. The thirteenth stanza highlights the point that by the grace of *Devī*, even the impossible worldly desires of devotees get fulfilled.[301] But the *samaya mārga* emphatically advises to seek Her grace for higher spiritual purposes alone.

The fourteenth stanza says -

> "Fifty-six rays shine in the *mūlādhāra* comprised of the element of Earth (*Pṛthvi tattva*), fifty-two rays shine in the *maṇipūra* of the essence of Water (*Āpas tattva*), sixty-two in the *svādhiṣṭhāna* (the *Agni* or *Tejas tattva*) being of the nature of fire, fifty-two in the *anāhata* of the character of air (*vāyu tattva*); seventy-two rays in the *viśuddhi* of the form of ether (*ākāśa tattva*) and sixty-four in the *ājñā (manas tattva)*. Far above all these shine the pair of Thy lotus feet."[302]

This stanza points out that the various manifestations of *Śiva* and *Śakti*, related to the different centres of the *kula* path, are only so many rays *(mayūkhā-s)* emerging from the feet of the Goddess. The total number of important manifestations or rays associated with each centre is also given in the stanza. To comprehend the full significance of this stanza we must look into the possible reasons for terming the *śrīvidyā tantra* of *samaya mārga* as the *'candra kalā vidyā'*. This *tantra* makes repeated mention of the moon, its rays, its phases *(kalā),* its reflection as also the sun, the fire and their rays.

Vedic literature generally describes consciousness as light *(prakāśa* or *jyotiḥ)*. Taking cue from this, the moon *(candra)* has been taken as the nearest simile for describing the nature and manifestations of the highest consciousness. It is common knowledge that the moon is seen in its different phases or digits *(kalā)* on different nights, both during the bright and the dark fortnights. There are fifteen digits or phases of the moon, starting from the *pratipadā* to the *pūrṇimā* or full-moon in the bright fortnight *(śukla pakṣa)*. In the night of the new-moon or *amāvasyā* the moon is not seen at all. However, despite the varying digits or *kalās* of the moon, the fact is that in reality the light of the moon is not at all affected by it and the moon retains its full splendour all the while. Only the viewers of the moon see the apparent variations in the moon and its light, in its various digits, caused by the shadow of the earth on the moon. As such, the appearance of the various degrees of the moonlight occurs due to the obstructive shadows, as viewed from particular angles.

This worldly experience has been beautifully used by the early masters of *śrīvidyā* or *candra vidyā* to explain the nature of consciousness in the light of advaitika philosophy. Pure consciousness, which may be compared with the pure light of the moon or *candra*, always maintains its real nature and is not affected by the apparent variations. These apparent variations are caused by the extent of ignorance or *avidyā* enveloping the viewer. Just like the new moon *(amāvasyā)*, the inanimate objects *(jaḍa padārtha)* do not reflect or reveal the light of consciousness at all, despite the fact that they are fundamentally identical with the highest consciousness or *Brahman*. At the other end, there are the 'liberated-while-alive' persons, the *jīvanmukta* souls, in the state of *nirvikalpa samādhi* (the *nirbīja* or *dharmamegha samādhi* of the Yoga-sūtras). This may be compared to the fifteenth digit or *kalā* of the moon viz. the full-moon or *pūrṇimā*. It reveals the full light of the moon, the true nature of pure consciousness or *Brahman*. Yet, the distinction of the viewer and the viewed persists in this case too. As a result, as in the case of the moon, the waxing and waning of the moon's digits continues even after the full-moon or *pūrṇimā*. Similarly, the *jīvanmukta* person, despite the full and true knowledge of the pure consciousness or *Brahman*, continues to witness the varying manifestations of that immutable *Brahman* until the complete exhaustion of his *prārabdha karmas*. It is so because even the *jīvanmukta* is not completely free of his own distinguishing individuality or *ahaṅkāra* vis-à-vis *Brahman*. *Śrīvidyā* terms the highest state of consciousness i.e., the immutable transcendent nature of *Brahman* as the sixteenth digit, the *Ṣoḍaśī kalā*, of the moon. It transcends space and time and hence it does not wax or wane. All the other digits or *kalās* of the moon are said to be mere reflections of this *Parā śoḍaśī kalā*. That is, they are mere epistemic appearances arising, due to *avidyā,* out of the *Ṣoḍaśī kalā*. Similarly, the transcendent or *Para Brahman* is absolutely immutable, yet the various manifestations of consciousness or *cit*, in the form of numerous beings or *cidābhāsa-s* and their experiences, are only so many epistemic appearances of *Brahman* occurring due to *avidyā*. When the consciousness of the phenomenal being, the *jīva cit* or *cidābhāsa*, realizes its absolute and immutable identity with the *Ṣoḍaśī kalā* or *Para Brahman*, he loses his distinctive individuality as a *jīva* and thus transcends the possibility of experiencing again the varying manifestations of *Para Brahman,* i.e., the varying digits of the reflection of the transcendent *Ṣoḍaśī kalā*. The subject-object dichotomy, the distinction of the knower and the known, the viewer and the viewed, vanishes in the *Ṣoḍaśī kalā,* the *Para Brahman*. Thus, in the light of its advaitika philosophical backdrop, the justification of *śrīvidyā* or *śrītantra* being termed as *candra vidyā* becomes quite clear.

The fourteenth stanza also makes an explicit reference to the regions of fire *(agni khaṇḍa),* sun *(sūrya khaṇḍa)* and the moon *(candra khaṇḍa)*. Let us try to see the significance and justification of these regions and their names in the context of the advaitika backdrop of *śrīvidyā*. In the *śrīvidyā* terminology the gross, subtle and the causal worlds *(sthūla, sūkṣma* and *kāraṇa jagat),* are known as the regions of fire, sun and the moon or the *agni khaṇḍa, sūrya khaṇḍa* and *candra khaṇḍa* respectively. Now, in the advaitika philosophy the macrocosmic consciousness *(samaṣṭi cit)* of the gross universe or *sthūla jagat* is known as *Virāṭ* or *Vaiśvānara*. The term *'Vaiśvānara'* means fire, which is meaning of *'agni'* as well. The macrocosmic consciousness of the subtle universe or the *sūkṣma jagat* is called *Hiraṇyagarbha* or *Sūtrātman*. *'Hiraṇyagarbha'* means the sun, the same as the word *'sūrya'*. In terms of the Vedic philosophy of the five sheaths *(pañca kośa-s),* the gross world most explicitly manifests the *annamaya kośa;* the subtle world the *prāṇamaya, manomaya* and *vijñānamaya kośa-s* and the causal world the *ānadamaya kośa.*

Now, the fire, sun and the moon are all sources of light in the world. But fire, being the most intensely heated light form in ordinary human experience, has been aptly used to depict the gross universe in *śrīvidyā,* since it is at this level of existence that the *jīvas* most intensely suffer various pain and misery (due to ignorance of their identity with the transcendent *Brahman* or the *Ṣoḍaśī kalā*).

Sun is the source of all life-forces and reveals the world in our everyday experience. Also, the heat of sunlight becomes painful after a limit. Similarly, the three sheaths constituting the subtle body or *sūkṣma śarīra* of the *jīva,* namely the *prāṇamaya, manomaya* and the *vijñānamaya kośa-s,* control the various life-forces of the *jīva* and provide the necessary means of interacting with the world in terms of the various cognitive faculties. Also, the dualistic existence of *jīva* quite often engenders various kinds of subtle pain and misery, related with the internal cognitive faculties. All these things lie in the realm of the subtle universe or *sūkṣma jagat.* Hence, the justification of calling the subtle universe the region of the sun or *sūrya khaṇḍa* in the *śrīvidyā* tradition.

Now, the light of the moon is neither revealing like that of the sun, nor painful like the excessive heat of fire and the sun. Moonlight is very pleasant and soothing, and it is always seen during the night, when the objects of the world are more or less unrevealed in the darkness of the night. Similarly, the causal universe or *kāraṇa jagat* is the realm of the most explicit manifestation of the *ānandamaya kośa* or the blissful sheath. This sheath is also the causal body or *kāraṇa śarīra* of the *jīva,* containing all the seeds of past actions *(karma saṁsakāras)*. At the macrocosmic level of the causal world, *Māyā* or *Avyakta* is the repository of the causal forms of all the existing and potential objects and manifestations of consciousness *(cidābhāsa)*. This causal body of the *jīva* viz. the *ānandamaya kośa*, is also the individualized obstructive ignorance or *avidyā* of the *jīva* in one of its aspects. In his ordinary life, the *jīva* experiences the most intense and direct form of bliss or *ānanda* of the blissful sheath during the deep sleep state, where his consciousness is merged at the level of causal existence. Similarly, at the macrocosmic level, *māyā* (same as *prakṛti* and *avyakta*) is the source of bliss to *Īśvara* or *Akṣara*. Also, the individualized manifestation of *māyā* as *avidyā* leads to the individualized manifestation of the *jīva cidābhāsa* out of *Īśvara*. Thus, due to the similarities of (a) bliss or *ānanda,* (b) unrevealing and obstructive nature of *avidyā*, and (c) the latent existence of all objects, potential *cidābhāsas* and their *karma saṁsakāra-s,* the causal universe or *kāraṇa jagat* has been aptly called the *candra khaṇḍa* in *śrīvidyā*.

Coming back to the fourteenth stanza of the *S.L.*, it is clear that the lotus-like feet of the Goddess mentioned therein actually refers to the *nāda* level of existence, the level of the primordial duality of *Sadāśiva* and *Śuddha vidyā*. All the other levels and manifestations of duality are referred to as so many rays *(mayūkhā-s)* emanating from the *Devī's* feet and it is these rays of epistemic manifestations of duality that constitute the three realms of fire, sun and the moon *(agni, sūrya* and *candra khaṇḍa-s)*. In previous analyses, it has already been seen that it is out of the *nāda* level that the *bindu* and the three realms get epistemically projected. Thus, the comparison of the three realms with the rays emanating from the *Devī's* feet is quite natural. The stress on the point that the *Devī's* feet are far above, and not just above, the three realms, highlights two points. Firstly, there is the level of *bindu* between the *nāda* and the three realms. Secondly, the *nāda* transcends the space-time framework and it is thus a transcendent level, whereas the three realms are all immanent levels of existence, subject to space-time limitations.

The fifteenth, sixteenth and seventeenth verses of the *S.L.* describe specific meditations on some special forms of the *Devī* for the purpose of attaining excellence in literary expressions. According to the *Saubhāgyavardhinī*,[303] while the fifteenth verse gives the *sāttvika* meditation[304] on the first five letters of the *Devī's* fifteen-syllabled *(pañca daśākṣarī) mantra,* the sixteenth verse gives the *rājasika* meditation on the same.[305] The four objects and gestures associated with the *Devī's* four hands, as described in the fifteenth verse, signify different things. According to *Aruṇāmodinī*,[306] the rosary represents the saṁskṛta alphabet which in turn stands for the world of names *(śabda prapañca)*, the book represents all the objects of the world *(artha prapañca),* the *abhaya mudrā* signifies the removal of all ills generally afflicting phenomenal existence, and the *varada mudrā* signifies the boon of unalloyed bliss.[307]

The eighteenth verse says -

> "How many celestial courtesans including Urvaśī, with eyes bashful like those of frightened dear of the forest, do not become fascinated by one who meditates on the entire Heaven and Earth as submerged in the redness of the lustre of Thy body resembling the splendour of the rising (morning) Sun's rays?"[308]

The *Saubhāgyavardhinī* says that this verse gives the meditation on the second section, i.e., the *kāmarāja kūṭa,* of *Devī's pañcadaśākṣarī mantra.*[309] Further, this verse shows that for a person who knows and has realized the fact that both the gross and subtle worlds are but the very forms, although epistemic ones, of *Devī Tripurasundarī,* nothing remains difficult to attain. Given his wish, he can acquire anything whatsoever. But, a true votary of the *samaya mārga* would not be led astray by such temptations; he would only seek the realization of his absolute identity with the *Devī.*

The nineteenth verse is quite significant. It says -

> "O Queen of *Hara*! It is but a trifle that one who contemplates Thy *Manmatha-kalā*, taking the *bindu* to be the face, what is thereunder to be the breasts, and still underneath to be one half of *Hara* (i.e., a triangle), at once fascinates women (in general); (what is more) he very soon causes even *Trilokī* (the three worlds together) who has the Sun and the Moon as Her breasts, to swirl."[310]

Prima facie, this verse provides a *madana prayoga* i.e., a meditative application designed to bestow the fascination of the desired lady, and many commentators of the *S.L.* have restricted their comments on this verse to this context only. However, this verse has tremendous esoteric significance in the context of *samaya mārga*. The *manmatha kalā* or *kāma kalā* of *Devī Tripurasundarī* refers to the aspect wherein She is the ground and the substance of the whole mechanism responsible for the epistemic projection (and thus creation) of the three worlds. This verse gives the three divisions of the *kāma kalā* aspect of *Devī* - (1) the face, (2) the breasts i.e., the torso *(kuca yugam)* and (3) the waist down section of Her body. The face of *Devī's kāma kalā* corresponds with the *bindu*, which is the last *āvaraṇa* of the *śrīcakra*. This *āvaraṇa* is also called the *mahābindu* and it represents the *Sāmarasya* state of *Śiva-Śakti*, which is the same as *Parāśakti* and *Paramaśiva,* corresponding with the *śānta* and *śakti* components of *Aum.* The pair of breasts of the *Devī's kāma kalā* corresponds with the *āvaraṇa* preceding the *mahābindu* in the *śrīcakra* i.e., the *bindu.* This *bindu āvaraṇa* of *śrīcakra* represents the *nāda* level of (the primordial duality of) *Sadāśiva* and *Śuddha vidyā*, corresponding with the *nāda* component of *Aum.* The waist down section of *Devī's kāma kalā* corresponds with the *'harārdha'*. This *'harārdha'*, the one half of *Hara* or *Śiva,* is the *vimarśa* of *Śiva* i.e., *Śakti*. The triangle being the general representation of *Śakti*, *'harārdha'* refers to the triangle,[311] the *trikoṇa āvaraṇa* preceding the *bindu* in the *śrīcakra.* This *trikoṇa āvaraṇa* represents the *bindu* level of

Navātman Śiva and *Śakti,* which in turn correspond with the *bindu* component of *Aum.* Recalling the correspondence of the components of *Aum* with the nodal points in the *kula patha*, it is easy to see that the face, the breasts and the waist down section of *Devī's kāma kalā*, are represented by the *sahasrāra,* the *nāda* and the *bindu* levels of *kula patha* in the microcosm. Thus, the *manmatha kalā dhyāna* i.e., the meditation on the *kāma kalā* or the *manmatha kalā* constitutes meditation on the corresponding identities of the three sections of *kāma kalā* (the face, breasts and the waist down sections), the last three *āvaraṇas* of the *śrīcakra* (the *mahābindu, bindu* and *trikoṇa)*, the last three nodal points of the *kula patha (sahasrāra, nāda* and *bindu)* and the last four components of *Aum (śānta, śakti, nāda* and *bindu)*. The verse further points out the significance of such meditative devotion by saying that for the one practising such meditation, the three worlds personified as a woman, whose breasts are the sun and the moon, swirl to his fascination. What to say of the mortal ladies of the gross world or even the celestial damsels of the subtle world? This indication makes it clear that the devotee practising such meditation soon reaches the level of *bindu* in the *kula patha* and thus becomes a *jīvanmukta,* as only a *jīvanmukta* person, in his state of identity with the *Navātman Śiva*, can cause the *Navātman Śakti's* enticement. It must be so, as the *Navātman Śakti* alone is the feminine (*vimarśa* or objective) principle underlying and encompassing the three worlds, and She alone may justifiably be said to have the sun and the moon as Her breasts. Also, the sun and the moon are the sources of energy and nourishment to the world due to which they may be taken as the *Devī's* breasts.

The twentieth stanza of the *S.L.* says -

> "One, who in his heart, meditates on Thee as having an image of the moonshine *(candrakāntā)* stone with a multitude of rays of nectar pouring out of the limbs, by mere look, subdues the pride of serpents, like the lord of birds, and cures persons

> afflicted by bodily diseases through his nectar-*nāḍī* (nectar-ridden nerve)."[312]

This stanza highlights the extraordinary powers coming to the devotee of the *Devī Tripurasundarī* as a result of meditating on Her form. It says that such a devotee is capable of curing all kinds of snakebites and various other bodily diseases, with the help of his nectar-nerve *(sudhāsāra sirayā),* by just casting a glance at the afflicted person. It is notable that this stanza makes it clear that the rejuvenating effect can be exercised only through the nectar-nerve. This nectar-nerve is nothing but the pathway of the *kuṇḍaliṇī,* namely the *suṣumṇā* nerve running through the centre of the spinal column. The *kuṇḍaliṇī* pathway is not suffused with nectar in the case of ordinary human beings. Only in the case of *jīvanmukta* persons the *kuṇḍaliṇī* pathway is filled with nectar, because only when the *kuṇḍaliṇī* rises up to the *bindu* level there occurs the shower of nectar from the *nāda.* For such a *jīvanmukta* devotee it is enough to cast a glance upon the suffering person and conceive him to be cured, for the purpose of ending all types of bodily diseases. This is understandable since such a person has already realized the basic identity of his own consciousness with the *Devī* and *Śiva*, at the intuitive plane. As a result, he has also intuitively realized the unity of his own consciousness with other people's consciousness. As such, he can very easily cure other persons operating through his own consciousness. However, acquiring such curative powers should never be the aim of spiritual disciplines, according to the *samaya mārga.* Nonetheless, such supernormal powers do come to the sincere devotees of *Śakti* as a side-effect and these powers should be used only for the general welfare of humanity.

The next stanza, according to Kaivalyāśrama's *Saubhāgya-vardhanī*, presents the subtle inner meditation upon the *kāma kalā.*[313] It says -

> "Great men, who, with their minds bereft of impurity and illusion, look on Thy *kalā*, slender as a streak of lightning, of the essence of the Sun, the Moon and Fire, and abiding in the great forest of lotuses, standing far above even the six lotuses, derive a flood of infinite bliss."[314]

Lakṣmīdhara too says that the *kalā* mentioned in this stanza refers to the *sādākhyā kalā* of *Śakti*.[315] This *sādākhyā kalā* is also known as the *baindavī kalā* because it corresponds with the centre of *śrīcakra*. Moreover, there are many pointers in this stanza itself, e.g., this *kalā* is described as the essence of the sun, moon and fire, i.e., as the essence of the gross, subtle and causal worlds. The ultimate essence of the three worlds is the transcendent *Brahman* alone, corresponding with the *śakti* and *śānta* components of *Aum*. This stanza also says that this *kalā* abides in the great forest of lotuses, which means it abides in the *sahasrāra* or the thousand-petalled lotus that is located at the top end of the *kuṇḍalinī* pathway. Further, this stanza says that it is standing far above even the six lotuses. This means it is much above the level of the *ājñā cakra* and it is truly so because between the *ājñā* and the *sahasrāra* lie the points of the *Brahma granthi, bindu* and *nāda*. This stanza also indicates that only those persons who have perfectly cleansed their minds of all impurities and illusions can be capable of meditating upon *sādākhyā kalā*. The result of such meditation is the intuitive experience of the infinite bliss of the *(cidānandamayī)* blissful *Śakti*. The description of the *sādākhyā kalā* as a slender streak of lightning is very significant. Up to the *Brahma granthi*, the rise of the *kuṇḍalinī* is very gradual and requires deliberate meditative efforts on the part of the devotee. The *Brahma granthi* is the level of the manifestation of *Śiva* and *Śakti* in the aspect of *Īśvara* and *Māyā* respectively. At this level, the individuality of the *jīva* persists explicitly since *Īśvara* is the macrocosmic aggregate of all *jīva*-defined consciousness at the causal level. However, at the *bindu* level of *Navātman Śiva* and *Nava-prakṛtyātmaka Śakti*, there is no explicit manifestation of the *jīvas*, yet they do persist as potential seeds. Once the *kuṇḍalinī* rises up to the *bindu*, the *jīva* becomes a *jīvanmukta*. After rising up to the *Brahma granthi*, the rise of *kuṇḍalinī* is sudden and automatic, needing no effort from the devotee. Hence, the comparison with the sudden flash of lightning. The individualized consciousness of the *jīva* ceases to explicitly function beyond the *Brahma granthi*. Therefore, the *jīva* is able to feel the ascent of *kuṇḍalinī* as a sudden flash of lightning at the level of *Brahma granthi* only. Beyond that, the *jīva* cannot cognize as an individualized consciousness. However, at the *bindu* level, the *jīva* temporarily loses his individuality in the consciousness of *Navātman Śiva* and thus enjoys the ineffable bliss of his counterpart *vimarśa Śakti*. At the level of *bindu,* because of his temporary mergence in *Navātman Śiva,* the *jīva* also gets a strong intuitive conviction about the primordial and transcendent duality of *Śiva* and *Śakti* at the *nāda* level, as also about the absoluteness and non-duality of the *Sāmarasya* state of *Śiva-Śakti* and the *nirguṇa Brahman* at the level of *sahasrāra*. However, it is only an intuitive realization and not an absolute existential mergence as yet. That is possible only through *videhamukti*. Therefore, the *sādakhyā kalā* has been aptly compared with a slender streak of lightning. The sudden ascent of the *kuṇḍalinī* is the last explicit impression available to the individualized *jīva*-consciousness. Beyond that, the experience of infinite bliss is impersonal, as far as the *jīva* is concerned. However, the residual impression of that impersonal blissful experience remains with the *jīva's* consciousness even when the *kuṇḍalinī* descends from the *bindu*.

The twenty-second stanza of *S.L.* says -

> "When one, desirous of earnestly beseeching Thee with the words, 'O *Bhavāni* ! mayest Thou cast Thy merciful glance on me, Thy slave', pronounces the words, '*Bhavāni tvam*', (may I be Thou), that very moment, Thou bestowest on him the status identically Thine own, rendered lusturous by the brilliant crowns worn by *Mukunda, Brahman* and *Indra*."[316]

This stanza beautifully brings out the efficacy of devotion towards *Śakti* in bringing about the highest kind of liberation. Out of the four kinds of liberation possible for the devotee - *sālokya, sārūpya, sāmīpya* and *sāyujya*[317] - the liberation mentioned in this stanza refers to *sāyujya* i.e., absorption in the deity itself. Lakṣmīdhara, in his commentary on the *S.L.*, has pointed out that the word *'bhavāni'* as a verb in the first person of the imperative mood would also mean 'let me become'. Although the stanza makes it clear in its very first line that the devotee intends to use the word *'bhavāni'* as an address to the *Śakti*, yet due to its possible alternative meaning as soon as the first two words *'bhavāni tvam'* are uttered by the devotee, the *Devī* rushes forth to grant him absorption in Herself *(sāyujya mukti)*.[318] All the commentators have compared the role of the *mahāvākyas*, such as *'Tat tvam asi'*, *'Ahaṁ brahmāsmi'*, etc., in causing the realization of *Brahman*, with the role played by *'bhavāni tvam'* in this stanza. However, there is some notable difference between these two cases. The *mahāvākyas* have to be deliberately and repeatedly meditated upon during the stage of *nididhyāsana*[319] by the spiritual aspirant with the express aim of intuitively realizing one's own identity with the highest *Brahman*. However, even this repeated effort does not succeed until the state of *nirvikalpa samādhi* is achieved.[320] Thus, the onus of making efforts to realize *Brahman* as one's own inner self lies with the aspirant himself while making use of the *mahā- vākyas*. On the other hand, in this stanza Śaṅkara makes it clear in the first line itself that the word *'bhavāni'* is being used as an address of *Śakti* and not as a *mahāvākya* intended to cause the realization of one's identity with *Brahman*. Thus, there is no deliberate intention of realizing identity with the deity. The intention of the devotee is only to get the loving and merciful glance of his deity, the *Devī Tripurasundarī*. Despite this, even before the devotee succeeds in uttering the whole sentence, the *Devī* Herself comes forward to grant *sāyujya* to the devotee. She cannot possibly misunderstand the intended statement of the devotee, in spite of the alternative grammatical meaning. When Śaṅkara says that even when only the first two words are uttered by the devotee and the *Devī* comes forward to grant *sāyujya*, it appears that Śaṅkara just wanted to highlight the immediacy of *Devī's* grace and nothing more. The expression *'bhavāni tvam'* in the devotee's supplication before the *Devī,* as authored by Śaṅkara, also shows that in the *samaya mārga* tradition of *śrīvidyā,* despite the apparent deity-devotee distinction, the devotee always practices advaitika devotion *(advaita bhakti)*. It is so because in this tradition even before a person attains *jīvanmukti* he has to be theoretically aware of the status of *Śakti*, as well as of *Śiva*, as the absolute ontological reality even in the face of all kinds of apparent multiplicity. However, this theoretical belief transforms into an intuitive conviction as a result of the spiritual realization attained through the ascent of the *kuṇḍalinī* up to the *bindu* level. Thus, a primary belief in the presuppositions of advaitika devotion, along with its sincere practice, is the means for the intuitive realization of the highest truth, which is the same as the *Parāśakti* and *Paramaśiva*. Śaṅkara has beautifully used the expression *'bhavāni tvam'* in this stanza to show the advaitika content of devotion in the *samaya mārga*, as also to show how this advaitika devotion is both the means and the goal of the votary of this tradition. The alternative possible meaning of the first two words may also be taken as an example of Śaṅkara's poetic excellence. However, the real thrust seems to be that Śaṅkara wanted to highlight the efficacy of devotion, especially advaitika devotion, to *Śakti* in the attainment of the highest possible realization and liberation. He wants to say that devotion is the most effective way of attaining liberation.[321] Of course, in the *samaya mārga* tradition of *śrīvidyā* the devotee has to be very clear about the status and nature of *Devī Tripurasundarī,* viz. that She is the sole immanent as well as the transcendent reality, that She is the same as the *Para Brahman*. Thus, in this stanza Śaṅkara wonderfully extols the role of devotion to *Śakti* in the attainment of the highest advaitika liberation, so much so that the advaitika devotional approach even excels the Vedic *mahā vākya* approach to liberation.

The twenty-third stanza of *S.L.* says -

> "I fancy that the other (half) as well, of *Śaṁbhu's* frame, has been absorbed by Thee with Thy mind, not satisfied with having absorbed that left one; for, this, Thy form, is entirely of a red colour, has three eyes, is slightly bent with (the weight of) the breasts, and wears over its crown the crescent-moon."[322]

In this stanza Śaṅkara has made use of the *ardhanārīśvara* form of *Śiva* and *Śakti* to convey his opinion regarding the mutual relationship of *Śiva* and *Śakti*. The *ardhanārīśvara* is taken as a symbol of the *Sāmarasya* state of *Śiva* and *Śakti*. It is the interpenetrative union of *Śiva* and *Śakti* at the transcendent and non-dual level of *saguṇa Brahman,* which is but the other aspect of the *nirguṇa Brahman*. It corresponds with the *sahasrāra* level of the *kuṇḍaliṇī* pathway. The *Sāmarasya* state of *Śiva* and *Śakti* corresponds with the *śakti* component of *Aum*. In the *Sāmarasya* state there is perfect mingling of *Śiva* and *Śakti* and as such there is no duality at this level. The *ardhanārīśvara* form, representing the *Sāmarasya* state, has three eyes, a crescent moon on the forehead, a pale white colour in the right half of the body, a single breast in the left half of the body and the colour of the rising sun in the left half of the body. Thus, the right and the left halves of the *ardhanārīśvara* form symbolize the *Śiva* and *Śakti* elements respectively. However, in this stanza Śaṅkara has beautifully expressed his own feelings regarding the mutual relationship of *Śiva* and *Śakti* in their *Sāmarasya* state. He says that it seems even the right half of the *ardhanārīśvara* form has been usurped by *Śakti* since the whole body of *ardhanārīśvara* has acquired a reddish complexion and it has not one but two breasts. The implication of this description is two-fold. Firstly, this description aptly shows that there is no separation between the *Śiva* and *Śakti* elements in the *Sāmarasya* state. There is no duality at this level, not even the epistemic duality of *Śiva* and *Śakti*. Secondly, this description clearly suggests that at this level of reality, the *Śakti* aspect absolutely dominates the *Śiva* aspect, so much so that there is no noticeable separate *Śiva* element at all. This *Sāmarasya* state is the active and non-dual aspect of the transcendent *Brahman*. It is responsible for generating the first vibration of epistemic relativity. This has been amply indicated by Śaṅkara in the very first stanza of *S.L.* The dominating role of *Śakti* at the *Sāmarasya* level also justifies its correspondence with the *śakti* component of *Aum*. But, the most significant implication of this description is that it is the *Śakti* element which is responsible for starting the process of epistemic involutions through the various hierarchies. The *Śiva* element only follows suit, as the counterpart consciousness, through those hierarchies. That is, from the *Sāmarasya* level down to the gross material level of existence, the *Śakti* element, i.e., the objective principle *(vimarśa bhāva)* takes the epistemic lead and the corresponding *Śiva* element, i.e., the subjective principle *(prakāśa bhāva),* follows it epistemically. This precedence of *Śakti* or objectivity is there not only through the involutionary process, but it is also there throughout the evolutionary progress at the epistemic plane, starting from the lowest gross material level to the highest *Sāmarasya* level. This shows the necessity and inevitability of seeking *Śakti*'s blessings in epistemically evolving up to the level of the non-dual transcendent *Brahman*. As such, it also shows the need and value of devotion *(bhakti)* to *Śakti* in attaining the highest liberation, apart from matters pertaining to the phenomenal realm. Manju has noted the role of devotion as facilitator of realizational knowledge through the purification of mind.[323] The rise of *kuṇḍalinī* through its various centres *(cakra-s)* and the accompanying resultant evolution of the epistemic subjectivity of the *jīva* also confirm that it is the *Śakti* element, represented by the *kuṇḍalinī,* that precedes the *Śiva* element in the path of epistemic evolution. Similarly, the descent of the *kuṇḍalinī* is responsible for bringing down the epistemic level of subjectivity for the *jīva* through the various centres of the *kuṇḍalinī* pathway. Thus, in this stanza, Śaṅkara has shown that at all the levels of duality, whether transcendent (i.e., *nāda*) or immanent (i.e., *bindu* and below), it is the *Śakti* element *(vimarśa bhāva)* that decides the epistemic level of the corresponding *Śiva* element *(prakāśa bhāva)*. Further, even at the non-dual transcendent level of the active aspect of *Brahman*, namely the *Sāmarasya* level or the *śakti* component of *Aum,* the *Śakti* element overwhelmingly dominates the *Śiva* element. Only the passive non-dual transcendent aspect of *Brahman*, namely the *nirguṇa Brahman* or the *śānta* component of *Aum,* has the quiescent *Śiva* aspect dominating over the *Śakti* aspect. However, it must be kept in mind that the *nirguṇa* and the *saguṇa* aspects of *Brahman* are not two separate realities, even epistemically. They are merely the active and the passive forms of the same non-dual transcendent *Brahman*. Thus, through this description Śaṅkara has shown that the *Sāmarasya* state of *Śiva* and *Śakti* is a non-dual transcendent level of reality, embodying the epistemic activity of *Śakti* in an overwhelming manner.

The twenty-fourth stanza of *S.L.* says -

> "*Brahmā* creates the universe, *Hari* sustains it and *Rudra* dissolves it. Annihilating them, *Īśvara* conceals himself as well. *Sadāśiva* approves of them, pursuant to Thy command conveyed through Thy creeper-like (curved) eye-brows moved but for a moment."[324]

In this stanza Śaṅkara makes clear the role of *Śakti* in the creation, sustenance and dissolution of the phenomenal universe. *Brahmā* is endowed with the responsibility of creating the worlds, *Viṣṇu* with that of preserving it and *Rudra* with that of dissolving it at the appropriate time. The epistemic levels of *Brahmā*, *Viṣṇu* and *Rudra* are all below that of the *bindu* i.e., the level of *Navātman śiva* or *Maheśvara* and *Nava-prakṛtyātmaka śakti*. *Bindu* is the primordial level of immanent duality. Since all the forms of immanent duality spring forth epistemically from the *bindu,* therefore, *Īśa* or

Maheśvara causes all of them to disappear into his own form.[325] After that, the form of *Maheśvara* himself gets dissolved into that of the transcendent *Sadāśiva,* which corresponds with the *nāda* level. *Nāda* is the first level of epistemic duality and it consists of the transcendent forms of *Śiva* and *Śakti*, namely *Sadāśiva* and *Śuddha vidyā* respectively. The transcendent and immutable nature of *Sadāśiva* (and *Śuddha vidyā*) is clearly suggested in this stanza by pointing out that *Sadāśiva* is the silent witness to the complete (epistemic) dissolution of the entire phenomenal realm, including the *bindu* level of *Navātman śiva* and *śakti*. Further, the last line of the stanza also makes it clear that ultimately the whole process of dissolution is caused by the slightest wish to that effect by the *Śuddha vidyā,* the counterpart of *Sadāśiva. Sadāśiva* is witness to the momentary movement of the *Devī's* eyebrows, representing Her wish for the cosmic dissolution, and this is the necessary and sufficient condition for the epistemic dissolution of the phenomenal realm. Similar is the case with the epistemic creation of the phenomenal universe, starting from the *bindu* level of *Maheśvara* and *Māyā śakti* and ending at the gross material level, corresponding with the *mūlādhāra kulkuṇḍa* or the *kula sahasrāra.*

The twenty-fifth stanza of *S.L.* says -

> "O spouse of *Śiva*! the homage rendered to Thy feet becomes by itself the homage rendered to the three gods born of Thy three guṇa-s. It is, therefore, meet that these (gods) ever stand by the jewelled seat on which Thy feet rest, with their folded hands adorning their crowns."[326]

In this stanza Śaṅkara makes it clear that the devotee of *Śakti* need not make any separate propitiation of *Brahmā, Viṣṇu* and *Rudra* since they are only the separate personifications of the three *guṇas,* viz. *sattva, rajas* and *tamas,* residing in the *Devī*. That is, they are all virtually encapsulated in the form of the *Devī*. Therefore, one who is devoted to *Śakti* is effortlessly propitiating all the other deities as well. The various deities, including the three prominent ones, are but the personifications of the various powers of *Śakti*. Thus, *Śakti* is the common ground and the immanent nature of all the other deities. As such, it is clearly desirable to be devoted to *Śakti* alone instead of propitiating the various deities separately. The last two lines of the stanza show that the three main deities are always in close proximity of the *Devī,* carrying out Her wishes with utmost devotion *(bhakti)*. The word *'bhakti'* derives from the sanskrit root *'bhaj'* which means 'to serve'. As such, being a devotee or *bhakta* of a deity implies the loving willingness to serve that deity by carrying out its wishes to one's utmost capacity.

The twenty-sixth stanza says -

> "O Queen of chastity! *Viriñci* goes back to the five elements; *Hari* ceases to exist; *Kināśa* meets with destruction; *Kubera* perishes; the array of the ever-wakeful eyes of *Mahendra* is also closed (for ever); in this great deluge, this Lord of Thine (alone) has His diversion."[327]

In this stanza Śaṅkara describes the great dissolution by saying that even the traditionally acclaimed immortal gods such as *Brahmā, Viṣṇu* etc. meet their ends during the great dissolution. But, even amidst this immense destruction, the spouse of *Śakti*, namely *Sadāśiva,* continues to survive and enjoy the blissful beauty of the *Devī*. Ānandagiri makes it clear that the spouse of *Śakti* mentioned here stands for *Sadāśiva,* who survives even the great deluge *(mahā pralaya)*.[328] Here, mentioning *Śiva* as the spouse of *Śakti* implies the duality and complementarity of *Śiva* and *Śakti*, whereas their persistence even during the great deluge shows their transcendent and immutable nature. As such, this stanza makes reference to the *nāda* level, consisting of *Sadāśiva* and *Śuddha vidyā*. It must be noted that even though the *nāda* level is an offshoot of the *Sāmarasya* level, yet being transcendent, it also represents the immutable duality of *Śiva* and *Śakti*. Further, this stanza says that it is the chastity of *Śakti* which is responsible for the blissful survival of *Śiva* even during the great deluge. That is, it is *Śakti* who is responsible for the persistence of Her counterpart subjectivity principle *(prakāśa bhāva),* namely *Sadāśiva.* Thus, this stanza also highlights the point that in matters of epistemic evolution and involution, it is the *Śakti* element that takes the lead and then the counterpart *Śiva* element follows suit. Since *Śakti* stops its epistemic evolution at the *nāda* level during the great deluge, therefore *Sadāśiva* continues to enjoy the bliss of *Śakti* even at that time. Thus, *nāda* is the immutable and transcendent level of the primordial duality of *Śiva* and *Śakti*, manifesting themselves epistemically as *Sadāśiva* and *Śuddha vidyā.* As such, in addition to the transcendent non-dual reality of *Brahman*, consisting of both the *nirguṇa* and *saguṇa* aspects, there is also the immutable and transcendent dualistic level of *nāda,* consisting of *Sadāśiva* and *Śuddha vidyā.* Thus, the immutable eternal transcendent reality of *Brahman* has both its non-dualistic and dualistic levels. The non-dualistic level refers to the *śakti* and *śānta* components of *Aum* (the same as the *Śiva-Śakti Sāmarasya* state or *saguṇa Brahman,* and the *nirguṇa Brahman*), whereas the dualistic level refers to the *nāda,* consisting of *Sadāśiva* and *Śuddha vidyā.*

The twenty-seventh stanza of *S.L.* says -

> "Let my prattle be the repitition of Thy *mantra*, my manual work be the gestures *(mudrās)* offered in Thy worship, my movements be Thy circumambulation, my food and drink be the oblations offered in fire *(agni)*, my resting be prostrations to Thee, and all my actions that give comfort to me be dedication to Thee. Let all my activity be Thy worship."[329]

This stanza is very significant because it describes the kind of advaitika devotion practised by a *jīvanmukta* i.e., a person who has already perfected his devotion to *Śakti* and has thus realized intuitively the nature of the highest reality viz. the *Parāśakti.* Lakṣmīdhara, in his commentary on the *S.L.*, clearly terms the description given in this stanza as that of a *jīvanmukta.*[330] It is also noteworthy that the use of the word *'yanme'* in the last line of the stanza clearly shows that Śaṅkara has provided this description of a *jīvanmukta's* advaitika devotion as a firsthand account and not as an outsider's observation. He has acknowledged the nature of his own devotional state by identifying with the description provided in this stanza, which is reflected by the word *'yanme'*.

This stanza also clearly shows that even in the case of a *jīvanmukta's* perfect devotion there are two distinct elements. Firstly, the *jīvanmukta* is well aware of the yet persisting epistemic distinction between himself and his deity. Secondly, he is also intuitively convinced about the all-encompassing absolutist nature of his deity, namely *Śakti*. One might wonder whether Śaṅkara accepts the persistence of epistemic dualities even after the *nirvikalpa samādhi* i.e., after a person becomes a *jīvanmukta*. However, he is quite emphatic in maintaining that even after having the highest spiritual realization in the *nirvikalpa samādhi,* the *jīvanmukta* continues to face the various kinds of epistemic dualities at the phenomenal level. His phenomenally limited self continues to have the impression of being the agent and experiencer of actions and their results respectively, but these impressions are said to be attenuated in the case of a *jīvanmukta* person.[331] Such attenuation of dualistic impressions *(vāsanā-s)* obtains due to the overwhelming impression of the *nirvikalpa samādhi* in which one comes across the intuitive realization of the non-dual and transcendent nature of reality. The greater the frequency and duration of the *nirvikalpa samādhi*, the stronger is the non-dualistic impression left by it in the *jīvanmukta's* mind.[332] This non-dualistic impression then overrides the various dualistic actions and experiences in such a manner that not for a single moment does the *jīvanmukta* forget the fundamental non-dualistic nature of reality and therefore, despite experiencing all kinds of epistemic duality, he never actually believes in the illusory projections of duality constituting the phenomenal realm, including his own limited phenomenal self or *jīva cidābhāsa*.

Once the *nirvikalpa samādhi* is attained there is total annihilation of the *sañcit* and *āgāmī* karmic impressions, but there is the persistence of the *prārabdha karmas*. The *prārabdha karmas* continue to fructify through the lifetime of a *jīvanmukta* person. That is, the experiences deriving from the *prārabdha karmas* are definitely faced by the *jīvanmukta.*[333] However, despite being rooted in his limited phenomenal self, he neither believes in the reality of those experiences nor does he appropriate them as belonging to his self. The *jīvanmukta* dedicates all his actions and experiences to the *Devī,* who is the same as the highest transcendent reality. Vinoba Bhave has pointed out this absence of *ahaṅkāra* and the resulting natural devotional dedication of all activities to God.[334] So, what is the nature of liberation or *mokṣa* for a *jīvanmukta?* Śaṅkara says his liberation consists in being rid of the cosmic illusion *(mithyā jñāna)* as a result of his experience of the *nirvikalpa samādhi.*[335] Even though the illusions projected by *māyā* continue to appear before him, he is not for a moment misled by them, as noted by Manju.[336] Rather, he witnesses the immanence and absolutist nature of the *Devī* even in that epistemic projection of duality. Once a person knows the trick behind a magical show, he can never be fooled by it again. Even when that magic is being performed before him, he is always aware of the magician as well as the reality lying behind the magical facade.

As such, a *jīvanmukta* is always aware of the absoluteness of the highest reality i.e., the immanent and transcendent nature of *Śiva* and *Śakti*. Along with this, he also continues to face the cosmic illusion of duality projected by *māyā,* in which he continues to perform actions and experience their results, stemming from his *prārabdha karma-s*. However, despite his continuing phenomenal existence, the impression of the *nirvikalpa samādhi* makes him realize the entire cosmic illusion as an epistemic sport taking place within the absolute reality, at the behest of the absolute itself. As such, he realizes the entire phenomenal realm lying within the *Devī* alone, where all the particular phenomena are but the epistemic embodiments of the *Devī's* consciousness and energy. Therefore, it is but natural that a *jīvanmukta,* not in the least appropriates to himself the experiences resulting from his *prārabdha karmas.* As such, he most naturally and instinctively dedicates all his thoughts, speeches and actions, as well as his limited phenomenal self *(jīva cidābhāsa),* to his deity, the immanent and transcendent *Śakti*. This is the state of the person who has attained the highest spiritual knowledge *(parā vidyā),* which is the same as the highest devotion *(parā bhakti).* This is the perfection of advaitika-devotion *(advaita bhakti).* The highest knowledge and the highest devotion are one and the same.[337] No wonder, Śaṅkara identifies himself with this state.

The next stanza says -

> "O Mother! all the denizens of the celestial regions, such as *Vidhi, Śatamakha* and others, perish even after drinking nectar, which is reputed to confer immunity from terrible old age and death. If the period of the life of *Śaṁbhu,* who has swallowed virulent poison, is beyond computation, it is all due to the peculiar virtue of Thy *Tāṭaṅka-s* (ear-ornaments)."[338]

This stanza points out the irony that although *Brahmā, Indra* and the other gods are said to have consumed nectar *(amṛta),* capable of granting immunity from old age and death, yet they too die at the time of the great deluge *(mahā pralaya).* On the other hand, *Śiva*, despite the consumption of the *halāhala* poison, never dies, not even during the great deluge. This stanza attributes *Śiva*'s immortality to the virtue of the *Devī's* ear ornaments. In traditional Indian culture the ear ornaments of a woman signify that her husband is alive. Therefore, the eternal form of *Devī Tripurasundarī*, along with Her ear ornaments in the form of the sun and the moon,[339]ensures and signifies that Her spouse, Lord *Śiva*, never dies. It is important to understand that the immortality of *Śiva* flows from the *Devī's* nature and not vice-versa. This is very important philosophically and spiritually. The presentation of

Śiva and *Śakti* as spouses in the *tantra* tradition highlights the point that they are always inseparable, two yet one. *Śiva* stands for consciousness or *prakāśa*, whereas *Śakti* stands for the form with which that consciousness identifies itself, namely *vimarśa*. Thus, all the manifestations of consciousness, from the highest *Brahman* to the lowest phenomenal being are the joint epistemic projections of *Śiva* and *Śakti*. This stanza shows that only that consciousness which has the transcendent form of *Śakti* as its *vimarśa*, is absolutely beyond the possibilities of old age and death. All spatio-temporal epistemic manifestations of *Śakti*, up to the level of *Nava prakṛtyātmaka Śakti* (at the *bindu* level), are destroyed sooner or later. Therefore, the points of consciousness identifying with them necessarily suffer death as well. However, the *Śuddha vidyā* form of *Devī Tripurasundarī*, corresponding with the *nāda* level in the *kuṇḍalinī* path, is beyond the space-time framework. It is the transcendent and immortal form of the *Devī*. Therefore, the consciousness identifying with the *Devī's* form at the *nāda* level inevitably turns out to be eternal and immortal. Such consciousness is the same as that of *Sadāśiva*, the transcendent form of *Śiva*, corresponding with the *nāda* level. When an aspirant succeeds in raising his *kuṇḍalinī* up to the *nāda* level, his consciousness *(prakāśa)* takes the transcendent form of the *Devī* as its own identification *(vimarśa)*. As a result, the aspirant becomes one with *Sadāśiva*, which amounts to the eternity of his consciousness and its identificational counterpart. Thus, the identification with the transcendent form of the *Devī* is the cause of the eternity of the concerned consciousness. Once again Śaṅkara shows in this stanza that it is the form of *Śakti* that determines the form of consciousness or *Śiva* at any given level of epistemic manifestation. Hence, it is but appropriate to hold that in the context of epistemic evolution and involution, *Śiva* and *Śakti* are the passive and active principles respectively, complementing one another to make up one unit, as described in the very first stanza of *S.L.*

The twenty-ninth stanza of *S.L.* says -

> "Glorious are the words of Thy attendents - "Avoid the crown of *Brahmā* in front, Thou may stumble on the hard crest of the slayer of *Kaitabha*; keep off the crown of *Jambha's* foe", when they lie prostrate (before Thee) and as Thou starteth in haste to receive *Bhava* (Thy consort) coming to Thy abode."[340]

This stanza clearly highlights the superior position of the *Devī* as compared to all the other gods such as *Indra, Brahmā, Viṣṇu*, etc. It also graphically depicts the love and affection of the *Devī* towards *Śiva*, Her spouse. However, through this depiction Śaṅkara has once again emphasized the complementarity of *Śiva* and *Śakti* through all the stages of spiritual realization. When the *jīva* raises his level of consciousness by successively meditating over the immediately higher levels of *vimarśa,* i.e., the objective counterpart of his consciousness, the *kuṇḍalinī* ascends from the lower to higher levels in the *suṣumṇā*. The *kuṇḍalinī* goes on rising from one level to another through the continuous meditative effort of the *jīva* until it reaches the level of *Brahma granthi*, after which the *jīva* does not have to exert meditatively any more since then the *kuṇḍalinī* rises on its own to reach the level of *bindu*. *Bindu* is the level of the epistemic manifestation of *Navātman Śiva* and *Nava-prakṛtyātmaka Śakti*, the level where the *jīva*-consciousness temporarily merges in the consciousness of *Śiva*, the level where his consciousness intuitively realizes the universal immanence and transcendence of *Śiva* and *Śakti*. This is the level of consciousness which grants *jīvanmukti* to the *jīva*. The rise of the *kuṇḍalinī* between the *Brahma granthi* and the *bindu* is sudden and automatic. This sudden ascent is the home coming of *Śiva*, which makes the *Devī* rush to receive Him. This rise of consciousness beyond the *Brahma granthi* is sudden and automatic and it is immediately conjoined with the manifestation of *Śakti* at the *bindu* level, in the form of its objective counterpart *(vimarśa)*. Thus, once the *jīva* has succeeded in raising the *kuṇḍalinī* up to the *Brahma granthi*, his consciousness suddenly merges in the consciousness of *Navātman Śiva*, which has the *Nava-*

prakṛtyātmaka Śakti as its objective counterpart *(vimarśa)*. In fact, Śaṅkara has even used the term *'abhyutthāne'*, which means 'ascent' or 'rise', to describe the home coming of *Śiva*. When it is noted that *Śiva* stands for the principle of consciousness in the *tantra* tradition, the spiritual and philosophical significance of this stanza becomes quite clear. This matter has also been described earlier in the twenty-first stanza of *S.L.*

The thirtieth stanza says -

> "(O Goddess !) who art eternal and art served all around by the rays, *Aṇimā* and others emanating from Thine own frame ! What is there to wonder at, if the fire of the great Deluge should perform the ritual of offering lights before whosoever conceives Thee always as 'I am (Thou)', treating the wealth of *Tri-nayana* as mere straw ?"[341]

This stanza addresses the *Devī* as *'nityā'*, which means the eternal and immutable one. As such, the reference is to the transcendent aspect of the *Devī*, corresponding with the *nāda* level manifestation of *Devī* as the *Śuddha vidyā*. In this aspect, the *Devī* is the objective counterpart *(vimarśa bhāva)* of *Sadāśiva*. The eight supernatural powers (*siddhi-s*) such as *aṇimā*, *garimā*, *laghimā*, etc. are like so many rays of light emerging from the *Devī's* body, especially her feet. Since these *siddhi-s* are effective at the phenomenal plane only, their level of existence is much lower as compared to the transcendent form of the *Devī*. Therefore, they are said to be emanating from the lowest portion of the *Devī's* body, namely Her feet.

Śaṅkara has shown the nature of advaitika devotion in this stanza, as also the results following from its practice and perfection. He says that a person who always meditates upon the identity of his own self with the transcendent form of the *Devī*, as given in this stanza, surely realizes the fundamental identity of his own self with the transcendent *Śakti*. As a result, he effortlessly masters all the supernatural powers of the phenomenal realm. However, due to his realization of the transcendent aspect of *Devī*, he is no longer bewildered and attracted by the beauties of the phenomenal realm. Constant meditation in the form of *'tvām aham'* or 'I am Thou', where 'Thou' refers to the transcendent *Devī* as the grounds of all phenomenal entities, has the potential of uplifting the consciousness of the votary to the levels of *bindu* and *nāda*. While being physically alive at the gross plane, the *jīva's* consciousness can rise only up to the *bindu* level, the level of *Navātman Śiva* or *Maheśvara* and *Navaprakṛtyātmaka Śakti* or *Māyā śakti*. However, when he is no longer bound to any phenomenal body, then his consciousness merges in the consciousness of *Sadāśiva*, corresponding with the *nāda* level. Then, it finds the transcendent form of the *Devī* as its own objective counterpart *(vimarśa bhāva)*. When being merged in *Sadāśiva* at that level, even the fire of the great deluge *(pralayāgni)* cannot affect him since that fire can destroy only phenomenal things. Thus, the stanza says that it is no wonder that even the fire of great deluge appears as camphor lights before such a perfected practitioner of advaitika devotion. It is also no wonder, says Śaṅkara, that even the wealth of *Trinayana* is like a mere straw before such a perfected devotee, i.e., the devotee of *Devī* who has intuitively realized his identity with the transcendent form of *Devī,* namely *Parāśakti,* by raising his *kuṇḍaliṇī* up to the *bindu* level. The word *'Trinayana'* refers to *Maheśvara Śiva,* the immediate source of the whole phenomenal realm consisting of the causal, subtle and the gross worlds. The sun, moon and fire are said to be the three eyes of *Maheśvara*. In the *samaya* tradition of *tantra* the fire, sun and moon represent the gross, subtle and causal realms respectively. Thus, the word *'Trinayana'* refers to *Śiva* as the source of all the three phenomenal realms, which is the manifestation of *Śiva* as *Maheśvara*. The wealth of *Trinayana* thus stands for the entire phenomenal realm. However, to the devotee who has raised his consciousness up to the *bindu* level and thus intuitively realized his identity with the *nāda* level of *Śiva* and *Śakti*, the entire phenomenal realm is nothing but an epistemic projection grounded in the reality of *Śiva* and *Śakti*, and therefore the entire phenomenal realm carries no independent worth in his eyes.

The thirty-first stanza of *S.L.* says -

> "*Paśupati*, having deluded all the worlds with the sixty-four *Tantra-s* which have as their sole purpose the conferring of the several *Siddhi-s* attributed to each, has once again brought down to this world, on account of Thy persuasion, Thy *Tantra*, which, of its own accord, would bring about the several ends and aims of human existence."[342]

In this stanza Śaṅkara has clearly enunciated the comparative superiority of the *samaya tantra* i.e., the *śrīvidyā* vis-à-vis all the other traditional *tantra-s*. The *tantra* traditions have been classified into three categories, namely *kaula mārga, miśra mārga* and *samaya mārga*. The sixty-four *tantra-s* mentioned in this stanza belong to the *kaula mārga*. The practice of these *tantra-s* generally involves elements of the *vāma mārga* or the *apsavya mārga*.[343] Lakṣmīdhara quotes these sixty-four *tantra-s* in his commentary on the *S.L.* by referring to the *Vāmakeśvara tantra*.[344] He also gives the principal objectives being served by the practice of these *tantra-s*. The *miśra mārga tantra-s* consist of the eight *candra kalā vidyās*.[345] These *tantra-s* too expound the *śrīvidyā,* but there is a significant difference between their exposition and that by the *samaya mārga*. The *miśra mārga tantra-s* may be practised either through the *dakṣiṇa mārga* or the *vāma mārga*. This means it can be practised by both *brahmins* and non-*brahmins*.[346] However, the *samaya mārga* can be practised only by the *brahmins*. Thus, it can be practised only through the *dakṣiṇa mārga*. The *samaya mārga* tradition is based on the five sacred texts authored by the seers Vaśiṣṭha, Sanaka, Śuka, Sanandana and Sanatkumāra.[347] These texts are jointly called the *śubhāgama pañcaka*.

The sixty-four *tantra*-s of the *kaula mārga* are capable of granting various *siddhi-s* or supernatural powers. However, all these *siddhis* pertain to the phenomenal realm only, i.e., to the realm of epistemic dualities. As such, they are incapable of granting any higher spiritual realization. They cannot rid the votary from the cycle of transmigrations. As a result, the *tantras* of the *kaula mārga* should be practised only by those people who wish to apply them for the purpose of attaining various phenomenal objectives. Obviously, people aiming for the highest spiritual realization over and above all worldly desires, namely the *brahmins*, would never opt for the practices of the *kaula mārga*. The *miśra mārga tantras* are capable of providing spiritual as well as phenomenal goals. As such, it can be practised by both the *brahmins* and the non-*brahmins,* but the *brahmins* can adopt only the *dakṣiṇa mārga* whereas the non-*brahmins* are free to adopt even the *vāma mārga.*[348] The *samaya mārga* tradition aims exclusively at the highest spiritual realization, in accordance with the upaniṣads.[349] Therefore, its successful practice can end the transmigratory cycle. As such, only the *brahmins* are eligible to practice it since any person who has as his sole and supreme objective the highest possible spiritual realization, is truly a *brahmin* only. This stanza says that *Paśupati* i.e., *Śiva* has deluded the world with the sixty-four *tantra-s*. These *tantra-s* are designed to fulfill various phenomenal desires though their *siddhi-s*. As such, their avowed goal is very different from the upaniṣadika aim of realizing one's identity with *Brahman*. These *tantra-s* do not lead one out of the realm of epistemic dualities. In this way, Śaṅkara says, *Śiva* has deluded the world with the sixty-four *tantra-s.*[350] Moreover, these sixty-four *tantra-s* provide their own separate *siddhi-s* and this means that a person having many worldly desires would be greatly confused in deciding over his choice of the specific *tantra* or *tantra-s* to be practised. Ānandagiri, a prominent disciple of Śaṅkara, points out in his commentary on the *S.L.* that whereas these sixty-four *tantra-s* can provide different goals in a separate manner only, the practice of *samaya mārga* can provide all the worldly and spiritual objectives in a comprehensive manner. Therefore, the *samaya mārga* is clearly superior and preferable to the other sixty-four *tantra-s.*[351] He also says that whereas the sixty-four *tantra-s* cannot grant liberation, the practice of *samaya mārga* provides liberation along with the other needs and objectives.[352] Therefore, the *samaya mārga* is preferable to the *kaula mārga.*

As far as the *miśra mārga,* consisting of the eight *candra kalā vidyā-s,* is concerned, Lakṣmīdhara points out that although it talks of the sixteen *nityā-s* and prescribes various propitiatory practices, it treats them as separate deities. Thus, the realm of epistemic duality persists even in the spiritual objectives promised by the *miśra mārga.* This means even though the *miśra mārga* provides for both spiritual and worldly objectives, its promised spiritual goal is not in total conformity with the Vedic picture of advaitika realization, especially as coming up in the upaniṣads. Therefore, quoting *Īśvara*, Lakṣmīdhara declares that both the *kaula mārga* and the *miśra mārga* should be rejected by the *brahmins*[353] i.e., by the people who wish to have the highest spiritual realization as promised in the Vedas. *Brahmins* should therefore adopt the *samaya mārga* alone.[354] Lakṣmīdhara also indicates the manner in which the *samaya mārga* conforms with the non-dualistic framework of the upaniṣads. He says that in the *śubhāgama pañcaka* the sixteen *nityā devīs* are presented as being subsumed under the transcendent *Nityā* i.e., the *Mahātripurasundarī.*[355] It says that at the *śakti* and *śānta* levels, corresponding with the *Mahābindu,* there is absolute non-duality and that is depicted in the *Sāmarasya* state of *Śiva* and *Śakti*. With respect to this *Sāmarasya* state, all the other levels of existence (starting with *nāda* and ending at the gross material plane) are nothing but epistemic projections of duality of varying orders. Therefore, the *samaya mārga* tenets and practices alone are in complete harmony with the non-dualistic upaniṣadika framework.

This conformity of the *samaya mārga* with the upaniṣadika framework has been made all the more clear by Śaṅkara's choice of terms in describing the *samaya mārga* as the *'sva-tantra'* of the *Devī* and the *kaula mārga tantra-s* as *'para tantra'*. The word *'tantra'* derives from the *saṁskṛta* root *'tan'* which also means 'to stretch, to expand, to widen out'. As such, *'tantra'* basically means the whole framework that has resulted from the expansion of some central entity. Since Śaṅkara is addressing all the hymns of the *S.L.* to the transcendent *Śakti*, the *Parāśakti,* when he designates the *samaya mārga* as *'sva tantra'* i.e., 'own *tantra'* of the *Devī,* he implies that in the *samaya mārga* the transcendent form of the *Devī,* epitomizing the non-dual *Sāmarasya* state of *Śiva* and *Śakti*, is the fundamental ontological reality upholding the entire epistemic projection of the phenomenal world of duality. On the other hand, the term *'para tantra'* or 'others' *tantra'* used to refer to the sixty-four *tantra-s* of the *kaula mārga* signify that they take the phenomenal world to be an expansion of some entity other than the transcendent *Śakti*. In accordance with this indication, these *tantra-s* view the origination of the phenomenal world either from the *nāda* level or from the *bindu* level of *Śiva-Śakti* dualism. They do not start with the non-dual level of *Śiva-Śakti Sāmarasya.* As a result, they clearly do not conform with the non-dualistic framework of the upaniṣads. Thus, *samaya mārga* is the most suitable *tantra* for the followers of the Vedic tradition. Moreover, because of the realization that the entire phenomenal world is just an epistemic projection of the *Parāśakti,* the votary of *samaya mārga* effortlessly attains all his phenomenal goals along with the most cherished objective of the highest liberation in the form of an intuitive realization of one's own identity with the transcendent *Sāmarasya* state of *Śiva* and *Śakti*.

The thirty-second verse of the *S.L.* says -

> "O Mother! *Śiva*, *Śakti*, *Kāma* and *kṣiti*; and then, *Ravi, Śītakiraṇa, Smara, Haṅsa* and *Śakra*; and thereafter, *Parā, Māra* and *Hari*; these (three sets of) syllables, when conjoined severally at their ends with the three *Hṛllekhā-s,* become the components of Thy name."[356]

This verse is very important since it gives an indication of the various syllables of the most important *mantra* or sacred chant in the *samaya* tradition. Most commentators agree that even though only fifteen syllables are indicated here, the verse really intends to give the sixteen syllabled *mantra* of the *śrīvidyā* tradition. The profound mystical significance of the sixteenth syllable is cited as the reason for not giving its explicit description in the verse. It is to be received only directly from a qualified preceptor. The importance and secrecy attached with this syllable may be compared with the fourth section of the famous *Gāyatrī mantra.* Its importance in this tradition may also be comprehended from the fact that the very name of this *tantra* tradition, *'śrīvidyā',* derives from this sixteenth syllable.

There are two versions of the sixteen syllabled *mantra* in the *śrīvidyā* tradition. One of them starts with the letter *'ka'* and is thus known as the *'kādi vidyā',* whereas the other one starts with the letter *'ha'* and is thus known as the *'hādi vidyā'.* The difference between them is only in the first three syllables. In the case of *kādi vidyā* they are *'ka', 'e'* and *'ī',* whereas in the case of *hādi vidyā* they are *'ha', 'sa'* and *'ka'.* Lakṣmīdhara holds this stanza to indicate the *kādi vidyā.*[357] However, Kaivalyāśrama[358] and Ānandagiri[359] think that it indicates the *hādi vidyā.* Synthesizing the two interpretations of the verse, Kāmeśvara Sūrī[360] and Rāma Kavi[361] believe that this stanza indicates both the versions of the sixteen syllabled *mantra.* Rāma Kavi also points out that whereas the *hādi vidyā* emphasizes the *Paramaśiva,* the passive aspect of the absolute, the *kādi vidyā* emphasizes the *Parāśakti,* the active aspect of the absolute.[362] The active and the passive aspects of the absolute are signified by the *śakti* and the *śānta* aspects of *Aum* respectively. They are merely the different aspects of the same absolute, mutually complementing and yet indistinguishable.

This stanza also points out that the various syllables of the *mantra* are indicative of the various deities mentioned in the stanza. Since all the deities are nothing but the various partial epistemic manifestations of the absolute *Śakti*, therefore the whole sequence of their representative syllables depicts the various manifestations of the absolute *Śakti*. In this context, this stanza presents the sixteen syllabled *mantra* as the name of the absolute *Śakti*, the *Devī Tripurasundarī*. This *mantra* consists of four different sections or *khaṇḍa-s*. The first section, called the *agni khaṇḍa* or the fire-region, consists of four syllables. In *kādi vidyā* they are *'ka'*, *'e'*, *'ī'* and *'la'*. In *hādi vidyā* they are *'ha'*, *'sa'*, *'ka'* and *'la'*. The fire region of the *mantra* bears subtle corresponding identity with various aspects of the world and thus it represents them at the *mantra* level. Constant meditation over this section of the *mantra* has the potential of giving one the intuitive realization of these corresponding identities. The fire region of the *mantra* corresponds with the waking state, the gross realm, the various activities of the waking-self or *Viśva,* the *tamo guṇa,* the section of the *suṣumṇā* from its base up to the *maṇipūra cakra,* the *'a'* syllable of *'Aum'* and the volitional power or *kriyā śakti*. With respect to the *śrīcakra,* it corresponds with the three outer *bhūpura-s,* the three circles, the sixteen-petalled lotus and the eight-petalled lotus. The second section, called the *sūrya khaṇḍa* or the solar region, consists of five syllables viz. *'ha'*, *'sa'*, *'ka'*, *'ha'* and *'la'*. This section bears a corresponding identity with the dreaming state, the subtle realm, the various activities of the dream-self or *Taijasa,* the *rajo guṇa,* the section of *suṣumṇā* between the *svādhiṣṭhāna* and the *anāhata cakras,* the *'u'* syllable of *Aum* and the conational power or *icchā śakti*. With respect to the *śrīcakra,* the solar region corresponds with the *catur- daśāra* or the fourteen-angled *cakra* and the *bahir daśāra* or the outer ten-angled *cakra*. Between the fire region and the solar region there is the syllable *'hṛīṁ'* which bears correspondence with the gross level macrocosmic consciousness or *Virāṭ* and the *Rudra granthi,* a nodal point in the *kuṇḍalinī* pathway situated between the *maṇipūra* and *svādhiṣṭhāna cakra-s*. The third section, called the *soma khaṇḍa* or the lunar region, consists of three syllables viz. *'sa'*, *'ka'* and *'la'*. Between the solar and the lunar regions lies the syllable *'hṛīṁ',* which bears correspondence with the subtle level macrocosmic consciousness or *Hiraṇyagarbha,* and the *Viṣṇu granthi,* a nodal point in the *kuṇḍalinī* pathway situated between the *anāhata* and the *viśuddhi cakra-s*. The lunar region bears a corresponding identity with the dreamless sleep state, the causal realm, the various activities of the deep sleep-self or *Prājña*, the *sattva guṇa,* the section of *suṣumṇā* spanning across the *viśuddhi* and *ājñā cakra,* the *'m'* syllable of *Aum* and the cognitive power or *jñāna śakti*. With respect to the *śrīcakra,* the lunar region of the *mantra* corresponds with the inner ten-angled *cakra* and the eight-angled *cakra*. The fourth section of the *mantra,* called the *citcandrakalā khaṇḍa* or the ever-resplendent-moon region, consists of only one syllable and that is the *Ramā bīja*. Between the third and the fourth sections of the *mantra* there is the syllable *'hṛīṁ',* which bears correspondence with *Īśvara* or the causal level macrocosmic consciousness, and the *Brahma granthi,* situated between the *ājñā cakra* and the *bindu*. The fourth section of the *mantra* bears a corresponding identity with the state of consciousness transcending the three ordinary states (and thus called the *turīya* or fourth state), the realm transcending the causal realm, the realm beyond the three *guṇa-s,* the *kuṇḍalinī* pathway covering the *bindu, nāda* and *sahasrāra;* the *bindu, nāda, śakti* and *śānta* components of *Aum,* and the pure witness-consciousness. With respect to the *śrīcakra,* the fourth section of the *mantra* corresponds with the innermost triangle *(trikoṇa),* the visible centre or *bindu* and invisible centre or *mahābindu*. This section represents the ever-resplendent-lunar region, the *parā kalā,* the *sādākhyā kalā,* the *citcandra kalā* of the absolute *Śakti*. It represents the immutable absolute consciousness of the *Sāmarasya* state of *Śiva* and *Śakti*. The first fifteen syllables of the *mantra* are the partial manifestations or imperfect reflections of the sixteenth syllable. The sixteen syllables represent the sixteen *nityā devīs,* where the sixteenth *Nityā* stands for the transcendent *Sādākhyā kalā*. Thus, by meditatively understanding the significance and symbolism of the sixteen-syllabled *mantra,* one can easily elevate one's level of consciousness and attain the highest liberation.

The thirty-third stanza of the *S.L.* says -

> "O Goddess eternal! having placed this triad of *Smara, Yoni* and *Lakṣmī* before Thy *Mantra*, some (devotees of Thine), bent on the boundless enjoyment of Beatitude, worship Thee with rosaries strung with *Cintāmaṇi* beads, while offering hundreds of oblations with streams of *Surabhi's* ghee, on the fire of *Śiva* (triangle)."[363]

This stanza suggests a variation in the *Devī* mantra given in the previous stanza. If the previous stanza is taken to give the *kādi vidyā*, as believed by Lakṣmidhara, then this stanza would suggest placing the *bīja mantra-s* of *Smara, Yoni* and *Lakṣmī*, namely *klīṁ, hrīṁ* and *śrīṁ*, before the *kādi vidyā*.[364] However, if the previous stanza is believed to give the *hādi vidyā*, then this stanza would suggest the substitution of the first three syllables with the letters representing *Smara, Yoni* and *Lakṣmi*, namely *'ka', 'e'* and *'ī'* respectively.[365] The meditation over this mantra gives the votary *mahā bhoga*, i.e., immense bliss and beatitude. This *mahā bhoga* could also mean the immense bliss of realizing one's own identity with the *Devī*. Unlike the *kaula-s*, the followers of *samaya* tradition do not perform external worship of the *Devī*.[366] All the rituals are performed internally through meditation. Thus, the *Devī* is to be meditatively brought down from Her abode in the *sahasrāra* to the *anāhata cakra*, where the devotee is to offer Her oblations. Such meditative worship is capable of providing all the worldly pleasures as well as the highest bliss of liberation in due course. The practice of such meditative worship is thus capable of giving *nirvikalpa samādhi*.[367] This stanza also suggests that the meditation over the *Devi's* mantra has to be done with the help of a rosary having the *mātṛkā-s* (sanskrit alphabet letters) as its beads, where the last letter *'kṣa'* is not to be crossed. Such a rosary is referred to as the *'akṣa mālā'*. According to Kaivalyāśrama, the *kuṇḍalinī* is to be meditatively visualized as the *mātṛkā māla* spreading between the *mūlādhāra* and the *sahasrāra* and the *Devī* is to be worshipped with the feeling of basic identity with Her form. Such internal worship with the *kādi vidyā* grants all phenomenal and spiritual beatitude, as also the highest bliss of liberation.[368] Ānandagiri also believes that this stanza indicates the *kādi mantra*, which is capable of granting all phenomenal and heavenly pleasures, as well as the highest liberation in the form of realizing absolute identity with the *Parāśakti*.[369] According to Ānandagiri, the internal worship is to be performed with the belief that one's own self is in identity with the *Devī*. The karmic residues of various worldly experiences are to be offered as oblations by the votary in the fire of *'śivo'ham'*. Such worship leads to the absolute exhaustion of all *karmas* and thus paves the way to the highest realization and liberation.[370]

The thiry-fourth stanza of *Saundarya laharī* is very significant since it emphasizes the nature of relationship between *Paramaśiva* and *Parāśakti*. The stanza may be roughly translated as -

> "O glorious *Devī* ! Thou art the body of *Śaṁbhu* with the Sun and the Moon as Thy breasts. O Goddess! I conceive Thy soul to be the pure *Navātman (Śaṁbhu)*. Hence, the relationship of the principal and the accessory, in the case of Ye both, exists in common, who as Transcendent Bliss and Transcendent (Consciousness) stand equipoised."[371]

This stanza aims to show the fundamental ontological identity of *Paramaśiva* and *Parāśakti* by pointing out that any effort to identify either of them as the principal *(śeṣī)* or the accessory *(śeṣa)* will be in divergence with their true nature. Ānandagiri has clearly brought out the content of this stanza in accordance with the *samaya* tradition. According to him the first line of the stanza says that *Parāśakti* is the body of *Paramaśiva.* Moreover, in the context of *śrīvidyā,* the *Parāśakti* is believed to have a corresponding identity with the *mantra* of the *Devī* and therefore, that *mantra* itself is also taken as the very body of *Paramaśiva.*[372] Then, the second line of the stanza refers to the pure *Navātman Śiva* as the soul of that body which is identified with *Parāśakti.* While explaining this line Ānandagiri says that the concept of a body is always in relation with that of a soul. A soul requires a body to exhibit its presence at the tangible level, whereas a body is able to exhibit consciousness only when it is associated with a soul. Thus, both of them have an essential complementarity with respect to one another. The simile of the body and the soul has been used by Śaṅkara to bring out explicitly the necessary complementarity of *Śiva* and *Śakti*. This necessary complementarity, which actually stems from their ontological identity, has also been indicated in the very first stanza of *S.L.* Ānandagiri says that because of this it is not possible to categorize them as the principal and the accessory. Moreover, if one should insist upon such categorization, then it is possible for both of them to be treated either as the principal or as the accessory because of their basic ontological identity. Therefore, Ānandagiri concludes that just as in the case of *dvandva samāsa,* where both the terms have equal importance, both the *Paramaśiva* and *Parāśakti* are equally principal.[373] Ānandagiri goes on to explain the last line of the stanza by elaborating the meaning of *'samarasa parānanda parayoḥ'*. At the absolute level of reality, there is perfect equilibrium or *Sāmarasya* between *Śiva* and *Śakti*, symbolizing the subjective and objective principals respectively. All their characteristics co-mingle and there is perfect interpenetration, rather identity. *Sāmarasya* is explained in terms of identity *(ekātmya)*. In this *Sāmarasya* there is neither the subject nor the object, neither *Śiva* nor *Śakti*. There is only the non-dual Absolute. This Absolute, the *Brahman*, is the same as the transcendent Bliss.[374] The bliss experienced during the state of *nirvikalpa samādhi* is the manifestation of this very bliss of the *Sāmarasya* state, even though it might be just a microscopic particle of that absolute Bliss. The difference is only in terms of degree and not in terms of quality, as in the case of a vast ocean and a drop of water belonging to that ocean.

Kaivalyāśrama too agrees that it is neither possible nor appropriate to treat either *Paramaśiva* or *Parāśakti* as the principal and the other as the accessory, since both of them are equipoised in the

Sāmarasya state, just as the twin terms in the case of *dvandva samāsa* carry equal importance.[375]

Lakṣmīdhara gives both the *samaya* tradition interpretation and the *pūrva kaula* tradition interpretation of this stanza. While explaining it from the *samaya* viewpoint, he also emphasizes the equipoise, equal importance and interpenetration of *Śiva* and *Śakti*.[376] This is the *Sāmarasya* state of *Śiva* and *Śakti*, where they are actually indistinguishable as two distinct realities. It is the highest ontological absolute which alone manifests itself sometimes as the passive principal and sometimes as the active principal, better known as the *nirguṇa* and *saguṇa Brahman* respectively. Again, they are the same as the *Paramaśiva* and *Parāśakti* respectively. They are the passive and the active aspects of the same reality, which is the sole ontological absolute. This *Sāmarasya* of *Śiva* and *Śakti* upholds the ontological absolutism underlying the traditions of *śrīvidyā* and advaitism.

According to Lakṣmīdhara, the *pūrva kaula* tradition interprets the equipoise of *Śiva* and *Śakti* not only in terms of their ontological identity but also on two other counts. Firstly, according to them, during the creation, sustenance and destruction of the universe the *Śakti* aspect of the absolute reality remains the principal and the *Śiva* aspect of the absolute becomes the accessory. However, during the great dissolution *(mahā pralaya)* the *Śiva* aspect becomes the principal and the *Śakti* aspect the accessory. This way, *Śiva* and *Śakti* become even and they have equal importance. This is their equipoise. Secondly, *Śiva* and *Śakti* are also equipoised in terms of their nine-fold functional aspects.[377] *Śiva* and *Śakti* are characterized by their nine-fold functional aspects at the macrocosmic epistemic level, corresponding with the *bindu* in the pathway of the *kuṇḍaliṇī*. Therefore, at this level they are called the *Navātman Śiva* and the *Navātmā Śakti* or the *Nava-prakṛtyātmaka Śakti*. The nine *vyūha-s* characterizing the *Navātman Śiva* are - *kāla* or time, *kula* or colours, *nāma* or conventional names, *jñāna* or knowledge, *citta* or the internal faculty, *nāda* or the sound vibration (consisting of *parā, paśyantī, madhyamā* and *vaikharī), bindu* or the six *kuṇḍalinī cakra-s, kalā* or the letters of the *saṁskṛta* alphabet, and *jīva-s* or the souls.[378] Similarly, the *Navātmā Śakti* is characterized by nine *vyūha-s* viz. *vāmā, jyeṣṭhā, raudrī, ambikā, icchā, jñānā, kriyā, śāntā* and *parā*. Out of these nine *vyūhas* the first four are represented by the four triangles pointing in one direction of the *śrīcakra,* whereas the last five are represented by the five triangles pointing in the other direction.[379] Thus, the *pūrva kaula* tradition justifies the equal importance and equipoise of *Śiva* and *Śakti* with reference to both their ontological identity at the absolute level and their functional equality at the epistemic level of *Navātman Śiva* and *Navātmā Śakti*.

The thirty-fifth stanza describes the universal immanence of *Śakti* as follows -

> "O youthful spouse of *Śiva*! Thou art the Mind, Thou the ether, Thou the air, Thou the fire, Thou the Water, and Thou the Earth. When Thou hast transformed Thyself (thus), there is nothing beyond. Thyself, with a view to manifesting Thyself in the form of the Universe, inwardly assumest the form of Consciousness and Bliss."[380]

In this stanza Śaṅkara extols the immanence of *Śakti* by pointing out that it is *Śakti* alone who has transformed Herself into the five basic elements, as well as the sixth element viz. mind. These six elements are responsible for the creation of the gross elements, and then all of them appear in the form of the subtle and gross material universe. However, all these transformations are only of an epistemic nature.[381] All these basic elements of the macrocosm are also represented at the microcosmic level as the various *cakra-s* having different elemental aspects as their dominant features, i.e., the mind element is represented in the *ājñā cakra,* ether in the *viśuddhi cakra,* air in the *anāhata,* fire in the *svādhiṣṭhāna,* water in the *maṇipūra* and earth in the *mūlādhāra cakra*. Thus, it is *Śakti* alone who is immanent in the whole universe.[382] As such, *Śakti* is verily the underlying reality upholding the various appearances of the universe. All the apparent individual entities are actually superimposed *(adhyasta)* upon the basic substantial reality, namely *Śakti*, and this *Śakti* appears in the form of the *kuṇḍalinī* at the microcosmic plane.[383] Kaivalyāśrama too shows the immanence and complete universality of *Śakti* while commenting on this stanza. He explicitly states that there is absolutely nothing existing apart from or beyond *Śakti*.[384] In a similar manner Kāmeśvara Sūrī emphasizes the universal immanence of *Śakti* and points out that the use of the word *'pariṇāma'* in this stanza should not be presented as a justification for the separate ontological status of the various subtle and gross elements. He explains the use of the word by saying that in the ordinary worldly existence, prior to the *nirvikalpa samādhi,* the various elements and their compounds do appear as separately existing; yet they are epistemic superimpositions of the transcendental kind *(vivarta paraḥ)*. Thus, nothing apart from *Śakti* exists truly even in the ordinary material universe.[385] He even points out that it is the wish of *Śakti* alone which brings about the epistemic creation of the whole universe. Not only this, even the distinct appearances of *Śiva* and *Śakti* also result from the very same wish, since both the subjective and the objective polarities are required for the epistemic projection of the universe. However, from the viewpoint of absolute ontological reality, *Śiva* and *Śakti* are one and the same.[386] This absolute reality is the highest *Brahman*, that is at once both the *nirguṇa* and the *saguṇa Brahman,* both *Paramaśiva* and *Parāśakti*.

While commenting on this stanza Ānandagiri explains the identity of *Śakti* with the whole universe on the lines of the ontological identity of the actual rope and the snake which is epistemically superimposed *(adhyasta)* upon that rope. The existence of snake is only in terms of its ontological identity with the rope and thus, separate from the rope, it has no true existence at all.[387] The created universe is both real and unreal only in a similar sense. Ānandagiri also says that the appearance of *Śakti* as the spouse or active counterpart of *Śiva,* also takes place only when in the absolute state of *Sāmarasya* there occurs the wish of manifesting oneself as the manifold; otherwise, the non-dual *Sāmarasya* state, depicted by the *ardhanārīśvara* form, alone is the true ontological absolute.[388] The appearance of *Śakti* as being separate from *Śiva* and thus the appearance of reality being bipolar in nature is also ultimately a matter of epistemic superimposition, which has however been brought about by the absolute non-dual reality itself in the first place.

From the thirty-sixth to the forty-first stanza of the *S.L.* Śaṅkara describes the six *cakra-s* one by one, from the *ājñā* to the *mūlādhāra.* These *cakra-s* represent the various evolutionary stages of the epistemically projected universe, wherein different aspects of the subjective and objective principles, namely *Śiva* and *Śakti*, are manifested. The whole sequence of the epistemic projection of the macrocosmic universe is duly represented in the microcosm as the pathway of the *kuṇḍalinī*. The microcosmic *cakra-s* in the *kuṇḍalinī* pathway bear a corresponding identity with the different macrocosmic epistemic levels. Different elemental essences typify the *cakra-s,* starting from the *ājñā* down to the *mūlādhāra.* That is, the *manas tattva* or mind-essence is associated with the *ājñā cakra;* the *ākāśa* or ether element with the *viśuddhi cakra;* the *vāyu* or air element with the *anāhata cakra;* the *tejas* or fire element with the *svādhiṣṭhāna cakra,* the *āpas* or water element with the *maṇipūra cakra,* and the *pṛthivī* or earth element with the *mūlādhāra cakra.* These six stanzas primarily refer to the six macrocosmic elemental stages which are symbolized as the six *cakra-s* in the *Śakti*'s cosmic form. It is so because the whole of the epistemically projected universe is nothing but the very form and body of *Śakti*. However, due to the corresponding similarities, rather identities, obtaining between the macrocosm and the microcosm, these six stanzas also describe in a secondary sense the various microcosmic *cakra-s,* along with the forms of *Śiva* and *Śakti* manifested therein. The description of these *cakra-s,* both macrocosmic and microcosmic, as also of their respective presiding *Śiva-Śakti* manifestations, is very important for the meditative spiritual practices of the followers of the *samaya mārga*. For that matter, it is not totally irrelevant even for the followers of the *kaula mārga,* both *pūrva kaula* and *uttara kaula*. At this point, it is important to bear in mind that the status of the *jīva* as a separate individual soul is functionally effective only up to the *ājñā cakra*. As such, active meditative worship and devotion is actually possible only up to the level of consciousness represented by the *ājñā cakra*. Beyond that, the consciousness of the *jīva* ceases to operate in its individual capacity. Beyond the *ājñā,* at the level of the *Brahma granthi,* the *jīva* remains just as an essential constituent of the *Īśvara*-consciousness. Therefore, while describing the internal meditative worship for the followers of the *samaya mārga*, Śaṅkara has indicated only the six *cakra-s* situated between the *ājñā* and the *mūlādhāra*.

Describing the *ājñā cakra,* the thirty-sixth stanza says -

> "I bow to *Paraśaṁbhunātha* resting in Thy *ājñā-cakra* enveloped by *Paracit* on the sides and having the splendour of crores of suns and moons. Having worshipped whom with devotion, one lives in the *sahasrāra*, the land of eternal moonshine, which is out of reach of the Sun, Moon and Fire and far beyond the ken of all and devoid of light."[389]

In this stanza the *ājñā cakra* is being described as the abode of *Para śaṁbhunātha* and *Cit Parāmbā*. The *ājñā cakra* is the *mānasa cakra* i.e., the *cakra* depicting the evolutionary stage of the mind element. It is this mind element that immediately provides the stuff for the epistemic projection of the essences of the other five elements, viz. ether, air, fire, water and earth, at the levels of their respective *cakra-s*. Lakṣmīdhara interprets the word *'tava'* as referring to the *śrīcakra* and thus the term '*tavājñā cakrasthaṁ*' is taken as referring to the four *Śiva cakra-s* of the *śrīcakra,* correspondingly located between the eyebrows of the aspirant.[390] However, Kaivalyāśrama understands this term as referring to the *ājñā cakra* of the *Devī,* which is of the form of two-petalled lotus and it is located between the eyebrows.[391] He elaborates further and says that by meditatively worshipping the *Śiva-Śakti* manifestations in the *ājñā cakra* one's consciousness transcends the dualistic realm to reach the level of the thousand-petalled lotus or *sahasrāra,* which is the realm of infinite light, lying much beyond the regions of the sun, moon and the fire.[392] Kāmeśvara Sūrī not only interprets *'tavājñā cakrasthaṁ'* as the two-petalled lotus situated between the eyebrows of the *Devī*, but also criticizes Lakṣmīdhara for his different interpretation.[393] In addition to this, he also gives the novel interpretation that all the various *cakra-s*, their elemental essences and the various *Śiva-Śakti* manifestations therein fall within the ambit of the *Parāśakti's* command.[394] By the meditative worship of *Paraśaṁbhunātha* and *Cit Parāmbā* in the *ājñā cakra*, one's consciousness rises up to the non-dualistic level of the *sahasrāra*, gaining absolute identity or *sāyujya* with the *Parāśakti.*[395] Ānandagiri too agrees that by such meditative worship of *Paraśaṁbhunātha* and *Cit Parāmbā* in the *ājñā cakra,* one gains access and abode in the ever resplendent non-dual realm represented by the *sahasrāra* and this realm is absolutely beyond all kinds of phenomenal miseries, changes and illusions.[396]

The thirty-seventh stanza, describing the *viśuddhi cakra* and its presiding deities, says -

> "I worship, in Thy *viśuddhi*, *Śiva*, clear as pure crystal and generating *Vyoman,* as also the Goddess, whose functions are the same as *Śiva*'s; in virtue of the lustre of them both assuming equality of status with the moon-beams, the Universe, rid of its internal darkness, delights like a she-partridge."[397]

In this stanza Śaṅkara refers to the *viśuddhi cakra* in the cosmic form of the *Devī*, wherein the presiding manifestations of *Śiva* and *Śakti* are called *Vyomeśvara* and *Vyomeśvarī* respectively. This *cakra* is the ethereal centre, representing the epistemic projection of the elemental essence of ether or *ākāśa tattva*, in the sequence of involution. It is only after this level that the other four elemental essences are epistemically created. As such, in the sequence of epistemic involution, the *viśuddhi cakra* is the level where all the other four elemental essences, viz., earth, water, fire and air, are found to be epistemically merged into the ethereal essence. This stanza also significantly describes the *Śakti* as being functionally at par with *Śiva*, where *Śiva* has been described as *'vyoma janakaṁ'*, the creator or father of ether. Therefore, it shows that the epistemic projection of ether-essence involves the equal participation of both *Śiva* and *Śakti*. This is equally true for all the other epistemically created entities as well. It is so because any epistemic projection is possible only in the dichotomous framework of the subject and the object, which are represented here by *Śiva* and *Śakti* respectively. Further elaborating on this, Ānandagiri points out that *Śakti* is at par with *Śiva* not only in the epistemic creation of ether, but also in terms of having likewise names e.g., *Vyomeśvarī*, as also in terms of being the cause of the epistemic creation, sustenance and dissolution of the universe. In addition, both of them are ontologically identical in the *Śiva-Śakti Sāmarasya* state, which is the same as the highest *Brahman*.[398] Moreover, the bipolar epistemic projection of *Śiva* and *Śakti* out of the *Sāmarasya* state is the result of the same primordial transcendent *spanda* or vibration. As for the purpose of their propitiation in the *viśuddhi cakra*, Ānandagiri makes it amply clear that it is a necessary stage in the path leading to the realization of one's identity with the *Paramaśiva* and *Parāśakti*.[399] This stanza also tells us that by raising one's *kuṇḍalinī*, and thereby consciousness, up to the *viśuddhi cakra,* the internal darkness of ignorance is destroyed by the divine luster of *Śiva* and *Śakti* witnessed there. The destruction of ignorance is to the extent of witnessing the ethereal essence as the source, as well as the point of merger, of the other four elemental essences. The building blocks of the tangible gross and subtle worlds are witnessed as merged into the *ākāśa tattva.*

Describing the *anāhata cakra*, Śaṅkara says -

> "I worship that unique pair of swans, subsisting entirely on the honey of the blooming lotus of wisdom (the *anāhata*) and gliding over the *Mānasa* of great minds; from whose mutual cackle, there results the exposition of the eighteen *vidyā-s*, and which extracts all the good from the bad, even as it would, milk from the water (which dilutes it)."[400]

The *anāhata cakra* described in this stanza is the centre representing the level of the elemental air-essence in the sequence of epistemic evolution as well as involution of the universe. Each and every level of this epistemic chain is associated with its own unique manifestation of the *Śiva-Śakti* couple. In the case of the *anāhata cakra* they manifest themselves as *Haṁseśvara* and *Haṁseśvarī.*[401] The meditative worship of these forms of *Śiva* and *Śakti* in the *anāhata cakra,* firstly, enables one to progress towards realizing the blissful *Brahman* upholding the epistemic universe, just like the famed swans who have the capacity to separate the milk from the diluting water,[402] and secondly, it provides an intuitive understanding of the different kinds of worldly knowledge.[403] The votaries of the *samaya mārga* meditate over the *Śiva-Śakti* manifestations in the *anāhata* for the purpose of raising their consciousness level for realizing their identity with the transcendent *Śiva-Śakti Sāmarasya* and in this connection Lakṣmīdhara quotes from Śaṅkara's commentary on Gauḍapāda's *Subhagodaya* where he says that in the *anāhata cakra, Samaya* and *Samayā* i.e., *Śiva* and *Śakti* also appear in the form of a flame and its luminosity.[404] The votaries witnessing the swan-couple enjoying themselves in the *anāhata cakra* are described as the 'great ones' because they have been successful in getting rid of the numerous worldly desires.[405] Referring to *Yoginīcakra*, Ānandagiri comments that the entire universe itself is the lake in which the *Śiva-Śakti* swan-couple enjoy themselves as the blissful consciousness manifesting in the hearts of all sentient beings.[406]

The next stanza describes the *svādhiṣṭhāna cakra,* which is also the centre representing the elemental essence of fire or *tejas.* It says -

> "Oh Mother! I bow to the *Saṁvarta* resting in the *Agni tattva* in Thy *Svādhiṣṭhāna cakra* and also to that magnanimous *Samayā*, whose glance drenched with pity, renders a cooling treatment when His exceedingly furious stare burns the worlds."[407]

The *Śiva-Śakti* manifestations presiding over the fire centre, namely the *svādh-iṣṭhāna cakra,* are known as *Saṁvarteśvara* and *Samayāmbā* respectively.[408] These *Śiva-Śakti* manifestations, forming a balanced couple, are together responsible for the dissolution of the created worlds as well as for their recreation respectively. While *Saṁvarteśvara* burns up all the seven phenomenal spheres, *Samayāmbā* gives them a new lease of life by reprojecting them epistemically due to Her infinite mercy.[409]

The next stanza, describing the *maṇipūra cakra,* says -

> "I worship that redoubtable dark-blue cloud, abiding forever in Thy *maṇipūra*, endowed with lightning in the form of *Śakti*, whose lustre controverts darkness, with a rainbow caused by sparkling of variegated gems set in the jewels (of the *kuṇḍalinī*), and showering rain over the worlds scorched by *Hara* (fire) and *Mihira* (the Sun)."[410]

The *maṇipūra cakra* is the level representing the elemental essence of water or *āpas.*[411] In this *cakra* the presiding manifestations of *Śiva* and *Śakti* are known as *Megheśvara* and *Saudāminī.*[412] *Śiva* is comparable to the dark clouds full of water and *Śakti* is the lightning accompanying those clouds. However, the lustre of *Śakti* in this *cakra* is not momentary, unlike the case of ordinary lightning, rather it is permanent. Hence, *Śakti* as manifest in this *cakra,* is also known as *Sthira saudāminī.*[413] This *cakra* is known as the *maṇipūra* because it refers to the bow-like brilliant lustre of the *Śakti* which encircles *Megheśvara Śiva.*[414] Another explanation of the name of this *cakra* as *'maṇipūra'* is offered by Ānandagiri according to which just as the ocean is full of various gems, similarly this *cakra* is full of life-sustaining potential since it represents the water element.[415] The epistemic creation corresponding with the *maṇipūra cakra* level is treated as the *miśra loka* i.e., a realm which is characterized by both light and darkness.[416] While *Megheśvara* appears as the dark clouds, its characterizing *Saudāminī* (lightning) provides the illuminating brilliance. This brilliance may be also understood as the lustre of the *kuṇḍalinī śakti* at the level of *maṇipūra cakra*. In the process of the epistemic evolution of the various elemental essences, beginning with the mind element at the *ājñā cakra,* by the time the *maṇipūra* level arrives the sun-rays emanating from above the *anāhata* get combined with the fire of the *svādhiṣṭhāna* and they then convert the water of the *maṇipūra* into dark clouds that drench the worlds and provide all worldly life forms.[417] Ānandagiri has beautifully explained that the same *Śiva-Śakti*, in their different aspects, are responsible for both the evolution and involution of the universe, just as the same sun is responsible for both scorching the earth as also for generating the clouds that drench the scorched earth.[418]

The last stanza of the *Ānanda-laharī* section of the *S.L.*, viz. the forty-first stanza, refers to the *mūlādhāra cakra* and describing the *Śiva-Śakti* manifestations there, it says -

> "I conceive, in Thy *mūlādhāra*, the Deity dancing the great *Tāṇḍava,* replete with the nine sentiments, along with *Samayā* intent upon *Lāsya*, as *Navātman*. This world came to own its father and mother in these two, with their manifest grace for the act of Creation."[419]

The *mūlādhāra cakra* is the centre of the elemental essence of earth or *pṛthivī*. The presiding *Śiva-Śakti* manifestations in this *cakra* are known as *Mahānaṭeśvara* and *Samayāmbā* respectively.[420] The manifestation of *Śakti* in this *cakra* is also known as *Lāsyeśvarī.*[421] In this *cakra* the *Śiva-Śakti* manifestations have been described as being engaged in a divine cosmic dance. *Śiva* is engaged in *tāṇḍava,* whereas *Śakti* is engaged in *lāsya,*[422] thus complementing one another as their counterparts. The reference to the *Mahānaṭeśvara* as *'Navātmānaṁ'* in this stanza can be understood as indicative of his possessing all the nine *rasa-s* or emotive varieties while doing the *tāṇḍava* dance, or alternatively it may be indicative of the *Nava vyūhātmaka Śiva* who manifests at the *bindu* level, immediately above the *Brahma granthi* in the *kuṇḍalinī* pathway.[423] The reference to *Śakti* as *Samayā* in this stanza is also quite significant because the reference to *Śiva* and *Śakti* as *Samaya* and *Samayā* is on the basis of their five-fold similarities or *'pañca vidha sāmyaṁ'.*[424] These similarities are - similarity of abode *(adhiṣṭhāna sāmyaṁ),* similarity of state or position *(avasthāna sāmyaṁ),* similarity of activity *(anuṣṭhāna sāmyaṁ),* similarity of form *(rūpa sāmyaṁ)* and similarity of name *(nāma sāmyaṁ).* The meditation over these five-fold similarities of *Śiva* and *Śakti* throughout the various levels of epistemic projections, resulting from their transcendent ontological identity in the *Sāmarasya* state, forms the crux of *samaya mārga.* The importance of these five *sāmya-s* is also indicated by the term *'samaya mārga'.* In the case of the *mūlādhāra cakra* the similarity of abode is with reference to the *mūlādhāra cakra* where both the *Mahānaṭeśvara* and *Lāsyeśvarī* reside. Their similarity of state is with reference to their being engrossed in complementary dance forms. Their similarity of activity refers to both of them being involved in the creation of the worlds, thus becoming the cosmic parents. Their similarity of form may be understood as both having a pink hue, and also as both having the nine-fold cosmic projective aspects, indicated by their names, the *Nava-vyūhātmaka Śiva* and the *Nava-prakṛtyātmaka Śakti,* or simply the *Navātman Śiva* and *Navātmā Śakti.* Their similarity of name also gets reflected through their names as *'Navātman'.* It is also true with reference to their names *Samaya* and *Samayā,* or even *Mahānaṭeśvara* and *Lāsyeśvarī.* The previous five stanzas pertaining to the other five *cakra-s* too reflect these five-fold similarities between *Śiva* and *Śakti* and Lakṣmīdhara has elaborated on them.[425] The followers of the *samaya mārga* meditatively worship the *Samaya* and the *Samayā*. They primarily worship and meditate upon the absolute as the *Śiva-Śakti Sāmarasya,* which has its microcosmic corresponding identity with the *(mahā-) bindu* in the *sahasrāra cakra.*[426] Along with this, they also contemplate upon four kinds of corresponding identities, which are firstly, that between the six microcosmic *cakra-s* and the corresponding *cakra-s* of the *śrīcakra;* secondly, the identity of the *sahasrāra* with the *bindu sthāna* in the *śrīcakra;* thirdly, the identity of *Paramaśiva* (who is identical with *Parāśakti)* with the *bindu* in the *śrīcakra;* and lastly, the fifteen or sixteen-syllabled *śrīvidyā mantra* with the entire *śrīcakra.*[427] At some places, six kinds of corresponding identities have been mentioned for the purpose of meditative worship by the votaries of *samaya mārga.* These identities pertain to the mutual correspondences among the *nāda, bindu* and *kalā.* The *Sādākhyā tattva* or the *Śiva-Śakti Sāmarasya* is itself transcendent to all these three, viz. *nāda, bindu* and *kalā.* The meditation on these identities leads to the realization of one's identity with the transcendent absolute.[428] This stanza significantly calls *Mahānaṭeśvara* and *Lāsyeśvarī* the parents of this universe since at all the levels of epistemic creation the twin principles of *Śiva* and *Śakti* are involved in it. Their *tāṇḍava* and *lāsya* may be viewed both as the cosmic creative process as well as the expression of their joy arising from the creation of the universe after the spell of the preceding cosmic dissolution.[429] In the six stanzas describing the six *cakra-s,* Śaṅkara has started with the *ājñā cakra* and concluded with the *mūlādhāra cakra.* This order of description of the *cakra-s* is in agreement with the order of involution of the various elemental essences as mentioned in the upaniṣads. This order also explains the position of the *āpas cakra* i.e., the *maṇipūra* as lying below the *tejas cakra* i.e., the *svādhiṣṭhāna.* This order of the elemental centres or *cakra-s* is at variance with the order accepted by the Yoga tradition wherein the *svādhiṣṭhāna* is taken as lying below the *maṇipūra cakra*.[430]

The first forty-one stanzas of the *S.L.* discussed so far constitutes the *Ānanda-laharī* section of the *S.L.* The section succeeding the *Ānanda-laharī* is called as the *Saundarya-laharī* section. At the same time, both the sections taken together constitute the *Saundarya-laharī* text. The content of the *Ānanda-laharī* section is deeply philosophical and mystical in character, whereas the second section of the text is an illustration of Śaṅkara's aesthetic genius. There he elaborately describes the dazzling beauty of the *Devī Tripurasundarī* in Her personalized form. Such description cannot be regarded as a mere poetic and aesthetic exercise. It has a higher purpose. That purpose is, making possible the spiritual progress of people, having ordinary intellect and emotions, in the direction of divine realization. The deep philosophical and mystical content of the *Ānanda-laharī* section can be properly appreciated only by persons of highly refined intellect and philosophical insight. The latter section of *S.L.* aims to provide an aesthetic and emotive motivation to turn the minds of ordinary people towards the supreme beauty, grace and power of the *Devī,* so that they may be freed from their unending mental obsessions of the worldly kind. Such mental reorientation gradually crystallizes into the all-absorbing desire and effort to come face to face with the divine form of the *Devī Tripurasundarī*. This mode of spiritual discipline and its ultimate culmination in the realization of one's identity with the *Parāśakti* and *Paramaśiva* has already been indicated by Śaṅkara in the twelfth stanza of *S.L.* where he says that the celestial damsels, in their eagerness to behold and appreciate the divine beauty of the *Devī,* easily realize their identity with *Paramaśiva* i.e., they attain *sāyujya* with the absolute reality.[431] Apart from this there is also the emotive path to the divine realization for people of ordinary intellect. When a person develops faith in the words of his *Guru* or preceptor, as also in the words of the Vedas, he also develops the intense desire to realize the transcendent reality, which is also manifest everywhere in the universe. He comes to acquire initial faith in the omniscience, omnipotence, omnipresence and the infinite bliss and beauty of the divine reality. Yet, when he does not find himself progressing towards the desired spiritual realization, he becomes aware of his shortcomings and helplessness. This awareness deals a serious blow to his ego or *ahaṅkāra.* As a result, he takes refuge in the infinite grace of the *Devī* and surrenders his ego before Her. He devotionally beseeches Her grace and mercy and this, according to Śaṅkara, brings about the necessary spiritual trick since the infinitely merciful *Devī* never ignores the supplications of Her devotees. She Herself raises the consciousness level of the devotee such that he may realize his basic identity with the *Śiva-Śakti Sāmarasya.* Thus, the devotional approach is also capable of leading one to the same realization which is sought through meditation over the Vedic *mahā- vākya-s.* All this has been indicated by Śaṅkara in the twenty-second stanza of the *S.L.*[432]

It is in the light of the above-mentioned aesthetic and emotive approaches to the realization of the transcendent reality that the second section of the *S.L.*, beginning with the forty-second stanza, has to be studied. For the purpose of the present study, it would be sufficient to take up just a few representative stanzas from this section for seeing their brilliant aesthetic and emotive exposition.

The forty-ninth stanza says -

> "The glance of Thine eyes is all-victorious, being all-pervasive *(Viśālā),* showering prosperity *(Kalyāṇī),* clearly brilliant *(sphuṭaruci),* invincible by blue lotuses *(ayodhyā),* the fountain-head of the stream of mercy *(dhārā),* indescribably sweet *(madhurā),* enjoying bliss in *Śiva*'s company *(bhogavatī),* protector of devotees *(avanti)* and excelling in expanse many a city. Hence certainly Thy glance is fit to be referred to by the respective appellations."[433]

This stanza describes the various qualities of the *Devī's* eyes. It is all-pervasive due to the omnipresence and immanence of *Devī* at all points in the cosmos. Her eyes are full of mercy as She is the cosmic mother of all beings. They are also full of sweetness because, being the *Śakti* principle, they witness the universal presence of *Śiva* at all points in the universe and even beyond it.

The next stanza says-

> "The eye on Thy fore-head turns a little red, actuated by jealousy on seeing the bee-like side-glances that are eager to enjoy the nine sentiments and not leaving Thy pair of ears, that are solely delighting in the honey of the bunch of compositions of great poets."[434]

This stanza beautifully points out that the *Devī* is ever eager to listen to and enjoy the devotional compositions, *stuti-s*, of the devotees which are sung in praise of Her infinite graceful qualities. The fifty-third stanza, describing the three eyes of the *Devī*, shows their nature of manifesting the three basic *guṇas - sattva, rajas* and *tamas* - of the world.[435] As such, they are also described as being responsible for the creation of the universe through the creation of their respective representative deities, namely *Visṇu, Brahmā* and *Rudra.* In a similar vein the fifty-fifth stanza says-

> "Oh ! Daughter of the king of mountains! The sages have said that the world gets dissolved and created with the closing and opening of Thy eyes (respectively). I conjecture that Thy eyes have dispensed with winking in order to save from dissolution this entire world which has had its origin through the opening of Thine eyes."[436]

This stanza beautifully describes the merciful nature of the *Devī* because of which the universe is able to sustain itself. It has also described the *Devī* as the cause of the epistemic creation and dissolution of the universe by referring to the creation and dissolution of the universe as being respectively occasioned by the opening and closing of the *Devī's* eyes.

The fifty-seventh stanza beautifully describes the knowledge based devotional appeal of the devotee to the *Devī*. It says -

> "O Spouse of *Śiva* ! may Thou graciously bathe even me, who stands helpless at a far off distance, with Thy far-reaching glance, beautiful like the slightly blossomed blue lily. This (mortal) will derive the summum bonum of existence from such (action). By such action, no loss is after all sustained by Thee. The snow-beamed (Moon) sheds the selfsame lustre on a forest as well as on a mansion."[437]

This stanza has indicated the importance of understanding the *jīva's* utter helplessness in the absence of the merciful glance of the *Devī* because it is this understanding alone that leads to the devotional appeal to the *Devī* for Her merciful divine intervention. The epistemic realm of creation of the world and the *jīva's* bondage fall within the *Devī's* jurisdiction. Therefore, it is utter foolishness to think that one may transcend the bindings of that realm without securing the gracious concurrence of the *Devī*.

The ninetieth stanza says -

> "Let my soul (me), having the (six) sense organs as feet, become a (six-footed) honey -bee, plunging deep in this, Thy foot, which is always bestowing on the helpless, wealth according to their desires, scattering abundant honey in the form of a swell of beauty and which is charming like a cluster of *mandāra* flowers."[438]

This stanza describes the devotee's yearning for being incessantly able to meditate on the *Devī's* feet by focussing one's attention on the *Devī* through all the six sense-organs. Such all-absorbing meditation on the *Devī* is said to fulfill all the worldly desires of the devotee, in addition to the liberating spiritual realization of one's identity with the *Śiva-Śakti Sāmarasya*. Thus, devotional meditation on the *Devī* grants both phenomenal and spiritual rewards of the highest kind since She is both the ultimate immanent and transcendent reality.

The ninety-fifth stanza of the *S.L.* says -

> "Thou art the harem of the foe of the (three) *Pura-s*. Therefore, the privilege of adoring Thy feet is unattainable by the fickle-minded. Hence it is that these gods, with *Śatamakha* as their leader, have been reduced to a status equal to that of the psychic powers, *Aṇimā* and others, standing near Thy doorway."[439]

This stanza beautifully puts across the point that nobody except *Śiva* himself is capable of truly beholding and enjoying the beauty and grandeur of the *Devī Tripurasundarī,* since *Śiva* alone is the spouse of *Śakti*. As such, one can be in the true proximity of the *Devī* only through the realization of one's identity with *Śiva*, where *Śiva* represents the absolute and cosmic consciousness. Leave alone the enjoyment of the beauty of the *Devī,* it is not possible for the ordinary *jīvas* to even contemplate in a proper devotional manner the *Devī's* feet. Even that requires long penance and great mental purification, as indicated by Śaṅkara in the introductory stanza of *S.L.*[440] Even the king of gods, *Indra*, is able to acquire a status comparable only with the various psychic powers, such as *Aṇimā* etc., who are stationed at the doorway of the *Devī's* palace. In other words, even a relative proximity to the *Devī's* place is capable of granting various worldly and celestial majesties. Therefore, the bliss experienced by a true devotee of the *Devī* is understandably inexpressible.

The ninety-seventh stanza brings out the various manifestations of the *Devī,* along with Her transcendent absolute aspect. It says -

> "O Queen of *Parabrahman!* the knowers of the *Āgama-s* call only Thee as the goddess of letters who is the wife of *Druhiṇa;* they call only Thee as *Padmā* who is the wife of *Hari;* they call only Thee the partner of *Hara,* the daughter of the mountain; while Thou perplexest the world, as the transcendent fourth

> entity unattainable, and with Thy boundless splendour, as the great illusory being and the fountain of all chastity."[441]

This stanza wonderfully shows in a crisp manner how it is the supreme *Devī* alone who is both the immanent and the transcendent reality, both the basic ontological as well as the epistemic illusory aspects of the universe. She alone is the power upholding the creation, sustenance and dissolution of the universe, since She alone manifests as the spouses of *Brahmā, Viṣṇu* and *Maheśa*. She alone is the indescribable absolute fourth quarter of *Brahman* viz. the *Turīyā*. That is, She alone is the transcendent absolute *Brahman*. She alone manifests as the wonderful cosmos, which becomes possible only due to Her power of projecting cosmic illusions. She is the inseparable power of *Brahman,* as pointed out by C.D. Sharma.[442] In short, She alone is the alpha and omega of the cosmos.

The ninety-ninth stanza, describing the multi-faceted bliss enjoyed by the *Devī's* devotee, says -

> "Thy devotee diverts himself with *Saraswatī* and *Lakṣmī,* i.e., becomes enlightened and (opulent), and thus excites the jealousy of *Vidhi* and *Hari* (their husbands); shatters *Rati's* chastity with his beautiful frame; and, endowed with long life, tastes the sweetness of what is called exquisite Bliss, bereft of the ignorance incidental to mortals."[443]

This stanza tells us that the true devotee of *Devī Tripurasundarī* experiences all-round phenomenal and spiritual bliss. He is blessed with both knowledge and riches. He enjoys a long and healthy life and most importantly he enjoys spiritual bliss in the intuitive realization of his identity with the transcendent *Śiva-Śakti Sāmarasya*. The devotee's life is characterized by the constant witnessing of the *Devī's* cosmic immanent and transcendent aspects. He beholds the immutable unity of *Devī's* form amidst the infinite multiplicity of the world. Though living in the world, he finds himself merged in the all-pervasive presence of the supreme *Śakti*, the *Devī Tripurasundarī*.

Devotion (Bhakti) as Depicted in Saundarya-laharī

The study of *S.L.* gives a clear picture of advaitika devotion. Some of the important and distinguishing features of advaitika devotion, as emerging from the *S.L.*, are as follows.

1. The *S.L.* makes it amply clear that the transcendent *Brahman (Para Brahman)* is the sole and absolute non-dual Reality. Thus, it upholds the ontological absolutism of *advaita* philosophy. Furthermore, the *S.L.* makes it clear that the one and the same transcendent *Brahman* may be indicated in both a positive and a negative manner, as the *Brahman* with attributes and *Brahman* without attributes, the *saguṇa* and *nirguṇa Brahman*, the *sākāra* and *nirākāra Brahman* respectively. They merely highlight the active and passive aspects of the same transcendent *Brahman*, without infringing upon its absolute and non-dual status. The transcendent *Brahman* is shown as the state of indistinguishable interpenetration of *Paramaśiva* and *Parāśakti*. This state is also known as the *Sāmarasya* or *Yugnaddha* state of *Śiva* and *Śakti*. It is the very nature of *Parāśakti*, the active aspect of the transcendent *Brahman*, to initiate the chain of epistemic projections and superimpositions. This is also known as the *līlā*, the sport of *Parāśakti*.

2. The *S.L.* also shows that the first level of epistemic relativism and superimposition is the dualism of *Sadāśiva* and *Śuddha vidyā*. This primordial duality is the first case of epistemic superimposition *(adhyāsa)*. The unique feature of this dualism is that it allows for only the two principles of *Sadāśiva* and *Śuddha vidyā*. Furthermore, despite the operation of epistemic relativism and superimposition, *Sadāśiva* and *Śuddha vidyā* are always fully aware of the higher transcendent Reality of their own interpenetrative non-duality. This primordial level of epistemic manifestation of the transcendent *Brahman* is also known as the *nāda*. So, even though the *nāda* level consists of duality and epistemic superimposition, it does not suffer from the usual limitations and delusions resulting from it. It is due to this fact that this level is also known as the *Śuddha vidyā* level, the level of Pure Knowledge, and not as the level of least ignorance *(avidyā)*. But, just like ignorance *(avidyā)*, knowledge *(vidyā)* also presupposes dualism, and the *nāda* level therefore consists of the duality of *Sadāśiva* and *Śuddha vidyā*.

3. The next level of epistemic manifestation, which is projected by the *nāda* level, is known as the *bindu*. This level of epistemic manifestation allows for the epistemic projection of infinite *jīva-s* and the various phenomenal principles, such as - space, time, vibration, volition, desire, etc., out of *Sadāśiva* and *Śuddha vidyā*. The manifestation of *Śiva* and *Śakti* at the *bindu* level is characterized by their association with the nine *vyūha-s* and nine *prakṛti-s* respectively. So they are also known as the *Navātman Śiva* and *Śakti* at this level of manifestation. The *bindu* level depicts the first level of epistemic projection of *jīvātman-s*, and therefore, it also stands as the last limit of sustaining the epistemic projection of *jīvātman-s* during the course of evolutionary progress of the consciousness of *jīva-s*. The *bindu* level is that manifestational level of *Śiva* and *Śakti*, out of which creation *(sarga)* of the universe takes place, and into which the whole universe dissolves to reside in its seed state during the period of cosmic dissolution *(pralaya)*.

4. Further down the chain of epistemic projections, come three important manifestational levels of *Śiva* and *Śakti*. These are - **a.** the macrocosmic causal world *(kāraṇa jagat)* Consciousness or *Īśvara*, and the whole causal world as constituted by *Māyā*; **b.** the macrocosmic subtle world *(sūkṣma jagat)* Consciousness or *Hiraṇyagarbha*, and the whole subtle world and **c.** the macrocosmic gross world *(sthūla jagat)* Consciousness or *Virāṭ*, and the whole gross world. These three levels, along with the levels of *bindu*, *nāda* and *Para Brahman* are the same as the seven components of *'Aum'*. They are -- *A*, *U*, *M*, *bindu*, *nāda*, *śakti* and *śānta*. The last two components of *'Aum'* depict the active and the passive aspects of the transcendent *Brahman*. The seven components of *'Aum'* cover both the immanent and the transcendent aspects of Reality. At the microcosmic level of *jīva*, the seven components of *'Aum'* have a corresponding identity with the various nodal points lying in the evolutionary path of the *kuṇḍalinī* (the microcosmic aspect of *Śakti* in the subtle body of the *jīva*).

5. The *S.L.* gives the dominant elemental aspects of the six centres lying in the path of the *kuṇḍalinī*. As such, the dominant elemental aspect of the *mūlādhāra*, the *maṇipūra*, the *svādhiṣṭhāna*, the *anāhata*, the *viśuddhi* and the *ājñā cakras* are the earth, water, fire, air, ether and mind elements *(tattva-s)* respectively. During the course of spiritual evolution, the *kuṇḍalinī* rises through these six centres *(ṣaṭ cakra)*. During this upward movement of the *kuṇḍalinī*, the elemental aspect of different centres is very significant in defining the objective counterpart lying before the consciousness of *jīva* at a given level of spiritual evolution. This sequential elemental dissolution *(tāttvika laya krama)*, effected by the rise of the *kuṇḍalinī*, is a very significant feature of spiritual evolution, as indicated in the *S.L.*

6. The *S.L.* shows that the state of *jīvanmukti*, 'liberation-while-alive', is achieved by the *jīva* when the *kuṇḍalinī* rises up to the *bindu* level. Śaṅkara's *Vivaraṇa* on the *Yoga-sūtra Vyāsa-bhāṣya* too gives an elaborate discussion on the *nirvikalpa* or *nirbīja samādhi*, which heralds the state of *jīvanmukti*. Both the Vivaraṇa and the *S.L.* make it clear that the epistemic projection of *jīva* is not annihilated even for a *jīvanmukta*. This holds true even during the state of *nirvikalpa samādhi*. So, the state of *jīvanmukti* does not imply the merger of *jīva* in the transcendent *Brahman*. The epistemic projection of a *jīva* persists until the exhaustion of the *prārabdha karmas* of a *jīvanmukta*. The *S.L.* also indicates that once a *jīva* acquires the state of *jīvanmukti* by raising the *kuṇḍalinī* up to the *bindu*, he spontaneously attains the knowledge of the nature and reality of both the *nāda* and the transcendent *Brahman*. Consequently, he is no more deluded by *avidyā* and the phenomenal categories of the world. He is always aware of the absolute reality and non-duality of the transcendent *Brahman*.

7. After the exhaustion of his *prārabdha karmas*, the *jīva cidābhāsa* of a *jīvanmukta* person is annihilated once and forever. It may get annihilated either in the Consciousness of *Sadāśiva* at the level of *nāda*, or in the Consciousness of the transcendent non-dual *Brahman*, that is, the *Sāmarasya* state of *Śiva* and *Śakti*. This final liberation is known as *videhamukti*. It is the nature of the devotional orientation of a *jīvanmukta* person that decides whether his *cidābhāsa* would get annihilated in *Sadāśiva* or in the *Sāmarasya* state i.e., the transcendent *Brahman*.

8. The *S.L.* illustrates the *samaya* tradition of *Śrī-tantra*. It is the hallmark of this tradition that it does not go against the śruti-s and believes primarily in the internal meditative worship of the *Śrīcakra*. *Śrīcakra* is a special symbol of this tradition, which represents the different levels of epistemic manifestations of *Śiva* and *Śakti*, as also the transcendent non-dual Reality, the *Para Brahman*. The various sections *(āvaraṇa-s)* of the *Śrīcakra* symbolize the various levels of epistemic manifestations and thus have a corresponding identity with the various nodal points in the path of *kuṇḍaliṇī*, in the context of the microcosm. Such a corresponding identity holds in the case of the macrocosm as well. As such, the various centres in the path of the *kuṇḍaliṇī* together constitute the internal *Śrīcakra* at the microcosmic level, whereas the transcendent *Brahman* together with all the epistemic manifestational levels constitute the macrocosmic *Śrīcakra*. *Samaya* tradition advocates the internal worship of *Śrīcakra* by meditatively realizing the corresponding identity of the microcosm and the macrocosm. Such internal meditative worship and devotion arouses the *kuṇḍaliṇī* and grants the progressive realization of the identity of the microcosm and the macrocosm.

9. Although the *samaya* tradition of *Śrī-tantra* lays primary emphasis on the internal meditative worship of the *Śrīcakra* to arouse the *kuṇḍalinī*, it does not rule out the utility of other means, such as, the use of various sacred syllables *(mantra-s)*, hymns *(stotra-s)*, symbolic diagrams *(yantra-s)*, external worship of *Śrīcakra*, as also the worship of various manifestations of *Śiva* and *Śakti*. The *S.L.* presents an elaborate scheme of sacred syllables to be used in both the internal and the external worship of the *Śrīcakra* and gives it a very important place in the overall scheme of spiritual practices. Similarly, the external worship of *Śrīcakra* and the use of hymns to propitiate *Śiva* and *Śakti* is given great importance.

10. The state of perfect devotion, as envisaged in the *S.L.*, is the type of devotion entertained by a *jīvanmukta* person. A *jīvanmukta* has the spontaneous knowledge of his own non-duality with the transcendent *Brahman*. Therefore, his devotional attitude towards the highest Reality can be justifiably called non-dualistic devotion or advaitika devotion. Such devotion is also known as transcendent devotion *(parā bhakti)*. It transcends the delusive nature of the phenomenal categories, and always remains awake to the reality of the transcendent non-dual *Para Brahman,* or the *Sāmarasya* state of *Śiva* and *Śakti*. All the mental, verbal and physical actions *(karma)* of the person possessing such transcendent devotion do not entangle him, as they are not guided by his own limited ego *(ahaṅkāra)*. As a result, all his actions automatically become so many offerings to the transcendent Reality.

11. The *S.L.* makes it clear that *Śiva* and *Śakti* are always together at all the levels of epistemic manifestations. The transcendent *Brahman* is also treated as the *Sāmarasya* state of *Śiva* and *Śakti*. *Śiva* represents the aspect of consciousness, cognition, the subject principle, whereas *Śakti* stands for the objective aspect lying before that consciousness. *Śiva* is *prakāśa*; *Śakti* is *vimarśa*. The transcendent non-dual nature of *Para Brahman* makes it clear that both *Śiva* and *Śakti*, *prakāśa* and *vimarśa*, are ultimately one and the same. The belief in their duality, the subject-object dichotomy is the hallmark of dualism and constitutes ignorance *(avidyā)*. The very beginning of the *Brahma sūtra Śāṅkara bhāṣya* refutes the apparent duality of the subject and the object, and thus rejects any real distinction of *Śiva* and *Śakti*. The non-dual reality of the *Sāmarasya* state of *Śiva* and *Śakti* alone is the absolute transcendent *Brahman*. Everything else is a result of various levels of epistemic superimpositions.

Chapter IV

Depiction of Devotion in Prasthānatraya-Bhāṣya-s

In the previous chapter a survey of the *Saundarya-laharī (S.L.)* was made with the purpose of understanding the concept of devotion *(bhakti)* as discussed therein. For the purpose of such survey and analysis, four parameters of devotion had been used to keep the study focused on the desired theme. As a result of such study, the broad concept of devotion, as depicted in the *S.L.*, had emerged.

Now, in this chapter, an attempt shall be made to discuss selectively some representative passages from Śaṅkara's *bhāṣya-s* on the *Prasthānatraya*, which consists of his commentaries on the *Brahma sūtra,* the eleven principal *upa-niṣads* and the *Bhagvadgītā*. The selective reference and analysis of these passages would be designed to bring out the concept of devotion *(bhakti)* as depicted in these works of Śaṅkara. Moreover, all these discussions would also try to locate the similarities and dissimilarities between the concept of devotion as discussed in the *Prasthānatraya bhāṣyas* and the *S.L.* of Śaṅkara. Further, as in the case of *S.L.* in the previous chapter, the selection of passages and their discussion in the case of Śaṅkara's *Prasthānatrya bhāṣya-s* would be in the light of the four crucial parameters of the concept of devotion *(bhakti)*, namely (a) the concept of deity *(Iṣṭa)*, (b) the concept of devotee *(bhakta)*, (c) the means of devotion *(bhakti sādhana)*, and (d) the state of perfect devotion and its result. The ensuing analysis and discussion are not meant to be an exhaustive one. Rather, it is meant exclusively to indicatively bring out the conceptual continuity and compatibility between Śaṅkara's *S.L.* and his commentaries on the

Prasthānatraya, especially with respect to the concept of devotion *(bhakti)*, understood in the earlier mentioned sense.

Devotion (Bhakti) in the Brahma-sūtra-bhāṣya of Śaṅkara

> "From every point of view, however, there is no difference as regards the appearance of one thing as something else. And in accord with this, we find in common experience that the nacre appears as silver, and a single moon appears two."[444]

In this passage, while discussing the nature of epistemic superimposition *(adhyāsa)* that is responsible for the ordinary sense-based cognition of the world, Śaṅkara concludes by stating that despite various possible ways of approaching epistemic superimposition it is quite certain that it essentially consists in the presentation of something in a manner that is not in tune with its true and persisting nature. This *adhyāsa* is also a basic feature of the cosmic *māyā*. The mutual superimposition of the subject and the object in the phenomenal world is the most prominent example of this cosmic *adhyāsa*. It is due to this beginningless cosmic *adhyāsa* only that the ordinary world appears to have sprung up in the manner cognizable to our normal senses. The *Māyā* which projects such superimposition is verily the power or *śakti* of *Brahman* itself. Therefore, the epistemic creation of the world is said to be resulting from the wish of *Brahman* only. The absolute *Brahman* appears as the pluralistic phenomenal world due to the power of *Brahman* itself. The same idea comes up in the *S.L.* as well when *Devī Tripurasundarī*, also described as the spouse of *Para Brahman*, is pointed out as the transcendent fourth entity *(turīyā)* who is putting the whole world through the cosmic illusion.[445] Thus, the idea of the appearance of the phenomenal world in the matrix of cosmic epistemic superimposition or *adhyāsa*, as well as the inalienable power of *Brahman*, namely *Śakti*, being responsible for such illusion, is common to both the *S.L.* and the *Brahma sūtra bhāṣya* of Śaṅkara.

Discussing the necessary eligibility conditions for a proper inquiry into the nature of the absolute *Brahman*, Śaṅkara says -

> "The answer is: They are discrimination between the eternal and the non-eternal; dispassion for the enjoyment of the fruits (of work) here and hereafter; a perfection of such practices as control of the mind, control of the senses and organs, etc; and a hankering for liberation. Granted the existence of these, *Brahman* can be deliberated on or known even before or after an inquiry into virtuous deeds, but not otherwise."[446]

In this passage Śaṅkara has pointed out the various spiritual disciplines that need to be practised with reasonable perfection so that the eligibility for inquiry into *Brahman* may be acquired. Although at the basic ontological level the individual soul *(jīva)* is identical with *Brahman,* yet it is not possible to successfully enquire into the nature of either *Brahman* or the Self with an internal organ that has not been duly purified of the mundane dross. Just as a mirror covered with dust cannot reflect anything, similarly an internal organ that has not been purified and controlled by the practice of the necessary disciplines is totally incapable of understanding and realizing the true nature of the highest *Brahman*. On the other hand, the person possessing a pure internal organ is entitled to inquire into the nature of *Brahman*, irrespective of whether he has gone through the various stages *(āśrama-s)* of life or not. Also, for a person having pure heart and mind resulting from the sustained practice of these disciplines, the realization of the nature of *Brahman* and the self is not at all difficult or far-fetched. In the *S.L.* the *Devī Tripurasundarī* has been presented as the inalienable eternal power *(śakti)* of the absolute *Brahman*. As such, She is verily identical with the absolute *Brahman*, or rather, the absolute *Brahman* itself is the transcendent aspect of this *Śakti*. As a result of such ontologically absolute nature of *Śakti*, any deliberation on Her nature invites the same eligibility conditions as in the case of inquiry into *Brahman*. Śaṅkara has described the necessity of these eligibility conditions in a somewhat indirect manner in the very first stanza of the *S.L.*[447] The *S.L.* also says that only people whose minds are free from impurity and illusions can truly comprehend and intuitively realize the absoluteness of *Śakti*, encompassing both its immanent and transcendent aspects.[448] The *S.L.* further says that this transcendent *Śakti* is ever unattainable by those who do not have the necessary spiritual strength of the mind and the heart.[449] Thus, the eligibility conditions for inquiry into *Brahman* in the case of Śaṅkara's commentary on *Brahma sūtra* are clearly reflected as the pre-requisites for approaching *Śakti* in the case of *S.L.*

Discussing the nature of relationship between *Brahman* and the phenomenal world, Śaṅkara states in his *bhāṣya* -

> "(So the meaning of the whole aphorism is): That omniscient and omnipotent source must be *Brahman* from which occur the birth, continuance, and dissolution of this universe that is manifested through name and form, that is associated with diverse agents and experiences, that provides the support for actions and results, having well-regulated space, time, and causation, and that defies all thoughts about the real nature of its creation."[450]

In this passage Śaṅkara points out that *Brahman* alone can be accepted as the cause of the creation, sustenance and dissolution of the cosmos. *Brahman* alone is responsible for the epistemic projection of the cosmos exhibiting various kinds of dualities. Not only this, *Brahman* itself, in fact, appears through the different names and forms at the level of the phenomenal world. Despite all this, *Brahman* also always remains the transcendent absolute lying far beyond the dualistic realm.

All these aspects of *Brahman* are amply reflected at various points in the *S.L.*, although they are in the matrix of the *Śiva-Śakti* terminology. The second stanza of *S.L.* beautifully describes *Śakti* as the cause of the cosmic creation, sustenance and dissolution by saying that the tiniest speak of dust from Her feet provides the necessary ontological stuff with respect to which the three principal gods - *Brahmā, Viṣṇu* and *Maheśa* - are able to perform their respective duties of the creation, sustenance and dissolution of the worlds.[451] Further, the *S.L.* describes how *Śiva* and *Śakti* are manifested microcosmically in both their transcendent and immanent aspects in terms of the various plexuses (*cakra*-s) situated along the path of the *kuṇḍalinī*.[452] Thus, apart from the fact that *Śiva-Śakti* are both the immanent and the transcendent realities, there is also a detailed corresponding manifestation of that macrocosmic reality at the microcosmic level of the individual soul (*jīva*). In another stanza the primordial *Śakti* is described as being the essence, that is, the ontological reality of the three levels of the created dualistic realm, namely the causal, subtle and the gross worlds; but at the same time, it is also said to be the transcendent absolute lying far beyond the realm of these three worlds.[453] The twenty-fourth stanza clearly states that it is in accordance with the wishes of the primordial *Śakti*, *Devī Tripurasundarī*, that the (epistemic) creation, sustenance and dissolution of the cosmos takes place through the agencies of *Brahmā, Viṣṇu* and *Rudra*.[454] The *S.L.* further indicates how, on the one hand, the epistemic manifestations of all subject-object duality are but the different manifestations of the *Śiva-Śakti* dualism (as *prakāśa* and *vimarśa*), and on the other hand, the *sāmarasya* state, i.e., the inseparable homogeneous state of *Śiva* and *Śakti*, depicts the transcendent non-dual Reality characterized by absolute bliss and consciousness.[455] At another point, the *S.L.* states how the five subtle elements along with the mind, constituting the building blocks of the epistemically created objective world, are essentially the manifestations of *Śakti* only; and how the subjective world of bliss and consciousness too is nothing but the particularized epistemic manifestation of *Śakti* alone.[456] *Śakti* as the cause of the epistemic creation and dissolution of the cosmos has been wonderfully depicted in the fifty-fifth stanza where they are stated to be dependent upon the opening and closing of the *Devī's* eyes, which means their existence and appearance rests on the corresponding perception by the *Devī* in Her mind.[457] At another point, *S.L.* describes the primordial *Śakti*, *Devī Tripurasundarī*, as being manifest in the forms of the power *(śakti)* associated with the agencies responsible for the cosmic creation, sustenance and dissolution; but at the same time She is also the transcendent fourth entity *(turīyā)* who puts the whole world through the illusion of epistemic projections.[458]

Describing the inevitable effect of the intuitive realization of one's identity with the absolute *Brahman*, Śaṅkara says in his *bhāṣya* -

> "Hence a man who has realized his own identity with *Brahman* cannot continue to have the worldly state just as before, whereas the man who continues to have the worldly state just as before has not realized his identity with *Brahman*."[459]

The person who has attained the intuitive realization of the identity of the Self and *Brahman* is inevitably and immediately transformed at the epistemic plane. That person can no longer continue to see oneself and the world in the manner that came naturally to him or her until the moment of the supreme intuitive realization. His bodily existence does continue to exist as long his *prārabdha karmas* require it, but he no longer believes in the cosmic illusion of phenomenal world, just as the person who knows that the apparent snake is only a rope, can never be afraid of it. He has already learned to see through the magic of the magician.

These ideas can be found in the *S.L.* as well. In the moment of intuitive realization of the fundamental identity of one's Self with the *Śiva-Śakti Sāmarasya* state, also referred to as the *'Sādākhyā Kalā'* of the *Devī*, the *kuṇḍalinī* reaches the *bindu* centre and as a result of this ascent of *kuṇḍalinī* the subtle illuminative nectar flowing from this centre drenches all the subtle nerves of the body.[460] As a result of such intuitive realization of the transcendent *Śakti*, the person is inwardly immersed in the infinite transcendent bliss of the *Devī*.[461] Even when the person comes out of the highest *samādhi*, the impression of that experience of transcendent bliss persists in the mind and thus uplifts the nature of his remainder bodily existence as well. It becomes but natural for him to appreciate all his body related actions and thoughts as being the various modes of worshipping the transcendent yet omnipresent *Śakti*.[462] He does not believe in the reality of his separate ego-sense *(ahaṅkāra)*. This is the necessary nature of the liberated-while-alive person, the *jīvanmukta*. Such a person goes beyond all sense of mortality so much so that even the great dissolution of the cosmos cannot shake him.[463] Such a *jīvanmukta* person enjoys his remainder phenomenal existence basking in the light of spiritual enlightenment and transcendent bliss.[464] His post-realization phenomenal existence becomes a divine sojourn.

While discussing the pattern of dissolution, rather epistemic evolution, Śaṅkara says -

> "Hence we say: As compared with this order of creation, dissolution ought to have a reverse order. For the common experience is that the order in which a man ascends a staircase, is reversed when he comes down. Besides, it is seen that pots, plates etc., which originate from earth, are reduced to earth again when they disintegrate; and ice, hail, etc. formed from water return to water. Hence also this is logical that earth which originates from water, should at the end of its period of continuance as earth, return to water; and water which is born out of fire, should merge in fire. It is also to be understood that the whole creation enters thus in this order successively into the finer and finer causes, and ultimately merges into *Brahman* which is the supreme cause and the acme of fineness. For it is not proper that a product should merge into the cause of its cause by skipping over its own cause.[465]

In this passage Śaṅkara has clearly pointed out the intimate connection between the order of creation and the order of dissolution of the various basic elements. The sequence of elemental dissolution is just the reverse order of the sequence of elemental creation. Of course, in the context of advaitism, this creation and dissolution signifies the epistemic involution and evolution of the various elements. The transcendent reality is the starting point of the process of epistemic involution and therefore it is also the necessary culminating point of the process of cosmic evolution. From *Brahman* the world comes about and in *Brahman* alone it merges ultimately.

All this is discussed elaborately in the *S.L.* The discussion is there both in terms of the macrocosm *(brahmāṇḍa)* and the microcosm *(piṇḍāṇḍa)*. *Tantra* philosophy accepts the corresponding similarity, rather identity, of the macrocosm and the microcosm and this basic tenet of *tantra* philosophy is elaborately illustrated in the *S.L.* of Śaṅkara.

The pathway of the *kuṇḍalinī* represents the whole spectrum of epistemic evolution and involution in the microcosm. Whereas the thousand-petalled lotus, *sahasrāra*, represents the transcendent non-dual absolute, also designated as the *sāmarasya* state of *Śiva* and *Śakti*, the *mūlādhāra cakra* stands for the subtle earth element. The epistemic appearance of *Śiva-Śakti* duality signifies the epistemic appearance of subject-object distinction in the ontological absolute. This *Śiva-Śakti* distinction manifests in various forms at the different points of the pathway of *kuṇḍaliṇī* i.e., the *kula patha*. In the *sahasrāra* alone there is no such distinction, since it signifies the *Śiva-Śakti sāmarasya* state that is the same as the transcendent *Brahman*. In this *kula patha,* the *ājñā, viśuddhi, anāhata, svādhiṣṭhāna, maṇipūra* and *mūlādhāra cakra-s* respectively signify the mind, ether, air, fire, water and earth elemental essences. The level of the *kuṇḍaliṇī* in this *kula patha* shows the prevailing consciousness level of the *jīva* and hence the rise of *kuṇḍaliṇī* from the *mūlādhāra* to the *sahasrāra,* piercing through the various elemental centres, stands for the entire sequence of epistemic evolution for the *jīva*-consciousness.[466] It may as well be described as the *'tāttvika laya krama'*.

The *S.L.* is quite emphatic in pointing out that the true form of the *Devī*, i.e., the non-dual transcendent form, is beyond the whole spectrum of epistemic manifestation of the various elemental essences.[467] As such, *S.L.* makes it clear that this transcendent *Śakti* is the sole originating point of epistemic involution and therefore, also the sole culminating point of epistemic evolution. *S.L.* states clearly how in the state of great deluge *(mahā pralaya)* everything merges back in the consciousness of *Navātman Śiva* to remain there in a latent form until the time of the next cosmic creation.[468] Thus it shows how the cosmos is epistemically created through the conjoint efforts of *Navātman Śiva* and *Navaprakṛtyātmaka Śakti*, also known as *Maheśvara Śiva* and *Māyā*. Since the transcendent *Śakti* is the primal point of epistemic involution, therefore for the *jīva* who has realized his identity with this *Śakti,* there is nothing to fear even from the great deluge.[469] The ontological base of the epistemic involutions naturally outlasts the epistemic evolution of the various involutes. The fact that the creation and dissolution of the world refer to the same epistemic process, albeit in reverse orders, and also the fact this process actually pertains to the transcendent reality of *Śiva-Śakti Sāmarasya*, has been beautifully depicted in the *S.L.* when Śaṅkara says that the genesis and dissolution of the worlds lies in the opening and closing of the *Devī's* eyes.[470]

Discussing the implications of the omnipresent immanence of the absolute reality in its manifestation as the omnipotent God, Śaṅkara says-

> "During the state of ignorance, when the individual soul is blinded by the darkness of ignorance and cannot understand itself to be different from the assemblage of body and organs, it derives its transmigratory state, consisting in its becoming an agent and experiencer, from the behest of the supreme Self who presides over all activities and resides in all beings, and who is the witness (of all), imparts intelligence (to all), and is the

supreme Lord. Liberation, too, results from realization that is vouchsafed by Him out of His grace.

Why? That is what is stated in the Vedic texts. Although the individual being is impelled by such defects as attachment and is endowed with the accessories of activity, and although in ordinary experience, such activities as agriculture are not recognized as caused by God, still it is ascertained from the Vedic texts that God is the directing (i.e., ultimate efficient) cause behind all activities. To this effect occurs the text: "It is He who makes him do good works whom He would raise above these worlds, and it is He who makes them do evil works whom He would drag down"(Kau. III. 8), as also "He who dwells in the sound and controls the soul from within" (Ś.B. XIV. vi. 7.30, Bṛ. III. vii. 3-23), and other texts of this kind."[471]

In this passage it has been amply highlighted by Śaṅkara that until the attainment of highest intuitive realization one tends to think that the agency for phenomenal and spiritual efforts is entirely one's own but the fact remains that the ultimate efficiency belongs to the indwelling immanent God alone. He goes to the extent of proclaiming that even the highest realization becomes possible only by the grace of God. One may persist in one's spiritual efforts but their final fruition is entirely a matter of God's grace. All kinds of bliss and suffering, knowledge and ignorance flow from God alone as He is the ultimate cause. The way to win God's grace is to acknowledge His omnipresence and omnipotence and thus surrender before His wishes in the sincerest possible way.

All these ideas echo throughout the *S.L.* In fact, such unsurpassable omnipotence of God is truly the most important factor for precipitating devotion *(bhakti)* and surrender to God, as long as one has not been vouchsafed the intuitive realization of non-dualism. After such a realization, while the body continues due to *prārabdha karmas*, one exhibits the highest form of knowledge and devotion, namely *advaita bhakti* or non-dualist devotion. The introductory stanza of *S.L.* states that without the cooperation of *Śakti*, even *Śiva* cannot stir and therefore it is no wonder that without the necessary mental purification one cannot be eligible to even salute the omnipotent *Śakti*, who is both the immanent and transcendent Reality.[472] Elaborating on the omnipotent will of *Śakti*, *S.L.* clearly states that it is ultimately Her grace and mercy alone that is responsible for providing one with wealth, intelligence, worldly knowledge, spiritual realization, as well as desires of all kinds.[473] *S.L.* beautifully shows how the *Devī* grants the highest realization of non-dualism to the devotee who surrenders before Her and beseeches Her mercy.[474] At the cosmic plane too, the deities responsible for creating, sustaining and destroying the worlds are all acting at the behest of *Śakti* alone.[475] The *S.L.* has beautifully expressed the devotee's sense of helplessness as well as the supreme faith of the devotee in the omnipotence of divine mercy, as a result of which the devotee naturally prays to the *Devī* for Her merciful glance.[476] The greatness of enlightened devotion to *Śakti* or to any form of the immanent absolute, has been summarized in the *S.L.* where it is said that the worthy devotee of *Śakti* enjoys wealth, health, knowledge, as well as the highest spiritual realization.[477]

Discussing the latent presence of divine powers in the soul, Śaṅkara says-

> "*Opponent*: Do you mean that the soul has no attribute similar to God's?
>
> *Vedāntin*: Not that it has not; but though present, this similarity remains hidden, since it is screened off by ignorance. That similarity, remaining hidden, becomes manifest in the case of some rare person who meditates on God with diligence, for whom the darkness of ignorance gets removed, and who becomes endowed with mystic powers through the grace of God, like the regaining of the power of sight through the potency of medicine by a man who had lost it through the

disease called *timira*. But it does not come naturally to all and sundry."[478]

According to this passage, even though the bound soul does not show the various divine qualities associated with God despite being an inalienable constituent of God, it is not that it can never manifest those qualities. For that, meditation over God is required, which attracts the grace of God and then those divine powers get manifest in that individual soul.

The *S.L.* is also full of passages having a similar content. It says that the *Devī's* feet, for those who meditate on them, has the intrinsic nature of providing immunity from fear, as well as granting boons transcending one's desires.[479] Meditation on the *Devī* is capable of winning from Her the fulfillment of both worldly and spiritual desires of the devotee, so much so that it can even grant immense natural attraction of the opposite sex, if it be the desire of the devotee.[480] However, the devotee who has controlled his senses and purified his mind would only strive for the highest spiritual realization, namely identity with the *Śiva-Śakti sāmarasya*. The *S.L.* mentions special meditations over the *Devī* which have the potential of granting immense intellectual acumen.[481] It also describes the meditation over *Devī* which is capable of granting one the mystic power of eliminating all kinds of snake-poisons and fever related diseases by a mere look.[482] The *S.L.* declares in an emphatic and conclusive manner the superiority of the *Śrīvidyā tantra* vis-à-vis all the other *tantras* due to its potential of granting all the phenomenal and spiritual desires, right from the mundane to the highest realization of non-dualism, as per the beseeching desire of the *Devī's* devotee.[483] According to *S.L.*, meditation on the *Śiva-Śakti* forms manifesting in the *anāhata cakra* grants the devotee spiritual discrimination and mastery over all phenomenal disciplines.[484]

Describing the nature and the means of the transcendent intuitive realization, while commenting on the *Brahma sūtra*, Śaṅkara says-

> "Moreover, the *Yogins* realize, during *saṁrādhana*, this Self (i.e., *Brahman*) which is free from the entire universe of phenomenal manifestation and is supersensuous. *Saṁrādhana* means the act of devotion, contemplation, deep meditation, and such other practices (e.g., *japa* etc.)."[485]

In this passage Śaṅkara has mentioned the nature of the Self as being transcendent to the phenomenal universe of names and forms. This immediately indicates the supersensuous nature of the Self, which is the same as *Brahman*. However, the direct intuitive realization of the existence and nature of the transcendent reality comes during *saṁrādhana*, which signifies the superconscious state of the mind, namely *samādhi*, resulting from the sustained and intense practice of meditation, contemplation, devotion, etc.

Similar ideas about the nature of the transcendent reality and its means of realization can be found in the *S.L.* The transcendent nature of *Parāśakti* and *Paramaśiva* is indicated from the fact that the thousand-petalled lotus, *sahasrāra*, is described as their abode and this *sahasrāra* lies above the five basic elemental *cakras* as well as the mind related *cakra*.[486] The *S.L.* also states clearly that the meditative realization of the transcendent *Devī* requires the devotee's mind to be free from all illusions and impurities. Only then the devotee is able to meditate on the *Parāśakti* at the level of the *sahasrāra cakra*, which lies beyond the various elemental *cakras* in the *kuṇḍalinī* pathway. Thus, the intuitive realization of the non-dual aspect of the *Devī* is possible only when the devotee's mind is able to transcend the various ideas associated with the phenomenal realm. The resultant realization of the transcendent *Śakti* bestows the devotee with the intuitive experience of infinite and ineffable bliss.[487] The *S.L.* has also beautifully expressed the efficacy of the devotional pleas made to the *Śakti* by the devotee, especially when that devotion is grounded in the knowledge of the omnipresence and omnipotence of that *Śakti*. Such devotion has the capacity of winning the divine mercy of *Śakti* that gives the devotee an intuitive realization of his or her identity with the transcendent

Śakti.[488] Such devotion culminates in the same realization that comes through the perfect meditation on the *upaniṣadika mahāvākyas*.

The *S.L.* has also indicated the devotee's perception of his various activities in the world, where each and every action, speech and thought becomes a devotional dedication to the omnipresent *Śakti*.[489] Such a mental state, when deliberately practised, signifies an exalted devotional practice. However, when such a mental state becomes natural for the devotee, as a result of the intuitive realization of omnipresence of *Śakti*, it signifies the fruition of perfect devotion at the phenomenal plane. In other words, that is the outlook of a *jīvanmukta* devotee. All the activities of such a devotee are dedicated to *Śakti* alone. Thus, being non-egocentric activities, they do not have the capacity of generating any *karmic* bondage. The *S.L.* has indicated the nature and result of transcendent devotion or *parā bhakti*. This supreme devotion consists in the constant meditation on the absoluteness of *Śakti* and thus also on the basic identity of one's own Self and the supreme *Śakti*.[490] The realization of one's basic identity with the transcendent *Śakti* grants one immunity from even the great deluge *(mahā pralaya)* of the universe, along with the enjoyment of infinite bliss.

The *S.L.* has also described the nature of the transcendent and absolute aspect of *Śiva* and *Śakti*. It is the non-dual interpenetrative aspect of *Śiva* and *Śakti*, called their *sāmarasya* state or *yugnaddha* state, which is essentially of the nature of infinite and absolute transcendent bliss and consciousness.[491] Thus, the *S.L.* too describes the nature of the highest Reality as being absolute, transcendent, non-dual, blissful and conscious.

Indicating the nature of difference and non-difference between the supreme Self and the individual self, Śaṅkara says in the *Brahma sūtra bhāṣya* -

> "Now, in the face of this dual mention, if non-difference alone be accepted to the exclusion of difference, the mention of

difference will be left without any substance. So from the mention of both difference and non-difference, the reality here must be like the snake and its coil. As in the illustration, the snake in itself is non-different, but it differs in its having a coil, or a hood, or an extended posture; so also is the case here (with *Brahman*).

Or this is to be understood on the analogy of light and its substratum. Just as the sunlight and its substratum, the sun, are luminous, and not entirely different, both being equally effulgent, and yet they are thought of as different, similar is the case here."[492]

In this passage Śaṅkara has tried to show the sense of distinction and identity subsisting between the supreme Self, i.e., *Brahman*, and the individual Self or *jīva*. He shows through the examples of a snake and its coil and the case of light and its substratum that the sense of distinction is only epistemic and functional in nature, but the sense of identity or non-duality pertains to their basic ontological nature. That is, some special epistemic functionality in some point of the infinite *Brahman* alone is responsible for the sense of distinction between the *jīva* and *Brahman*. When devoid of such epistemic functionality, as in the state of *samādhi*, there is perfect identity between the *jīva* and *Brahman*, rather, there is no sense of *jīva* in that state at all.

There are various passages in the *S.L.* which show the difference and non-difference between the individual soul and supreme Self. The *S.L.* describes this supreme Self as the *sāmarasya state* of *Śiva* and *Śakti*, which has also been described as *Paramaśiva* and *Parāśakti*. The reference to the various *cakras* in the pathway of the *kuṇḍaliṇī*, along with the description of *Śiva-Śakti* manifestations in those centres, brings out the sense of identity and difference between the *jīva* and the supreme reality. The various *cakras* are representative of the different epistemic levels of the *jīva*-consciousness. When this consciousness is operative at the dualistic phenomenal plane, whether causal, subtle or gross, the *Śiva-Śakti* manifestations are epistemically distinct and this is in evidence in the case of the six lower *cakras*. This epistemic distinction and functionality of *jīva*-consciousness in terms of the subject-object polarity represents the sense of epistemic distinction between the *jīva* and the absolute reality at the levels of six lower *cakras*. However, the sphere of the seventh and highest *cakra*, namely the *sahasrāra*, is the microcosmic representation of the non-dual transcendent Reality, that can be variously described as *Para Brahman* or *Paramaśiva* or *Parāśakti*. As such, according to *S.L.*, the rise of the *kuṇḍaliṇī* from the *mūlādhāra* up to the *sahasrāra* is the microcosmic representation of the various stages of the *jīva*-consciousness in terms of the various degrees of epistemic illusions involved.[493] Thus, there is a gradual attenuation of the sense of epistemic distinction involving the *jīva*-consciousness until it becomes totally absent at the *sahasrāra* level to reveal the absolute ontological identity of the *jīva* with the transcent *Parāśakti* and *Paramaśiva*.

At another place the *S.L.* has beautifully described both the aspects of difference and non-difference with respect to the *jīva* and the supreme *Śakti* in the context of the pleas of mercy made by the devotee to the *Parāśakti*.[494] In the aspect of difference, the *jīva* is bound by his *karmic* impressions and this makes the divinity of his Self seem limited in various respects. The devotee acknowledges this fact of epistemically generated limitations, but he also accepts and believes in the omnipotence and infinite mercy of the supreme *Śakti*, which is the absolute and transcendent Reality. As a result, for a true devotee who has his devotional faith grounded in the upaniṣadika knowledge, the easiest way out of this phenomenal and *karmic* quagmire is to appeal for mercy before the supreme *Parāśakti*. The sincere devotional appeal for mercy by the devotee immediately elicits a divine response from supreme *Śakti*, who facilitates the removal of all epistemic obstructions to the realization of the identity of the self of devotee with the supreme Self, namely the *Parāśakti*. Thus, the appeals for mercy by the devotee, although based in the sense of difference, eventually leads to the realization of non-difference or identity with the supreme transcendent *Parāśakti*, which is the same as the *Para Brahman* of the upaniṣads.

In another stanza, the *S.L.* says that a devotee who has the intuitive realization of his own identity with the transcendent *Śakti* easily transcends the entire phenomenal realm of duality such that even the great deluge *(mahāpralaya)* of the universe is not able to affect him at all.[495] Thus, the *S.L.* explicitly emphasizes the basic ontological identity of the *jīva* and the transcendent *Parāśakti*.

Discussing the nature of relationship between the non-dualistic knowledge of the absolute and the various worldly and spiritual actions that are necessarily based in epistemic duality, Śaṅkara says in his *bhāṣya* on the *Brahma sūtra* -

> "......., therefore the answer is being given, "All religious activities are also necessary" etc. As a matter of fact, knowledge needs the help of all the duties of the various stages of life, and it is not a fact that there is absolutely no dependence on them (for purification of heart).
>
> *Opponent*: Is it not contradictory to say that knowledge depends and yet does not depend on other duties?
>
> We *(Vedāntins)* answer that there is no contradiction. For once knowledge has emerged, it does not depend on any other factor for producing its (own) result (viz. liberation); but it does depend on others for its own emergence."[496]

In this passage it has been stated clearly that the realization or knowledge of identity of the self with the absolute reality is the culminating point of spiritual journey. Prior to this realization one is inevitably operating at the level of duality. Such epistemic existence at the dualistic plane logically creates sufficient space for all sorts of religious, devotional and meditative practices, along with the concept of a personified form of the absolute reality. Thus, the devotional framework of the *S.L.* is in perfect consistency and harmony with the non-dualist framework of the upaniṣads, as brought out by Śaṅkara in his commentaries. It is in this context that the *S.L.* describes how the devotee's appeal for mercy before the supreme *Devī* results in the highest intuitive realization of non-duality with that transcendent *Śakti*.[497] Similarly, the *S.L.* describes the rise of the *kuṇḍalinī* through the various *cakras* and its final ascent to the *sahasrāra cakra* as the various stages of spiritual evolution. It also describes various kinds of meditative practices to be performed for obtaining the highest knowledge and realization of non-duality.[498] But, logically, all meditative practices are possible only in the realm of duality. Furthermore, *S.L.* also describes how the devotee mentally dedicates all his actions, thoughts and speech to the supreme *Śakti*[499] and this devotional practice is an effective means for obtaining the highest realization of non-duality. However, the practice of such devotional practices as a means definitely requires a preliminary understanding and faith in the omnipresence and omnipotence of the supreme *Śakti*.

In his commentary on the *Brahma sūtra* Śaṅkara has mentioned how it is logically necessary to accept the fact that even after the intuitive realization of non-duality, the fructifying karmas *(prārabdha karmas)* cannot be checked immediately. They go on to complete their due fructification and this accounts for the state of *jīvanmukti*. He says -

> "*Vedāntin*: The answer is: It cannot be that knowledge can arise without the help of some residual results of actions that have begun to bear fruit. And when it is granted that knowledge is based on that medium (viz. the body produced by the residual results), it is but natural that knowledge has to wait (for its result) till the acquired momentum of that medium exhausts itself out as in the case of a wheel of a potter; for there is nothing to stop it in the intervening period. As for the knowledge of the Self as the non-performer of any act, that

> destroys the result of works by first sublating false ignorance. This false ignorance, even when sublated, continues for a while owing to past tendencies like the continuance of the vision of two moons. Furthermore, no difference of opinion is possible here as to whether the body is retained (after knowledge) for some time or not by the knowers of *Brahman*. For when somebody feels in his heart that he has realized *Brahman* and yet holds the body, how can this be denied by somebody else?"[500]

The *S.L.* too describes how the devotee enjoys the bliss of the realization of non-duality by raising the *kuṇḍalinī* up to the level which lies beyond the *ājñā cakra*.[501] This is the duality based meditative practice in which the *jīvanmukta* devotees engage repeatedly for enjoying the bliss of non-dualistic realization. Furthermore, the *S.L.* also describes how the *jīvanmukta* devotee, after having the intuitive realization of the omnipresence of the *Parāśakti*, finds all his worldly actions, thoughts and speeches naturally dedicated to the supreme *Śakti*.[502]

Devotion (Bhakti) in the Upaniṣad-bhāṣya-s of Śaṅkara

> "Following on the creation of the cosmos, verily these two paths did emerge - the path of *karma* being the earlier one, and the other being renunciation, consisting in the giving up of the three kinds of desire (for son etc.), in accordance with the latter path of detachment. Of these, the path of renunciation is the more excellent."[503]

In this passage, while commenting on the *Īśā upaniṣad,* Śaṅkara talks of the two paths available in this world - the path of *karma* and the path of renunciation. The path of *karma* basically stands for pursuing various actions designed to provide numerous phenomenal objects, whether gross material or subtle in nature. On the other hand, for the follower of the path of renunciation, the realization of the transcendent nature of the self has to be the sole and primary objective and this means there should not be any hankering for various phenomenal objects. In this sense, it necessarily involves the renunciation of the phenomenal pleasure-oriented attitudes and activities.

Passages conforming to these ideas are also available in the *S.L.* The very first stanza of the *S.L.* indicates that only after many births of ethical and religious lives one can possibly become eligible for approaching and saluting the primordial *Śakti*, i.e., *Devī Tripurasundarī*.[504] This *Śakti* is both the transcendent ontological absolute as well as the immanent ontological reality of the phenomenal realm. This transcendent non-dual and absolute *Śakti* is the presiding deity of the *śrīvidyā* tradition and therefore this tradition is totally consistent with the non-dualistic interpretation of the Vedas. As such, the *S.L.* naturally lays clear emphasis on the realization of the transcendent, universal and non-dual aspect of *Śakti*, as opposed to the goal of achieving various phenomenal objectives.

At another place the *S.L.* shows how the adepts of the *śrīvidyā* tradition, being devoid of the mental impurities of phenomenal desires, immerse themselves in the non-dual transcendent bliss of the primordial *Śakti* while meditating on the higher centres of the *kuṇḍalinī* pathway.[505] Here also, it has been indicated that only those persons who have eliminated their phenomenal desires can have the intuitive realization of the transcendent, non-dual and absolute nature of *Śakti*.

Discussing the universal immanence of the transcendent absolute, Śaṅkara says:

> "....... - he, who realizes the unconditioned Self in all beings thus, *tataḥ*, by virtue of that vision; *na vijugupsate*, feels no hatred, does not hate. This is only a restatement of a known fact. For, this is a matter of experience that all revulsion comes to one who sees something as bad and different from oneself, but for one who sees only the absolutely pure Self as a

continuous entity, there is no other object that can be the cause of revulsion."[506]

That is, the intuitive realization of the universal immanence of the transcendent non-dual reality totally transforms the attitude and behaviour of the concerned person. Such a person becomes a *jīvanmukta* and for such a person all the objects and activities pertaining to the phenomenal realm are nothing but so many phenomenal manifestations of the transcendent absolute.

Similar ideas can be easily located in the *S.L.* For example, the *S.L.* says that the five basic subtle elements, as well as the mind, are just the phenomenal manifestations of so many rays emanating from the transcendent form of the *Devī's* feet.[507] These elements being the basic building blocks of the phenomenal realm, it goes without saying that the entire phenomenal universe is but the immanent manifestation of the transcendent non-dual form of *Devī Tripurasundarī*.

At another place the *S.L.* states even more explicitly how the various subtle elements and the mind are but the phenomenal immanent transformations of the transcendent *Devī* and thus, how all the objects and subjects of the phenomenal universe are the immanent forms of the *Devī*.[508] The *S.L.* also indicates the attitude of the *jīvanmukta* person who has had the intuitive realization of the transcendent absolute and the universal immanent aspects of the primordial *Śakti*. For such a person, all the mental, verbal and physical actions become so many devotional offerings at feet of the *Devī*.[509] For such a person, the *Devī* truly manifests Herself as *Tripurasundarī*, the deity whose beauty and splendour encompasses the three realms of the phenomenal universe viz. the causal, subtle and gross worlds.

Discussing the transcendent and immanent aspects of *Brahman,* Śaṅkara says -

> "In the divine context, *Brahman* has the attribute of revealing Itself quickly like lightning and winking; and in the context of the soul, It has the attribute of manifesting Itself simultaneously with the states of the mind."[510]

In this passage Śaṅkara indicates that intuitive realization of the non-dual and transcendent aspect of *Brahman* is instantaneous and illuminative, whereas in its immanent aspect *Brahman* manifests through the various cognitive states of the mind.

Similar references to the transcendent and immanent aspects of *Śakti* in the form of *Devī Tripurasundarī* can be located in the *S.L.* It says that the great devotees of the *Devī* intuitively realize the transcendent aspect of *Śakti* as if it were an instantaneous streak of lightning and also as the ontological essence of three regions of the sun, moon and fire, lying far above the six lotus *cakras*.[511] In the *śrīvidyā* tradition the sun, moon and fire regions represent the gross, subtle and causal realms of the phenomenal universe at the microcosmic plane and the six lotus-*cakras* represent the various important levels of *jīva* consciousness while operating at the plane of phenomenal duality. At another place, indicating the universal immanence of the supreme *Śakti*, the *S.L.* clearly says that all the objects and subjects of the realm of phenomenal duality are but the various manifestations of the sole supreme *Śakti* viz. *Parāśakti*.[512] This transcendent *Parāśakti* is identical with *Paramaśiva* and this *sāmarasya* state of *Śiva* and *Śakti* is the transcendent non-dual absolute.

Discussing the various pre-requisites for the intuitive realization of the non-dual *Brahman*, Śaṅkara says in the *upaniṣad bhāṣya* -

> "*Tapaḥ*, the concentration of the body, the senses, and the mind; *damaḥ*, cessation (from sense-objects); *karma*, rites, Agnihotra etc. (are the means); for it is found that the

knowledge of *Brahman* arises in a man who has attained the requisite holiness by means of purification of the heart through these. For it is a matter of experience that, even though *Brahman* is spoken of, there is either non-comprehension or miscomprehension in the case of one who has not been purged of his sin, as for instance, in the cases of Indra and Virocana (Ch. VIII.vii-xii)."[513]

In this passage Śaṅkara has brought out the inevitable need of various purificatory practices for the purpose of *Brahman* realization. Without the purity of the mind and heart the knowledge of the non-dual *Brahman* is absolutely impossible.

Similar passages can be found in the *S.L.* as well. In the *śrīvidyā* tradition the transcendent aspect of *Devī Tripurasundarī* is nothing but the non-dual *Brahman*. In this context, all the numerous devotional practices of the *śrividyā* tradition are ultimately aimed at the intuitive realization of identity with the non-dual *Parāśakti*. The very first stanza of *S.L.* clearly states that nobody can make even a preliminary advance towards the realization of identity with the *Parāśakti* unless and until the necessary mental purification has already been accomplished.[514] One cannot have even a preliminary and theoretical understanding of the authority and divinity of *Śakti* unless the necessary mental purification has taken place. Hence, one does not become eligible to even salute the supreme *Śakti* without the requisite purification. The necessity of such purity of mind and heart has also been indicated in the *S.L.* while describing the devotee's intuitive realization of the transcendent aspect of *Śakti*.[515] *S.L.* goes to the extent of suggesting that for achieving the necessary mental purification the devotee should dedicate all his thoughts and actions to the supreme *Śakti* believing in the universal immanence of the supreme *Śakti*.[516] Such absolute dedication to the universal *Śakti* easily purifies the mind and this in turn facilitates the realization of one's identity with the absolute and transcendent *Śakti*, the *Parāśakti*.

Discussing the nature of relationship between the transcendent absolute and the phenomenal world, Śaṅkara says -

> "Whatever great or atomic thing there be in the world, can be so by being possessed of its reality through that eternal Self. When deprived of that Self, it is reduced to unreality."[517]

In this passage Śaṅkara has emphasized that all the entities of the phenomenal realm possess a relative kind of reality solely because all of them are ontologically grounded in the transcendent ontological absolute. That is, despite the epistemically projected nature of the phenomenal realm, it is actually the immanent form of the transcendent absolute Self.

Such relationship between the transcendent absolute and the phenomenal world has also been described in the *S.L.* in various ways. In the *śrīvidyā* terminology of the *S.L.* the non-dual and transcendent aspect of *Śiva* and *Śakti* is called the *Sāmarasya* state of *Śiva* and *Śakti* and it is also described as *Parāśakti* or *Paramaśiva*. While describing the devotee's intuitive realization of the non-dual and transcendent aspect of *Śakti* in the microcosmic context, the *S.L.* explicitly states that this transcendent *Śakti* alone is the ontological essence of the fire, sun and moon regions, representing the gross, subtle and causal realms, along with the fact that this supreme *Śakti*, in its purest aspect as the non-dual absolute, is also transcendent to the region of the six lotuses (*cakras*) in the microcosm, which jointly represent the entire phenomenal universe.[518] The *S.L.* also describes all this with reference to the macrocosm, where it is stated clearly that it is the supreme *Śakti* alone that has epistemically transformed itself into all the objective and subjective entities of the phenomenal realm, comprising of the gross, subtle and causal worlds.[519]

Shedding light on the mystery of the true reason for the intuitive realization of the transcendent and non-dual nature of the Self, Śaṅkara says in his *upaniṣad bhāṣya* -

"*Ayam ātmā*, this Self; *na labhyaḥ*, is not to be attained, is not to be known; *pravacanena*, through the acquisition of many Vedas; and *na medhayā*, not through the intellect - through the power of grasping the meaning of texts; *na bahunā śrutena*, not through much hearing - alone. How is It then to be known? This is being said: *Yam eva*, that (Self) indeed which is his (i.e., aspirant's) own Self; which *eṣaḥ*, this one, the aspirant; *vṛṇute*, prays to; *tena*, by that - by that very Self which is the seeker (himself); the Self Itself is *labhyaḥ*, can be known, i.e., It becomes known to be such and such. The meaning is that to a desireless man who seeks for the Self alone, the Self becomes known of Its own accord. How is It known? This is being said: *eṣaḥ*, this Self; *tasya*, of that seeker of the Self; *vivṛṇute*, reveals; *svām*, Its own - Its real; *tanūm*, body, i.e., Its own nature."[520]

In this passage Śaṅkara has demystified the mystery of realization and stated that actually it happens only when the seeker of the Self takes refuge in the transcendent, divine and merciful aspect of the Self and prays to It for such realization and then the transcendent Self, out of its own sweet will, reveals Its true nature before that seeker of the Self. That is, while a *jīva* is bound to the realm of phenomenal illusion, it is not possible to go beyond it by force, by making use of any phenomenal means whatsoever, as those things, actions and thoughts would themselves be lying within the illusory realm. Only that which lies beyond such illusory realm can make possible the sublation of the *jīva's* illusion and the only such reality is the transcendent and non-dual aspect of the Self, as well as the personal manifestation of that absolute, since It is the controller of the phenomenal realm and thus It is not in any way restricted by the phenomenal illusion.

The necessity of devotion to the transcendent supreme *Śakti* in Her various manifestations for the purpose of highest spiritual realization has been highlighted by *S.L.* in various ways. The devotee's prayer to the supreme *Śakti* for Her divine grace is grounded in the devotee's firm faith in *Śakti*'s omnipotence. As such, even though the devotee is entangled in the dualistic realm of phenomena, when he approaches and prays to *Śakti* for Her divine grace then that supreme *Śakti*, out of Her infinite mercy, immediately facilitates the devotee's realization of identity with the non-dual absolute, which is the same as the higher *Brahman* or *Parāśakti* or *Paramaśiva* or the *Śiva-Śakti sāmarasya.*[521]

At another place in the *S.L.*, Śaṅkara has described the nature of advaitika devotion *(advaita bhakti)* along with its result.[522] Advaitika devotion consists in the firm faith of the devotee regarding the omnipresence and omnipotence of *Śakti*, amounting to the ontological absoluteness of *Śakti*. When a devotee approaches the supreme *Śakti* with such a non-dualist devotional frame of mind, he easily wins the grace of *Śakti* and overcomes the cosmic illusion of duality, realizing the transcendent non-dual aspect of *Śakti* along with Her universal immanence in the phenomenal realm.

Discussing the sequential epistemic projection or phenomenal creation of the various basic elements, Śaṅkara says -

> "From that *Brahman* which is identical with the Self, *ākāśaḥ*, space; *sambhūtaḥ*, was created. *Ākāśa* means that which is possessed of the attribute of sound and provides space for all things that have forms. *Ākāśa*, from that space; *vāyuḥ*, air - which has two attributes, being possessed of its own quality, touch, and the quality, sound, of its cause *(ākāśa)*. The verb 'was created', is understood. *Vāyuḥ*, from that air; was created *agniḥ*, fire - which has three attributes, being possessed of its own quality, colour, and the two earlier ones (of its cause, air). *Agneḥ*, from fire; was produced, *āpaḥ*, water - with four attributes, being endowed with its own quality, taste, and the three earlier ones (of fire). *Adbhyaḥ*, from water; was produced *pṛthivī*, earth - with five attributes, consisting of its own quality, smell, and the four earlier qualities (of its cause, water)."[523]

The five basic elements mentioned here serve as the material building blocks of the phenomenal realm. They individually represent different levels of epistemic involution and that too in a sequential fashion.

Similar passages are available in the *S.L.* However, the *S.L.* goes a step further and brings out the spiritual implications of such sequential projection of the basic elements and describes it in terms of the elemental nature of various *cakras* through which the *kuṇḍalinī* ascends and descends in the microcosm. The ascent of the *kuṇḍalinī* through the various elemental *cakras* and its culmination in the *sahasrāra cakra* shows the elemental sublation sequence or *tāttvika laya krama* representing, at the microcosmic plane, the step by step elevation of the plane of consciousness of the *jīva* until it rises up to the non-dual consciousness identifying itself with the *sāmarasya* state.[524] The *S.L.* also describes the epistemic involution of the various basic elements in a sequential fashion at the macrocosmic level out of the supreme *Śakti*. Not only the basic elements that serve as the building blocks of all the phenomenal objects, but the phenomenal subjects too are the various epistemic manifestations of the same *Śakti*.[525]

Discussing the blissful nature of *Brahman* and the effect of the realization of identity with such *Brahman*, Śaṅkara says in the *upaniṣad bhāṣya* -

> "*Rasaḥ* stands for anything that is a means for satisfaction, i.e., a source of joy, such as sweet and and sour things which are well known to be so in the world. *Rasam labdhvā*, getting a thing of joy; *ayam bhavati*, one becomes; *ānandī*, happy. A nonentity is not seen in this world to be a cause of happiness. Inasmuch as those Brāhmaṇas who have realized *Brahman* are seen to be as happy as one is from obtaining an external source of joy - though, in fact, they do not take help of any external means of happiness, make no effort, and cherish no desire -, it follows, as a matter of course, that *Brahman* is, indeed, the

> source of their joy. Hence there does exist that *Brahman* which is full of joy and is the spring of their happiness."[526]

Brahman is by nature pure and infinite bliss. The bliss of *Brahman* is absolutely intrinsic and unconditional and therefore one who realizes his basic identity with *Brahman* effortlessly and endlessly enjoys the infinite bliss of *Brahman*.

Passages similarly describing the infinitely blissful nature of the supreme *Śakti* can be found in abundance in the *S.L.* The supreme *Śakti* has been referred to as the *'cid ānanda laharī'* or 'the ocean of Consciousness and Bliss'.[527] The *S.L.* also describes how the devotee having realization of identity with the transcendent *Śakti* or *Parāśakti* finds himself immersed in the pure and infinite bliss of the transcendent *Śakti*.[528] For a person enjoying such pure and infinite bliss all the enjoyable things of the phenomenal universe become insignificant and lose their attraction when compared to the divine bliss of *Parāśakti*.[529]

Discussing the epistemic nature of the phenomenal world of duality, which is projected in and through the transcendent non-dual Self, Śaṅkara says in the *upaniṣad bhāṣya* -

> "Therefore there is nothing incongruous in saying that the omniscient Being creates the universe by virtue of Its oneness with the materials - viz. name and form - which are identified with Itself. Or the more reasonable position is this: Just as an intelligent juggler, who has no material, transforms himself, as it were, into a second self ascending into space, similarly the omniscient and omnipotent Deity, who is a supreme magician, creates Himself as another in the form of the universe."[530]

Here Śaṅkara is pointing out that there is nothing incompatible between the transcendent and non-dual ontological absolute and the phenomenal world of duality, since the creation of the dualistic realm is only epistemic in nature. However, this epistemic projection is grounded in the ontological absolute alone and it is the wish of that conscious absolute which brings about the epistemic projection of the phenomenal world.

The primordial *Śakti*, *Devī Tripurasundarī*, has also been variously described in both Her transcendent non-dual aspect and Her universal immanent aspect. At one place, the *S.L.* describes how the perfect devotee intuitively realizes the transcendent and non-dual absolute aspect of *Śakti*, in the form of *Parāśakti* or the *sāmarasya* state of *Śiva-Śakti*, as being the ontological essence of the entire phenomenal realm consisting of the causal, subtle and gross worlds.[531] This *Parāśakti* permeates the entire dualistic realm through Her immanent form. While being so, She is at the same time essentially transcendent to the entire phenomenal realm because shorn of all traces of epistemic projection, She retains Her transcendent non-dual form of absolute Bliss and Consciousness.

At another place, the *S.L.* describes that it is the transcendent *Śakti* Herself who epistemically manifests in the form of the various phenomenal objects and subjects, in accordance with the primary epistemic projection of the *Śiva-Śakti* duality, which is representative of the subject-object duality.[532] This *Śiva-Śakti* duality is to be found throughout the phenomenal realm, from the highest to the lowest level of epistemic manifestation. The various important levels of *Śiva-Śakti* manifestation are represented as the various *cakras* in the *suṣumṇā* pathway of the *kuṇḍalinī* in the case of the microcosm. Only the thousand-petalled lotus of the *sahasrāra cakra* is representative of the transcendent and non-dual *sāmarasya* state of *Śiva-Śakti*, also referred to as the *Parāśakti* or *Paramaśiva*.

Highlighting the basic identity of the transcendent non-dual absolute and the omniscient, omnipotent God, Śaṅkara says -

> "That Entity, thus dealt with, when freed from all distinctions created by the limiting adjuncts, is without stain, without taint, without action, quiescent, one without a second, to be known as 'Not this, not this' (Bṛ. III.ix. 26), by the elimination of all attributes, and (It is) beyond all words and thoughts. That very

> Entity, which is the omniscient God - because of the association with the limiting adjunct of very pure intelligence - and is the ordainer of the common seed of all the unmanifested universe, assumes the name of *antaryāmī* (the Inner Controller) by virtue of being the Guide."[533]

The transcendent non-dual absolute alone is free from all traces of epistemic projections and limiting adjuncts. The first epistemic projection presents the duality of *Śiva* and *Śakti*, representing the subjective and objective principles i.e., the duality and complementarity of *prakāśa* and *vimarśa*. This primary level of *Śiva-Śakti* duality corresponds with the *nāda* or central point of the *śrīcakra* and it symbolizes the level of *Sadāśiva* and *Śuddha Vidyā*. It also corresponds with the second highest point in the *kuṇḍalinī* pathway, called the *bindu*.

The transcendent and dualistic forms of the same Reality have been described in the *S.L.* in various ways. The *S.L.* says that *Śakti*, in Her transcendent and non-dual aspect as *Parāśakti*, is the ocean of infinite Bliss and She is also the ontological essence of the entire phenomenal realm.[534] The *S.L.* also describes how it is the same *Śakti* who is approached by the devotee with pleas of divine grace and who responds by facilitating the devotee's realization of his identity with the transcendent *Parāśakti*, the absolute Bliss and Consciousness.[535] Indicating the nature and effect of advaitika devotion, grounded in the faith of one's own identity with the deity namely *Śakti*, the *S.L.* beautifully shows that the deity-devotee relationship, which is possible only within the phenomenal realm of epistemic duality, is actually not at all incompatible with the basic ontological identity of deity and devotee at the transcendent level of *Parāśakti*.[536] As such, it is the same *Śakti* who is both the deity for the devotee and also the transcendent *Parāśakti*. The deity *Śakti* and the non-dual *Parāśakti* are one and the same in the basic ontological sense.

Śaṅkara explains with the help of various examples how the transcendent absolute is ontologically involved in the epistemic manifestation of the world of duality. He says -

> "just as it is in these cases, so *akṣarāt*, from the Imperishable, of the foregoing characteristics, that does not depend on any other auxiliary; *sambhavati*, originates; *iha*, here, in this phenomenal creation; *viśvam*, the entire Universe - both similar and dissimilar. As for the citing of many illustrations, it is meant for easy comprehension."[537]

The *S.L.* also states that it is the transcendent *Parāśakti* alone that manifests epistemically in the form of the various objects and subjects of the phenomenal realm of duality.[538] The epistemic creation and dissolution of the phenomenal realm by the transcendent *Parāśakti* has been beautifully depicted in the *S.L.* as resulting from the opening and closing of the *Devī*'s eyes, thereby highlighting the point that creation and dissolution are just the plays of *Parāśakti's* consciousness.[539] The *S.L.* depicts *Śakti* both as the transcendent fourth entity or *Turīyā,* as well as the functional energy responsible for the creation, sustenance and dissolution of the phenomenal world.[540]

Discussing the nature and effect of the intuitive realization of one's own identity with the non-dual absolute Reality, Śaṅkara says -

> " *Ca*, and; *asya*, one's, of the man whose doubts have been solved, whose ignorance has been removed; *karmāṇi*, the actions - that preceded the rise of illumination but had not yielded results in earlier lives, as also those actions that accompany the rise of illumination; *kṣīyante*, get dissipated; but not so the actions that produced the present life, since they have already begun to bear their fruits. (All this happens) *tasmin dṛṣṭe parāvare,* when that One, the omniscient and transcendent - who is both *para*, the high, as the cause, and *avara*, the low, as the effect - is seen directly as 'I am this'.

> The idea is that one becomes free on the eradication of the causes of the wordly state."[541]

Similar ideas echo throughout the *S.L.* By raising the *kuṇḍaliṇī* beyond the six lotuses in the *suṣumṇā* pathway, the devotee realizes the transcendent non-dual *Parāśakti* as being identical with one's own Self, as also the fact that this *Parāśakti* alone is the ontological essence of the whole phenomenal realm.[542] Moreover, such a realized devotee enjoys the ineffable bliss of the transcendent *Parāśakti*. Such a devotee realizes that the transcendent *Śakti* alone is the immanent reality manifesting as the entire phenomenal realm consisting of the gross, subtle and causal worlds.[543] Such a realized devotee becomes free from the bondage of all his unfructified *karmas*. However, the *prārabdha* or fructifying *karmas* continue to give their results but even during this period no fresh *karma* has the power to bind that devotee since his realization of identity with the omnipresent *Śakti* results in the mental dedication of all of his *karmas* as so many devotional offerings at the feet of the transcendent *Śakti*.[544]

Explaining the transcendent and immanent aspects of the Self in terms of four quarters *(pāda-s)*, Śaṅkara says in the *upaniṣad bhāṣya* -

> "*Saḥ ayam ātmā*, that Self that is such, that is signified by *Om* and exists as the higher and lower *Brahman*; is *catuṣpāt*, possessed of four quarters, like a *(kārṣā-paṇa)* coin, but not like a cow. As the Fourth *(Turīya)* is realized by successively merging the earlier three, starting from Viśva, the word *pāda* (in the cases of *Viśva, Taijasa* and *Prājña*) is derived in the instrumental sense of that by which something is attained, whereas in the case of the *Turīya* and word *pāda* is derived in the objective sense of that which is achieved."[545]

Similar ideas come up in the context of *Śakti* at various points in the *S.L.* In the *śrīvidyā* tradition, the fire, sun and moon regions represent the gross, subtle and causal worlds respectively and the

S.L. clearly says that *Śakti,* as the transcendent *Parāśakti,* is the ontological substratum of all these three realms, as well as the fact that this *Parāśakti* alone is the immanent reality manifesting in the three regions of the phenomenal universe.[546] The secret fifteen syllabled *mantra* of *śrīvidyā* tradition is also divisible into three parts, where each one of them has a corresponding identity with one of the three phenomenal regions.[547] The sixteenth syllable of the *śrividyā mantra* is said to possess a corresponding identity with the transcendent non-dual aspect of *Śakti* viz. the *Parāśakti*. This syllable is a profound secret which is never to be revealed to an ineligible person. The *S.L.* also describes the transcendent *Parāśakti* as the unattainable fourth entity or *Turīyā.*[548]

Indicating the nature of the transcendent absolute, Śaṅkara says -

> "In *'prapañcopaśamam*, the one in whom all phenomena have ceased', etc. are being denied the attributes of the states of waking etc. Hence It is *śāntam*, unchanging; *śivam*, auspicious. Since It is *advaitam*, non-dual, free from illusory ideas of difference; therefore *manyante*, (they) consider It to be; the Turīya, *caturtham*, the Fourth, being distinct from the three quarters that are mere appearances."[549]

Similar descriptions can be located in the *S.L.* While indicating the transcendent aspect of *Śakti*, called the *Parāśakti* or the *Śiva-Śakti sāmarasya,* the *S.L.* describes the transcendent *Śakti*, or *Parāśakti*, as being one with the *Paramaśiva* and being of the nature of infinite consciousness and bliss.[550] The transcendent *Śakti* is far above the level of the basic elemental essences and this fact is also represented at the microcosmic plane in the level corresponding with the *Parāśakti*, namely the *sahasrāra cakra,* being far above all the other *cakras* which jointly represent the entire dualistic phenomenal realm.[551] The transcendent *Śakti* is the ontological essence of the entire phenomenal realm and thus the *Parāśakti* is immanent in the entire phenomenal realm.[552] This *Parāśakti* is of the form of pure and infinite bliss and consciousness.[553] This *Parāśakti* is the inscrutable fourth entity *(Turīyā)* that is the ontological ground of the epistemic projection of the phenomenal realm.[554]

Elaborating the significance and meaning of the performance of various spiritual and worldly practices during the bright and the dark fortnights, Śaṅkara says in the *upaniṣad bhāṣya* -

> "Since they look upon Prāṇa, identified with the bright fortnight, as everything, therefore, *ete ṛṣayaḥ*, these seers, who realize Prāṇa; *śukle iṣṭam kurvanti*, perform their sacrifice (really) in the bright fortnight, even though they may be performing it in the dark half, because they do not perceive any dark fortnight existing apart from Prāṇa. On the other hand, whereas the others do not see Prāṇa, and as a result see only that which is marked by darkness and obstructs vision. Therefore *itare*, the others; *kurvanti*, perform; (their sacrifice, really) *itarasmin*, in the other half, in the dark fortnight, although they may be doing so in the bright half."[555]

In this passage it comes out clearly that some activity is to be treated as being performed in the bright fortnight only if the performer is well aware of the immanent presence of the universal and divine element in the various things associated with that activity. If the performer is not aware of such immanence, then all of his activities can only be considered as being performed in the dark fortnight.

Due to the basic harmony of the *śrīvidyā* tradition with the advaitika tradition, there is a natural emphasis on the need of performing all activities, whether spiritual or worldly, during the bright fortnight *(śukla pakṣa)*. That is, a votary of *śrīvidyā* is expected to perform all kinds of activities with the inner awareness of universal immanence of the divine *Śiva* and *Śakti*. This idea has been expressed in various ways in the *S.L.* An adept practitioner of the *śrīvidyā* tradition is able to effortlessly dedicate all his worldly and spiritual activities as so many devotional offerings at the feet of the transcendent *Śakti* on account of his firm faith and knowledge that the divine *Śakti* is immanent in each and every subject and object of the phenomenal realm.[556] The *S.L.* also says explicitly that it is the *Parāśakti* alone who has epistemically transformed into all the subjects and objects of the phenomenal realm.[557] Moreover, the *S.L.* also tells us that the *śrīvidyā* tradition is unique in comparison with the various other *tantra* traditions due to its advaitika framework, which leads to the effortless achievement of the various worldly and spiritual goals of life, even when the votary sticks deliberately only to the ideal of realizing intuitively one's identity with the transcendent *Śakti*.[558]

Resolving the apparent conflict of the ideal of realizing one's identity with the transcendent Reality while being totally enmeshed in the phenomenal realm as an individual *jīva*, Śaṅkara says in the *upaniṣad bhāṣya* -

> "As the supreme *Brahman* cannot be (directly) indicated by words etc. and is devoid of all distinctions created by attributes - and as It is (on that account) beyond the organs - therefore the mind by itself cannot explore It. But to those who meditate on *Om*, which is camparable to the image of Viṣṇu and others and on which is fixed the idea of *Brahman* with devotion, that *Brahman* becomes favourable (and reveals Itself). This is understood on the authority of scriptures."[559]

In this passage it is stated clearly that while being engrossed in the phenomenal realm one cannot, on his own, positively express, understand and experience the transcendent absolute. While being so, it is not even possible to actually meditate on the non-dual Reality per se. As such, the only way out is to use some symbol for that transcendent Reality and approach it with the appeal of revealing its transcendent and non-dual nature before the votary. The *śrīvidyā* tradition is an explicit illustration of this methodology since the divine *Śakti*, *Devī Tripurasudarī*, is presented as both the transcendent non-dual *sāmarasya* state as well as the reality immanent at all the points of the phenomenal realm. The *S.L.* echoes all this at various points. At one place the *S.L.* describes how the devotee of *Śakti* easily wins Her grace when he earnestly prays for Her merciful glance, as a result of which the devotee attains the intuitive realization of his identity with the transcendent and non-dual *Parāśakti*.[560] At another place the *S.L.* indicates the nature and effect of *advaita bhakti* and says that whosoever devotionally approaches the universal *Śakti* with a firm faith in his own basic identity with the *Devī* easily comes to have the intuitive realization of that kind and as a result effortlessly transcends the phenomenal illusion of duality.[561]

Indicating the omnipotent governance of the transcendent Reality, Śaṅkara says,

> "It is this Immutable which is like a boundary wall that preserves the distinctions among things- keeps all things within their limits; hence the sun and moon do not transgress the mighty rule of this Immutable. Therefore, Its existence is proved. The unfailing sign of this is the fact that heaven and earth obey a fixed order; this would be impossible were there not a conscious, transcendent Ruler."[562]

In this passage it has been pointed out that the phenomenal world exhibits a certain order only due to the universal governance of the transcendent Reality, which is the ontological substratum of the entire phenomenal realm. Similarly, the universal rule of the primordial *Śakti* has been pointed out in the *S.L.* in various ways. The *S.L.* clearly shows that the activities performed by *Brahmā, Viṣṇu* and *Maheśa,* namely creation, sustenance and destruction of the worlds, becomes possible only by getting the necessary energy and direction from the transcendent *Śakti*.[563] The supreme control of the transcendent *Śakti* has also been shown in a different perspective in the *S.L.* and in this context the epistemic nature of phenomenal realm has been highlighted with reference to the *Devī*'s consciousness.[564] As such, the genesis and dissolution of the phenomenal realm has been depicted as being the effects of *Śakti*'s cognition of that nature and this has been poetically described as being the effect of the *Devī*'s opening and closing of Her eyes.

Describing the stark contrast between the ideal of self-realization and that of phenomenal objectives, Śaṅkara says,

> "*Then he, having been mortal, becomes immortal,* being divested of desires together with their root. It is practically implied that desires concerning things other than the Self fall under the category of ignorance, and are but forms of death. Therefore, on the cessation of death, the man of realization becomes immortal. *And attains Brahman,* the identity with *Brahman*, i.e., liberation, living *in this very body.*"[565]

In a similar fashion the *śrīvidyā* tradition lays emphasis on the exclusive desirability of the ideal of self-realization, as opposed to the numerous goals of phenomenal gratification. The *S.L.* contains various passages reflecting such an ideal of intuitive realization, which is to be achieved by approaching the transcendent and immanent *Śakti* through the method of *advaita bhakti*. In this special kind of devotion, the devotee, believing firmly in the omnipresence of *Śakti*, dedicates all his activities at the feet of the *Devī* for Her pleasure.[566] With such a devotional frame of mind, there remains practically no possibility of continuation of hankering after various phenomenal objects and experiences. Further, when the votary has firm faith in his basic identity with the transcendent non-dual *Śakti,* it means he firmly believes that the entire phenomenal realm of duality is an illusory trifle and if so, there can be no possibility of persisting with the desire for phenomenal objectives.[567]

Pointing out *Brahman* as the cause of the creation, sustenance and dissolution of the phenomenal universe, Śaṅkara says

> "How can all be *Brahman*? Therefore, the text says, *'Tajjalān'*:- Because all (creation), through a succession of fire, water, food, etc. is born from that *Brahman*, therefore it is called *tajja*; and it is *talla* because, through a reverse process

> of that very order of birth, it gets merged in that very *Brahman*, becomes wholly identified with that; (and it is *tadana* because) it continues to live, to function on that very *Brahman* during the state of (its) existence. Thus, the world, in the three states, is non-different from *Brahman* because it is not perceived apart from It. Therefore this world is surely That itself."[568]

In the *śrīvidyā* tradition the transcendent *Śakti* viz. *Parāśakti* is just the same as the transcendent *Brahman*. It is only this *Parāśakti* which manifests Herself in the form of the various basic constituents of the subjects and objects comprising the entire phenomenal realm.[569] The universal immanence of the bliss and consciousness of *Parāśakti* in the entire phenomenal realm follows from the fact that this whole realm is an epistemic projection and cognition that is ontologically grounded in the transcendent *Parāśakti* and in this context the *S.L.* has depicted the creation and dissolution of the universe as following from the opening and closing of the *Devī*'s eyes.[570]

Discussing the immediate and final result of the intuitive realization of one's identity with the transcendent absolute, Śaṅkara says,

> "*Tasya,* for him, for this one who has such a teacher and becomes freed from the bondage of ignorance; *ciram,* the delay; is *tāvat eva,* for that long only, in the matter of attaining the true nature of his own Self which is Existence. This part of the sentence remains understood. How long is the delay? That is being answered: *Yāvat,* as long as; *na vimokṣye,* he does not become freed. From the force of the context it follows that *vimokṣye* stands for *vimokṣata* by change of person. The meaning is that the delay is for that long till the body falls after the enjoyment of the fruits of action due to which it was born. *Atha,* then, at that very time; *sampatsye,* he becomes merged in Existence."[571]

In this passage Śaṅkara has clearly stated that the immediate result of realization of the transcendent non-dual Reality is the attainment of *jīvanmukti*. However, the *prārabdha karma-s* of the *jīvanmukta* person continue to maintain the physical life of that person until those *karma-s* are fully exhausted through their due fructifications. Only after that, the final liberation or *videhamukti* becomes possible wherein there is complete and irreversible mergence in the transcendent Reality.

These concepts find an echo in the *S.L.* too. As a result of intuitively realizing the transcendent non-dual nature of *Śakti*, the devotee intuitively experiences the ineffable non-dual bliss of *Parāśakti* and this is the experience of a *jīvanmukta* person.[572] Not only this, even the physical and subtle body of the *jīvanmukta* person starts exhibiting signs of divine rejuvenation, as a result of the shower of nectar from the *sahasrāra cakra*.[573] Further, although the *jīvanmukta* person continues to perform and experience various actions and their results, he no longer appropriates them to himself and instead, he naturally dedicates all of them, as devotional offerings, at the feet of *Parāśakti* because of his realization of the omnipresent immanence of the transcendent *Parāśakti*.[574]

Discussing the basic identity of the transcendent Reality and the ontological reality supporting the phenomenal realm, Śaṅkara says,

> "This is what is stated: The supreme Self is nondual. Not only does It, like a potter, take up Itself alone as the material cause comparable to a lump of clay. What then? By virtue of activating Its own powers, It comes to be called the Projector or the Controller."[575]

The *S.L.* also exhibits similar ideas in the context of the primordial transcendent *Śakti*. It is the *Parāśakti* alone that transforms Herself to manifest phenomenally in the form of the various subjects and objects of the dualistic realm.[576] The creation, sustenance and dissolution of the phenomenal realm is totally epistemic in nature and it takes place in the consciousness of *Parāśakti* through Her mere wish.[577] This *Parāśakti* alone is operative as the energy responsible for the creation, sustenance and dissolution of the worlds and She is also the non-dual transcendent *Turīyā*, the real projector of the cosmic illusion of duality.[578]

Discussing the importance of performing actions for the pleasure of God, Śaṅkara says,

> "However, when people perform actions for God without hankering for rewards, then these become the means for Liberation through the stages of being the source of purification of the mind - which is the cause of Knowledge, the means to Liberation."[579]

That is, when actions are performed as devotional offerings for God, there is an absence of desire for appropriating their results and this makes those actions non-binding in nature. Instead, such actions lead to the purification of the mind and a purified mind is the direct means for the realization of one's identity with the transcendent non-dual absolute. Such a realization amounts to liberation and thus performing actions, without hankering for their results, and presenting them as offerings before God ultimately leads to self-realization and liberation. All this has also come up in the *S.L.* while describing the way in which a perfect devotee performs various actions in the world.[580] He dedicates each and every action of his at the feet of the *Devī*. For such a perfect devotee all the sense organs are always immersed in interacting with the various immanent forms of *Parāśakti* and this kind of devotion may be aptly called advaitika devotion.[581]

Devotion (Bhakti) in the Gītā-bhāṣya of Śaṅkara

In the *Bhagavadgītā bhāṣya*, while pointing out the mutual exclusion of the non-dual knowledge of the Self with various duality based phenomenal actions, Śaṅkara says,

> "Therefore, it is not possible for anyone to show that in the scripture called the *Gītā* there is any combination, even in the least, of Knowledge of the Self with rites and duties enjoined by the *Śrutis* or the *Smṛtis*. But in the case of a man who had

engaged himself in rites and duties because of ignorance and defects like attachment, and then got his mind purified through sacrifices, charities or austerities (see Bṛ. 4.4.22), there arises the knowledge about the supreme Reality - that all this is but One, and *Brahman* is not an agent (of any action). With regard to him, although there is a cessation of rites and duties as also of the need for them, yet, what may appear as his diligent continuance, just as before, in those rites and duties for setting an example before people - that is no action in which case it could have stood combined with Knowledge. Just as the actions of Lord *Vāsudeva*, in the form of performance of the duty of a *Kṣatriya*, do not get combined with Knowledge for the sake of achieving the human goal (Liberation), similar is the case with the man of Knowledge because of absence of hankering for results and agentship. Indeed, a man who has realized the Truth does not think 'I am doing (this)' nor does he hanker after its result."[582]

In this passage Śaṅkara has made it absolutely clear that at any given point of time a person may either be believing in his own agency or he may be convinced about the universal and non-dual nature of the Self, in which case there cannot be any sense of agency for various actions and also no personal hankering after their results.

This necessary dichotomy of actions and the knowledge of the universal Self has also been indicated in the *S.L.* In the *samaya* tradition of *śrīvidyā*, of which the *S.L.* is a prominent representative text, *Śakti* is seen as the transcendent absolute as well as the divinity universally immanent in the phenomenal realm. Even the initial recognition and faith in such nature of the *Śakti* requires a great amount of mental purification, which makes even the preliminary faith in one's identity with the transcendent non-dual *Parāśakti*, the sufficient condition for giving up the idea of one's agency of actions as well as the desire for enjoying their results.[583] In such a pre-realization state the devotee of *Śakti* deliberately desists from the idea of one's agency of actions and the desire for their results by mentally dedicating his various actions as so many offerings at the feet of the *Devī*.[584] This mental dedication of all the *karma-s* may be seen as the practice of *advaita bhakti* as a means to the intuitive realization of one's identity with the non-dual *Parāśakti*. However, in the post-realization state of the devotee, while the physical life continues due to the fructifying *prārabdha karma-s*, such comprehensive mental dedication of all *karma-s* at the feet of *Śakti* becomes natural and inevitable, because of the firm knowledge of identity of one's self with the *Parāśakti*. This is the culmination of advaitika devotion, taking place naturally in the case of a *jīvanmukta* devotee. It is for the attainment of such transcendent devotion *(parā bhakti)* that the *S.L.* depicts the devotee praying to the *Devī* for the state wherein his mind and sense organs are incessantly and completely immersed in the omnipresence of *Śakti* and thus his entire life becomes a devotional offering to the *Parāśakti*.[585]

Discussing the inevitability and desirability of performing various enjoined rites and duties in the pre-realization state, without any personal hankering for their results, for the purpose of the necessary mental purification, Śaṅkara says,

> "Therefore, before one attains the fitness for steadfastness in Knowledge, rites and duties, even though they have (limited) utility as that of a well, pond, etc., have to be undertaken by one who is fit for rites and duties."[586]

It is in this context that the *S.L.* shows the uniqueness of the *samaya* tradition, as compared to all the other *tantra-s,* in terms of its basic compatibility with the path of knowledge because of its basic tenet of the ontological identity of one's self with the transcendent *Parāśakti*.[587] This basic tenet of the *śrīvidyā* tradition logically translates into giving up the desire for personal appropriation of the results of *karma-s* because, firstly, the omnipresence of *Śakti* goes against the concept of one's separate individual agency, and secondly, all of one's actions are to be dedicated devotionally at the feet of the *Devī*. As such, even in the pre-realization state, the devotee of the *samaya* tradition practices the forsaking of all *karmic* results for the purpose of dedicating them to the omnipresent *Śakti*.[588]

Highlighting the superiority of actions dedicated to God, Śaṅkara says,

> "Then again, as against action performed with equanimity of mind for adoring God, *karma*, action undertaken by one longing for the results; is, *hi*, indeed; *dūreṇa*, quite, by far; *avaram*, inferior, very remote; *buddhi-yogāt*, from the yoga of wisdom, from actions undertaken with equanimity of mind, because it (the former) is the cause of birth, death, etc."[589]

In this passage the 'equanimity of mind' referred to stands for the firm conviction about the nature of Reality, which is taken to be non-dual and absolute in its character.

Similar ideas can be located in the *S.L.* as well. Depicting the nature of transcendent devotion *(parā bhakti)* or advaitika devotion *(advaita bhakti)*, the *S.L.* describes the attitude of the perfect devotee, who treats each and every action, thought and speech of himself as a devotional offering laid down before the transcendent *Parāśakti*.[590] Such a mental attitude springs from the conviction about the universal, transcendent, immanent and non-dual nature of *Parāśakti*. In the pre-realization state this conviction is of the nature of faith grounded in the authority of verbal testimony of one's *Guru* and the spiritual tradition. However, in the post-realization state of the devotee this conviction acquires the nature of intuitive knowledge about the non-dual transcendent nature of *Śakti* and one's own basic identity with *Śakti*.

Moreover, the *S.L.* establishes the superiority of the *samaya* tradition of *śrīvidyā* vis-à-vis the other *tantra* traditions primarily on the grounds of it being a *'sva-tantra'* tradition, which signifies the ontologically absolutist framework of *śrīvidyā*. [591] As such, the deity in *śrīvidyā*, *Devī Tripurasundarī*, is both the transcendent form of *Śakti* (*Parāśakti*) as well as the *Śakti* immanent in the three worlds of the phenomenal realm viz. the gross, subtle and causal worlds and hence Her name *'Tri-pura-sundarī'* i.e., 'the divinity whose beauty and splendour permeates the three worlds.' In such an absolutist framework there remains no logical possibility of sticking to the concept of one's individuality in the basic ontological sense. As such, it becomes imperative for the votary of this tradition to dedicate to the omnipresent *Śakti* whatever one may seem to be performing at the phenomenal plane. Hence, the *samaya* tradition is intrinsically superior to the other *tantra* traditions having various phenomenal objects and states as their avowed objectives. All actions performed for the pleasure of the omnipresent non-dual *Śakti* do not become binding in nature, rather they lead to the purification of the mind, the direct means of realizing one's identity with the transcendent *Parāśakti*.

Showing the nature of relationship between the means of spiritual realization and the actual state of spiritual realization, Śaṅkara says,

> "For in all the scriptures without exception, dealing with spirituality, whatever are the characteristics of the man of realization are themselves presented as the disciplines for an aspirant, because these (characteristics) are the result of effort. And those that are the disciplines requiring effort, they become the characteristics (of the man of realization)."[592]

The means of spiritual realization are to be practised diligently by the spiritual aspirant till the moment of actual realization. However, once the realization has taken place, whatever things were earlier practised with much effort as spiritual disciplines, all of them become the natural characteristics of the man of realization. Thus, all those thoughts and behaviours which are deliberate in the pre-realization state turn out to be effortless and natural in the post-realization state.

All this is also applicable to the *samaya* tradition of *śrīvidyā*. Since the *S.L.* is a representative text of this tradition it shows all this in the context of the practice and perfection of advaitika devotion or *advaita bhakti*. For example, the spiritual discipline of raising the *kuṇḍalinī* through the various *cakra-s* is crucial for having the non-dual realization of *Parāśakti*, but once that realization has taken place the ascent of the *kuṇḍalinī* through the various *cakra-s* becomes effortless, frequent and rather instinctively natural for the *jīvanmukta* devotee.[593] Similarly, whereas the spiritual practice of dedicating all of one's *karmas* at the feet of the *Devī* is faith based and rather deliberate in the pre-realization state, it becomes an effortless natural characteristic of the perfect devotee in the post-realization state.[594]

Discussing the nature and reason for the diverse response of the supreme deity or the transcendent Reality to the different kinds of devotees, Śaṅkara says,

> "Therefore, by granting fruits to those who hanker after fruits; by granting Knowledge to those who follow what has been stated (in the scriptures) and are seekers of Liberation, but do not hanker after rewards; and by granting Liberation to those who are men of wisdom and are monks aspiring for Liberation; and so also by removing the miseries of those who suffer, - in these ways I favour them just according to the manner in which they approach Me. This is the meaning. On the other hand, I do not favour anybody out of love or aversion, or out of delusion."[595]

In this passage it is stated clearly that the supreme deity, who is both the immanent as well as the transcendent Reality, responds to various devotees only in accordance with the desire and attitude with which they approach It. Thus, the same supreme deity sometimes provides various phenomenal objects, sometimes relief from some acute suffering, sometimes knowledge and sometimes liberation, always in accordance with the nature of the devotees' desires and nature of devotion.

In the *śrividyā* tradition, *Śakti* is both the transcendent non-dual Reality, the *Turīyā Parāśakti*, as well as the reality immanent in the three worlds of the phenomenal realm i.e., the *Devī Tripurasundarī*. The *S.L.* highlights how the *Devī* grants various boons to the different devotees having diverse needs and desires.[596] The *Devī* even grants various phenomenal pleasures and worldly knowledge when so desired by the devotee.[597] The very same *Śakti* also grants the realization of one's identity with the transcendent *Parāśakti* when the devotee desires liberation as a result of perfect mental purification. [598] The *S.L.* indicates the superiority of *śrīvidyā* tradition also in terms of its capability of catering to each and every desire of the devotee, ranging from the gross material up to the highest spiritual realization of non-duality.[599] Thus, the devotee of *Śakti* acquires all the phenomenal and spiritual goods, including liberation, through the divine grace of *Parāśakti*.[600]

Indicating the various stages of spiritual progress and the reason of immediate liberation i.e., *jīvanmukti*, Śaṅkara says,

> "Immediate Liberation of the monks who are steadfast in full realization has been stated. And the Lord has said, and will say, at every stage that karma-yoga undertaken as a dedication to *Brahman*, to God, by surrendering all activities to God, leads to liberation through the stages of purification of the heart, attainment of knowledge, and renunciation of all actions."[601]

In this passage it has come out clearly that even though the realization of knowledge is the immediate cause of attaining the state of *jīvanmukti*, yet such realization itself does not take place without the necessary long preparation for it. Firstly, there has to be the practice of performing all the *karma-s* without hankering for their results and thus dedicating them to *Brahman* or to God. The sustained practice of this discipline leads to the purification of the mind and heart, which in turn heralds the intuitive realization of one's identity with the transcendent Reality. Once this realization has taken place, there occurs the natural renunciation of all actions, in terms of being convinced about the illusoriness of one's sense of ego, and that is nothing but the state of *jīvanmukti*. Thus, it can be seen that the detached performance of *karma-s* and their dedication to God has to be practised consciously as a means of spiritual advancement and then, as a result of it, all the other stages in the attainment of liberation take place naturally at the appropriate points of time.

Thus, the spiritual discipline of dedicating all of one's *karma-s* to God is the most important means of spiritual advancement and this has been duly highlighted in the *S.L.* while depicting the mental state of the votary of the *samaya mārga*.[602] This dedication of all *karma-s*, when done consciously on the basis of faith and testimony, constitutes the practice of *advaita bhakti* as a means to the highest spiritual realization. However, when this dedication becomes natural, springing from the realization of non-duality, then it becomes a manifestation of the perfection of *advaita bhakti* which can then be truly called transcendent devotion or *parā bhakti*. Such transcendent devotion is just the other facet of the state of *jīvanmukti*. As such, it is the spiritual objective of the votary of *samaya mārga* that he may realize the state where all the sense organs and mind are completely immersed in the service of the omnipotent *Śakti* in an effortless manner.[603]

Discussing the nature of *Prakṛti* in its higher and lower forms, Śaṅkara says,

> "O mighty-armed one, *iyam*, this; is *aparā*, the inferior (Prakṛti) - not the higher, (but) impure, the source of evil and having the nature of worldly bondage. *Viddhi*, know; *anyām*, the other, pure; *prakṛtim*, Prakṛti; *me*, of Mine, which is essentially Myself; which, *tu*, however; is *parām*, higher, more exalted; *itaḥ*, than this (Prakṛti) already spoken of; *Jīva-bhūtam*, which has taken the form of individual souls, which is

characterized as 'the Knower of the body (field)', and which is the cause of sustenance of life; and *yayā*, by which Prakṛti; *idam*, this; *jagat*, world; *dhāryate*, is upheld, by permeating it."[604]

In this passage it has been clearly shown that the higher *Prakṛti* is actually just the same as the transcendent *Brahman* and it is this which appears in the form of various individual souls at the phenomenal plane. This higher *Prakṛti*, although transcendent, also permeates the entire phenomenal realm as the immanent reality. On the other hand, the various basic non-conscious constituents of the phenomenal realm constitute the lower form of *Prakṛti* and this *Prakṛti* signifies the realm of phenomenal illusion and *karmic* bondage. However, even this lower *Prakṛti* is just an epistemic illusion projected over the ontological substratum of the higher *Prakṛti*.

The *S.L.* also talks of *Śakti* as both the transcendent and the immanent Reality. In its transcendent aspect *Śakti* is *Parāśakti*, which is identical with the transcendent *Paramaśiva*. Both of them represent the non-dual state of *Śiva-Śakti Sāmarasya*, which is just the same as the non-dual supreme *Brahman*. *Brahman* in its passive and quiescent aspect may be called *Paramaśiva*, but the same *Brahman* in its active and projective aspect is called *Parāśakti* and therefore they are merely two aspects of the same non-dual absolute.[605] Moreover, this transcendent *Parāśakti* alone manifests Herself immanently in the form of various objective constituents of the phenomenal realm, as well as in the form of various conscious subjects or *jīva-s*.[606] This *Śakti* alone is both the transcendent fourth entity *(Turīyā)* and the immanent reality responsible for the epistemic creation, sustenance and dissolution of the phenomenal universe.[607]

Discussing the excellence of the man of knowledge *(jñānī)* and the nature of his devotion, Śaṅkara says,

> "*Teṣām*, of them, among the four; *jñānī*, the man of Knowledge, the knower of Reality, is *nitya-yuktaḥ*, endowed with constant steadfastness as a result of being a knower of Reality; and he also becomes *eka-bhaktiḥ*, endowed with one-pointed devotion, because he finds no one else whom he can adore. Consequently, that person of one-pointed devotion *viśiṣyate*, excels, becomes superior, i.e., he surpasses (the others)."[608]

Out of the four classes of devotees, namely the afflicted or *ārta,* the seeker of knowledge or *jijñāsu,* the seeker of wealth or *arthārthī* and the man of knowledge or *jñānī,* it is the *jñānī* who excels all the others. A *jñānī* has testimony and faith-based conviction about the non-dual and omnipresent nature of Reality, prior to the intuitive realization of that Reality. However, after such realization, the *jñānī* gets firmly established, at the intuitive plane, in the non-dual omnipresent Reality. However, in both the pre-realization and the post-realization states, the *jñānī* is convinced about his identity with the transcendent and yet universally immanent Reality, as a result of which he finds nothing apart from that supreme Reality whom he can adore. Therefore, he becomes endowed with one-pointed devotion or *'eka bhakti'*.

Such one-pointed devotion is nothing but *advaita bhakti* since it stems from the firm belief in the omnipresent immanence of the transcendent Reality. In the *śrīvidyā* tradition this transcendent Reality is seen as the primordial non-dual *Parāśakti*. Therefore, such *advaita bhakti*, characteristic of the *jñānī,* is the hallmark of the *śrividyā* tradition. The *S.L.*, therefore, beautifully highlights the nature and nuances of such non-dualistic devotion. On the one hand, it consists of dedicating all the *karma-s* at the feet of the primordial *Śakti* for Her pleasure and winning Her grace.[609] On the other hand, the complete surrender of one's ego at the feet of the omnipresent *Śakti* for winning Her grace through the practice of *advaita bhakti* easily brings about the intuitive realization of one's identity with the non-dual transcendent *Parāśakti*.[610]

Emphatically concluding the basic ontological identity of the unconditioned transcendent *Brahman* and the conditioned lower *Brahman*, Śaṅkara says,

> "The purport is this: Indeed, that power of God through which *Brahman* sets out, comes forth, for the purpose of favouring the devotees, etc., that power which is *Brahman* Itself, am I. For, a power and the possessor of that power are non-different. Or, *brahman* means the conditioned *Brahman*, since It (too,) is referred to by that word. 'Of that *Brahman*, I Myself, the unconditionrd *Brahman* - and none else - am the Abode.' "[611]

This passage highlights that the power of *Brahman*, which is responsible for the epistemic creation, sustenance and destruction of the phenomenal universe, is none other than the supreme and transcendent non-dual *Brahman*. They are two aspects of the same Reality. The ontological and passive aspect of that Reality is known as the transcendent *Brahman* or *Para Brahman*, whereas the epistemically active aspect of that same Reality is known as the lower and immanent *Brahman* or the *apara Brahman* and also as the conditioned *Brahman* or *saguṇa Brahman*. These two aspects are also known as the formless *Brahman* or *nirākāra Brahman* and the *Brahman* with form or *sākāra Brahman*.

The *S.L.* too similarly highlights these two aspects of Reality. In the *śrīvidyā* terminology of *S.L.*, *Śiva* stands for the ontological, passive and subjective aspects, whereas *Śakti* stands for the epistemic, active and objective aspects of the supreme Reality. In the realm of epistemic duality, the basic subject-object distinction and their essential complementarity reflects the ontological identity underlying the epistemically distinct manifestations of *Śiva* and *Śakti*.[612] On the other hand, the essential identity of *Śiva* and *Śakti* at the transcendent level has also been highlighted, which indicates the fact that they are just two aspects of the same supreme Reality.[613] This transcendent Reality is what is called *Paramaśiva*, or the *Parāśakti*, or the *Śiva-Śakti Sāmarasya*, or the *Ṣoḍaśī kalā* (i.e., the sixteenth digit of) of *Śakti*, or the 'Ocean of Consciousness and Bliss' *(cid-ānanda-laharī)*.[614]

On the basis of the study of afore-mentioned numerous passages from the *Prasthānatraya bhāṣya-s* of Śaṅkara and their comparison with the relevant sections of the *S.L.*, it becomes clear that there is a perceptible inner harmony between the tenets of advaitism, as emerging from the *Prasthānatraya bhāṣyas* of Śaṅkara, and the *samaya* tradition of *śrīvidyā*, as expounded in the *S.L.* There are, surely, some differences in the emphasis of using various terms but this does not undermine the basic conceptual consistency between them. These two traditions can be seen as diverse attempts to approach the same supreme Reality, consisting of its transcendent and immanent aspects, from two different viewpoints. Whereas advaitism tries to emphasize the transcendent ontological aspect of that Reality, the *śrīvidyā* tradition seeks to highlight the epistemic, projective and active aspects of that very same Reality.

Chapter V

Advaitika Devotion as the Essence of Tantrādvaita

The earlier chapters have dealt with the commonly acclaimed Advaitika and Tāntrika texts of Śaṅkara, as well as Gauḍapāda, with the objective of understanding the philosophical frameworks illustrated in them. Also, efforts were made to examine the compatibility of the philosophical frameworks exhibited in them. The broad picture emerging from this examination has given us the impression that there is a basic coherence between these two classes of texts. In fact, there is ample room to argue for a conceptual complementarity obtaining between the philosophical frameworks illustrated in these two classes of texts. There is strong case for treating these two classes of texts in a holistic manner for gaining a comprehensive understanding of the philosophical and spiritual frameworks of Śaṅkara and Gauḍapāda. In order to distinguish this holistic approach from the prevailing contemporary approach to Advaitism, I humbly propose the term 'Tantrādvaita' to signify the complementarity of the Advaitika and Tāntrika elements in the philosophy of Śaṅkara and Gauḍapāda. Now, in the framework of Tantrādvaita, *advaita-bhakti* or advaitika devotion plays a very important role since it represents the inevitable means for progressing towards the highest non-dualistic realization, as well as the outlook of a liberated-while-alive or *jīvanmukta* person. Therefore, the present chapter would seek to focus on the various aspects of advaitika devotion in the holistic framework of Tantrādvaita.

The previous chapters in the present work have dealt with various philosophical issues, textual analyses and comparisons to bring out the inner compatibility and mutual need between the non-dualistic and devotional aspects of Śaṅkara's thinking as reflected in his *Saundarya-laharī (S.L.)* and the commentaries on the *Prasthānatraya*, namely the *Brahma sūtra*, the eleven principal *upaniṣads* and the *Bhagavadgītā*. But the mute question is - 'How does an intellectually brilliant and reflective person like Śaṅkara come to accept the need and desirability of advaitika devotion?' An attempt to answer this question promises to shed light on the various aspects and stages of advaitika devotion *(advaita bhakti)*.

The starting point of Śaṅkara's philosophical and spiritual journey has been well indicated in the introductory passage of the *Brahma sūtra bhāṣya* where it is observed that the common understanding of the intrinsic nature of the subject and the object, along with that of their mutual relationship, presents a sort of paradox.[615] The mutual overlapping of the subjective and objective natures is not a peripheral issue that can be possibly ignored. Rather, this paradoxical phenomenon happens to be the guiding principle of almost all phenomenal thoughts and activities, both morally appropriate and inappropriate. This observation immediately prompts the reflective mind to look for an apt explanation of it.

The reflective mind also comes across another puzzling observation. This is the observation of the near universal quest by all the sentient beings, from the simplest to the most sophisticated and evolved ones, for realizing a state of the most intense and enduring existence, knowledge, power and bliss. This quest is not only universal but also instinctive. The significant point is that such instinctive and universal quest persists despite the commonly known phenomenal constraints and inevitable truths in this regard. For example, the quest for infinite existence retains its alluring charm despite the knowledge of inevitability of death. Or, the quest for pure and permanent bliss continues universally despite the knowledge of the changing and corruptible nature of all phenomena.[616] Such contradiction between these quests and the nature of the phenomenal world presents a queer, natural and universal paradox. Obviously, the reflective mind screams for an appropriate solution to this paradox.

The creative rational mind throws up various alternative models and solutions to resolve these paradoxes. These various models presuppose the subject-object distinction based dualistic framework.[617] However, it becomes clear in the course of time that these various alternative models suffer from numerous discrepancies and even logical inconsistencies. The present author has discussed these problems elsewhere also.[618] As such, it becomes difficult to accept them as full and proper explanations of these paradoxes, which characteristically reflect the nature of the phenomenal world. Śaṅkara's rejection of the various orthodox and heterodox systems of philosophy in his commentary on the *Brahma sūtra* is an illustration of the problems afflicting different dualistic philosophies. In general terms, it can be seen that there can be no logical possibility of any finality in a dualistic framework either with reference to knowledge, or to bliss, or to existence, etc.[619] This logical limitation, although stemming from the nature of subject-object distinction, percolates down to the levels of rational understanding, linguistic expressions and emotional experiences.[620] The logical inevitability and practical necessity of even more or less ad-hoc explanations of the phenomenal world is accepted, even though reluctantly, by even modern science and philosophy. The phenomenal faith in logic, language and rationality fails in finding a full and final solution to the paradox called the phenomenal world.

It is in this context that the significance of verbal testimony or *śabda* can be properly understood. Verbal testimony is the valid means of knowledge which, being supra-rational in nature (especially in the Vedic context), provides knowledge that is unattainable through the ordinary means of knowledge.[621] S.N. Dasgupta has pointed out the higher status of Vedic testimony as compared to reason.[622] The authority of verbal testimony does not flow from logic and rationality. It comes from the trustworthiness of the persons involved with it. Be they the ancient Vedic seers *(ṛṣi-s)* or the masters of the *tantra* tradition, their non-selfish, benevolent and ascetic character rules out the possibility of any positive or negative ulterior motive for misleading the masses. In such a scenario, there are far more reasons for accepting, rather than rejecting, the knowledge based on verbal testimony.

According to Śaṅkara, the Vedic *śabda* presents an explanation of the phenomenal world, its characteristics and paradoxes in terms of a non-dualistic or advaitika framework, upholding the ontological absolutism of *Brahman*.[623] Similarly, the verbal testimony associated with the *samaya* tradition of *tantra* also explains the phenomenal world and its characteristics in terms of an ontologically absolutist but epistemically pluralistic framework, taking recourse to the transcendent non-dual state of *Śiva-Śakti Sāmarasya* and the immanent dualistic manifestations of *Śiva* and *Śakti* at the phenomenal plane.[624] The *samaya* tradition of *tantra* is in full harmony with the non-dualistic Vedic framework. This is why Śaṅkara, the author of various *bhāṣya-s* upholding advaitism, has also authored the *Saundarya laharī,* an exemplary discourse in praise of the highest Reality, that is both the transcendent absolute and the phenomenal universe.[625] Thus, the *śabda* associated with both the Vedic tradition and the *tantra* tradition of *samaya mārga* presents a non-dualist and absolutist explanation of the phenomenal world.

Thus, while on the one hand, there is the logical impossibility of finding a full and final solution to the various phenomenal puzzles in a dualistic framework, on the other hand, the testimonies of the Vedic and *tāntrika* traditions claim to provide a supra-rational explanation to those puzzles, but in a non-dualistic framework. While there seems to be cogent reasons for having faith in the acceptability and validity of these testimonies, it is also a fact that ordinary understanding, based in logic, language and rationality, cannot appropriate it in a direct manner. Moreover, the non-dualistic framework, presented as a solution by these spiritual traditions, does not apparently cohere with our dualistic understanding of the phenomenal world at all.

That is, a person may either choose to be forever restricted by the logical limitations of a dualistic framework or he may try to find ways and means of properly comprehending the non-dualistic framework, as presented by the Vedic and *tāntrika śabda* traditions. The inquisitive reflective mind would naturally like to go for the latter choice. In this context, the possibility of a personal and intuitive realization of the non-dual absolute, as also one's own identity with that absolute, as promised by these traditions, becomes very significant and extremely crucial.[626] That is, these traditions do promise a most direct verification of their non-dualist claim. Ramakant Tripathi has noted the enormous importance of the possibility of such realization at the phenomenal plane itself.[627] However, such conclusive verification is promised only at the end of a long and disciplined spiritual journey, the first pre-requisite of which is faith in the spiritual tradition and one's personal preceptor or *Guru*.[628]

As such, the spiritual aspirant of intuitive realization of the non-dual absolute prepares himself for undertaking a grand spiritual experiment. The hypothesis of this grand experiment is the non-dualist and absolutist framework of Reality presented by the Vedic and *samaya tantra* traditions. The object of this experiment is the subjective consciousness of the spiritual aspirant himself. As such, accepting the tenets of these traditions as a hypothesis for spiritual experimentation means a full-hearted acceptance of these tenets at the intellectual, emotional and behavioural planes. That is, he willingly argues, emotes and behaves in conformity with the basic tenets of these absolutist traditions.[629] However, all this willing acceptance and behaviour is done for the explicit goal of attaining oneself the intuitive realization of the absolute Reality.

Thus, the aspirant develops faith in the testimony of these *śabda* traditions. That is, he acquires a testimony-based conviction about the transcendent and absolutist nature of the supreme Reality and also, a similar conviction about his own ontological identity with that non-dual Reality. However, despite developing such non-dualistic convictions and continuously practising the prescribed spiritual disciplines, the aspirant's desired intuitive realization remains elusive.[630] That is, despite the necessary hypothetical conviction and practice of various spiritual disciplines, one does not immediately achieve an intuitive realization of the supreme non-dual Reality and one's identity with It.

At this stage, the spiritual aspirant suddenly becomes acutely aware of the strength of the cosmic epistemic projection of phenomenal duality. The bondage of the aspirant appears to be insurmountable. He recognizes his own utter helplessness in overcoming the cosmic illusion of duality, despite his utmost efforts. The theoretical conviction of the non-dual and transcendent nature of Reality proves incapable of resolving this sense of spiritual helplessness.

It is at this juncture that the aspirant suddenly realizes the supermacy of the divine *Śakti* or the eternal power of *Brahman*.[631] Surendranath Bhattacharya[632] and P.K. Sundaram[633] have pointed out the positivity *(bhāva-rūpa)* of this *Śakti*. The devotee therefore comes to realize the futility of his egotistical spiritual efforts. He sees clearly that only that principle which is responsible for the cosmic projection of duality and the resultant bondage, can be truly capable of and responsible for the withdrawal of that epistemic projection and the resultant liberating intuitive realization. He thus surrenders his ego at the feet of the divine *Śakti* and flings himself at Her mercy, beseeching Her grace, so that he may successfully transcend the cosmic illusion of duality.[634]

With the testimony-based conviction in the transcendent non-dual yet universally immanent nature of the divine *Śakti*, who is identical with the supreme *Brahman*, the spiritual aspirant becomes a devotee or *bhakta* of *Śakti*.[635] Such a devotee has a non-dualistic conviction about the nature of Reality, that includes both himself and the transcendent yet immanent *Śakti*.[636]

This spiritual frame of mind of the aspirant exhibits, what we may call, 'advaitika devotion' or *'advaita bhakti'*. As such, advaitika devotion may be taken as the spiritual culmination of the theoretical testimony-based philosophy of non-dualism or advaitism. Vinoba has pointed out this natural development.[637] Such advaitika devotion, on the part of the devotee having an advaitika conviction, easily wins the divine grace of the transcendent and immanent *Śakti*,[638] as a result of which, perfect purity and concentration of the aspirant's mind becomes possible and then, the highest intuitive realization of the supreme *Brahman* or the *Śiva-Śakti Sāmarasya* follows as a necessary consequence of it. Thus, the practice of advaitika devotion facilitates the attainment of the highest intuitive realization of non-duality, which is just the same as attaining the highest liberation. That is, the highest realizational knowledge is never possible without the divine grace of the eternal power of *Brahman* i.e., the supreme *Śakti*. Thus, the full and final solution of the phenomenal puzzles is revealed to the aspirant and the devotee by the grace of *Devī*. However, this revelation is necessarily at the supra-rational intuitive plane. He is forever freed from the cosmic illusion of duality, realizing his basic identity with the transcendent non-dual absolute Reality.[639]

The term 'advaitika devotion' or *'advaita bhakti'* itself clearly suggests that there are two aspects of it viz. the aspect of advaitism and that of devotion *(bhakti)*. These two aspects are closely related and yet they maintain their distinct characteristics. They are neither absolutely distinct nor identical. Among them, the aspect of advaitism signifies the testimony based theoretical conviction about the non-dual nature of the supreme Reality and one's own identity with It. This non-dualist conviction culminates in the spiritual attitude of devotion *(bhakti)* towards the eternal, transcendent and yet immanent *Brahmaśakti*. In this devotional state the spiritual aspirant surrenders his ego before the wishes of the omnipotent divine *Śakti*. Each and every thought, speech and action of the devotee becomes a devotional offering at the feet of the divine *Śakti*.[640] Practising such devotion and also believing in the omnipresence, omnipotence and absoluteness of *Śakti*, the devotee prays for Her divine grace and intervention,[641] for it is in Her jurisdiction alone to either project or withdraw the cosmic illusion of duality in general or with reference to any specific *jīva cidābhāsa*.

In this manner, while advaitism provides the background conditions for the practice of such advaitika devotion, the practice of devotion itself at all the levels becomes the functional aspect of advaitika devotion. However, this functional aspect is again directed to win the grace of *Śakti* for the purpose of achieving the intuitive realization of the transcendent non-dual nature of Reality and one's basic identity with that Reality.[642] As such, the devotional aspect of advaitika devotion emerges as its dominant and explicit aspect. Devotion becomes the primary connotation of 'advaitika devotion'. On the other hand, advaitism stands for the implicit aspect, as also for the avowed realizational objective, of the practice of advaitika devotion. Advaitism may thus be taken as the secondary connotation of 'advaitika devotion'. The advaitika and devotional aspects of advaitika devotion are truly complementary in nature. While the advaitika conviction about the nature of Reality logically culminates in the aspirant's devotional attitude towards *Śakti*, such devotion itself also requires a prior belief in the advaitika framework as its necessary pre-condition. The two aspects of advaitika devotion always go together. As such, they may be called the twin aspects of advaitika devotion.

In the pre-realization state the aspirant's belief in advaitism is only theoretical and testimony based. That is, such belief in advaitism lacks direct experiential basis. Since the devotional attitude towards *Śakti* is the logical corollary of such advaitika belief, it follows that it also remains somewhat deliberate and volitional in nature. It cannot be taken as grounded in the direct intuitive knowledge of the omnipresence and omnipotence of *Śakti* and one's own basic identity with Her.

However, once the devotee wins the grace of *Śakti* and acquires the highest intuitive realization of the nature of supreme Reality and one's relationship with It, everything changes dramatically and so does the nature of advaitika devotion.[643] Even after such realization the physical body of the perfected devotee continues to exist at the phenomenal plane due to the momentum of the already fructifying *karmas*, called the *prārabdha karmas*.[644] This is called the 'liberated-while-alive' or *jīvanmukta* state of the devotee.[645] Unless and until there is complete fructification of the *prārabdha karmas*, the *jīvanmukta* devotee cannot attain the highest liberation, the 'bodiless liberation' or *videhamukti*, wherein there is the absolute sublation of all traces of epistemic duality. As such, it is clear that in the state of *jīvanmukti* there is a persistence of that trace of epistemic duality, qualifying the devotee's consciousness, which is necessary for sustaining the basic illusion of the individuality of the *jīva*, since otherwise the fructification of that *jīva's prārabdha karmas* would become logically impossible. H.S. Prasad has noted this logical requirement.[646] The highest level of consciousness accessible to the *jīvanmukta* devotee corresponds with the *bindu* level, situated right above the *Brahma granthi* in the pathway of the *kuṇḍalinī*. When the devotee's *kuṇḍalinī* rises up to the *bindu* level as a result of perfecting the highest kind of *samādhi*, i.e., the *nirbīja* or *dharmamegha* or *asamprajñāta* or *nirvikalpa samādhi*, the cosmic illusion of duality gets sublated before the consciousness of the devotee as long as that *samādhi* continues.[647] He gets an intuitive insight into the non-dual and absolute nature of Reality. He no longer needs the testimony of the Vedas or the *āgama-s* to believe in the non-dual and absolute nature of the supreme Reality. His personal realization itself becomes the unassailable and conclusive proof for the non-dual absolute nature of Reality. However, in spite of all this, the devotee's *prārabdha karmas* sustain the epistemic individuality of his consciousness. But, since the cosmic illusion already lies fully exposed before the *jīvanmukta* devotee, he is no longer led astray by such epistemic projection of duality, even though witnessing it.[648] That is, just as in the case of *Īśvara*, while the projective power *(vikṣepa śakti)* of the primordial *Śakti* remains effective before his consciousness, its obstructive power *(āvaraṇa śakti)* becomes totally ineffective before him.

In such a state of consciousness, the *jīvanmukta* devotee intuitively realizes the true nature of the divine *Śakti*.[649] He comes to realize that this eternal and absolute *Śakti* is none other than the transcendent *Brahman* itself.[650] The passive state of that supreme Reality is called the *nirguṇa nirākāra Brahman* or *Paramaśiva*, while the epistemically active aspect of that very Reality is known as the *saguṇa sākāra Brahman* or *Parāśakti*. In the traditional terminology of the *samaya mārga*, this supreme Reality is known as *Śiva-Śakti Sāmarasya* or the *Ṣoḍaśī kalā*, the sixteenth digit, of *Devī Tripurasundarī*.[651] In the post-realization state, i.e., the *jīvanmukta* state, the devotee becomes intuitively aware of both the transcendent and immanent aspects of *Śakti*. He becomes intuitively aware of the omnipresent, omnipotent and omniscient nature of the primordial *Śakti*. He becomes aware of the unsurpassable jurisdiction of the divine *Śakti*. He becomes aware of the universal immanence of the transcendent *Śakti* in each and every particle of the phenomenal realm, whether sentient or insentient. He becomes aware of *Śakti*'s sole control over the epistemic projection, sustenance and withdrawal of the cosmic illusion of duality and its associated epistemic obstruction of the knowledge of the non-dual absolute nature of Reality.[652] The present author has pointed out the aspects of identity and difference with respect to *Māyā* and *Śakti* elsewhere.[653] Having become intuitively aware of these aspects of *Śakti*, as a result of the rise of *kuṇḍaliṇī* up to the *bindu* level, the *jīvanmukta* devotee develops a natural all-consuming devotion *(parā bhakti)* towards the divine *Śakti*. All his thoughts and activities naturally become so many offerings at the *Devī's* feet.[654] He finds the presence of that *Śakti* alone everywhere. All volitions, all cognitions, all actions, all conscious and unconscious things are revealed as just so many phenomenal manifestations of the same transcendent and absolute *Parāśakti*. He finds himself seated in the eternal blissful bosom of the divine *Śakti*.[655] Such all-consuming natural devotion of the *jīvanmukta* devotee is the highest possible kind of devotion or *bhakti*.[656] It may be aptly called the transcendent devotion or *parā bhakti*. Thus, the post-realization advaitika devotion is actually the same as the highest possible devotion or *parā bhakti*.

In such transcendent advaitika devotion the aspects of advaitism and devotion are totally at par with each other since the very same intuitive realization of the non-dual (advaitika) nature of supreme Reality also naturally transforms into the transcendent devotion or *parā bhakti*. In the post-realization mental state of the devotee, the aspects of advaitism and devotion merge together to evolve into a higher realizational state where everything becomes natural and holistic. This transcendent devotion *(parā bhakti)* is identical with the highest realizational knowledge *(parama jñāna)*. In this state of transcendent knowledge and devotion the *jīvanmukta* sees the transcendent non-dual Reality immanent in the phenomenal realm of duality. He also sees the ontological identity of the phenomenal realm and the immutable blissful transcendent Reality. He finds the same Reality manifesting as both the subject and object at the phenomenal plane. He sees both knowledge and ignorance, bondage and liberation as nothing but the divine play *(līlā)* of the supreme *Śakti*.[657] K.H. Potter has noted the importance of theory of *līlā* in the advaitika framework.[658] Both pleasure and pain are revealed as the manifestations of the same blissful *Śakti*. Everything becomes but a vision of the blissful *Devī*, the *'Cidānanda-svarūpā'*. He sees all the three phenomenal planes *(tri-pura)* immersed in and manifesting the bliss, power, majesty and beauty *(saundarya)* of the divine *Śakti*. He thus realizes the infinite existence, beauty, bliss, power and consciousness of the *Devī Tripurasundarī*. Not only this, he also comes to realize the non-dual transcendent aspect of *Śakti*, in which She is the *Parāśakti*, identical with *Paramaśiva*. He comes to realize his basic identity with the transcendent non-dual *Śiva-Śakti Sāmarasya*. He realizes the same divine *Śakti* as both the immanent and the transcendent Reality. He sees his own ontological identity with that supreme *Śakti*. He witnesses the macrocosm in the microcosm and also the microcosm in the macrocosm. He experiences the truth of the famous dictum *'yat piṇḍe, tat brahmāṇḍe'*. He goes beyond the sense of distinction between knowledge and ignorance, pure and impure, merit and demerit, bondage and liberation, immanent and transcendent, duality and non-duality, pleasure and pain and lastly, even the distinction of the deity and devotee itself. This is the culmination of the supreme and sublime transcendent advaitika devotion, *parā bhakti*, or *parā advaita bhakti*.

This advaitika devotion, in both of its forms, the pre-realizational and the post-realizational, is the gist of Śaṅkara's philosophy and spiritualism. Śaṅkara was not only a brilliant philosopher but also, and more importantly, an exalted spiritual master. He gave a renewed vigour and direction to the Vedic philosophy and spiritualism. His works and life reflect his sincere practising of advaitika devotion.

His commentaries *(bhāṣya-s)* on the *Prasthānatraya* highlight the non-dualistic interpretation of the *śrutis* and the *smṛtis*. These interpretations provide the theoretical philosophical framework for the testimony-based understanding of the nature of the world and the supreme Reality. Some independent works of Śaṅkara also highlight such testimony based advaitika philosophy. All these works thus illustrate the advaitika aspect of advaitika devotion in the pre-realizational state of the aspirant. It provides the necessary intellectual and philosophical backdrop for the practice of advaitika devotion.

Śaṅkara's devotional works or *stotra* literature, such as the *Saundarya laharī,* the *Śivānanda laharī,* etc. highlight the devotional aspect of advaitika devotion in the pre-realizational state. They highlight the necessity of taking recourse to devotion *(bhakti)* towards the supreme *Brahma Śakti*. It does not matter for Śaṅkara as to which specific form of that divine *Śakti* one may accept as his personal deity *(iṣṭa)*. Therefore, Śaṅkara has written hymns in praise of *Śakti*, *Śiva*, *Viṣṇu,* etc. with the same vigour and devotion.[659] For him, all these were the different forms of the same *Brahma Śakti*. Furthermore, if one decides not to have devotion to any of these forms of *Brahma Śakti*, then he must at least accept his own preceptor or *Guru* as his personal deity, who is to be, therefore, regarded as a direct personification of the supreme *Brahman*. The *Guru* must be seen as one with the transcendent *Brahma Śakti* and as such one must have devotion to the *Guru* and one must surrender his ego at his feet. All this has been beautifully depicted in *Śrīdakṣiṇāmūrti stotra* of Śaṅkara. The upshot of all this is that it is imperative to surrender one's ego in a devotional manner before the supreme *Brahma Śakti*, in any of Her various manifest forms. She is equally immanent in all of them.

In keeping with the necessity of practising advaitika devotion, Śaṅkara established the four important temples dedicated to *Saraswatī* and *Viṣṇu* in the four corners of India for the purpose of providing the necessary spiritual direction to the masses. Further, he established the monastic order, affiliated to these four religious centres, for ensuring the availability of necessary philosophical and spiritual teachings for the masses. Significantly, he also established the *Kāñcī Kāmakoṭi Pīṭham* dedicated to the primordial *Śakti*, the *Devī Tripurasundarī*, and he spent a considerable time there.

All these textual and historical evidences prove beyond doubt that Śaṅkara espoused advaitika devotion as the highest philosophical, religious and spiritual ideal. The philosophy of non-dualism or advaitism is only the starting point of his spiritual journey that progresses through the practice of pre-realizational advaitika devotion to arrive at the intuitive realization of the transcendent non-dual Reality and then culminate in the *jīvanmukta's* natural state of transcendent advaitika devotion or *parā bhakti*.[660]

Illustration of Corresponding Identities in Tantrādvaita

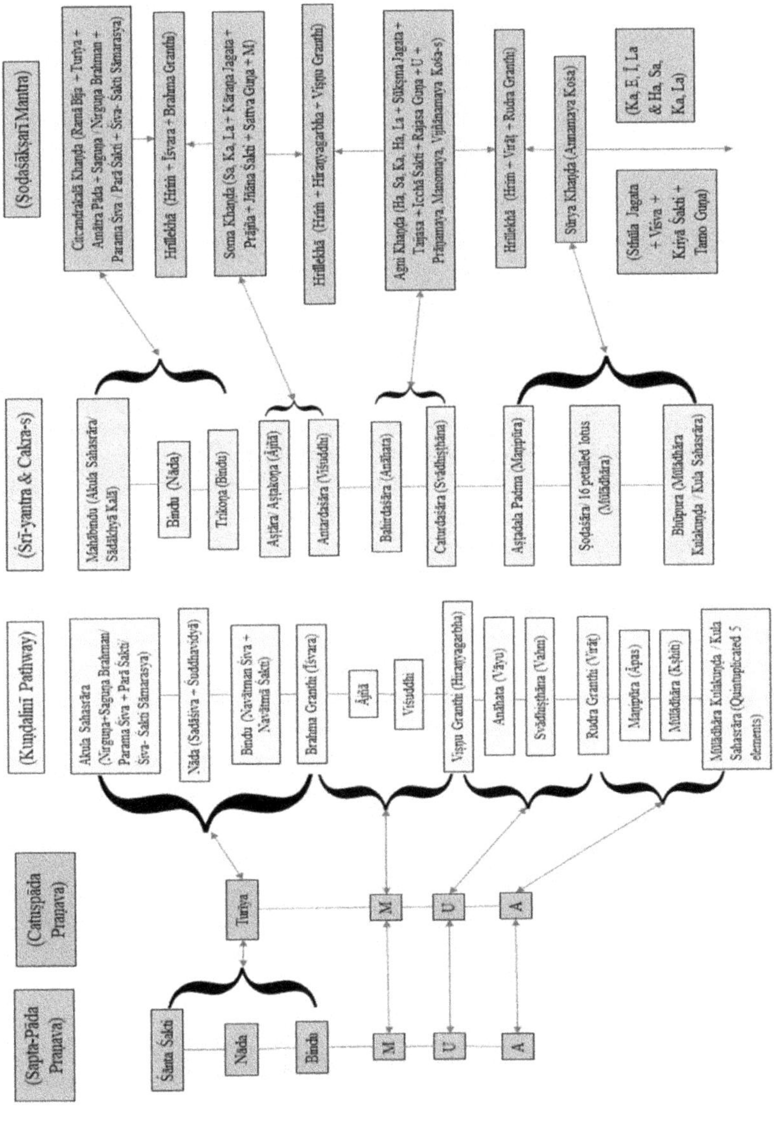

Notes and References

[1] Viv. Cd., vv.468, 470.

[2] T.R.V. Murti, The Central Philosophy of Buddhism, p.321.

[3] Bina Gupta, Percieving in Advaita Vedānta, p.67.

[4] ... janma māyopamaṁ teṣāṁ sā ca māyā na vidyate;

Mā. kā., IV-58, p.370;

also, U. Sā.(tr.), I-xi-5, p.126.

[5] Viv. Cd., v.405;

also, ...māyā mātram idaṁ dvaitam advaitaṁ paramārthataḥ;

Mā. Kā., I-17, p.213.

[6] M. Hiriyanna, Outlines of Indian Philosophy, p.339.

[7] B. S. Bh. I-i-1, pp.7-17;

also, Viv. Cd., v.405;

also, Mā. Kā., I-17, p.213;

also, asato māyayā janma tattvato naïva yujyate;

ibid., III-28, p. 301.

[8] N. V. Bannerjee, The Spirit of Indian Philosophy, p.226.

[9] tattva trayeṇa sā vividhā;

SVRS., aph.5, p.9;

also, U. Sā.(tr.), I-xvii-26,64;

also, Mā. Kā., I-1, p.185;

also, akāro nayate viśvam ukāraś cāpi taijasam,

makāraś ca punaḥ prājñaṁ nāmātre vidyate gatiḥ;

ibid., I-23, p.220.

[10] B. S. Bh., I-i-1, pp.7-32;

also, Viv. Cd., vv. 386,387;

also, Mā. Kā., IV-58, p.370;

ibid., III-27, p.300.

[11] K. C. Bhattacharya, 'Studies in Vedāntism' in Studies in Philosophy, p.43.

[12] Bṛ.Up.Bh., II-iv-5, p.193;

also, Viv. Cd., vv.56, 59, 62;

also, Mā. Kā., I-17, p.213;

ibid., III-48, p.320.

[13] Ramakant Tripathi, Brahmasūtra-Śāṅkara bhāṣya (catuḥsūtrī), p.19.

[14] Bṛ.Up.Bh., IV-iv-21, ll.10-3, p.369;

also, U. Sā. (tr.), I-xviii-23,188,195;

also, Viv. Cd., vv.353, 358, 360, 361;

also, Pañcī., pp.5-7.

[15] Viv. Cd., vv.267, 279, 416, 418, 428, 429;

also, Subh., v.52;

also, U. Sā. (tr.), I-xviii-207, 222.

[16] N.S.S. Raman, Methodological Studies in the History of Religions, p.128f.

[17] Viv. Cd., v.108;

also, B. S. Bh., I-i-2, pp.85f;

also, ...māyaiṣā tasya devasya yayā saṁmohitaḥ svayam,

Mā. Kā., II-19, p.243;

also, ibid., II-12,13, pp.237f.

[18] V. P., IX-25, p.161;

also, Bṛ.Up.Bh., IV-iv-21, ll.10-3, p.369;

also, Pañcī., pp.5-7;

also, Viv. Cd., vv.353, 358, 360, 361;

also, U. Sā. (tr.), I-xviii-23,188,195.

[19] Viv. Cd., vv.298, 300, 301, 306;

also, Pañcī., pp.5-7.

[20] ...sahasrāre padme subhaga subhagodeti subhage,

paraṁ saubhāgyaṁ yat tad iha tava sāyujya padavī;

Subh., v.51, p.300.

[21] Bṛ.Up., II-iv-5, p.193;

also, Bṛ.Up.Bh., p.193, lines 9-11.

[22] Bṛ.Up.Bh., IV -iv -21, p.369, lines 10-13.

[23] Bṛ.Up.Bh., IV -iv -13, p.366, lines 9-16;

also, V.P., IX-25, p.161.

[24] B.S.Bh., I-i-1, pp.7-17.

[25] H.S. Prasad, 'Dreamless Sleep and Soul: a controversy between Vedānta and Buddhism' in Asian Philosophy, p.72.

[26] B.S.Bh., II-iii-45, 46.

[27] B.S.Bh., I-i-1.

[28] kāryānumeyā sudhiyaiva māyā yayā jagat sarvam idaṁ prasūyate;

Viv.Cd., v.108, p.39.

[29] janma sthiti bhaṇgaṁ yataḥ sarvajñāt sarva śakteḥ kāraṇād bhavati ...;

B.S.Bh., I-i-2, pp.85f.

[30] ibid., I-i-2, pp.85f.

[31] avyakata nāmnī parmeśa śaktir anādy avidyā triguṇātmikā parā;

Viv. Cd., v.108, p.39.

[32] ibid., loc.cit.

[33] niratiśayopādhi saṁpannaś ceśvaro nihīnopādhi saṅpannāñ jīvān praśāstīti..;

B.S.Bh., II-iii-45, p.623;

also, Viv.Cd., v.110, p.40;

also, Bh.G., VII-14, p.326;

also, Bh.G.Bh., VII-14, p.115.

[34] N.S.S. Raman, Methodological Studies in the History of Religions, p.130.

[35] māyā mātram idaṁ dvaitam advaitaṁ paramārthataḥ...;

Viv.Cd., v.405, p.153;

also, ...ekmeva advyaṁ brahma neha nānāsti kiñcana;

ibid., v.468, p.174.

[36] T.M.P. Mahadevan, The Philosophy of Advaita, p.119.

[37] D.M. Dutta, The Six Ways of Knowing, p.72.

[38] Bṛ.Up.Bh., II-iv-5, p.193, lines 9-11;

also, ibid., IV-iv-21;

also, V.P., IX-25, p.161.

[39] B.S.Bh., I-i-2, pp.85f;

also, Viv.Cd., v.243, p.94.

[40] Brian Carr,'Śaṅkarācārya' in Companion Encyclopedia of Asian Philosophy, p.192.

[41] V.P., IX-25, p.161;

also, Viv.Cd., v.46, p.17;

also, Bṛ.Up.Bh., II-iv-5, p.193, lines 9-11.

[42] K.C. Bhattacharya, 'Studies in Vedāntism' in Studies in Philosophy, p.39.

[43] B.S.Bh., I-i-2;

also, Viv.Cd., v.108, p.39.

[44] Bh.G., XII-2, p.475;

also, Bh.G.Bh., XII-2, p.172.

[45] Bh.G., VII-17, XII-2, pp.328, 475;

also, Bh.G.Bh., VII-17, XII-2, pp.115f,172.

[46] Bh.G., XII-6,7, p.479;

also, Bh.G.Bh., XII-6,7, p.174;

also, Viv.Cd., v.300, p.114.

[47] Viv.Cd., vv.27,28;

also, Bh.G., VII-17,18, XII-8;

also, Bh.G.Bh., VII-17,18, XII-8, pp.115f,174.

[48] K.H. Potter, Encyclopedia of Indian Philosophy, p.78.

[49] atha śākta mantrāgama jijñāsā;

SVRS., aph.1, p.2.

[50] The texts on *tantra* are collectively known as *āgama* texts.

[51] The term refers to all matters related with *Śakti,* the Omnipotent Primordial Energy.

[52] makaraṁ mananaṁ prāhuḥ trakaraḥ trāṇam ucyate,

manana trāṇa saṅyukto mantra iti abhidhīyate;

SVRS. Bh., aph.1, p.3.

[53] ...jīva ātma saṅjñayoḥ aikyaṁ mantra iti abhidhīyate;

ibid., loc. cit.

[54] ātmaivākhaṇḍākāraḥ;

SVRS., aph.2, p.6.

[55] SVRS. Bh., aph.2, p.7, lines 2-3.

[56] jīvātmanaḥ tu akhaṇḍākāratvaṁ bhrānti tayā vyavahṛta jīvahṛta jīvatva vicāre yathā bhrāntis tadvat;

SVRS. Bh., aph.2, p.7.

[57] caitanya svarūpā cit śaktiḥ;

SVRS., aph.3, p.7.

[58] saiveyam anāmākhyā śrīvidyā;

ibid., aph.4, p.9.

[59] ya iyam eva cit sā anāmākhyā prathamā vidyā.... ;

SVRS. Bh., aph.4, p.9, line 4.

[60] tatva trayeṇa sā vividhā;

SVRS., aph.5, p. 9.

[61] In the *samaya* tradition of *tantra* the moon, sun and fire regions represent the causal, subtle and gross (material) worlds respectively.

[62] koṇa patra samuccayaṁ cakram;

SVRS., aph.6, p.17.

[63] ibid., aph.7, p.18.

[64] ibid., aph.8, p.22.

[65] atha cintāmaṇi gṛha sthitā tripurasundarī mahāvidyā anuttarā;

ibid., aph.15, p.34.

[66] .... trayāṇāṁ purāṇāṁ triṣu lokeṣu tasyā devyāḥ saundaryeṇa samudāyaḥ tasmāt tripurasundarī..... ;

SVRS. Bh., aph.15, p.34.

[67] Vinoba Bhave, Gītā Pravacana, p.99.

[68] The *Sāmarasya* state refers to the interpenetrative indistinguishable unity of *Śiva* and *Śakti,* also known as the transcendent *Brahman*. It is beyond the realm of all kinds of duality.

[69] SVRS., aph.16, p.35.

[70] tayā mantrā anekāś ca tathā yantra tantrāṇi;

ibid., aph.17, p.36.

[71] vividha bhaktir vividhopāsanam;

ibid., aph.18, p.36.

[72] tasmāt phalāny anekāni;

ibid., aph.19, p.36.

[73] bhavāni tvāṁ vande bhava mahiṣi sac cit sukha vapuḥ parākārāṁ devīm amṛta laharīṁ baindavakalām, mahākālātītāṁ kalita saraṇī kalpit tanuṁ sudhā sindhor antaravasatim aniśaṁ vāsara mayīm;

Subh., v.1, p.1.

[74] hṛdayasthāpi lokānam adṛśyā mohanātmikā,

nāma rūpa vibhāgaṁ ca yā karoti sva līlayā;

Subh. Bh., v.1, p.6.

[75] nirvibhāga citiś ca śiva śakti sāmarasyam;

ibid., v.1, p.3.

[76] The microcosm *(piṇḍa)* is a miniature form of the macrocosm *(bhrahmāṇḍa)*, being respectively the individualistic and cosmic aspects of highest reality. *"Yat piṇḍe tat brahmāṇḍe"*, i.e., whatever is in the microcosm, is in the macrocosm (also, vice-versa) -- is a basic tenet of *tantra* philosophy.

[77] pūrṇatvaṁ sarva-bhāvānāṁ yasyā nālpaṁ na vādhikam;

Subh. Bh., v.1, p.6, line 4;

hṛdayasth-āpi lokānam adṛśyā mohanātmikā,

nāma rūpa vibhāgaṁ ca yā karoti sva-līlayā;

ibid., v.1, p.6, line 1-2.

[78] ...sphurati bahir antar bhagvatī parānandakārā paraśiva parā...;

Subh., v.2, p.11.

[79] N.K. Devaraja, 'Self and Freedom: The Vedāntic and Phenomenological

Perspectives' in Philosophy, Grammar and Indology, p.83.

[80] ...suṣumnāṁ saṅyojya ślathayati ca ṣaḍ granthi śaśinaṁ,

tavājñā cakrasthaṁ vilayati mahāyogi samayī;

ibid., v.3, p.17;

also, Cf. v.4.

[81] ...paraṁ tattvātītaṁ milita vapur indoḥ para kalā;

ibid., v.5, p.28.

[82] ...sudhā sindhau tasmin sura maṇi gṛhe sūrya śaśinor agamye raśmīnāṁ samaya sahite tvaṅ viharase;

ibid., v.7, p.38.

[83] tri khaṇḍaṁ te cakraṁ.................prabhṛti tava ṣaṭ cakra sadanam;

ibid., v.8, p.43.

[84] ...tvac caraṇagā mahākālas tasmān na hi tava śive kāla kalanā;

ibid., v.9, p.47.

[85] ibid., v.10, p.52.

[86] ....catuś cakraṁ śaivaṁ nivasati bhage śāktikamume ...;

ibid., v.11, p.60.

[87] ...tritaya vibhavaikyaṁ para śive tad evaṁ ṣoḍhaikyaṁ bhavati..;

ibid., v.12, p.65.

[88] ibid., v.13, p.70.

[89] ibid., v.17, p.93.

[40] ...śubhākhyāḥ pañcaitāḥ śruti saraṇi siddhāḥ prakṛtayo,

mahā vidyās tāsāṁ bhavati paramārthā bhagavatī;

ibid., v.18, p.98.

[41] The *śubhāgama pañcaka* are the saṁhitas of Vaśiṣṭha, Śuka, Sanaka, Sanandana and Sanatkumāra.

[92] Subh., v.19, p.104.

[93] ibid., v.20, p.113.

[94] ibid., v.23, p.129.

[95] ....pare sādākhye 'smin nivasati caturdhaikya kalanāt...;

Subh., v.24, p.135.

[96] ibid., v.25, p.139.

[97] imāstāḥ ṣoḍaśyās tava ca saraghāyāṁ śaśi kalā svarūpāyāṁ līnā nivasati...;

ibid., v.26, p.146.

[98] ....maṇi dhanur itīdaṁ samayinaḥ...;

ibid., v.28, p.159.

[99] ...viśuddhy ākhye cakre viyad uditam āhuḥ samayinaḥ...;

ibid., v.29, p.165.

[100] ...sahasrāre cakre nivasati kalā pañca daśakaṁ...;

ibid., v.30, p.169.

[101] kalāyāḥ ṣoḍaśyāḥ pratiphalita bimbena sahitaṁ,

tadīyaiḥ pīyūṣaiḥ punar adhikam āhlādita tanuḥ...;

ibid., v.31, p.174.

[102] ..śuciḥ svādhiṣṭhāne ravir upari saṁvit sarsije,

śaśī cājñā cakre hari hara vidhi granthaya ime;

ibid., v.32, p.180.

[103] ...sūrya śaśinau tamasy ādhāre tau yadi tu militau sā tithir amā,

tad ājñā cakrasthaṁ śiśira kara bimbaṁ ravi nibhaṁ,

dṛḍhavyālīḍhaṁ sad vigalita sudhā sāra visaram;

ibid., v.33, p.186.

[104] ibid., v.34, p.191.

[105] tato gatvā jyotsnāmaya samaya lokaṁ samayināṁ,

parākhyā sādākhyā jayati śiva tattvena militā....;

ibid., v.35, p.198.

106 ...tvaṁ ṣaḍ viṁśā bhavasi śivayor melana vapuḥ...;

ibid., v.36, p.206.

107 ....kriyā'vasthā rūpaṁ prakṛtir abhidhā pañcaka samaṁ...;

ibid., v.39, p.223.

108 bhaven mūlādhāraṁ tad upari tanaṁ cakram api tad,

dvayaṁ tāmisrākhyaṁ .... vāmākhyaṁ matam api parityājyam ubhayam;

ibid., v.42, p.240.

109 nava vyūhaṁ kaula prabhṛtika mataṅ tena sa vibhur

navātmā devo'yaṁ jagad udayakṛd bhairava vapuḥ,

navātmā vāmādi prakṛtibhir iyaṁ baindava vapu

mahādevī tābhyāṁ janaka jananī maj jagad idam;

ibid., v.44, p.250.

110 ...tadevaiko bindur bhavati jagad utpattikṛd ayam;

ibid., v.46, p.263.

111 ...mahāntaḥ sevante sakala jananīṁ baindava gṛhe,

śivākārāṁ nityām amṛta jharikām aindava kalām;

Subh., v.49, p.280.

112 idaṁ kaulotpatti sthiti layakaraṁ padma nikaraṁ,

tri khaṇḍaṁ śrī cakraṅ manur api ca teṣāṁ ca milanam,

tad aikyaṁ ṣoḍhā vā bhavati ca caturdheti ca tathā,

tayoḥ sāmyaṁ pañca prakṛtikam idaṅ śāstram uditam;

ibid., v.50, p.298.

113 ...sahasrāre padme subhaga subhagodeti subhage,

paraṁ saubhāgyaṁ yat tad iha tava sāyujya padavī;

Subh., v.51, p.300.

114 ...tayā viddho yogī vicarati niśāyām api divā,

divā bhānū rātrau vidhur iva kṛtārthī kṛta matiḥ;

ibid., v.52, p.306.

115 bahiṣ prajño vibhur viśvo hy antaḥ prajñas tu taijasaḥ,

ghana prajñas tathā prājña eka eva tridhā smṛtaḥ;

Mā. Kā., I-1, p.185.

116 ...ānandabhuk tathā prājñas tridhā bhogaṁ nibodhat ;

ibid., I-3, p.191.

117 ...vedaitad ubhayaṁ yastu sa bhuñjāno na lipyate;

ibid., I-5, p.192.

118 nivṛtteḥ sarva duḥkhānām īśānaḥ prabhur avyayaḥ;

ibid.,I-10, p.206.

119 kārya kāraṇa baddhau tāviṣy ete viśva taijasau,

prājñaḥ kāraṇa baddhas tu dvau tau turye na sidhyataḥ;

ibid., I-11, p.207.

120 Ramakant Tripathi, Spinoza in the Light of the Vedānta, p.103-4.

121 ... prājñaḥ kiñca na saṁvetti turyaṁ tat sarva dṛk sadā;

Mā.Kā., I-12, p.208.

122 dvaitasyāgrahṇaṁ tulyam ubhayoḥ prājña turyayoḥ,

bīja nidrā yutaḥ prājñaḥ sā ca turye na vidyate; ibid., I-13, p.209.

123 anādi māyayā sup to yadā jīvaḥ prabudhyate,

ajam anidram asvapnam advaitaṅ budhyate tadā;

ibid., I-16, p.211.

124 ..māyā mātram idaṁ dvaitam advaitaṁ paramārthataḥ;

ibid., I-17, p.213.

[125] ...upadeśād ayaṁ vādo jñāte dvaitaṁ na vidyate;

ibid., I-18, p.213.

[126] ibid., I-22, p.220.

[127] akāro nayate viśvam ukāraś cāpi taijasam,

makāraś ca punaḥ prājñaṁ nāmātre vidyate gatiḥ;

ibid., I-23, p.220.

[128] praṇavo hy aparaṁ brahma praṇavaś ca paraḥ smṛtaḥ;

ibid., I-26, p.224.

[129] sarvasya praṇavo hy ādir madhyam antas tathaiva ca,

evaṁ hi praṇavaṁ jñātvā vyaśnute tad anantaram;

Mā.Kā., I-27, p.225.

[130] amātro'anant amātraś ca dvaitasyopaśamaḥ śivaḥ,

oṅkāro vidito yena sa munir netaro janaḥ;

ibid., I-29, p.226.

[131] vaitathyaṁ sarva bhāvānāṁ svapne āhur manīṣiṇaḥ;

ibid., II-1, p.227.

[132] ādāvante ca yan nāsti vartamāne'api tat tathā,

vitathaiḥ sadṛśāḥ santo'vitathā iva lakṣitāḥ;

ibid., II-6, p.231.

[133] ibid., II-7, p.232.

[134] ibid., II-9, p.235.

[135] kalpayaty ātmanā' 'ātmānam ātmā devaḥ sva māyayā,

sa eva budhyate bhedān iti vedānta niścayaḥ;

ibid., II-12, p.237;

also, vikaroty aparān bhāvān antaś citte vyavasthitān,

niyatāṁś ca bahiś citta evaṁ kalpayate prabhuḥ;

ibid., II-13, p.238.

[136] jīvaṁ kalpayate pūrvaṁ tato bhāvān pṛthag vidhān;

ibid., II-16, p.240.

[137] aniścitā yathā rajjur andhakāre vikalpitā,

sarpa dhārādibhir bhāvais tad vad ātmā vikalpitaḥ;

ibid., II-17, p.242.

[138] niścitāyāṁ yathā rajjvāṁ vikalpo vinivartate,

rajjur eveti cādvaitaṁ tad vad ātma viniścayaḥ;

ibid., II-18, p.242.

[139] ...māyaiṣā tasya devasya yayā saṁmohitaḥ svayam;

ibid., II-19, p.243.

[140] svapna māye yathā dṛṣṭe gandharva nagaraṁ yathā,

tathā viśvam idaṁ dṛṣṭaṁ vedānteṣu vicakṣaṇaiḥ;

ibid., II-31, p.250.

[141] na nirodho na cotpattir na baddho na ca sādhakaḥ,

na mumukṣur na vai mukta ity eṣā paramārthatā;

ibid., II-32, p.251.

[142] bhāvair asadbhir evāyam advayena ca kalpitaḥ,

bhāvā apy advayenaiva tasmād advayatā śivā;

ibid., II-33, p.256.

[143] yathā na jāyate kiṅcij jāyamānaṁ samantataḥ;

ibid., III-2, p.265.

[144] ātmā hy ākāśavaj jīvair ghaṭākāśair iveditaḥ...;

ibid., III-3, p.267.

[145] ghaṭādiṣu pralīneṣu ghaṭākāśādayo yathā,

ākāśe saṅpralīyante tadvaj jīvā ihātmani;

Mā.Kā., III-4, p.268.

[146] yathaik asmin ghaṭākāśe rajo dhūmādibhir yute,

na sarve saṅprayujyante tadvaj jīvāḥ sukhādibhiḥ;

ibid., III-5, p.269.

[147] nākāśasya ghaṭākāśo vikārāvayavau yathā,

naivātmanaḥ sadā jīvo vikārāvayavau tathā;

ibid., III-7, p.274.

[148] saṅghātāḥ svapnavat sarve ātmamāyā visarjitāḥ,

ādhikye sarva sāmye vā nopapattir hi vidyate;

ibid., III-10, p.277.

[149] rasādayo hi ye kośā......teṣām ātmā paro jīvaḥ....;

ibid., III-11, p.278.

[150] jīvātmanoḥ pṛthaktvaṁ yat prāg utpatteḥ prakīrtitam,

bhaviṣyad vṛttyā gauṇaṁ tan mukhyatvaṁ hi na yujyate;

ibid., III-14, p.281.

[151] mṛl loha visphuliṅgādyaiḥ sṛṣṭir yā coditā 'nyathā,

upāyaḥ so 'vatārāya nāsti bhedaḥ kathaṅcana;

ibid., III-15, p.283.

[152] māyayā bhidhyate hy etan nānyathā 'jaṅ kathañcana,

tattvato bhidyamāne hi martyatām amṛtaṁ vrajet;

ibid., III-19, p.289.

[153] bhūtato'bhūtato vā'pi sṛjyamāne samā śrutiḥ,

niścitaṁ yukti yuktaṁ ca yat tad bhavati netarat;

ibid., III-23, p.293.

[154] sato hi māyayā janma yujyate na tu tattvataḥ,

tattvato jāyate yasya jātaṁ tasya hi jāyate;

ibid., III-27, p.300.

[155] asato māyayā janma tattvato naiva yujyate,

bandhyā putro na tattvena māyayā vā'pi jāyate;

ibid., III-28, p.301.

[156] akalpakam ajaṁ jñānaṁ jñeyābhinnaṅ pracakṣate,

brahma jñeyam ajaṁ nityam ajenājaṁ vibudhyate;

ibid., III-33, p.305.

[157] ibid., III-34, p.306.

[158] līyate hi suṣupte tan nigṛhītaṁ na līyate,

tad eva nirbhayaṁ brahma jñānālokaṅ samantataḥ;

ibid., III-35, p.307.

[159] ajam anidram asvapnam anāmakam arūpakam,

sakṛd vibhātaṁ sarvajñaṁ nopacāraḥ kathañcana;

ibid., III-36, p.308.

[160] manaso nigrahāyat tam abhayaṁ sarva yogināṁ,

duḥkha kṣayaḥ prabodhaś cāpy akṣayā śāntir eva ca;

ibid., III-40, p.314.

[161] duḥkhaṁ sarvam anusmṛtya kāma bhogān nivartayet,

ajaṁ sarvam anusmṛtya jātaṁ naiva tu paśyati;

ibid., III-43, p.316.

[162] laye saṁbodhayec cittaṁ vikṣiptaṁ śamayet punaḥ,

sakaṣāyaṁ vijānīyāt sama prāptaṁ na cālayet;

ibid., III-44, p.317.

[163] nāsvādayet sukhaṁ tatra niḥsaṅgaḥ prajñayā bhavet,

niścalaṁ niścarac cittam ekī kuryāt prayatnataḥ;

ibid., III-45, p.317.

[164] yadā na līyate cittaṁ na ca vikṣipyate punaḥ,

aniṅganam anābhāsaṁ niṣpannaṁ brahma tat tadā;

ibid., III-46, p.318.

[165] svasthaṁ śāntaṁ sanirvāṇam akathyaṁ sukham uttamam;

ibid., III-47, p.319.

[166] ...etat tad uttamaṁ satyaṁ yatra kiñcin na jāyate;

ibid., III-48, p.320.

[167] jarā maraṇa nirmuktāḥ sarve dharmāḥ svabhāvataḥ,

jarā maraṇam icchantaś cyavante tan manīṣayā;

ibid., IV-10, p.329.

[168] ibid., IV-16, p.334.

[169] ...evaṁ hi sarvathā buddhair ajātiḥ paridīpitā;

ibid., IV-19, p.336.

[170] pūrvāparā parijñanam ajāteḥ paridīpakam...;

ibid., IV-21, p.338.

[171] svato vā parato vā'pi na kiṅcid vastu jāyate,

sad asat sadasad vā'api na kiṅcid vastu jāyate;

ibid., IV-22, p.339.

[172] nimittaṁ na sadā cittaṁ saṅspṛśaty adhvasu triṣu,

animitto viparyāsaḥ kathaṁ tasya bhaviṣyati;

ibid., IV-27, p.346.

[173] tasmān na jāyate cittaṁ citta dṛśyaṁ na jāyate,

tasya paśyanti ye jātiṅ khe vai paśyanti te padam;

ibid., IV-28, p.347.

[174] upalambhāt samācārād asti vastutva vādinām,

jātis tu deśitā buddhair ajātes trasatāṁ sadā;

ibid., IV-42, p.358.

[127] jāty ābhāsaṁ calābhāsaṁ vastvābhāsaṁ tathaiva ca,

ajācalam avastutvaṁ vijñānaṁ śāntam advayam;

ibid., IV-45, p.361.

[176] ṛju vakrādikābhāsam alāta spanditaṁ yathā,

grahaṇa grāhakābhāsaṁ vijñāna spanditaṁ tathā;

ibid., IV-47, p.362.

[177] ...kṣīṇe hetu phalāveśe saṅsāraṁ na prapadyate;

ibid., IV-56, p.369.

[178] Pandeya, R. C. and Manju, 'Pūrva Mīmāṁsā and Vedānta' in Companion

Encyclopedia of Asian Philosophy, p.183f.

[179] saṁvṛtyā jāyate sarvaṁ śāśvataṁ nāsti tena vai,

sad bhāvena hy ajaṁ sarvam ucchedas tena nāsti vai;

Mā.Kā., IV-57, p.369.

[180] dharmā yā iti jāyante jāyante te na tattvataḥ,

janma māyopamaṁ teṣāṁ sā ca māyā na vidyate;

ibid., IV-58, p.370.

[181] nājeṣu sarva dharmeṣu śāśvatāśāśvatābhidhā,

yatra varṇā na vartante vivekas tatra nocyate;

ibid., IV-60, p.372.

[182] na kaścij jāyate jīvaḥ saṁbhavo'sya na vidyate,

etat tad uttamaṁ satyaṁ yatra kiṅcin na jāyate;

Mā.Kā., IV-71, p.377.

[183] ādi buddhāḥ prakṛtyaiva sarve dharmāḥ suniścitāḥ,

yasyaivaṁ bhavati kṣāntiḥ so'mṛta tatvāya kalpate;

ibid., IV-92, p.396.

[184] B.K. Matilal, Logic, Language & Reality, p.288.

[185] Refer to section 4, chapter 1, for a detailed discussion of the explicit and implicit aspects of advaitika devotion.

[186] There are thirty-five glosses of Saundarya-laharī extant in various parts of India and Nepal, out of which only one attributes its authorship to a person other than Śaṅkara. Cf. S. laharī, Introduction, p.xi.

[187] śivaḥ śaktyā yukto yadi bhavati śaktaḥ prabhavituṁ,

na cedevaṁ devo na khalu kuśalaḥ spanditum api;

atas tvām ārādhyāṁ hari hara viriñcādi bhir api,

praṇantuṁ stotuṁ vā katham akṛtapuṇyaḥ prabhavati; S. laharī, v.1, p.8.

[188] P.T. Raju, Structural Depths of Indian Thought, p.395.

[189] sa eṣa neti nety ātmā ....na riṣyati; Bṛ.Up.(tr.), IV-v-15, p.543;

also,

turīyā kāpi tvaṁ duradhigama niḥsīma mahimā,

mahāmāyā viśvaṁ bhramayasi para brahma mahiṣi; S.L., v.97, p.II-277a;

also,

"Hence the conclusion is that the phenomenal expressions, imagined on *Brahman*, are denied, and *Brahman* stands out as outside the negation."; B. S. Bh. (tr.), III-ii-22, p.627;

also,

manasaivānudraṣṭavyam, neha nā nāsti kiñcana; Bṛ.Up.(tr.), IV-iv-19, p.517;

also,

ekadhaivānudraṣṭavyam etad pramayaṁ dhruvam,

virajaḥ para ākāśād aja ātmā mahān dhruvaḥ; ibid., IV-iv-20, p.517;

also,

nāntaḥ prajñaṁ na bahiṣ prajñaṁ nobhayataḥ prajñaṁ na prajñāna ghanaṁ na prajñaṁ

nāprajñaṁ. adṛṣṭam avyavahāryam agrāhyam alakṣaṇam acintyam avyapadeśyam

ekātma pratyayasāraṁ prapañcopaśamaṁ śāntaṁ śivam advaitaṁ caturthaṁ manyate

sa ātmā sa vijñeyaḥ;

Mā.Up.(tr.), 7, p.200;

also,

paraṁ tattvātītaṁ milita vapur indoḥ para kalā; Subh., v.5, p.28;

also,

jñātṛ jñeya jñāna śūnyam anantaṁ nirvikalpam,

kevalākhaṇḍa cinmātraṁ paraṁ tattvaṁ vidur budhāḥ; Viv. Cd., v.239, p.92.

190 ataḥ śeṣaḥ śeṣīty ayam ubhaya sādhāraṇatayā,

sthitaḥ saṅbandho vāṅ samarasa parānanda parayoḥ; S. laharī, v.34, p.138;

also,

paraṁ tattvātītaṁ milita vapur indoḥ para kalā; Subh., v.5, p.28;

also,

sudhā sindhau tasmin suramaṇi gṛhe sūrya śaśinor

agamye raśmīnāṁ samaya sahite tvaṅ viharase; ibid., v.7, p.38.

also,

śivākāre mañce parama śiva paryaṅka nilayāṁ

bhajanti tvāṁ dhanyāḥ katicana cid ānanda laharīm; S. laharī, v.8, p.44.

191 ity ato'smat pratyaya gocare viṣayiṇi cid ātmake yuṣmat pratyaya gocarasya

viṣayasya tad dharmāṇāṁ cādhyāsaḥ;

B.S.Bh., 1-1-1, pp.7-10;

also,

sarvathāpi tvanyasyānya dharmāvabhāsatāṁ na vyabhicarati; ibid., 1-1-1, p.32.

[192] aspandamānam alātam anābhāsam ajaṁ yathā,

aspandamānaṁ vijñānam anābhāsam ajaṁ tathā; Mā. Kā., IV-48, p.363;

also,

alāte spandamāne vai nābhāsā anyatobhuvaḥ,

na tato'nyatra nispandānn ālātaṁ praviśanti te; ibid., IV-49, p.364.

Spanda, in the context of consciousness, stands for an internal epistemic activity within pure consciousness, which leads to an appearance of polarization in the form of subject *(jñātā)* and object *(jñeya)*. Presence or absence of *spanda* in the non-dual pure consciousness is responsible for the epistemic appearance or disappearance of duality respectively. The operation of epistemic superimposition *(adhyāsa)* requires *spanda* or vibration in pure consciousness.

[193] In advaitism the highest reality refers to the transcendent non-dual consciousness or the *nirākāra Brahman*, which is just the same as the *saguṇa sākāra Brahman*, also known as the *Śiva-Śakti Sāmarasya* in the *samaya tantra*. It is the highest reality since it involves no trace of epistemic superimposition and so there can be no further sublation of illusion at this level. With reference to this reality there are many levels of epistemic superimpositions, where each one is grounded in its preceding level of reality. In this manner, the transcendent *Brahman* alone is the ultimate ontological ground of various epistemically superimposed levels of reality.

[194] akāraḥ sarva varṇāgryaḥ prakāśaḥ paramaḥ śivaḥ;

Subh. Bh., v.36, p.208;

also,

vaśati prakāśate svayaṁ prakāśa iti, yadvā, svasmin prapañcaṁ prakāśayatīti śivaḥ;

yadvā'śīṁ svapna'ity asmād dhātoḥ śiva śabdo niṣpannaḥ;

S.L.Bh. (Lakṣmīdharā), v.1, p.I-2.

195 nityaḥ sarvagataḥ sūkṣmaḥ sadānando nirāmayaḥ,

vikāra rahitaḥ sākṣī śivo jñeyaḥ sanātanaḥ; Subh. Bh., v.2, p.16.

196 eka eva prakāś ākhyaḥ paraḥ ko'pi maheśvaraḥ,

yasya śaktir vimarś ākhyā sā nityā gīyate budhaiḥ; Subh. Bh., v.20, p.114;

also,

vimarśa rūpiṇī nityā ṣoḍaśī yā prakīrtitā; ibid., v.26, p.148;

also,

akāraḥ sarva varṇāgryaḥ prakāśaḥ paramaḥ śivaḥ,

hakāro'ntyaḥ kalā rūpo vimarś ākhyaḥ prakīrtitaḥ,

ubhayoḥ sāmarasyaṁ yat parasminnahami sphuṭam; ibid., v.27, p.155

197 bhajanti tvāṁ dhanyāḥ katicana cidānanda laharīm; S. laharī, v.8, p.44;

also,

mahāntaḥ paśyanto dadhati param āhlāda laharīm; ibid., v.21, p.93;

also,

bhavāni tvāṁ vande bhava mahiṣi sac cit sukha vapuḥ,

parākārāṁ devīm amṛta laharīṁ baindava kalām; Subh., v.1, p.1.

198 supra 188.

199 *Samaya tantra* or *samaya mārga* is that tradition of *tantra* which is perfectly in tune with the Vedic philosophy, aiming for the highes *mokṣa* described in the upaniṣads. It emphasizes the importance of meditating upon the immanence of the trandcendent non-dual

reality, along with one's own basic identity with that absolute reality. This tradition is based on the works of five great seers, called the *śubhāgama pañcaka*. These seers are Vaśiṣṭha, Śuka, Sanaka, Sanandana and Sanatkumāra.

200 tvam eva svātmānaṁ pariṇamayituṁ viśva vapuṣā,

cid ānandākāraṁ śiva yuvati bhāvena bibhṛṣe; S. laharī, v.35, p.140;

also,

vadanty eke santaḥ paraśiva pade tattva milite,

tatas tvaṁ ṣaḍviṅśā bhavasi śivayor melan vapuḥ; Subh., v.36, p.206.

201 avyakta nāmni parameśa śaktir anādy avidyā triguṇātmikā parā,

kāryānumeyā sudhiyaiva māyā yayā jagat sarvam idaṁ prasūyate;

Viv. Cd., v.108, p.39;

also,

"It has been said earlier that a kaleidoscopic phenomenal creation can very well stem out from the same *Brahman* on account of Its being endowed with multifaroius powers. *Opponent* : How, again, is it known that the supreme *Brahman* is endowed with diverse powers? *Vedāntin* : That is being answered: "The supreme Deity is possessed of all powers, it having been revealed thus." It has to be accepted that the supreme Deity is endowed with all powers."

B.S.Bh. (tr.), II-i-30, pp.358f.

202 tanīyāsāṁ pāṅsuṁ tava ....bhasitod dhūlana vidhim;

S. laharī, v.2, p.26.

203 *Vimarśa* stands for the reflective objectivity required to manifest the illuminative power or *prakāśa śakti* of *Śiva*. As such, when the primordial vibration takes place in pure conscoiusness, the subject-object polarity is epistemically projected, in which *Śiva* and *Śakti* represent the illuminative *(prakāśa)* and reflective *(vimarśa)* aspects.

[204] Cf. S. laharī, v.41, p.157.

[205] Cf. Subh., v.44, p.250.

[206] Prapañcasāra tantra, I-41, p.16.

[207] supra 203, 204.

[208] akāraś cā'py ukāraś ca makāro bindur eva ca,

nādaś ca śaktiḥ śāntaś ca tāra bhedāḥ samīritāḥ;
Prapañcasāra tantra, II-60-1, p.36.

[209] supra 207.

[210] supra 207.

[211] avidyānām antas timira mihira dvīpa nagarī ....mura ripu varāhasya bhavatī;

S. laharī, v.3, p.30.

[212] Manju, Advaitavāda aura Śūnyavāda, p.81.

[213] ....maheśi smṛte bodha rūpe'py abodha svarūpe;

Prapañcasāra tantra, v.67, p.159.

[214] tvad anyaḥ pāṇibhyām abhaya varado..............tava hi caraṇāv eva nipiṇau;

S. laharī, v.4, p.34.

[215] Mā.Up.(tr.), 8, p.214;

also,

ibid., 12, p.221.

[216] supra 207.

[217] The macrocosmic subject aspect in this case is called *Virāṭ* and the corresponding object aspect is the gross universe *(sthūla jagat),* whereas the microcosmic subject and object aspects are *Vaiśvānara* and the gross body *(sthūla śarīra)* respectively.

also,

Cf. Mā.Up.(tr.), 3, p.176.

[218] The gross universe stands for the totality of all tangible and material entities.

[219] Cf. Mā.Up.(tr.), 10-11, pp.216f;

also,

The subtle and causal level macrocosmic subjects are known as *Hiraṇyagarbha* and *Īśvara* respectively, which have as their corresponding objective aspects the subtle and the causal worlds respectively. The subtle and causal microcosmic subjects are *Taijasa* and *Prājña* respectively, which have as their objective aspects the subtle and causal bodies respectively.

[220] It is the sum of all subtle bodies and objects of the universe.

[221] It is the sum of all causal bodies and objects in the universe.

[222] This is the last limit of immanent dualism.

[223] Cf. Pañcīkaraṇam.

[224] It is the microcosmic manifestation of *Śakti*. It moves along the *suṣ umṇā* nerve in the subtle body. Its level of rise in the *suṣumṇā* pathway reflects the level of conscoius-ness of the *jīva.*

[225] The *Rudra granthi, Viṣṇu granthi, Brahma granthi* and the *bindu* are situated just a little above the *maṇipūra cakra, anāhata cakra, ājñā cakra* and the *Brahma granthi* respectively.

[226] In the *samaya* tradition *Śiva* and *Śakti* symbolically represent the subjective and objec-tive aspects of any cognitive process. *Śiva* stands for the cognitive and illuminative aspect or the *prakāśa* aspect of any cognition, whereas *Śakti* represents the cognized, illumined and reflective aspect or the *vimarśa* aspect of any cognition. In all pheno-menal cognitions the subject-object dichotomy is there and that is represented by the *Śiva-Śakti* dualism at all the planes of phenomenal existence, whether gross, subtle or causal. Only at the level of transcendent *Brahman* the dichotomy of subject and object is completely sublated and therefore it is said in the *samaya* tradition that in the tran-scendent state of *Śiva-Śakti Sāmarasya* there is no distinction between them at all.

[227] haris tvām ārādhya ....hi mohāya mahatām;

S. laharī, v.5, p.36.

[228] The *tantra* traditon of *kaula mārga* treats both material and spiritual aspirations as acceptable. Unlike the *samaya mārga* it does not treat the highest spiritual realization alone as the desirable goal. Also, unlike the *samaya mārga,* it advocates the external worship of *Śakti* with the help of various symbols. Further, it aslo gives a special place to the *pañca makāras* in the worship of *Śakti*.

[229] Maurice Winternitz, History of Indian Literature, vol. I, p.246.

[230] dhanuḥ pauṣpaṁ maurvī ....jagad idam anaṅgo vijayate;

ibid., v.6, p.40.

[231] kvaṇat kāñcī dāmā ....pura mathitur āho puruṣikā;

ibid., v.7, p.41.

[232] ataḥ aho ahaṁ bhāvaḥ - āho puruṣikā ahaṅkāra iti yāvat;

S.L.Bh. (Lakṣmīdharā), v.7, p.I-86.

[233] S. laharī, p.43.

[234] Such samādhi stands for the highest possible intuitive realization of the non-dual, absolute and transcendent nature of reality. The subject-object dichotomy of con-sciousness is sublated in this state. Attaining this state one becomes a *jīvanmukta.* All his karma-seeds get burnt up, except the fructifying ones or the *prārabdha karma.*

[235] Y.S.V., I-51, II-29,30 and 31.

[236] Manju, Advaitavāda aura Śūnyavāda, p.73.

[237] *Prārabdha karmas* refer to those *karmas* which have already started fructifying, i.e., giving their results, and are responsible for the present phenomenal existence.

[238] The *nāda* point in the path of the *kuṇḍalinī* corresponds with the *nāda* component of *AUM*. It is the level of the primordial epistemic dualism, represented by the mani-festations of *Śiva* and *Śakti* as *Sadāśiva* and *Śuddha vidyā* respectively. At this level, there is no illusion but only the first epistemic projection of duality.

[239] *Sahasrāra* or the thousand-petalled lotus is the last station in the path of *kuṇḍalinī*. It corresponds with the *śakti* and *śānta* components of *AUM*, i.e., with the *turīya* or fourth quarter of *AUM*. It represents the non-dual and transcendent *Brahman*, the *para Brahman* or the *Śiva-Śakti Sāmarasya*.

[240] The devotional inclination towards the personal forms of *Śiva* and *Śakti* (at the *nāda* level), or towards the impersonal form of *Śiva* and *Śakti* as the transcendent *Sāmarasya* state, is crucial for the course of merger of the *jīva's* consciousness after the exhaustion of the fructifying or *prārabdha karmas*.

[241] *Videhamukti* stands for the final annihilation of the individuality of the *jīva cidābhāsa* and the resultant irreversible merger of one's consciousness in *Brahman*, either in its personal or impersonal aspect.

also,

Cf. Y.S.V., IV-34, p.417.

[242] S.L. (tr.), v.7, p.12.

[243] rāga svarūpa pāśāḍhyā krodhākārāṅkuśojjvalā,

manorūpekṣukodaṇḍā pañca tanmātra sāyakā; L.S., vv.54-55, p.191.

[244] icchā śaktimayaṁ pāśaṁ aṅkuśaṁ jñāna rūpiṇaṁ,

kriyā śaktimayaṁ bāṇa dhanuṣi dadhadujjvalaṁ;

S.L.(tr.), v.7, p.13.

[245] sudhā sindhor madhye ....katicana cid ānanda laharīm;

S.laharī, v.8, p.44.

[246] *Śrīcakra* symbolically represents the transcendent as well as the various immanent levels of the manifestatons of *Brahman*, or *Śiva* and *Śakti*.

[247] The nine *āvaraṇa-s* or *cakra-s* of the *śrīcakra* are the outermost quadrangular peri-meter or *bhūpura,* the sixteen-petalled lotus or *ṣ oḍaśāra,* the eight-petalled lotus or the *aṣṭa dala padma,* the

fourteen angles or *catur daśāra,* the outer ten angles or *bahir daśāra,* the inner ten angles or *antar daśāra,* the eight angles or *aṣṭ āra,* the triangle or *trikoṇa* and the centre point or *bindu.*

248 The correspondence existing between the various points of the *kuṇḍaliṇī* pathway and the *āvaraṇa-s* of the *śrīcakra* is as follows. The *kula sahasrāra* or the lower thousand petalled lotus corresponds with the *bhūpura* of *śrīcakra,* the *mūlādhāra cakra* with the *mekhalā traya* and *ṣoḍaśāra,* the *maṇipūra cakra* with the *aṣṭa dala padma,* the *svādhiṣṭhāna cakra* with the *catur daśāra,* the *anāhata cakra* with the *bahir daśāra,* the *viśuddhi cakra* with the *antar daśāra,* the *ājñā cakra* with the *aṣṭāra,* the *bindu* with the *trikoṇa,* the *nāda* with the *bindu* or centre-point, and the *sahasrāra* with the *mahā bindu* of the *śrīcakra.*

249 The yoga and *tantra* texts describe the *suṣumṇā* nerve as the most important nerve, extending from the base of the spine and going up to the cranium. However, it is said to be located in the subtle body and not the gross material body.

250 sṛṣṭi cakraṁ sudhā sindhuḥ saubhāgyaṁ sura vāṭikā

daśāra yugalaṁ ratna dvīpaṁ nīpa vanaṁ tathā,

cintāmaṇi gṛhaṁ ramyam aṣṭāraṁ parameśvari

trikoṇaṁ mañca rūpaṁ tu bindu cakraṁ sadāśivaḥ;

Subh. Bh., v.36, p.211.

251 bindu rūpaṁ paraṁ brahma sahasra dala saṅsthitam;

ibid., v.36, p.211.

252 sahasrāre padme saha rahasi patyā viharase;

S. laharī, v.9, p.49.

253 sudhā sindhau tasmin sura maṇi gṛhe sūrya śaśinor

agamye raśmīnāṁ samaya sahite tvaṅ viharse;

Subh., v.7, p.38.

254 ibid., v.36, p.206.

255 S. laharī, p.49.

[256] ibid., p.49;

also,

akāraḥ sarva varṇāgryaḥ prakāśaḥ paramaḥ śivaḥ

hakāro'ntya kalā rūpo vimarśākhyaḥ prakīrtitaḥ,

anayoḥ sāmarasyaṁ yat parasmin mahasi sphuṭam;

Subh. Bh., v.36, p.208.

[257] tasyābhyantara vartini śivākāre brahma viṣṇu rudreśvarākhyaiḥ caturbhiḥ śivaiḥ

mañca pāda catuṣṭayatāmāpannaiḥ;

S.L.Bh. (Tātparyadīpinī), v.8, p.I-97.

[258] tan mātrāvabhāsa kāle'paraṁ sāmarasyaṁ jīvan mukta gamyam. paramaṁ tu sāma-

rasyaṁ videha mukta mātra gamyam iti rahasyam;

Subh. Bh., v.36, p.209.

[259] supra 254.

[260] mahīṁ mūlādhāre kam api ....padme saha rahasi patyā viharase;

S. laharī, v.9, p.49.

[261] idānīṁ sūkṣma dhyānamāha-mahīm iti;

S.L.Bh. (Saubhāgyavardhanī), v.9, p.I-103.

[262] kaṁ udaka tattvam;

ibid. (Lakṣmīdharā), v.9, p.I-101.

[263] S. laharī, pp.57f.

[264] Subh., v.28, p.159.

[265] Mā.Up.(tr.), 4 and 5, pp. 179 and 181.

[266] śarīra dvaya kāraṇam ātmājñānaṁ sābhāsam avyākṛtam ity ucyate. etet kāraṇa śarīram ātmanaḥ;

Pañcī., p.3.

[267] Subh., v.5, p.28.

also,

Cf. S. laharī, p.53.

[268] Subh., vv.35,36, pp.198, 206.

[269] Cf. V.P., VIII-29,30, pp.122f.

[270] apañcīkṛta pañca mahā bhūtāni ....etet sūkṣma śarīram ātmanaḥ;

Pañcī., p.2.

[271] S.V.R., pp.104f.

[272] The causal world contains the seeds of the subtle and gross worlds and it is clearly an epistemic projection by *Īśvara,* effected with the cooperation of *māyā.*

[273] The blissful sheath is the primary objective counterpart of the *jīva cidābhāsa.* That is, at the microcosmic level, this sheath is the primary representation of the *Śakti* aspect with respect to the *jīva.* Therefore, the totality of all blissful sheaths constitutes the blissful form of *Māyā,* serving as the objective counterpart of *Īśvara.*

[274] Y.S.V., I-51, pp.171f.

[275] Cf. S. laharī, v.7, p.44.

[276] Merger of one's consciousness in that of *Sadāśiva* or the absolute non-dual *Brahman* is equally irreversible and free from all traces of *avidyā.* At the *nāda* level, the obstructive power *(āvaraṇa śakti)* of *māyā* is completely ineffective.

[277] tan mātrāvabhāsa kāle'paraṁ sāmarasyaṁ jīvan mukta gamyam;

Subh. Bh., v.36, p.209.

[278] paramaṁ tu sāmarasyaṁ videha mukta mātra gamyam iti rahasyam;

ibid., v.36, p.209.

[279] sudhā dhārā sāraiś caraṇa yuglāntar vigalitaiḥ ....kulakuṇḍe kuhariṇi;

S. laharī, v.10, p.60.

[280] ibid., p.61.

[281] teṣām apy upari tava pādāmbuja yugam;

ibid., v.14, p.75.

[282] rasāmnāyamahaḥ śabdo yāmaleṣu kalānidhau prasiddhaḥ;

S.L.Bh. (Lakṣmīdharā), v.10. p.I-111.

[283] prapañcaṁ mānasa sthānādi ṣaṭ cakra rūpaṁ kula pathaṁ siñcantī;

ibid. (Saubhāgyavardhanī), v.10, p.I-113.

[284] S.V.R., p.105.

[285] Subh., v.34, p.191.

[286] supra 273.

[287] caturbhiḥ śrīkaṇṭhaiḥ ....tava śaraṇa koṇāḥ pariṇatāḥ;

S.L., v.11, p.I-118a.

[288] ibid. (tr.), pp.23f.

[289] etac ca bhūpura trayaṁ ....śrīcakram etad uditaṁ para devatāyāḥ;

S.L.Bh. (Lakṣmīdharā), v.11, p.I-121.

[290] mūla prakṛtibhiḥ prapañcasya mūla kāraṇaiḥ; ibid., v.11, p.I-119;

also,

evaṁ piṇḍāṇḍaṁ utpannaṁ tadvat brahmāṇḍaṁ udbabhau; ibid., v.11, p.I-120.

[291] daśamī yonir ekaiva parā śaktis tad īśvarī." iti daśam yoniḥ baindava sthānam;

ibid., v.11, p.I-120;

also,

pañca bhūtāni śāktāni māyādīni śivasya tu,

māyā ca śuddha vidyā ca maheśvara sadāśivau;

ibid., v.11, p.I-120.

[292] trayaś catvāriṅśad vasu dala kalāśra tri valaya,

tri rekhābhiḥ sārdhaṁ tava śaraṇa koṇāḥ pariṇatāḥ; S. laharī, v.11, p.64;

also,

catuś catvāriṅśad vasu dala kalāśra tri valaya,

tri rekhābhiḥ sārdhaṁ tava śaraṇa koṇāḥ pariṇatāḥ; S.L., v.11, p.I-118a.

[293] supra 287.

[294] Although both the *bindu* and the *mahābindu* of *śricakra* are transcendent in nature, yet their distinction is quite clear as they respectively correspond with the primordial level of epistemic duality, of *Sadāśiva* and *Śuddha vidyā,* and the non-dual absolute reality i.e., the *Śiva-Śakti Sāmarasya.*

[295] evaṁ prakāśavirmātmakasya tattvasya prakāśāṅśa bhūtā vāmā jyeṣṭ hā raudryas

tisraḥ śaktayo brahma viṣṇu rudrāḥ puruṣāḥ, tat samaṣṭiḥ śāntātmika śaktiḥ turīyā

vimarśāṅśabhūtā;

S.V.R., śrīvidyāmantrabhāṣyam, p.294;

also,

etan mūla bhūtaṁ brahma tu turīya bindur ity ucyate;

ibid., śrīvidyāmantrabhāṣyam, p.298.

[296] Subh., v.11, p.60.

[297] ibid., v.23, p.129.

[298] tvadīyaṅ saundaryaṁ tuhina giri kanye ....giriśa sāyujya padavīm;

S.L., v.12, p.I-136.

[299] Even though a person may intuitively realize his basic identity with the transcendent reality, he has to retain his phenomenal body until the complete exhaustion of his fructifying or *prārabdha karmas.*

Thus, a jīva*nmukta* remains at the phenomenal plane as long as his *prārabdha karmas* are not fully exhausted.

300 For beholding the beauty and excellence of the *Devī,* epistemic duality is necessary. The devotees desirous of the eternal bliss of the *Devī's* company have their conscious-ness merged into that of *Sadāśiva,* consequent to the exhaustion of their *prārabdha karmas.* The level of *Sadāśiva* corresponds with that of *nāda* in the pathway of the *kuṇḍalinī.*

301 naraṁ varṣīyāṁsaṁ ....yuvatayaḥ;

S.L., v.13, p.I-141a.

302 kṣitau ṣaṭ pañcāśad dvi samadhika pañcād udake

hutāśe dvā ṣaṣṭiś catur adhika pañcāśad anile,

divi dviḥ ṣaṭ triṅśan manasi ca catuḥ ṣaṣṭir iti ye

mayūkhās teṣām apy upari tava pādāmbuja yugam;

ibid., v.14, p.I-146a.

303 The commentary on S.L. by Kaivalyāśrama.

304 prathama kūṭasya sāttvika dhyāna mahimānamāha -- śaraj jyotsneti;

S.L.Bh. (Saubhāgyavardhanī), v.15, p.I-172.

305 tasyaiva rājasa dhyānamāha -- kavīndrāṇām iti;

ibid., v.16, p.I-177.

306 The commentary on S.L. by Kāmeśvara Sūrī.

307 varo 'bhīṣṭa mudrā,...................dhṛta varādi mudrā bāhu catuṣṭ ayām ity arthaḥ;

S.L.Bh. (Aruṇāmodinī), v.15, p.I-172.

308 tanuc chāyābhis te taruṇa taraṇi śrī saraṇibhiḥ ....gīrvāṇa gaṇikāḥ;

S.L., v.18, p.I-187a.

309 madhya kūṭa dhyāna mahimānamāha -- tanuc chāyābhir iti;

S.L.Bh. (Saubhāgyavardhanī), v.18, p.I-188.

[310] mukhaṁ binduṁ kṛtvā kuca yugam adhas tasya tad adho

harārdhaṁ dhyāyed yo hara mahiṣi te manmatha kalām,

sa sadyaḥ saṅkṣobhaṁ nayati vanitā ity ati laghu

trilokīm apy āśu bhramayati ravīndu stana yugām;

S.L., v.19, p.I-192a.

[311] harārdhaṁ harasya ardhaṁ śaktiḥ trikoṇaṁ yonir iti;

S.L.Bh. (Lakṣmīdharā), v.19, p.I-192a.

[312] kirantīm aṅgebhyaḥ ....sukhyati sudhā dhāra sirayā;

S.L., v.20, p.I-200a.

[313] kāma kalāyāḥ sthūla dhyānam abhidhāya sūkṣma dhyānamāha -- taṭ illekheti;

S.L.Bh. (Saubhāgyavardhanī), v.21, p.I-205.

[314] taṭillekhā tanvīṁ tapana śaśi vaiśvānaramayīṁ

niṣaṇṇāṁ ṣaṇṇām apy upari kamalānāṁ tava kalām,

mahā padmāṭavyāṁ mṛdita mala māyena manasā

mahāntaḥ paśyanto dadhati paramāhlāda laharīm;

S.L., v.21, p.I-204a.

[315] tava bhavatyāḥ, kalāṁ sādākhyāṁ baindavī kalām;

S.L.Bh. (Lakṣmīdharā), v.21, p.I-205.

[316] bhavāni tvaṁ dāse mayi vitara dṛṣṭiṁ sakaruṇāṁ

iti stotuṁ vāñchan kathayati bhavāni tvam iti yaḥ,

tadaiva tvaṁ tasmai diśasi nija sāyujya padavīṁ

mukunda brahmendra sphuṭa makuṭa nīrājita padām;

S.L., v.22, p.I-209a.

[317] Cf. S.L. (tr.), p.47.

[318]'bhavāni tvaṁ' iti pada dvaye 'bhavāni' iti padasya loḍuttam puruṣaika vacanāntatvam avagamya tat sāmānādhikaraṇyena tvaṁ padasya anvaye mahā vākya prayogo'nena sādhakena prayukta iti matvā mahā vākya phalaṁ tādātmyaṁ diśati bhagvatī;

S.L.Bh. (Lakṣmīdharā), v.22, p.I-210.

[319] tato nididhyāsitavyo niścayena dhyātavyaḥ;

Bṛ.Up.Bh., II-iv-5, p.193.

[320] nirantarābhyāsa vaśāt tad itthaṁ pakvaṁ mano brahmaṇi līyate yadā, tadā samādhiḥ savikalpa varjitaḥ svato'dvay ānanda rasānubhāvakaḥ;
Viv.Cd., v.362, p.137.

[321] mokṣa kāraṇa sāmagryāṁ bhaktir eva garīyasi,

svarūpānusandhānaṁ bhaktir ity abhidhīyate;

ibid., v.31, p.11.

[322] tvayā hṛtvā vāmaṁ.................................kuṭila śaśi cūḍāla makutam;

S.L., v.23, p.I-215a.

[323] Manju, Advaitavāda aura Śūnyavāda, p.81.

[324] jagatsūte dhātā .... kṣaṇa calitayor bhrū latikayoḥ;

S.L., v.24, p.I-220a.

[325] tiraskurvan upasaṅharan etat dhātṛ hari rudrātmakaṁ tritayaṁ svam api svakīyam api vapuḥ dehaṁ īśaḥ maheśvara tattvaṁ tirayati antarhitaṅ karoti. īśvaraḥ dhātṛ hari rudrādīnātmany āropya svayam api sadāśiva tattve antarbhuta ity arthaḥ;

S.L.Bh. (Lakṣmīdharā), v.24, p.I-221.

[326] trayāṇāṁ devānāṁ .... śaśvan mukulita karottaṅsa makuṭ āḥ;

S.L., v.25, p.I-226a.

[327] viriñciḥ pañcatvaṁ vrajati harir āpnoti viratiṁ .... mahā saṅhāre'smin viharati sati tvat patir asau;

S.L., v.26, p.I-231a.

[328] ete sarve'py evaṁ pralayābhibhūtā .... asau khalu tvat patir iti kṛtvā asmin mahā saṅhāre'pi vilasati;

S.L.Bh. (Ānandagirīyā), v.26, p.I-233.

[329] japo jalpaḥ śilpaṁ sakalam api mudrā viracanā

gatiḥ prādakṣiṇya kramaṇam aśanādy āhuti vidhiḥ

praṇāmas saṅveśas sukham akhilam ātmārpaṇa dṛśā

saparyā paryāyas tava bhavatu yan me vilasitam;

S.L., v.27, p.I-236a.

[330] ye ye samayino yogīśvarā jīvan muktāḥ saṅsāra yātrā manuvartamānāḥ sādākhya tattvam anucintayantaḥ ātmaika pravaṇāḥ vartante teṣāṁ 'japo jalpaś śilpam' ity ādinā saparyā prakāro nirūpitaḥ;

S.L.Bh. (Lakṣmīdharā), v.27, p.I-237.

[331] jñāte vastuny api balavatī vāsanā'nādir eṣā

kartā bhoktāpy aham iti dṛdhā yā'sya saṅsāra hetuḥ,

pratyagdṛṣṭyā'tmani nivasatā sāpaneyā prayatnān

muktiṅ prāhus tad iha munayo vāsanā tānavaṅ yat;

Viv. Cd., v.267, p.104.

[332] "The inhibition holds steady for a time, and that time is experienced as progressively longer, increasing with each repitition. From that experience of the lengthening time of the steadiness of the inhibition, it is inferred that there is a *saṁskāra* produced by mind in the state of inhibiton."

Y.S.V., aph. I-51, pp.171f.

[333] prārabdhaṁ balavattaraṁ khalu vidāṁ bhogena tasya kṣayaḥ

samyag jñāna hutāśanena vilayaḥ prāk sañcit āgāminām .... ;

Viv. Cd., v.453, p.169.

334 Vinoba Bhave, Gītā Pravacana, p.161.

335 "When that *samādhi* called Raincloud of *Dharma*, corresponding with the maturing of right vision, comes about, *has been attained, Ignorance and other tatints are annihilated with their roots,* completely dissolved along with the *saṅskāra*-groups. .... When that illusion has faded away, no one is ever known to be (re-)born anywhere."

Y.S.V., aph. IV-30, p.411.

336 Manju, Advaitavāda aura Śūnyavāda, p.73.

337 "*Teṣāṁ,* of them, among the four; *jñānī,* the man of Knowledge, the Knower of Reality, is *nitya-yuktaḥ,* endowed with constant steadfastness as a result of being a knower of Reality; and he also becomes *eka-bhaktiḥ,* endowed with one-pointed devotion, because he finds no one else whom he can adore. Consequently, that person of one-pointed devotion *viśiṣyate,* excels, becomes superior, i.e., he surpasses (the others)."

Bh.G.Bh.(tr.), v.7-17, pp.328f.

338 sudhām apy āsvādya .... tava janani tāṭaṅka mahimā;

S.L., v.28, p.I-244.

339 "tāṭaṅka yugalībhūta tapanoḍupa maṇḍalā" iti sahasra nāma vacana ....;

S.L.Bh. (Aruṇāmodinī), v.28, p.I-245.

340 kirīṭaṁ vairiñcaṁ parihara puraḥ ....tava parijanoktir vijayate;

S.L., v.29, p.I-248a.

341 sva dehodbhūtābhir ghṛṇibhir aṇimādyābhir abhitoḥ

niṣevye nitye tvām aham iti sadā bhāvayati yaḥ,

kim āścaryaṁ tasya trinayana samṛdhiṁ tṛṇayataḥ

mahā saṅvartāgnir viracayati nīrājana vidhim;

ibid., v.30, p.I-253a.

342 catuṣ ṣaṣṭyā tantraiḥ .... sva tantraṁ te tantraṁ kṣiti talam avātītarad idam;

S.L., v.31, p.I-264a.

343 The *pañca makāras* are inherent to the practice of the *vāma mārga* tradition, but they are prohibited in the *savya mārga* or *dakṣiṇa mārga* tradition. For the brāhmins, the *dakṣiṇa mārga* alone is prescribed.

344 catuṣ ṣaṣṭiś ca tantrāṇi .... ca devī mata mataḥ param;

S.L.Bh. (Lakṣmīdharā), v.31, pp.I-265f.

345 candra kalā vidyāṣṭakaṁ .... vāmācāro nirūpitaḥ;

ibid., v.31, p.I-268.

346 The *brāhmaṇas* can be taken as those people who have as their primary goal the spiritual realization of the highest reality. On the other hand, the non-*brāhmaṇas* can be taken as those who give importance to various phenomenal goals over and above the goal of spiritual realization. Birth and the resultant circumstantial conditioning of the mind may contribute towards developing such a mental framework. However, in the final analysis, the decisive factor for categorizing someone as a *brāhmaṇa* or non-*brāhmaṇa* is his mental setup i.e., whether or not he accepts the highest spiritual realization as his primary goal and accordingly modifies his life in its light.The traditional requirement of knowing the Vedas for becoming a *brāhmaṇa* also highlights the basic aim of developing such an attitude since the Vedas and especially the upaniṣads deal with the nature of the highest reality. The term *'brāh- maṇa'* comes from '*Brahman*.' As such, Sir Monier Monier Williams too, in his dictonary, says that a person having divine knowlege or one who is fit to have such knowledge is called a *brāhmaṇa,* along with the

traditional meaning of the term as a person who belongs to the first order among the three twice-born castes, or to the first order among the traditional four orders of the Hindu society.

[347] śubhāgama pañcakaṁ nāma vāsiṣṭha saṁhitā, sanaka saṁhitā, śuka saṁhitā, sanandana saṁhitā, sanatkumāra saṁhitā, iti pañca saṁhitāḥ śubhāgama pañcakam;

S.L.Bh. (Lakṣmīdharā), v.31, p.I-269.

[348] candra kalā vidyāṣṭakaṁ tu kula samayānusāritvena miśrakam ity ucyate vidvadbhiḥ;

ibid., v.31, p.I-268;

also,

supra 338.

[349] śubhāgama tantra pañcake vaidika mārgeṇa iva anuṣṭhāna kalāpo nirūpitaḥ. .... ayam eva samayācāra iti vyavahriyate;

ibid., v.31, p.I-268.

[350] evaṁ catuṣ ṣaṣṭi tantrāṇi .... eveti rahasyam;

ibid., v.31, p.I-268.

[351] akhila puruṣārthaika ghaṭanā sva tantraṁ, ... sva tantram anyānapekṣam;

S.L.Bh. (Ānandagirīyā), v.31, p.I-272.

[352] athavā siddhi prasava para tantraḥ .... tat sva tanraṁ nāma tantram iti;

ibid., v.31, p.I-272.

[353] 'miśrakaṁ kaula mārgaṁ ca parityājyaṁ hi śāṅkari' .... ca parityājyam;

S.L.Bh. (Lakṣmīdharā), v.31, pp.I-268f.

[354] ataś ca śubhāgama pañcakam eva vaidikair ādaraṇīyam;

ibid., v.31, p.I-269.

[355] tatra śubhāgama pañcake ṣoḍaśa nityānāṁ pratipādanaṁ .... kathitaḥ;

ibid., v.31, p.I-269.

[356] śivaś śaktiḥ kāmaḥ kṣitir atha raviś śīta kiraṇaḥ

.... bhajante varṇās te tava janani nāmāvayavatām;

S.L., v.32, p.I-276a.

[357] S.L.Bh. (Lakṣmīdharā), v.32, p.I-276a.

[358] S.L.Bh. (Saubhāgyavardhanī), v.32, p.I-287.

[359] S.L.Bh. (Ānandagirīyā), v.32, p.I-291.

[360] S.L.Bh. (Aruṇāmodinī), v.32, pp.I-288f.

[361] sa ca mantro dvi prakāro bhavati hādiḥ kādiś ca. hādiḥ parameśvara vācakaḥ. kādis tu parameśvarī vācakaḥ, kāmarāja vidyā ity āmnāyate;

S.L.Bh. (Ḍiṇḍimbhāṣyam), v.32, p.I-292.

[362] supra 354.

[363] smaraṁ yoniṁ lakṣmīṁ .... śivāgnau juhvantaḥ surabhi ghṛta dhārāhuti śataiḥ;

S.L., v.33, p.I-295a.

[364] smaraṁ kāmarājaṁ, yoniṁ bhuvaneśvarīṁ, ... bhajanti sevante;

S.L.Bh. (Lakṣmīdharā), v.33, p.I-295a.

[365] smaraḥ kaḥ, yoniḥ ekāraḥ, ... eke niravadhi mahā bhoga rasikāḥ;

S.L.Bh. (Saubhāgyavardhanī), v.33, p.I-296.

[366] samayināṁ mantrasya puraścaraṇaṁ nāsti. japo nāsti. bāhya homo'pi nāsti. bāhya pūjā vidhayo na santy eva. hṛt kamala eva sarvaṁ yāvat anuṣṭheyam;

S.L.Bh. (Lakṣmīdharā), v.33, p.I-296.

[367] vibhūti nirvikalpa samādhi yogā dhanyāḥ ....
prabhavantīti bhāvaḥ;

S.L.Bh. (Saubhāgyavardhanī), v.33, p.I-297.

[368] manasā bhāvyamāna varṇa mālayā mūlādi brahma randhrāntaṁ kuṇḍalinī rūpaṁ vicintya .... so'ham iti vicintyamāna śivāgnau pūrṇāhutiṁ kurvāṇā antaryāga parāyaṇāḥ tvāṁ bhajanti. evaṁ vidhāntaryāgena paramāṁ siddhiṁ labhanta iti tātparyārthaḥ;

ibid., v.33, p.I-297.

[369] niravadhi mahā bhoga rasikāḥ .... tatra rasikāḥ;

S.L.Bh. (Ānandagirīyā), v.33, p.I-299;

also,

niravadhi mahā bhoga rasikāḥ, akhaṇḍānubhavānandātmaka svarūpa lābha lakṣaṇa parama puruṣārtha rasikāḥ;

ibid., v.33, p.I-300.

[370] dhyānāvaruddha manasā śiva śakti svarūpānandānubhavena .... śivāgnau śivo'ham iti pūrṇāhaṁ bhāva janita mahā prakāśe .... tā evāhutayaḥ.viṣaya vāsanā pralayaṁ prāpyantīty arthaḥ;

ibid., v.33, p.I-300.

[371] śarīraṁ tvaṁ śaṅbhoḥ śaśi mihira vakṣoruha yugaṁ

tavātmānaṁ manye bhagvati navātmānam anagham,

ataś śeṣaś śeṣīty ayam ubhaya sādhāraṇatayā

sthitas saṅbandho vāṅ samarasa parānanda parayoḥ; S.L., v.34, p.I-303a.

[372] he bhagvati, ..., tvaṁ śaṁbhoḥ śarīram asi. mantra svarūpā tvaṁ śaṁbhoḥ śarīram api tvam eva;

S.L.Bh. (Ānandagirīyā), v.34, p.I-309.

[373] śarīre ātmāpekṣāyāmāḥ - .... śivaś ca śaktiś ceti dvandve dvayor api pradhānatvaṁ dvandvasyobhaya pada pradhānatvād iti bhāvaḥ;

ibid., v.34, p.I-310.

[374] kiṁ lakṣaṇayoḥ samarasa parānanda parayoḥ, samo rasaḥ samarasam aikātmyaṁ, tena samullatito yaḥ para utkṛṣṭa ānandaḥ, tat parayoḥ ity arthaḥ;

ibid., v.34, p.I-310.

[375] tathā ca śivaś ca .... dvandvaḥ;

S.L.Bh. (Saubhāgyavardhanī), v.34, p.I-307.

[376] vāṁ yuvayoḥ samarasa parānanda parayoḥ .... ca tayoḥ;

S.L.Bh. (Lakṣmīdharā), v.34, p.I-304.

[377] ānandabhairava mahābhairavyoḥ ....tadā bhairavyāḥ śeṣatvam iti;

ibid., v.34, p.I-306.

[378] mahābhairavasya navātmeti saṁjñā, nava vyūhātmakatvāt. nava vyūhās tu .... jīva vyūhas syād iti te nava;

S.L.Bh. (Lakṣmīdharā)., v.34, p.I-304.

[379] vāmādayaḥ śaktayaḥ vāmā, jyeṣṭhā, ...bhagvatyāḥ navātmatvaṁ ucyate;

ibid., v.34, p.I-305.

[380] manas tvaṁ vyoma tvaṁ marud asi marut sārathir asi

tvam āpas tvaṁ bhūmis tvayi pariṇatāyāṅ na hi param,

tvam eva svātmānaṁ pariṇamayituṁ viśva vapuṣā

cid ānandākāraṁ śiva yuvati bhāvena bibhṛṣe;

S.L., v.35, p.I-314a.

[381] Manju, Bhāratīya Darśana me Parivartan kā svarūpa, pp.23-39.

[382] manaḥ manas tattvaṁ ājñā cakra sthitaṁ ....paraṁ na kiñcad astīty arthaḥ;

S.L.Bh. (Lakṣmīdharā), v.35, p.I-314a.

383 evaṁ prapañcaṁ kārya rūpaṁ ....sā ca ādhāra kuṇḍaliṇīty abhidhīyate;

ibid., v.35, p.I-315.

384 manas tvaṁ, vyom tvaṁ, ...sarvaṅ tvad rūpam evety arthaḥ;

S.L.Bh. (Saubhāgyavardhanī), v.35, p.I-315.

385 evaṁ rūpeṇa pañca bhūta sūkṣātmaka kārya kāraṇa rūpeṇa ....piṇḍāṇḍa brahmāṇḍayor eka rūpeṇa sarvatra tavaiva vartamānatvād iti bhāvaḥ;

S.L.Bh. (Aruṇāmodinī), v.35, p.I-317.

386 pariṇamayituṁ cid ānandayoḥ .... anyathā tvam evaikety abhiprāyaḥ;

ibid., v.35, p.I-317.

387 idaṁ sarvaṁ tvaṁ tvad ātmakaṁ tvad abhinnaṁ tvayy adhyastatvāt. .... paraṁ yad uktaṁ mana ādi tan nāsti;

S.L.Bh. (Ānandagirīyā), v.35, p.I-317.

388 samarasa parā tvaṁ .... śiva yuvati bhāvaṅ kṛtṛm bhāvaṁ nayasīti yāvat;

ibid., v.35, p.I-318.

389 tavājñācakrasthaṁ .... nirāloke 'loke nivasati hi bhā loka bhuvane;

S.L., v.36, p.I-321a.

390 tavājñācakrasthaṁ .... taveti padānvayād iti;

S.L.Bh. (Lakṣmīdharā), v.36, p.I-322.

391 tava ājñācakrasthaṁ .... cit parāmbayāvinābhūta vāmāṅgam;

S.L.Bh. (Saubhāgyavardhanī), v.36, p.I-322.

[392] yam ārādhyan bhaktyā .... sarva tejasāṁ kāla traye'pi nivāsa sthāne;

ibid., v.36, p.I-322.

[393] ājñā cakre bhavad rūpa manas tattvātmake .... tad vicāritābhidhānam;

S.L.Bh. (Aruṇāmodinī), v.36, p.I-323.

[394] he devi! tava bhavatyā ājñā cakre nideśācaraṇe tiṣṭatīti tam tvad ājñānuvarttinam ity arthaḥ;

ibid., v.36, p.I-323.

[395] bhā loka bhuvane nitya jyotsnāmaye loke sahasra kamale nivasati hi, tat sāyujyaṁ prāpya vartate khalu;

ibid., v.36, p.I-324.

[396] utkarṣe hetumāha - hi yasmat kāraṇāt, yaṁ bhaktyā ārādhyan lokaḥ upāsako janaḥ,...................... sakala saṁsāra bhaya vinirmukte loke nivasati;

S.L.Bh. (Ānandagirīyā), v.36, p.I-324.

[397] viśuddhau te śuddha sphaṭika viśadaṁ ....vilasati cakorīva jagatī;

S.L., v.37, p.I-327a.

[398] kiṁ lakṣaṇāṁ devīṁ, śiva samāna vyasaninīṁ ....; enām anārādhya śiva sāyujya padavī na prāpyat ity arthaḥ;

S.L.Bh. (Ānandagirīyā), v.37, p.I-329.

[399] supra 390.

[400] samunmīlat saṅvit kamala makarandaika rasikaṁ ....yad ādatte doṣād guṇam akhilam adbhyaḥ paya iva;

S.L., v.38, p.I-333a.

[401] sarveṣāṁ prāṇināṁ hṛdaya kamale haṅseśvarī haṅseśvara rūpaṁ haṁsa dvayam asti;

S.L.Bh. (Aruṇāmodinī), v.38, p.I-335.

[402] yad ādatte doṣāt sac cid ānanda rūpasya .... haṁso yathādatte tatheti;

S.L.Bh. (Saubhāgyavardhanī), v.38, p.I-335.

[403] yat kala kūjanaṁ sarva vidyā kāreṇa pariṇata iti. aṣṭādaśa vidyā rūpo yad ālāpa ity arthaḥ;

S.L.Bh. (Ānandagirīyā), v.38, p.I-336.

[404] upāsakāḥ parama haṁsa mithunaṁ saṁvit kamale upāsate iti samayaikadeśimatam. ata eva mahatāṁ mānasa caram ity uktam. bhagvatpāda mattaṁ tu - śikhi jvālā rūpaḥ parameśvaraḥ śikhinyā sva śaktyā saṅvalitaḥ anāhata cakre dīpāṁkuravat pratibhātīti. yathoktaṁ bhagvatpādaiḥ subhagodaya vyākhyāne - "śikhi jvālā rūpaḥ samaya iha saivātra samayā, tayos sambhedo me diśatu hṛdayābjaika nilayaḥ" iti. etad eva asmākam api abhimatam;

S.L.Bh. (Lakṣmīdharā), v.38, p.I-334.

[405] mahatāṁ mānasa caram; apākṛta sāṁsārika sukha spṛhāṇāṁ mahāśayānāṁ mānasa caram;

S.L.Bh. (Saubhāgyavardhanī), v.38, pp.I-334f.

[406] athavā carācarātmaka saṁsāra sarasi sakala prāṇi gaṇa hṛdaya kamale śiva śakti rūpaṁ cid ānandākāraṁ haṁsa mithunam asti. tad uktaṁ yoginī cakre - "......... hṛdaya kamala madhye haṁsa yugmaṁ namāmi" iti;

S.L.Bh. (Ānandagirīyā), v.38, p.I-336.

[407] tava svādhiṣṭhāne hutavaham adhiṣṭhāya nirataṁ ....dayārdrā yā dṛṣṭiḥ śiśiram upacāraṁ racayati;

S.L., v.39, p.I-340a.

[408] atha svādhiṣṭhāna cakrādhidevate saṁvartteśvara samayāmbākhye stauti - taveti;

S.L.Bh. (Aruṇāmodinī), v.39, p.I-341.

[409] taṁ prasidhaṁ saṁvartaṁ .... samayāmbām ity arthaḥ;

ibid., v.39, p.I-341.

[410] taṭittvantaṁ śaktyā .... hara mihira taptaṁ tri bhuvanam;

S.L., v.40, p.I-344a.

[411] maṇipūra sthāne jala tattvaṁ utpannam iti prāk pratipāditam;

S.L.Bh. (Lakṣmīdharā), v.40, p.I-345.

[412] atha maṇipūra cakra sthite megheśvara saudāminyambākhye devate stauti- taṭitvantam iti;

S.L.Bh. (Aruṇāmodinī), v.40, p.I-347.

[413] yathoktaṁ siddha ghuṭikāyām - 'maṇipūraika vasatiḥ ....bhāti sthira saudāminī śivā" iti;

S.L.Bh. (Lakṣmīdharā), v.40, p.I-345.

[414] maṇi śabdena maṇi dhanur ucyate, ... maṇipūram iti rahasyam;

ibid., v.40, p.I-345;

also,

śakter vidyut sādharmyamāha - timira parivṛtti sphuraṇayā................tadā valayākāreṇa megha maṇḍalaṅ saṁveṣṭya sphurati;

S.L.Bh. (Ānandagirīyā), v.40, p.I-348.

[415] meghatvaṁ samarthayati - tamaḥ śyāmaṁ, tena sajalatvam. ....jīvana pūrakatvād ity arthaḥ;

ibid., v.40, p.I-348.

[416] yad āhuḥ - "ādhāra sthānam andha tāmisram; ....nitya jyotsnāmayo lokaḥ" ity ādi;

S.L.Bh. (Aruṇāmodinī), v.40, p.I-347.

[417] anāhatopari sthita sūrya kiraṇāḥ .... jagat āplāvayantīti āgama rahasyam;

S.L.Bh. (Lakṣmīdharā), v.40, p.I-345.

[418] punaḥ kiṁ lakṣaṇaṁ hara mihira taptaṁ .... kalayābhiṣicyotpādayati;

S.L.Bh. (Ānandagirīyā), v.40, p.I-348.

[419] tavādhāre mūle saha samayayā .... janaka jananī maj jagad idam;

S.L., v.41, p.I-351a.

[420] mūlādhāra cakrādhiṣṭhāna devate samayāmbā mahānaṭeśvarākhye stuvan .....;

S.L.Bh. (Aruṇāmodinī), v.41, p.I-357.

[421] mahānaṭeśvaraḥ, lāsyeśvarī ca madhye pūjyau dhyeyau vā;

S.L.Bh. (Saubhāgyavardhanī), v.41, p.I-357.

[422] strī kartṛkaṁ nṛtyaṁ lāsyam ity ucyate. ....

puṁ kartṛkaṁ nṛtyaṁ tāṇḍavam ity ucyate;

S.L.Bh. (Lakṣmīdharā), v.41, p.I-351a.

[423] evaṁ vidhaṁ mahānaṭeśvarākhyaṁ devaṁ navātmānaṁ pūrvokta nava vyūhātmakaṁ ānandabhairava nāmānāṁ nava rasātmakaṁ nūtana śṛṅgāra rasa svarūpaṁ vā manye tarkayāmīty arthaḥ;

S.L.Bh. (Aruṇāmodinī), v.41, p.I-358.

[424] ata eva samayināṁ sahasra kamale samayāyāḥ samayasya ca śaṁbhoḥ pūjā. samayā nāma - śaṁbhunā sāmyaṁ pañca vidhaṁ yātīti samayā. samayatvaṁ śaṁbhor api -pañca vidhaṁ sāmyaṁ devyā saha yātīti. ataḥ .... yadvā - 'navātmānam' iti rūpa sāmyaṁ nāma sāmyaṁ ca pratipāditam iti dhyeyam;

S.L.Bh. (Lakṣmīdharā), v.41, pp.I-352f.

[425] ibid., v.41, p.I-353.

[426] ataḥ samaya pūjakāḥ samayinaḥ. teṣāṁ ṣaṭ cakra pūjā na niyatā, api tu sahasra kamala eva pūjā. .... tan madhya bindoḥ pañca viṁśati tattvātīta ṣaḍ viṁśātmaka śiva śakti melana rūpa sādākhyātmanā ca anusandhānam;

ibid., v.41, p.I-353.

[427] tathāhi - ādhārādi ṣaṭ cakrāṇāṁ trikoṇādi ṣaṭ cakratvena tādātmyam, bindu sthānasya caturaśra sahasra kamalatvena tādātmyaṁ bindu śivayos tādātmyam. ....caturdhā aikyaṁ samayināṁ samayāradhanam iti mahat rahasyam;

ibid., v.41, p.I-354.

[428] kecit tu ṣoḍhā aikyamāhuḥ. .... atra nāda bindu kalānāṁ paraspar-aikyānusandhānaṁ ṣoḍhā bhavatīti ṣoḍhā aikyamāhuḥ. evaṁ bhagavatīṁ ṣaḍ vidh-aikyena sambhāvya pūjayitvā sadākhyāyāṁ vilīno bhavati;

S.L.Bh. (Lakṣmīdharā)., v.41, p.I-354.

[429] ubhābhyāṁ naṭa naṭī rūpābhyāṁ svātmānaṁ mātā pitṛmantaṁ mene. yathā pitṛbhyāṁ janana pālana poṣaṇādinā poṣyamāṇāḥ putrādayaḥ ....tava dayayā sanāthābhyāṁ saha kṛtābhyāṁ sa svāmikābhyāṁ vā;

S.L.Bh. (Ānandagirīyā), v.41, p.I-359.

[430] atra bhagavatpādaiḥ ādhāra kamalādi kramaṁ vihāya ājñā cakrādi krameṇa avaroha krameṇa pūjā prakāraḥ kathitaḥ. ayamāśyaḥ - 'ātman ākāśas sambhūtaḥ. ākāśād vāyuḥ. vāyor agniḥ. agner āpaḥ. adbhayaḥ pṛthivī.' iti śrauta kramam avalambya avaroha krama uktaḥ. ata eva svādhiṣṭhānānantara bhāvinaḥ maṇipūrasya tad adaḥ pradeśe nirūpaṇaṁ yujyate. ādhāra svādhiṣṭhānāntaraṁ maṇipūrakāvasthānam iti sarva yoga śāstra siddham;

S.L.Bh. (Lakṣmīdharā), v.41, p.I-356.

[431] S.L., v.12, p.I-136.

[432] ibid., v.22, p.I-209a.

[433] viśālā kalyāṇī sphuṭa rucir ayodhyā kuvalayaiḥ .... dhruvaṁ tattan nāma vyavaharaṇa yogyā vijayate;

ibid., v.49, p.II-35.

[434] kavīnāṁ saṅdarbha stabaka makarandaika rasikaṁ ....asūyā saṅsargād alika nayanaṁ kiṅcid aruṇam;

ibid., v.50, p.II-41a.

[435] vibhakta traivarṇyaṁ vyatikarita līlāñjanatayā .... rajaḥ sattvaṁ bibhrat tama iti guṇānāṁ trayam iva;

ibid., v.53, p.II-60a.

[436] nimeṣonmeṣābhyāṁ pralayam udayaṁ yāti jagatī

tavety āhuḥ santo dharaṇi dhara rājanya tanaye,

tvad unmeṣāj jātaṁ jagad idam aśeṣaṁ pralayataḥ

paritrātuṁ śaṁke parihṛta nimeṣās tava dṛśaḥ;

ibid., v.55, p.II-70a.

[437] dṛśā drāghīyasyā dara dalita nīlotpala rucā ....vane vā harmye vā sama kara nipāto hima karaḥ;

ibid., v.57, p.II-79a.

[438] dadāne dīnebhyaḥ śriyam aniśam āśānusadṛśīṁ ....
nimajjan majjīvaḥ karaṇa caraṇaḥ ṣaṭ caraṇatām;

ibid., v.90, p.II-236a.

[439] purārāter antaḥpuram asi tatas tvac caraṇayoḥ ....tava dvāropānta sthitibhir aṇimādyābhir amarāḥ;

ibid., v.95, p.II-266a.

[440] ibid., v.1, p.I-1.

[441] girām āhur devīṁ druhiṇa gṛhiṇīm āgamavido

hareḥ patnīṁ padmāṁ hara sahacarīm adri tanayām,

turīyā kāpi tvaṁ duradhigama niḥsīma mahimā

mahāmāyā viśvaṁ bhramayasi para brahma mahiṣi;

ibid., v.97, p.II-277a.

[442] C.D. Sharma, A Critical Survey of Indian Philosophy, p.275.

[443] sarasvatyā lakṣmyā vidhi hari sapatno viharate

rateḥ pātivratyaṁ śithilayati ramyeṇa vapuṣā,

ciraṁ jīvann eva kṣapita paśu pāśa vyatikaraḥ

parānandābhikhyaṁ rasayati rasaṁ tvad bhajanvān;

S.L., v.99, p.II-290a

444 B.S.Bh. (tr.), I-i-1, p.3;

also,

sarvathāpi tvanyasyānya dharmāvabhāsatāṁ na vyabhicarati. tathā ca loke'nubhavaḥ - śuktikā hi rajatavad avabhāsate, ekaś candraḥ sa dvitīyavad iti;

B.S.Bh., I-i-1, pp.32-4.

445 girām āhur devīṁ druhiṇa gṛhiṇīm āgamavido

hareḥ patnīṁ padmāṁ hara sahacarīm adri tanayām,

turīyā kāpi tvaṁ duradhigama niḥsīma mahimā

mahāmāyā viśvaṁ bhramayasi para brahma mahiṣi;

S.L., v.97, p.II-277a.

446 B.S.Bh. (tr.), I-i-1, p.9;

also,

ucyate - nityānitya vastu vivekaḥ, ihāmutrāthabhoga virāgaḥ, śama damādi sādhana saṅpat mumukṣutvaṁ ca. teṣu hi satsu prāg api dharma jijñāsāyā ūrdhvaṁ ca śakyate brahma jijñāsituṁ jñātuṁ ca, na viparyaye. tasmād atha śabdena yathokta sādhana saṁpatyānantaryam upadiśyate;

B.S.Bh., I-i-1, pp.71-3.

447 śivaḥ śaktyā yukto yadi bhavati śaktaḥ prabhavituṁ,

na cedevaṁ devo na khalu kuśalaḥ spanditum api;

atas tvām ārādhyāṁ hari hara viriñcādi bhir api,

praṇantuṁ stotuṁ vā katham akṛtapuṇyaḥ prabhavati;

S. laharī, v.1, p.8.

448 taṭillekhā tanvīṁ tapana śaśi vaiśvānaramayīṁ

niṣaṇṇāṁ ṣaṇṇām apy upari kamalānāṁ tava kalām,

mahā padmāṭavyāṁ mṛdita mala māyena manasā

mahāntaḥ paśyanto dadhati paramāhlāda laharīm;

S.L., v.21, p.I-204a.

449 purārāter antaḥpuram asi tatas tvac caraṇayoḥ
....tava dvāropānta sthitibhir
aṇimādyābhir amarāḥ;

ibid., v.95, p.II-266a.

450 B.S.Bh.(tr.), I-i-2, p.14;

also,

asya jagato nāma rūpābhyāṁ vyākṛtasyāneka kartṛ bhoktṛ
saṁyuktasya pratiniyata deśa kāla nimitta kriyā phalāśrayasya
manasāpy acintya racanā rūpasya janma sthiti bhaṁgaṁ yataḥ
sarvajñāt sarvaśakteḥ kāraṇād bhavati tad brahmeti vākyaśeṣaḥ;

B.S.Bh., I-i-2, pp.85f.

451 tanīyāsāṁ pāṁsuṁ tava ....bhasitod dhūlana vidhim;

S. laharī, v.2, p.26.

452 mahīṁ mūlādhāre kam api maṇipūre hutavahaṁ

sthitaṁ svādhiṣṭhāne hṛdi marutam ākāśam upari,

mano'pi bhrū madhye sakalam api bhittvā kula pathaṁ

sahasrāre padme saha rahasi patyā viharase;

S.L., v.9, p.I-100a.

453 taṭillekhā tanvīṁ tapana śaśi vaiśvānaramayīṁ

niṣaṇṇāṁ ṣaṇṇām apy upari kamalānāṁ tava kalām,

mahā padmāṭavyāṁ mṛdita mala māyena manasā

mahāntaḥ paśyanto dadhati paramāhlāda laharīm;

S.L., v.21, p.I-204a.

454 jagatsūte dhātā .... kṣaṇa calitayor bhrū latikayoḥ;

ibid., v.24, p.I-220a.

[455] śarīraṁ tvaṁ śaṁbhoḥ śaśi mihira vakṣoruha yugaṁ

tavātmānaṁ manye bhagvati navātmānam anagham,

ataś śeṣaś śeṣīty ayam ubhaya sādhāraṇatayā

sthitas saṅbandho vāṁ samarasa parānanda parayoḥ;

ibid., v.34, p.I-303a.

[456] manas tvaṁ vyoma tvaṁ marud asi marut sārathir asi

tvam āpas tvaṁ bhūmis tvayi pariṇatāyāṁ na hi param,

tvam eva svātmānaṁ pariṇamayituṁ viśva vapuṣā

cid ānandākāraṁ śiva yuvati bhāvena bibhṛṣe;

ibid., v.35, p.I-314a.

[457] nimeṣonmeṣābhyāṁ pralayam udayaṁ yāti jagatī

tavety āhuḥ santo dharaṇi dhara rājanya tanaye,

tvad unmeṣāj jātaṁ jagad idam aśeṣaṁ pralayataḥ

paritrātuṁ śaṅke parihṛta nimeṣās tava dṛśaḥ;

ibid., v.55, p.II-70a.

[458] girām āhur devīṁ druhiṇa gṛhiṇīm āgamavido

hareḥ patnīṁ padmāṁ hara sahacarīm adri tanayām,

turīyā kāpi tvaṁ duradhigama niḥsīma mahimā

mahāmāyā viśvaṁ bhramayasi para brahma mahiṣi;

ibid., v.97, p.II-277a.

[459] B.S.Bh. (tr.), I-i-4, p.43;

also,

tasmān nāvagata brahmātma bhāvasya yathā pūrvaṁ saṁsāritvam. yasya tu yathā pūrvaṁ saṁsāritvaṁ nāsāvavagata brahmātma bhāva ity anavadyam;

B.S.Bh., I-i-4, pp.152f.

[460] sudhā dhārā sāraiś caraṇa yuglāntar vigalitaiḥ
..............kulakuṇḍe kuhariṇi;

S. laharī, v.10, p.60.

[461] taṭillekhā tanvīṁ tapana śaśi vaiśvānaramayīṁ

niṣaṇṇāṁ ṣaṇṇām apy upari kamalānāṁ tava kalām,

mahā padmāṭavyāṁ mṛdita mala māyena manasā

mahāntaḥ paśyanto dadhati paramāhlāda laharīm;

S.L., v.21, p.I-204a.

[462] japo jalpaḥ śilpaṁ sakalam api mudrā viracanā

gatiḥ prādakṣiṇya kramaṇam aśanādy āhuti vidhiḥ

praṇāmas saṁveśas sukham akhilam ātmārpaṇa dṛśā

saparyā paryāyas tava bhavatu yan me vilasitam;

ibid., v.27, p.I-236a.

[463] sva dehodbhūtābhir ghṛṇibhir aṇimādyābhir abhitoḥ

niṣevye nitye tvām aham iti sadā bhāvayati yaḥ,

kim āścaryaṁ tasya trinayana samṛdhiṁ tṛṇayataḥ

mahā savartāgnir viracayati nīrājana vidhim;

S.L., v.30, p.I-253a.

[464] sarasvatyā lakṣmyā vidhi hari sapatno viharate

rateḥ pātivratyaṁ śithilayati ramyeṇa vapuṣā,

ciraṁ jīvann eva kṣapita paśu pāśa vyatikaraḥ

parānandābhikhyaṁ rasayati rasaṁ tvad bhajanvān;

ibid., v.99, p.II-290a.

[465] B.S.Bh.(tr.), II-iii-14, pp.467f;

also,

evaṁ prāptaṁ tato brūmaḥ - viparyayeṇa tu pralaya kramo'ta utpatti kramād bhavitum arhati. tathāhi loke dṛśyate

......................nahi sva kāraṇa vyatikrameṇa kāraṇa kāraṇe kāryāpy ayo nyāyyaḥ;

B.S.Bh., II-iii-14, p.597.

466 mahīṁ mūlādhāre kam api maṇipūre hutavahaṁ

sthitaṁ svādhiṣṭhāne hṛdi marutam ākāśam upari,

mano'pi bhrū madhye sakalam api bhittvā kula pathaṁ

sahasrāre padme saha rahasi patyā viharase;

S.L., v.9, p.I-100a.

467 kṣitau ṣaṭ pañcāśad dvi samadhika pañcād udake

hutāśe dvā ṣaṣṭiś catur adhika pañcāśad anile,

divi dviḥ ṣaṭ triṅśan manasi ca catuḥ ṣaṣṭir iti ye

mayūkhās teṣām apy upari tava pādāmbuja yugam;

ibid., v.14, p.I-146a.

468 viriñciḥ pañcatvaṁ vrajati harir āpnoti viratiṁ .... mahā saṅhāre'smin

viharati sati tvat patir asau;

ibid., v.26, p.I-231a.

469 sva dehodbhūtābhir ghṛṇibhir aṇimādyābhir abhitoḥ

niṣevye nitye tvām aham iti sadā bhāvayati yaḥ,

kim āścaryaṁ tasya trinayana samṛdhiṁ tṛṇayataḥ

mahā saṅvartāgnir viracayati nīrājana vidhim;

ibid., v.30, p.I-253a.

470 nimeṣonmeṣābhyāṁ pralayam udayaṁ yāti jagatī

tavety āhuḥ santo dharaṇi dhara rājanya tanaye,

tvad unmeṣāj jātaṁ jagad idam aśeṣaṁ pralayataḥ

paritrātuṁ śaṅke parihṛta nimeṣās tava dṛśaḥ;

ibid., v.55, p.II-70a.

[471] B.S.Bh.(tr.), II-iii-41, pp.504f;

also,

avidyāvasthāyāṁ kārya karaṇa saṁghātāviveka darśino jivasyāvidyā timirāndhasya sataḥ parasmād ātmanaḥ karmādhyakṣāt sarva bhūtādhivāsāt sākṣiṇaś cetayitur īśvarāt tad anujñayā kartṛtva bhoktṛtva lakṣaṇasya saṁsārasya siddhiḥ, tad anugraha hetuken aiva ca vijñānena mokṣa siddhir bhavitum arhati. kutaḥ? tac chruteḥ. yadyapi doṣa prayuktaḥ sāmagrī saṁpannaś ca jīvaḥ, yadyapi ca loke kṛṣy ādiṣu karmasu neśvara kāraṇatvaṁ prasiddham; tathāpi sarvāsveva pravṛttiṣv īśvaro hetu karteti śruter avasīyate. tathāhi śrutir bhavati - 'eṣa hy eva sādhu karma kārayati taṁ yamebhyo lokebhya un ninīṣate. eṣa hy evāsādhu karma kārayati taṁ yam adho ninīṣate' (Kauṣī. 3-8) iti 'ya ātmani tiṣṭ hannātmānam antaro yamayati' iti caivaṅjātīyakā;

B.S.Bh., II-iii-41, p.620.

[472] śivaḥ śaktyā yukto yadi bhavati śaktaḥ prabhavituṅ,

na cedevaṁ devo na khalu kuśalaḥ spanditum api;

atas tvām ārādhyāṁ hari hara viriñcādi bhir api,

praṇantuṁ stotuṁ vā katham akṛtapuṇyaḥ prabhavati;

S. laharī, v.1, p.8.

[473] avidyām antas timira mihira dvīpa nagarī

jaḍānāṁ caitanya stabaka makaranda sruti jharī,

daridrāṇāṁ cintāmaṇi guṇanikā janma jaladhau

nimagnānāṁ daṅṣṭrā mura ripu varāhasya bhavati;

S.L., v.3, p.I-58a.

[474] bhavāni tvaṁ dāse mayi vitara dṛṣṭiṁ sakaruṇāṁ

iti stotuṁ vāñchan kathayati bhavāni tvam iti yaḥ,

tadaiva tvaṁ tasmai diśasi nija sāyujya padavīṁ

mukunda brahmendra sphuṭa makuṭa nīrājita padām;

ibid., v.22, p.I-209a.

[475] jagatsūte dhātā .... kṣaṇa calitayor bhrū latikayoḥ;

ibid., v.24, p.I-220a.

[476] dṛśā drāghīyasyā dara dalita nīlotpala rucā ....vane vā harmye vā sama kara nipāto hima karaḥ;

ibid., v.57, p.II-79a.

[477] sarasvatyā lakṣmyā vidhi hari sapatno viharate

rateḥ pātivratyaṁ śithilayati ramyeṇa vapuṣā,

ciraṁ jīvann eva kṣapita paśu pāśa vyatikaraḥ

parānandābhikhyaṁ rasayati rasaṁ tvad bhajanvān;

ibid., v.99, p.II-290a.

[478] B.S.Bh.(tr.), III-ii-5, p.595;

also,

kiṁ punar jīvasyeśvara samāna dharmatvaṅ nāsty eva? na nāsty eva. vidyamānam api tat tirohitam avidyādi vyavadhānāt. .... kasyacid evāvirbhavati

na svabhāvat eva sarveṣāṁ jantūnām;

B.S.Bh., III-ii-5, p.693.

[479] tvad anyaḥ pāṇibhyām abhaya varado.............tava hi caraṇāv eva nipiṇau;

S. laharī, v.4, p.34.

[480] naraṁ varṣīyāṁsaṁ ....yuvatayaḥ;

S.L., v.13, p.I-141a.

[481] ibid., v.16, p.I-176a;

also,

ibid., v.17, p.I-181a.

[482] kirantīm aṁgebhyaḥ ....sukhyati sudhā dhāra sirayā;

ibid., v.20, p.I-200a.

483 catuṣ ṣaṣṭyā tantraiḥ sakalam atisandhāya bhuvanaṁ

sthitas tat tat siddhi prasava para tantraiḥ paśupatiḥ,

punas tvan nirbandhād akhila puruṣārthaika ghaṭanā

sva tantraṁ te tantraṁ kṣiti talam avātītarad idam;

S.L., v.31, p.I-264a.

484 samunmīlat saṁvit kamala makarandaika rasikaṁ ....yad
ādatte doṣād guṇam akhilam adbhyaḥ paya iva;

ibid., v.38, p.I-333a.

485 B.S.Bh.(tr.), III-ii-24, p.629;

also,

api cainam ātmānaṁ nirasta samasta prapañcam avyaktaṁ
saṅrādhana kāle paśyanti yoginaḥ. saṁrādhanaṁ ca bhakti dhyāna
praṇidhānādy anuṣṭhānam;

B.S.Bh., III-ii-24, p.721.

486 mahīṁ mūlādhāre kam api maṇipūre hutavahaṁ

sthitaṁ svādhiṣṭhāne hṛdi marutam ākāśam upari,

mano'pi bhrū madhye sakalam api bhittvā kula pathaṁ

sahasrāre padme saha rahasi patyā viharase;

S.L., v.9, p.I-100a.

487 taṭillekhā tanvīṁ tapana śaśi vaiśvānaramayīṁ

niṣaṇṇāṁ ṣaṇṇām apy upari kamalānāṁ tava kalām,

mahā padmāṭavyāṁ mṛdita mala māyena manasā

mahāntaḥ paśyanto dadhati paramāhlāda laharīm;

ibid., v.21, p.I-204a.

488 bhavāni tvaṁ dāse mayi vitara dṛṣṭiṁ sakaruṇāṁ

iti stotuṁ vāñchan kathayati bhavāni tvam iti yaḥ,

tadaiva tvaṁ tasmai diśasi nija sāyujya padavīṁ

mukunda brahmendra sphuṭa makuṭa nīrājita padām;

ibid., v.22, p.I-209a.

[489] japo jalpaḥ śilpaṁ sakalam api mudrā viracanā

gatiḥ prādakṣiṇya kramaṇam aśanādy āhuti vidhiḥ

praṇāmas saṁveśas sukham akhilam ātmārpaṇa dṛśā

saparyā paryāyas tava bhavatu yan me vilasitam;

ibid., v.27, p.I-236a.

[490] sva dehodbhūtābhir ghṛṇibhir aṇimādyābhir abhitoḥ

niṣevye nitye tvām aham iti sadā bhāvayati yaḥ,

kim āścaryaṁ tasya trinayana samṛdhiṁ tṛṇayataḥ

mahā saṅvartāgnir viracayati nīrājana vidhim;

ibid., v.30, p.I-253a.

[491] śarīraṁ tvaṁ śaṁbhoḥ śaśi mihira vakṣoruha yugaṁ

tavātmānaṁ manye bhagvati navātmānam anagham,

ataś śeṣaś śeṣīty ayam ubhaya sādhāraṇatayā

sthitas saṁbandho vāṁ samarasa parānanda parayoḥ;

ibid., v.34, p.I-303a.

[492] B.S.Bh.(tr.), III-ii-27,28, p.631;

also,

tatraivam ubhaya vyapadeśe sati yady abheda evaikāntato gṛhyate, ...atha ca bheda vyapadeśabhājau bhavat evamihāpīti;

B.S.Bh., III-ii-27,28, p.722.

[493] mahīṁ mūlādhāre kam api maṇipūre hutavahaṁ

sthitaṁ svādhiṣṭhāne hṛdi marutam ākāśam upari,

mano'pi bhrū madhye sakalam api bhittvā kula pathaṁ

sahasrāre padme saha rahasi patyā viharase;

S.L., v.9, p.I-100a.

[494] bhavāni tvaṁ dāse mayi vitara dṛṣṭiṁ sakaruṇāṁ

iti stotuṁ vāñchan kathayati bhavāni tvam iti yaḥ,

tadaiva tvaṁ tasmai diśasi nija sāyujya padavīṁ

mukunda brahmendra sphuṭa makuṭa nīrājita padām;

ibid., v.22, p.I-209a.

[495] sva dehodbhūtābhir ghṛṇibhir aṇimādyābhir abhitoḥ

niṣevye nitye tvām aham iti sadā bhāvayati yaḥ,

kim āścaryaṁ tasya trinayana samṛdhiṁ tṛṇayataḥ

mahā saṁvartāgnir viracayati nīrājana vidhim;

ibid., v.30, p.I-253a.

[496] B.S.Bh.(tr.), III-iv-26, p.783;

also,

apekṣate ca vidyā sarvāṇy āśrama karmāṇi, nātyantam anapekṣaiva. nanu viruddham idaṁ vacanam apekṣate cāśrama karmāṇi vidyā nāpekṣate ceti. neti brūmaḥ; utpannā hi vidyā phala siddhiṁ prati na kiṁcid anyad apekṣate. utpattiṁ prati tvapekṣatte;

B.S.Bh., III-iv-26, p.898.

[497] bhavāni tvaṁ dāse mayi vitara dṛṣṭiṁ sakaruṇāṁ

iti stotuṁ vāñchan kathayati bhavāni tvam iti yaḥ,

tadaiva tvaṁ tasmai diśasi nija sāyujya padavīṁ

mukunda brahmendra sphuṭa makuṭa nīrājita padām;

S.L., v.22, p.I-209a.

[498] taṭillekhā tanvīṁ tapana śaśi vaiśvānaramayīṁ

niṣaṇṇāṁ ṣaṇṇām apy upari kamalānāṁ tava kalām,

mahā padmāṭavyāṁ mṛdita mala māyena manasā

mahāntaḥ paśyanto dadhati paramāhlāda laharīm;

ibid., v.21, p.I-204a.

[499] japo jalpaḥ śilpaṁ sakalam api mudrā viracanā

gatiḥ prādakṣiṇya kramaṇam aśanādy āhuti vidhiḥ

praṇāmas saṁveśas sukham akhilam ātmārpaṇa dṛśā

saparyā paryāyas tava bhavatu yan me vilasitam;

ibid., v.27, p.I-236a.

[500] B.S.Bh.(tr.), IV-i-15, p.840;

also,

ucyate - na tāvad anāśrityārabdha kāryaṁ karmāśayaṁ jñānotpattir upapadyate. āśrite ca kulāla cakravat pravṛtta vegasyāntarāle pratibandhāsaṁbhavād bhavati vega kṣaya pratipālanam. akartrātmabodho'pi hi mithyā jñāna bādhanena karmāṇy ucchinatti. bādhitam api tu mithyā jñānaṁ dvi candra jñānavat saṁskāravaśāt kaṁcit kālam anuvartata eva. api ca naivātra vivaditavyaṁ brahmavidā kaṁcit kālaṁ śarīraṁ dhriyate na vā dhriyata iti. kathaṁ hy ekasya sva hṛdaya pratyayaṁ brahma vedanaṁ deha dhāraṇaṁ cāpareṇa pratikṣeptuṁ śakyeta? ;

B.S.Bh., IV-i-15, pp.958f.

[501] taṭillekhā tanvīṁ tapana śaśi vaiśvānaramayīṁ

niṣaṇṇāṁ ṣaṇṇām apy upari kamalānāṁ tava kalām,

mahā padmāṭavyāṁ mṛdita mala māyena manasā

mahāntaḥ paśyanto dadhati paramāhlāda laharīm;

S.L., v.21, p.I-204a.

[502] japo jalpaḥ śilpaṁ sakalam api mudrā viracanā

gatiḥ prādakṣiṇya kramaṇam aśanādy āhuti vidhiḥ

praṇāmas saṁveśas sukham akhilam ātmārpaṇa dṛśā

saparyā paryāyas tava bhavatu yan me vilasitam;

ibid., v.27, p.I-236a.

[503] Īśā Up.Bh. (Eight Up.-I), 2, p.8;

also,

'imau dvāveva paṁthānau anuniṣkrāntatarau bhavataḥ kriyā pathaś caiva purastāt saṁnyāsaś cottareṇa' tayoḥ saṁnyāsa patha evātirecayati;

Īśā Up.Bh. (Īśādi. Bh.), 2, p.3.

[504] śivaḥ śaktyā yukto yadi bhavati śaktaḥ prabhavituṁ,

na cedevaṁ devo na khalu kuśalaḥ spanditum api;

atas tvām ārādhyāṁ hari hara viriñcādi bhir api,

praṇantuṁ stotuṁ vā katham akṛtapuṇyaḥ prabhavati;

S. laharī, v.1, p.8.

[505] taṭillekhā tanvīṁ tapana śaśi vaiśvānaramayīṁ

niṣaṇṇāṁ ṣaṇṇām apy upari kamalānāṁ tava kalām,

mahā padmāṭavyāṁ mṛdita mala māyena manasā

mahāntaḥ paśyanto dadhati paramāhlāda laharīm;

S.L., v.21, p.I-204a.

[506] Īśā Up.Bh. (Eight Up.-I), 6, p.14;

also,

sarva bhūteṣu cātmānaṁ nirveśeṣaṁ yastvanupaśyati, ...

ātmānam evātyaṁta viśuddhaṁ nirantaraṁ paśyato na ghṛṇā nimittam arthāntaram astīti prāptam eva;

Īśā Up.Bh. (Īśādi. Bh.), 6, p.5.

[507] kṣitau ṣaṭ pañcāśad dvi samadhika pañcād udake

hutāśe dvā ṣaṣṭiś catur adhika pañcāśad anile,

divi dviḥ ṣaṭ triṅśan manasi ca catuḥ ṣaṣṭir iti ye

mayūkhās teṣām apy upari tava pādāmbuja yugam;

S.L., v.14, p.I-146a.

[508] manas tvaṁ vyoma tvaṁ marud asi marut sārathir asi

tvam āpas tvaṁ bhūmis tvayi pariṇatāyāṁ na hi param,

tvam eva svātmānaṁ pariṇamayituṁ viśva vapuṣā

cid ānandākāraṁ śiva yuvati bhāvena bibhṛṣe;

ibid., v.35, p.I-314a.

[509] japo jalpaḥ śilpaṁ sakalam api mudrā viracanā

gatiḥ prādakṣiṇya kramaṇam aśanādy āhuti vidhiḥ

praṇāmas saṅveśas sukham akhilam ātmārpaṇa dṛśā

saparyā paryāyas tava bhavatu yan me vilasitam;

S.L., v.27, p.I-236a.

[510] Ke.Up.Bh. (Eight Up.-I), IV-5, p.86;

also,

ataḥ sa eṣa brahmaṇo' dhyātmam ādeśo, vidyun nimeṣaṇavad adhidaitaṁ druta prakāśana dharmi, adhyātmaṁ ca manaḥ pratyaya sama kālābhivyakti dharmi, ity eṣa ādeśaḥ;

Ke.Up.Bh. (Īśādi. Bh.), IV-5, p.94.

[511] taṭillekhā tanvīṁ tapana śaśi vaiśvānaramayīṁ

niṣaṇṇāṁ ṣaṇṇām apy upari kamalānāṁ tava kalām,

mahā padmāṭavyāṁ mṛdita mala māyena manasā

mahāntaḥ paśyanto dadhati paramāhlāda laharīm;

S.L., v.21, p.I-204a.

[512] manas tvaṁ vyoma tvaṁ marud asi marut sārathir asi

tvam āpas tvaṁ bhūmis tvayi pariṇatāyāṁ na hi param,

tvam eva svātmānaṁ pariṇamayituṁ viśva vapuṣā

cid ānandākāraṁ śiva yuvati bhāvena bibhṛṣe;

ibid., v.35, p.I-314a.

[513] Ke.Up.Bh. (Eight Up.-I), IV-8, p.92;

also,

tapaḥ kāyeṁdriya manasāṁ samādhānam. damaḥ upaśamaḥ. ....yatheṁdra virocana prabhṛtīnām;

Ke.Up.Bh. (Īśādi. Bh.), IV-8, p.96.

[514] śivaḥ śaktyā yukto yadi bhavati śaktaḥ prabhavituṁ,

na cedevaṁ devo na khalu kuśalaḥ spanditum api;

atas tvām ārādhyāṁ hari hara viriñcādi bhir api,

praṇantuṁ stotuṁ vā katham akṛtapuṇyaḥ prabhavati;

S. laharī, v.1, p.8.

[515] taṭillekhā tanvīṁ tapana śaśi vaiśvānaramayīṁ

niṣaṇṇāṁ ṣaṇṇām apy upari kamalānāṁ tava kalām,

mahā padmāṭavyāṁ mṛdita mala māyena manasā

mahāntaḥ paśyanto dadhati paramāhlāda laharīm;

S.L., v.21, p.I-204a.

[516] japo jalpaḥ śilpaṁ sakalam api mudrā viracanā

gatiḥ prādakṣiṇya kramaṇam aśanādy āhuti vidhiḥ

praṇāmas saṁveśas sukham akhilam ātmārpaṇa dṛśā

saparyā paryāyas tava bhavatu yan me vilasitam;

ibid., v.27, p.I-236a.

[517] Ka.Up.Bh. (Eight Up.-I), I-ii-20, p.153;

also,

aṇu mahad vā yad asti loke vastu tat tenaivātmanā nityenātmavat saṁbhavati. tad ātmanā vinirmuktam asat saṁpadyate;

Ka.Up.Bh. (Īśādi. Bh.), II-20, p.52.

[518] taṭillekhā tanvīṁ tapana śaśi vaiśvānaramayīṁ

niṣaṇṇāṁ ṣaṇṇām apy upari kamalānāṁ tava kalām,

mahā padmāṭavyāṁ mṛdita mala māyena manasā

mahāntaḥ paśyanto dadhati paramāhlāda laharīm;

S.L., v.21, p.I-204a.

[519] manas tvaṁ vyoma tvaṁ marud asi marut sārathir asi

tvam āpas tvaṁ bhūmis tvayi pariṇatāyāṁ na hi param,

tvam eva svātmānaṁ pariṇamayituṁ viśva vapuṣā

cid ānandākāraṁ śiva yuvati bhāvena bibhṛṣe;

ibid., v.35, p.I-314a.

[520] Ka.Up.Bh. (Eight Up.-I), I-ii-23, pp.157f;

also,

nāyamātmā pravcanenāneka veda svīkaraṇena labhyo jñeyo, nāpi medhayā graṁthārtha dhāraṇa śaktayā, na bahudhā śrutena kevalena. kena tarhi labhya ity ucyate - yam eva svātmānam eṣa sādhako vṛṇute prārthayate tenaiv ātmanā varitrā svayam ātmā labhyo jñāyate ity etat. niṣkāmaś cātmānam eva prārthayate, ātmanaiv ātmā labhyat ity arthaḥ. kathaṁ labhyat ity ucyate - tasyātmakāmasyaiṣa ātmā vivṛṇute prakāśayati pāramārthikīṁ tanūṁ svāṁ svakīyāṁ sva yāthātmyam ity arthaḥ;

Ka.Up.Bh. (Īśādi. Bh.), II-23, p.53.

[521] bhavāni tvaṁ dāse mayi vitara dṛṣṭiṁ sakaruṇāṁ

iti stotuṁ vāñchan kathayati bhavāni tvam iti yaḥ,

tadaiva tvaṁ tasmai diśasi nija sāyujya padavīṁ

mukunda brahmendra sphuṭa makuṭa nīrājita padām;

S.L., v.22, p.I-209a.

[522] sva dehodbhūtābhir ghṛṇibhir aṇimādyābhir abhitoḥ

niṣevye nitye tvām aham iti sadā bhāvayati yaḥ,

kim āścaryaṁ tasya trinayana samṛdhiṁ tṛṇayataḥ

mahā saṁvartāgnir viracayati nīrājana vidhim;

ibid., v.30, p.I-253a.

[523] Tai.Up.Bh. (Eight Up.-I), II-i-1, pp.320f;

also,

tasmād etasmād brahmaṇa ātma svarūpād ākāśaḥ saṁbhūtaḥ samutpannaḥ. .... abhdyaḥ svena gaṁdha guṇena pūrvaiś ca caturbhiḥ paṁcaguṇā pṛthivī saṁbhūtā;

Tai.Up.Bh. (Īśādi. Bh.), II-1, p.361.

[524] mahīṁ mūlādhāre kam api maṇipūre hutavahaṁ

sthitaṁ svādhiṣṭhāne hṛdi marutam ākāśam upari,

mano'pi bhrū madhye sakalam api bhittvā kula pathaṁ

sahasrāre padme saha rahasi patyā viharase;

S.L., v.9, p.I-100a.

[525] manas tvaṁ vyoma tvaṁ marud asi marut sārathir asi

tvam āpas tvaṁ bhūmis tvayi pariṇatāyāṁ na hi param,

tvam eva svātmānaṁ pariṇamayituṁ viśva vapuṣā

cid ānandākāraṁ śiva yuvati bhāvena bibhṛṣe;

ibid., v.35, p.I-314a.

[526] Tai.Up.Bh. (Eight Up.-I), II-vii-1, p.362;

also,

raso nāma tṛpti hetur ānandakaro madhurāmlādiḥ prasiddho loke. ....tasmād asti tat teṣām ānanda kāraṇaṁ rasavad brahma;

Tai.Up.Bh. (Īśādi. Bh.), II-7, p.375.

[527] sudhā sindhor madhye sura viṭapi vāṭī parivṛte

maṇi dvīpe nīpopavana vati cintāmaṇi gṛhe,

śivākāre mañce parama śiva paryaṅka nilayāṁ

bhajanti tvāṁ dhanyāḥ katicana cid ānanda laharīm;

S.L., v.8, p.I-91a.

[528] taṭillekhā tanvīṁ tapana śaśi vaiśvānaramayīṁ

niṣaṇṇāṁ ṣaṇṇām apy upari kamalānāṁ tava kalām,

mahā padmāṭavyāṁ mṛdita mala māyena manasā

mahāntaḥ paśyanto dadhati paramāhlāda laharīm;

ibid., v.21, p.I-204a.

[529] sva dehodbhūtābhir ghṛṇibhir aṇimādyābhir abhitoḥ

niṣevye nitye tvām aham iti sadā bhāvayati yaḥ,

kim āścaryaṁ tasya trinayana samṛdhiṁ tṛṇayataḥ

mahā saṁvartāgnir viracayati nīrājana vidhim;

ibid., v.30, p.I-253a.

[530] Ai.Up.Bh. (Eight Up.-II), I-i-2, p.22;

also,

tasmāt ātma bhūta nāma rūpodāna bhūtaḥ sansarvajño ....tathā sarvajño devaḥ sarva śaktir mahāmāya ātmānam evātmāntaratvena jagad rūpeṇa nirmimīte iti yuktataram;

Ai.Up.Bh. (Īśādi. Bh.), I-2, p.18.

[531] taṭillekhā tanvīṁ tapana śaśi vaiśvānaramayīṁ

niṣaṇṇāṁ ṣaṇṇām apy upari kamalānāṁ tava kalām,

mahā padmāṭavyāṁ mṛdita mala māyena manasā

mahāntaḥ paśyanto dadhati paramāhlāda laharīm;

S.L., v.21, p.I-204a.

[532] manas tvaṁ vyoma tvaṁ marud asi marut sārathir asi

tvam āpas tvaṁ bhūmis tvayi pariṇatāyāṁ na hi param,

tvam eva svātmānaṁ pariṇamayituṁ viśva vapuṣā

cid ānandākāraṁ śiva yuvati bhāvena bibhṛṣe;

ibid., v.35, p.I-314a.

[533] Ai.Up.Bh. (Eight Up.-II), III-i-3, pp.68f;

also,

tad etat pratyastamita sarvopādhi viśeṣaṁ san niraṁjanaṁ nirmalaṁ niṣkriyaṁ śāntam ekam advayaṁ neti netīti sarva viśeṣāpoha saṅvedyaṁ ....niyaṁtṛtvād antaryāmi saṁjñaṁ bhavati;

Ai.Up.Bh. (Īśādi. Bh.), V-3, p.34.

534 taṭillekhā tanvīṁ tapana śaśi vaiśvānaramayīṁ

niṣaṇṇāṁ ṣaṇṇām apy upari kamalānāṁ tava kalām,

mahā padmāṭavyāṁ mṛdita mala māyena manasā

mahāntaḥ paśyanto dadhati paramāhlāda laharīm;

S.L., v.21, p.I-204a.

535 bhavāni tvaṁ dāse mayi vitara dṛṣṭiṁ sakaruṇāṁ

iti stotuṁ vāñchan kathayati bhavāni tvam iti yaḥ,

tadaiva tvaṁ tasmai diśasi nija sāyujya padavīṁ

mukunda brahmendra sphuṭa makuṭa nīrājita padām;

ibid., v.22, p.I-209a.

536 sva dehodbhūtābhir ghṛṇibhir aṇimādyābhir abhitoḥ

niṣevye nitye tvām aham iti sadā bhāvayati yaḥ,

kim āścaryaṁ tasya trinayana samṛdhiṁ tṛṇayataḥ

mahā saṁvartāgnir viracayati nīrājana vidhim;

ibid., v.30, p.I-253a.

537 Mu.Up.Bh. (Eight Up.-II), I-i-7, p.85;

also,

yathaite dṛṣṭāntāḥ tathā vilakṣaṇaṁ salakṣaṇaṁ ca ....aneka dṛṣṭāntopādānaṁ tu sukhāvabodhānārtham;

Mu.Up.Bh. (Īśādi. Bh.), I-i-7, p.502.

538 manas tvaṁ vyoma tvaṁ marud asi marut sārathir asi

tvam āpas tvaṁ bhūmis tvayi pariṇatāyāṁ na hi param,

tvam eva svātmānaṁ pariṇamayituṁ viśva vapuṣā

cid ānandākāraṁ śiva yuvati bhāvena bibhṛṣe;

S.L., v.35, p.I-314a.

539 nimeṣonmeṣābhyāṁ pralayam udayaṁ yāti jagatī

tavety āhuḥ santo dharaṇi dhara rājanya tanaye,

tvad unmeṣāj jātaṁ jagad idam aśeṣaṁ pralayataḥ

paritrātuṁ śaṁke parihṛta nimeṣās tava dṛśaḥ;

ibid., v.55, p.II-70a.

540 girām āhur devīṁ druhiṇa gṛhiṇīm āgamavido

hareḥ patnīṁ padmāṁ hara sahacarīm adri tanayām,

turīyā kāpi tvaṁ duradhigama niḥsīma mahimā

mahāmāyā viśvaṁ bhramayasi para brahma mahiṣi;

ibid., v.97, p.II-277a.

541 Mu.Up.Bh. (Eight Up.-II), II-ii-8, p.132;

also,

asya vicchinna saṅśayasya nivṛttāvidyasya yāni vijñānotpatteḥ prāktanāni janmāntare cāpravṛtta phalāni .... tasmin parāvare sākṣād aham asmīti dṛṣṭe saṁsāra kāraṇocchedānmucyata ity arthaḥ;

Mu.Up.Bh. (Īśādi. Bh.), II-ii-9, p.519.

542 taṭillekhā tanvīṁ tapana śaśi vaiśvānaramayīṁ

niṣaṇṇāṁ ṣaṇṇām apy upari kamalānāṁ tava kalām,

mahā padmāṭavyāṁ mṛdita mala māyena manasā

mahāntaḥ paśyanto dadhati paramāhlāda laharīm;

S.L., v.21, p.I-204a.

543 kṣitau ṣaṭ pañcāśad dvi samadhika pañcād udake

hutāśe dvā ṣaṣṭiś catur adhika pañcāśad anile,

divi dviḥ ṣaṭ triṁśan manasi ca catuḥ ṣaṣṭir iti ye

mayūkhās teṣām apy upari tava pādāmbuja yugam;

S.L., v.14, p.I-146a.

[544]japo jalpaḥ śilpaṁ sakalam api mudrā viracanā

gatiḥ prādakṣiṇya kramaṇam aśanādy āhuti vidhiḥ

praṇāmas saṁveśas sukham akhilam ātmārpaṇa dṛśā

saparyā paryāyas tava bhavatu yan me vilasitam;

ibid., v.27, p.I-236a.

[545] Mā.Up.Bh. (Eight Up.-II), 2, pp.175f;

also,

so'yamātmā oṁkārābhidheyaḥ parāparatvena vyavasthitaś catuṣpāt kārṣāpaṇavan na gauriva .... turīyasya tu padyata iti karma sādhanaḥ pāda śabdaḥ;

Mā.Up.Bh. (Īśādi. Bh.), I-2, p.426.

[546] taṭillekhā tanvīṁ tapana śaśi vaiśvānaramayīṁ

niṣaṇṇāṁ ṣaṇṇām apy upari kamalānāṁ tava kalām,

mahā padmāṭavyāṁ mṛdita mala māyena manasā

mahāntaḥ paśyanto dadhati paramāhlāda laharīm;

S.L., v.21, p.I-204a.

[547] śivaś śaktiḥ kāmaḥ kṣitir atha raviś śīta kiraṇaḥ ....

.... bhajante varṇās te tava janani nāmāvayavatām;

ibid., v.32, p.I-276a.

[548] girām āhur devīṁ druhiṇa gṛhiṇīm āgamavido

hareḥ patnīṁ padmāṁ hara sahacarīm adri tanayām,

turīyā kāpi tvaṁ duradhigama niḥsīma mahimā

mahāmāyā viśvaṁ bhramayasi para brahma mahiṣi;

ibid., v.97, p.II-277a.

[549] Mā.Up.Bh. (Eight Up.-II), 7, p.205;

also, prapañcopaśamam iti jāgrad ādi sthāna dharmābhāva ucyate. ata eva śāntaṁ śivaṁ yato'dvaitaṁ bheda vikalpa rahitaṁ caturthaṁ turīyaṁ manyate. pratīyamāna pāda traya rūpa vailakṣ aṇyāt;

Mā.Up.Bh. (Īśādi. Bh.), I-7, p.434.

[550] sudhā sindhor madhye sura viṭapi vāṭī parivṛte

maṇi dvīpe nīpopavana vati cintāmaṇi gṛhe,

śivākāre mañce parama śiva paryaṅka nilayāṁ

bhajanti tvāṁ dhanyāḥ katicana cid ānanda laharīm;

S.L., v.8, p.I-91a.

[551] kṣitau ṣaṭ pañcāśad dvi samadhika pañcād udake

hutāśe dvā ṣaṣṭiś catur adhika pañcāśad anile,

divi dviḥ ṣaṭ triṁśan manasi ca catuḥ ṣaṣṭir iti ye

mayūkhās teṣām apy upari tava pādāmbuja yugam;

ibid., v.14, p.I-146a.

[552] taṭillekhā tanvīṁ tapana śaśi vaiśvānaramayīṁ

niṣaṇṇāṁ ṣaṇṇām apy upari kamalānāṁ tava kalām,

mahā padmāṭavyāṁ mṛdita mala māyena manasā

mahāntaḥ paśyanto dadhati paramāhlāda laharīm;

S.L., v.21, p.I-204a.

[553]manas tvaṁ vyoma tvaṁ marud asi marut sārathir asi

tvam āpas tvaṁ bhūmis tvayi pariṇatāyāṁ na hi param,

tvam eva svātmānaṁ pariṇamayituṁ viśva vapuṣā

cid ānandākāraṁ śiva yuvati bhāvena bibhṛṣe;

ibid., v.35, p.I-314a.

[554]girām āhur devīṁ druhiṇa gṛhiṇīm āgamavido

hareḥ patnīṁ padmāṁ hara sahacarīm adri tanayām,

turīyā kāpi tvaṁ duradhigama niḥsīma mahimā

mahāmāyā viśvaṁ bhramayasi para brahma mahiṣi;

ibid., v.97, p.II-277a.

[555]Pr.Up.Bh. (Eight Up.-II), I-12, pp.422f;

also,

.....yasmāc chukla pakṣātmānaṁ prāṇaṁ sarvam eva paśyanti, tasmāt prāṇa darśina eta ṛṣayaḥ kṛṣṇa pakṣe'pīṣṭṁ yāgaṁ kurvantaḥ śukla pakṣa eva kurvanti. .... itara itar asmin kṛṣṇa pakṣa eva kurvanti śukle kurvanto'pi;

Pr.Up.Bh. (Īśādi. Bh.), I-12, p.397.

[556]japo jalpaḥ śilpaṁ sakalam api mudrā viracanā

gatiḥ prādakṣiṇya kramaṇam aśanādy āhuti vidhiḥ

praṇāmas saṁveśas sukham akhilam ātmārpaṇa dṛśā

saparyā paryāyas tava bhavatu yan me vilasitam; S.L., v.27, p.I-236a.

[557]manas tvaṁ vyoma tvaṁ marud asi marut sārathir asi

tvam āpas tvaṁ bhūmis tvayi pariṇatāyāṁ na hi param,

tvam eva svātmānaṁ pariṇamayituṁ viśva vapuṣā

cid ānandākāraṁ śiva yuvati bhāvena bibhṛṣe;

ibid., v.35, p.I-314a.

[558]catuṣ ṣaṣṭyā tantraiḥ sakalam atisandhāya bhuvanaṁ

sthitas tat tat siddhi prasava para tantraiḥ paśupatiḥ,

punas tvan nirbandhād akhila puruṣārthaika ghaṭanā

sva tantraṅ te tantraṁ kṣiti talam avātītarad idam;

ibid., v.31, p.I-264a.

[559] Pr.Up.Bh. (Eight Up.-II), V-2, pp.470f;

also,

paraṁ hi brahma śabdādy upalakṣaṇānarhaṁ sarva dharma viśeṣa varjita mato na śakyam atīndriya gocaratvāt kevalena mansāvagāhitum. oṁkāre tu viṣṇvādi pratimā sthānīye bhakty āveśita brahma bhāve dhyāyināṁ tat prasīdatīty avagamyate śāstra prāmāṇyāt tathā'paraṁ ca brahma;

Pr.Up.Bh. (Īśādi. Bh.), V-2, pp.412f.

560 bhavāni tvaṁ dāse mayi vitara dṛṣṭiṁ sakaruṇāṁ

iti stotuṁ vāñchan kathayati bhavāni tvam iti yaḥ,

tadaiva tvaṁ tasmai diśasi nija sāyujya padavīṁ

mukunda brahmendra sphuṭa makuṭa nīrājita padām;

S.L., v.22, p.I-209a.

561 sva dehodbhūtābhir ghṛṇibhir aṇimādyābhir abhitoḥ

niṣevye nitye tvām aham iti sadā bhāvayati yaḥ,

kim āścaryaṁ tasya trinayana samṛdhiṁ tṛṇayataḥ

mahā saṁvartāgnir viracayati nīrājana vidhim;

ibid., v.30, p.I-253a.

562 Bṛ.Up.Bh.(tr.), III-viii-9, p.362;

also,

etaddhyakṣaraṁ sarva vyavasthā setuḥ sarva maryādā vidharaṇamato nāsyākṣarasya praśāsanaṁ .... "yena dyaur ugrā pṛthivī ca dṛḍhā" iti mantra varṇāt;

Bṛ.Up.Bh., III-viii-9, p.269.

563 tanīyāsāṁ pāṁsuṁ tava ....bhasitod dhūlana vidhim;

S. laharī, v.2, p.26.

564 nimeṣonmeṣābhyāṁ pralayam udayaṁ yāti jagatī

tavety āhuḥ santo dharaṇi dhara rājanya tanaye,

tvad unmeṣāj jātaṁ jagad idam aśeṣaṁ pralayataḥ

paritrātuṁ śaṅke parihṛta nimeṣās tava dṛśaḥ;

S.L., v.55, p.II-70a.

565 Bṛ.Up.Bh.(tr.), IV-iv-7, p.506;

also,

atha tadā martyo maraṇa dharmā sankāma viyogāt samūlato'mṛto bhavati. arthād anātma viṣayāḥ kāmā avidyā lakṣaṇā mṛtyava ity etad uktaṁ bhavati. ato mṛtyu viyoge vidvāñ jīvan nevāmṛto bhavati. atrāsminneva śarīre vartamāno brahma samaśnute brahma bhāvaṁ mokṣaṁ pratipadyata ity arthaḥ. ato mokṣo na deśāntara gamanādy apekṣate. tasmād viduṣo notkrāmanti prāṇā yathāvasthitā eva sva kāraṇe puruṣe samavanīyante. nāma mātraṁ hy avaśiṣyata ity uktam;

Bṛ.Up.Bh., IV-iv-7, p.361.

566 japo jalpaḥ śilpaṁ sakalam api mudrā viracanā

gatiḥ prādakṣiṇya kramaṇam aśanādy āhuti vidhiḥ

praṇāmas saṁveśas sukham akhilam ātmārpaṇa dṛśā

saparyā paryāyas tava bhavatu yan me vilasitam;

S.L., v.27, p.I-236a.

567 sva dehodbhūtābhir ghṛṇibhir aṇimādyābhir abhitoḥ

niṣevye nitye tvām aham iti sadā bhāvayati yaḥ,

kim āścaryaṁ tasya trinayana samṛdhiṁ tṛṇayataḥ

mahā saṁvartāgnir viracayati nīrājana vidhim;

ibid., v.30, p.I-253a.

568 Ch.Up.Bh.(tr.), III-xiv-1, pp.208f;

also,

kathaṁ sarvasya brahmatvam ityata āha - taj jalān iti. tasmād brahmaṇo jātaṁ tejo bannādi krameṇa sarvam. atas taj jam. tathā tenaiva janana krameṇa pratilomatayā tasminneva brahmaṇi līyate tadātmatayā śliṣyata iti tal lam. tathā tasminneva sthiti kāle'niti prāṇiti ceṣṭata iti. evaṁ brahmātmatayā triṣu kāleṣu aviśiṣṭaṁ tad vyatirekeṇa agrahaṇāt. ataḥ tad eva idaṁ jagat;

Ch.Up.Bh. (Īśādi. Bh.), III-xiv-1, p.178.

[569] manas tvaṁ vyoma tvaṁ marud asi marut sārathir asi

tvam āpas tvaṁ bhūmis tvayi pariṇatāyāṁ na hi param,

tvam eva svātmānaṁ pariṇamayituṁ viśva vapuṣā

cid ānandākāraṁ śiva yuvati bhāvena bibhṛṣe;

S.L., v.35, p.I-314a.

[570] nimeṣonmeṣābhyāṁ pralayam udayaṁ yāti jagatī

tavety āhuḥ santo dharaṇi dhara rājanya tanaye,

tvad unmeṣāj jātaṁ jagad idam aśeṣaṁ pralayataḥ

paritrātuṁ śaṅke parihṛta nimeṣās tava dṛśaḥ;

ibid., v.55, p.II-70a.

[571] Ch.Up.Bh.(tr.), VI-xiv-2, p.488;

also,

tasyāsyaivam ācāryavato muktāvidyābhinahanasya tāvad eva ....atha tadaiva satsaṁpatsye;

Ch.Up.Bh. (Īśādi. Bh.), VI-xiv-2, p.272.

[572] taṭillekhā tanvīṁ tapana śaśi vaiśvānaramayīṁ

niṣaṇṇāṁ ṣaṇṇām apy upari kamalānāṁ tava kalām,

mahā padmāṭavyāṁ mṛdita mala māyena manasā

mahāntaḥ paśyanto dadhati paramāhlāda laharīm;

S.L., v.21, p.I-204a.

[573] sudhā dhārā sāraiś caraṇa yuglāntar vigalitaiḥ

prapañcaṁ siñcantī punar api rasāmnāya mahasaḥ,

avāpya svāṁ bhūmiṁ bhujaganibham adhyuṣṭavalayaṁ

svam ātmānaṁ kṛtvā svapiṣi kulakuṇḍe kuhariṇi;

ibid., v.10, p.I-110a.

[574] japo jalpaḥ śilpaṁ sakalam api mudrā viracanā

gatiḥ prādakṣiṇya kramaṇam aśanādy āhuti vidhiḥ

praṇāmas saṁveśas sukham akhilam ātmārpaṇa dṛśā

saparyā paryāyas tava bhavatu yan me vilasitam;

ibid., v.27, p.I-236a.

[575] Śv.Up.Bh.(tr.), III-2, p.125;

also,

etad uktaṁ bhavati - advitīyaḥ paramātmā. na cāsau kumbhakāravad ātmānaṁ kevalaṁ .... kurvan sraṣṭā

niyantā vā'bhidhīyat iti;

Śv.Up.Bh., III-2, p.53.

[576] manas tvaṁ vyoma tvaṁ marud asi marut sārathir asi

tvam āpas tvaṁ bhūmis tvayi pariṇatāyāṁ na hi param,

tvam eva svātmānaṁ pariṇamayituṁ viśva vapuṣā

cid ānandākāraṁ śiva yuvati bhāvena bibhṛṣe;

S.L., v.35, p.I-314a.

[577] nimeṣonmeṣābhyāṁ pralayam udayaṁ yāti jagatī

tavety āhuḥ santo dharaṇi dhara rājanya tanaye,

tvad unmeṣāj jātaṁ jagad idam aśeṣaṁ pralayataḥ

paritrātuṁ śaṅke parihṛta nimeṣās tava dṛśaḥ;

ibid., v.55, p.II-70a.

[578] girām āhur devīṁ druhiṇa gṛhiṇīm āgamavido

hareḥ patnīṁ padmāṁ hara sahacarīm adri tanayām,

turīyā kāpi tvaṁ duradhigama niḥsīma mahimā

mahāmāyā viśvaṁ bhramayasi para brahma mahiṣi;

ibid., v.97, p.II-277a.

[579] Śv.Up.Bh.(tr.), Introduction, p.12;

also,

yadā punaḥ phala nirapekṣam īśvarārthaṁ karmānutiṣṭhanti tadā mokṣa sādhana jñāna sādhanāntaḥkaraṇa śuddhi sādhana pāramparyeṇa mokṣa sādhanaṁ bhavati;

Śv.Up.Bh., p.5.

580 japo jalpaḥ śilpaṁ sakalam api mudrā viracanā

gatiḥ prādakṣiṇya kramaṇam aśanādy āhuti vidhiḥ

praṇāmas saṁveśas sukham akhilam ātmārpaṇa dṛśā

saparyā paryāyas tava bhavatu yan me vilasitam;

S.L., v.27, p.I-236a.

581 dadāne dīnebhyaḥ śriyam aniśam āśānusadṛśīṁ ....

nimajjan majjīvaḥ karaṇa caraṇaḥ ṣaṭ caraṇatām;

ibid., v.90, p.II-236a.

582 Bh.G.Bh.(tr.), II-10, pp.42f;

also,

.....tasmād gītā śāstra īṣanmātreṇāpi śrautena smārtena vā karmaṇā ''tma jñānasya samuccayo .... tattva vittu nāhaṁ karomīti manyate na ca tat phalamamisaṁdhatte;

Bh.G.Bh., II-10, p.11.

583 śivaś śaktyā yukto yadi bhavati śaktaḥ prabhavituṁ

na cedevaṁ devo na khalu kuśalaḥ spanditum api;

atas tvām ārādhyāṁ hari hara viriñcādi bhir api,

praṇantuṁ stotuṁ vā katham akṛtapuṇyaḥ prabhavati;

S.L., v.1, p.I-1.

584 japo jalpaḥ śilpaṁ sakalam api mudrā viracanā

gatiḥ prādakṣiṇya kramaṇam aśanādy āhuti vidhiḥ

praṇāmas saṁveśas sukham akhilam ātmārpaṇa dṛśā

saparyā paryāyas tava bhavatu yan me vilasitam;

ibid., v.27, p.I-236a.

585 dadāne dīnebhyaḥ śriyam aniśam āśānusadṛśīṁ
.......................nimajjan majjīvaḥ karaṇa caraṇaḥ ṣaṭ caraṇatām;

S.L., v.90, p.II-236a.

586 Bh.G.Bh.(tr.), II-46, p.93;

also,

tasmāt prāg jñāna niṣṭhādhikāra prāpteḥ karmaṇy adhikṛtena kūpa taḍāgādy artha sthānīyam api karma kartavyam;

Bh.G.Bh., II-46, p.30.

587 catuṣ ṣaṣṭyā tantraiḥ sakalam atisandhāya bhuvanaṁ

sthitas tat tat siddhi prasava para tantraiḥ paśupatiḥ,

punas tvan nirbandhād akhila puruṣārthaika ghaṭanā

sva tantraṁ te tantraṁ kṣiti talam avātītarad idam;

S.L., v.31, p.I-264a.

588 japo jalpaḥ śilpaṁ sakalam api mudrā viracanā

gatiḥ prādakṣiṇya kramaṇam aśanādy āhuti vidhiḥ

praṇāmas saṁveśas sukham akhilam ātmārpaṇa dṛśā

saparyā paryāyas tava bhavatu yan me vilasitam;

ibid., v.27, p.I-236a.

589 Bh.G.Bh.(tr.), II-49, p.95;

also,

dūreṇāti viprakarṣeṇa hy avaraṁ nikṛṣṭaṁ karma phalārthinā kriyamāṇaṁ buddhi yogāt samat buddhi yuktāt karmaṇo janma maraṇādi hetutvād dhanaṁjaya;

Bh.G.Bh., II-49, p.31.

590 japo jalpaḥ śilpaṁ sakalam api mudrā viracanā

gatiḥ prādakṣiṇya kramaṇam aśanādy āhuti vidhiḥ

praṇāmas saṁveśas sukham akhilam ātmārpaṇa dṛśā

saparyā paryāyas tava bhavatu yan me vilasitam;

S.L., v.27, p.I-236a.

[591] catuṣ ṣaṣṭyā tantraiḥ sakalam atisandhāya bhuvanaṁ

sthitas tat tat siddhi prasava para tantraiḥ paśupatiḥ,

punas tvan nirbandhād akhila puruṣārthaika ghaṭanā

sva tantraṁ te tantraṁ kṣiti talam avātītarad idam;

ibid., v.31, p.I-264a.

[592] Bh.G.Bh.(tr.), II-55, p.102;

also,

sarvatraiva hy adhyātma śāstre kṛtārtha lakṣaṇani yāni tāny eva "sādhanāny upadiśyante yatna sādhyatvāt. yāni yatna sādhyāni sādhanāni lakṣaṇāni ca bhavanti tāni;

Bh.G.Bh., II-55, p.33.

[593] taṭillekhā tanvīṁ tapana śaśi vaiśvānaramayīṁ

niṣaṇṇāṁ ṣaṇṇām apy upari kamalānāṁ tava kalām,

mahā padmāṭavyāṁ mṛdita mala māyena manasā

mahāntaḥ paśyanto dadhati paramāhlāda laharīm;

S.L., v.21, p.I-204a.

[594] japo jalpaḥ śilpaṁ sakalam api mudrā viracanā

gatiḥ prādakṣiṇya kramaṇam aśanādy āhuti vidhiḥ

praṇāmas saṁveśas sukham akhilam ātmārpaṇa dṛśā

saparyā paryāyas tava bhavatu yan me vilasitam;

S.L., v.27, p.I-236a.

[595] Bh.G.Bh.(tr.), IV-11, p.183;

also,

ato ye phalārthinas tān phala pradānena. ye yathokta kāriṇastva phalārthino mumukṣavaś ca tāñ jñāna pradānena

.........na punā rāga dveṣa nimittaṁ moha nimittaṁ vā kaṁcid bhajāmi;

Bh.G.Bh., IV-11, p.63.

596 avidyām antas timira mihira dvīpa nagarī

jaḍānāṁ caitanya stabaka makaranda sruti jharī,

daridrāṇāṁ cintāmaṇi guṇanikā janma jaladhau

nimagnānāṁ daṁṣṭrā mura ripu varāhasya bhavati;

S.L., v.3, p.I-58a.

597 ibid., vv.15-18, pp.I-171a-187a.

598 bhavāni tvaṁ dāse mayi vitara dṛṣṭiṁ sakaruṇāṁ

iti stotuṁ vāñchan kathayati bhavāni tvam iti yaḥ,

tadaiva tvaṁ tasmai diśasi nija sāyujya padavīṁ

mukunda brahmendra sphuṭa makuṭa nīrājita padām;

ibid., v.22, p.I-209a.

599 catuṣ ṣaṣṭyā tantraiḥ sakalam atisandhāya bhuvanaṁ

sthitas tat tat siddhi prasava para tantraiḥ paśupatiḥ,

punas tvan nirbandhād akhila puruṣārthaika ghaṭanā

sva tantraṁ te tantraṁ kṣiti talam avātītarad idam;

ibid., v.31, p.I-264a.

600 sarasvatyā lakṣmyā vidhi hari sapatno viharate

rateḥ pātivratyaṁ śithilayati ramyeṇa vapuṣā,

ciraṁ jīvann eva kṣapita paśu pāśa vyatikaraḥ

parānandābhikhyaṁ rasayati rasaṁ tvad bhajanvān;

ibid., v.99, p.II-290a.

601 Bh.G.Bh.(tr.), V-26, p.267;

also,

samyag darśana niṣṭhānāṁ saṁnyāsināṁ sadyo muktir uktā karma yogaś ceśvarārpita sarva bhāveneśvare brahmaṇy ādhāya kriyamāṇaḥ sattva śuddhi jñāna prāpti sarva karma saṁnyāsa krameṇa mokṣāyeti bhagavān pade pade'bravīd vakṣyati ca;

Bh.G.Bh., V-26, p.92.

602 japo jalpaḥ śilpaṁ sakalam api mudrā viracanā

gatiḥ prādakṣiṇya kramaṇam aśanādy āhuti vidhiḥ

praṇāmas saṁveśas sukham akhilam ātmārpaṇa dṛśā

saparyā paryāyas tava bhavatu yan me vilasitam;

S.L., v.27, p.I-236a.

603 dadāne dīnebhyaḥ śriyam aniśam āśānusadṛśīṁ

....nimajjan majjīvaḥ karaṇa caraṇaḥ ṣaṭ caraṇatām;

S.L., v.90, p.II-236a.

604 Bh.G.Bh.(tr.), VII-5, pp.319f;

also,

aparā na parā nikṛṣṭā 'śuddhā 'narthakarī saṁsāra bandhanātmikeyam ito'syā yathoktāyās tvanyāṁ viśuddhāṁ prakṛtiṁ mamā ''tmabhūtāṁ viddhi me parāṁ prakṛṣṭāṁ jīvabhūtāṁ kṣetrajña lakṣaṇāṁ prāṇa dhāraṇa nimittabhūtāṁ he mahābāho yathā prakṛtyedaṁ dhāryate jagad antaḥ praviṣṭayā;

Bh.G.Bh., VII-5, p.112.

605 śivaś śaktyā yukto yadi bhavati śaktaḥ prabhavituṁ,

na cedevaṁ devo na khalu kuśalaḥ spanditum api;

atas tvām ārādhyāṁ hari hara viriñcādi bhir api,

praṇantuṁ stotuṁ vā katham akṛtapuṇyaḥ prabhavati;

S.L., v.1, p.I-1.

606 manas tvaṁ vyoma tvaṁ marud asi marut sārathir asi

tvam āpas tvaṁ bhūmis tvayi pariṇatāyāṁ na hi param,

tvam eva svātmānaṁ pariṇamayituṁ viśva vapuṣā

cid ānandākāraṁ śiva yuvati bhāvena bibhṛṣe;

ibid., v.35, p.I-314a.

[607]girām āhur devīṁ druhiṇa gṛhiṇīm āgamavido

hareḥ patnīṁ padmāṁ hara sahacarīm adri tanayām,

turīyā kāpi tvaṁ duradhigama niḥsīma mahimā

mahāmāyā viśvaṁ bhramayasi para brahma mahiṣi;

ibid., v.97, p.II-277a.

[608] Bh.G.Bh.(tr.), VII-17, pp.328f;

also,

teṣāṁ caturṇāṁ madhye jñānī tattvavit tattvavittvān nitya yukto bhavaty eka bhaktiś cānyasya bhajanīyasyādarśanād ataḥ sa eka bhaktir viśiṣyate viśeṣam ādhikyam āpadyate'tiricyata ity arthaḥ;

Bh.G.Bh., VII-17, pp.115f.

[609] japo jalpaḥ śilpaṁ sakalam api mudrā viracanā

gatiḥ prādakṣiṇya kramaṇam aśanādy āhuti vidhiḥ

praṇāmas saṁveśas sukham akhilam ātmārpaṇa dṛśā

saparyā paryāyas tava bhavatu yan me vilasitam;

S.L., v.27, p.I-236a.

[610] bhavāni tvaṁ dāse mayi vitara dṛṣṭiṁ sakaruṇāṁ

iti stotuṁ vāñchan kathayati bhavāni tvam iti yaḥ,

tadaiva tvaṁ tasmai diśasi nija sāyujya padavīṁ

mukunda brahmendra sphuṭa makuṭa nīrājita padām;

ibid., v.22, p.I-209a.

[611] Bh.G.Bh.(tr.), XIV-27, p.590;

also,

yathā ceśvara śaktyā bhaktānugrahādi prayojanāya brahma pratiṣṭhe pravartate sā śaktir brahmaivāhaṁ śakti śaktimator ananyatvād ity abhiprāyaḥ;

Bh.G.Bh., XIV-27, p.213.

612 śarīraṅ tvaṁ śaṁbhoḥ śaśi mihira vakṣoruha yugaṁ

tavātmānaṁ manye bhagvati navātmānam anagham,

ataś śeṣaś śeṣīty ayam ubhaya sādhāraṇatayā

sthitas saṁbandho vāṁ samarasa parānanda parayoḥ;

S.L., v.34, p.I-303a.

613 śivaś śaktyā yukto yadi bhavati śaktaḥ prabhavituṁ,

na cedevaṁ devo na khalu kuśalaḥ spanditum api;

atas tvām ārādhyāṁ hari hara viriñcādi bhir api,

praṇantuṁ stotuṁ vā katham akṛtapuṇyaḥ prabhavati;

ibid., v.1, p.I-1.

614 sudhā sindhor madhye sura viṭapi vāṭī parivṛte

maṇi dvīpe nīpopavana vati cintāmaṇi gṛhe,

śivākāre mañce parama śiva paryaṅka nilayāṁ

bhajanti tvāṁ dhanyāḥ katicana cid ānanda laharīm;

ibid., v.8, p.I-91a;

also,

taṭillekhā tanvīṁ tapana śaśi vaiśvānaramayīṁ

niṣaṇṇāṁ ṣaṇṇām apy upari kamalānāṁ tava kalām,

mahā padmāṭavyāṁ mṛdita mala māyena manasā

mahāntaḥ paśyanto dadhati paramāhlāda laharīm;

ibid., v.21, p.I-204a;

also,

śarīraṁ tvaṁ śaṁbhoḥ śaśi mihira vakṣoruha yugaṁ

tavātmānaṁ manye bhagvati navātmānam anagham,

ataś śeṣaś śeṣīty ayam ubhaya sādhāraṇatayā

sthitas saṁbandho vāṁ samarasa parānanda parayoḥ;

ibid., v.34, p.I-303a.

615 ity ato'smat pratyaya gocare viṣayiṇi cid ātmake yuṣmat pratyaya gocarasya viṣayasya tad dharmāṇāṁ cādhyāsaḥ, tad viparyayeṇa viṣ ayiṇas tad dharmāṇāṁ ca viṣaye'dhyāso mithyeti bhavituṁ yuktam; tathāpy anyonyasminn anyonyātmakatām anyonya dharmāṁś cādhyasy etaretarāvivekenātyanta viviktayor dharma dharmiṇor mithyā jñāna nimittaḥ satyānṛte mithunī kṛtya 'aham idaṁ' 'mamedam iti' naisargiko 'ya ṁ loka vyavahāraḥ;

B.S.Bh., I-i-1, pp.7-17.

616 vāsanā vṛddhitaḥ kāryaṁ kārya vṛddhyā ca vāsanā,

vardhate sarvathā puṁsaḥ saṁsāro na nivartate;

Viv.Cd., v.313, p.119.

617 Supra 615.

618 Rajesh Kumar Jha, 'Post-modernism and Advaitika Spirituality' in Reason, Dialectic

and Postmodern Philosophy, p.185-189.

619 sad ghanaṁ cid ghanaṁ nityam ānanda ghanam akriyam,

ekam evādvayaṁ brahma neha nānāsti kiñcana;

Viv.Cd., v.465, p.173;

also,

nirguṇaṁ niṣkalaṁ sūkṣmaṁ nirvikalpaṁ nirañjanam,

ekam evādvayaṁ brahma neha nānāsti kiñcana;

ibid., v.468, p.174.

620 tam etam avidyākhyam ātmānātmanor itaretarādhyāsaṁ puraskṛtya sarve pramāṇa prameya vyavahārā laukikā vaidikāś ca pravṛttāḥ, sarvāṇi ca śāstrāṇi vidhi pratiṣedha mokṣa parāṇi;

B.S.Bh., I-i-1, p.40.

621 yasya vākyasya tātparya viṣayībhūta saṁsargo mānāntareṇa na bādhyate, tad vākyaṁ pramāṇam;

V.P., IV-1, p.65;

also,

ata eva veda vākyānāṁ brahmaṇi prāmāṇyam;

ibid., IV-46, p.84.

622 S.N. Dasgupta, A History of Indian Philosophy, vol. I, p.434.

623 asya jagato nāma rūpābhyāṁ vyākṛtasyāneka kartṛ bhoktṛ saṁyuktasya pratiniyata deśa kāla nimitta kriyā phalāśrayasya manasāpy acintya racanā rūpasya janma sthiti bhaṅgaṁ yataḥ sarvajñāt sarvaśakteḥ kāraṇād bhavati tad brahmeti vākyaśeṣaḥ;

B.S.Bh., I-i-2, pp.85f;

also,

na dharma jijñāsāyām iva śrty ādaya eva pramāṇaṁ brahma jijñāsāyām, kiṁtu śruty ādayo'nubhavādayaś ca yathā saṁbhavam iha pramāṇaṁ; anubhavāvasānatvād bhūta vastu viṣayatvāc ca brahma jñānasya;

ibid., I-i-2, p.89.

624 pṛthivyāpas tejaḥ pavana gagane tat prakṛtayaḥ

sthitās tanmātrāstā viṣaya daśakaṁ mānasam iti,

tathā māyā vidyā tadanu ca maheśaḥ śiva itaḥ

paraṁ tattvātītaṁ milita vapur indoḥ para kalā;

Subh., v.5, p.28;

also,

vadanty eke santaḥ para śiva pade tattva milite

tatas tvaṁ ṣaḍviṁśā bhavasi śivayor melana vapuḥ; ibid., v.35, p.206.

625 manas tvaṁ vyoma tvaṁ marud asi marut sārathir asi

tvam āpas tvaṁ bhūmis tvayi pariṇatāyāṁ na hi param,

tvam eva svātmānaṁ pariṇamayituṁ viśva vapuṣā

cid ānandākāraṁ śiva yuvati bhāvena bibhṛṣe;

S.L., v.35, p.I-314a;

also,

girām āhur devīṁ druhiṇa gṛhiṇīm āgamavido

hareḥ patnīṁ padmāṁ hara sahacarīm adri tanayām,

turīyā kāpi tvaṁ duradhigama niḥsīma mahimā

mahāmāyā viśvaṁ bhramayasi para brahma mahiṣi;

ibid., v.97, p.II-277a.

626 na dharma jijñāsāyām iva śrty ādaya eva pramāṇaṁ brahma jijñāsāyām, kiṁtu śruty ādayo'nubhavādayaś ca yathā saṁbhavam iha pramāṇaṁ; anubhavāvasānatvād bhūta vastu viṣayatvāc ca brahma jñānasya;

B.S.Bh., I-i-2, p.89;

also,

śāstraṁ yuktir deśikoktiḥ pramāṇaṁ

cāntaḥ siddhā svānubhūtiḥ pramāṇam;

Viv.Cd., v.474, p.177;

also,

taṭa sthitā bodhayanti guravaḥ śrutayo yathā

prajñayaiva tared vidvānīśvarānugṛhītayā;

ibid., v.476, p.177.

627 Ramakant Tripathi, Brahmasūtra Śāṅkara-bhāṣya (catuḥ-sūtrī), p.24.

628 sati cānantaryārthatve yathā dharma jijñāsā pūrva vṛttaṁ vedādhyayanaṁ niyamenāpekṣata evaṁ brahma jijñāsāpi yat pūrva

kṛtaṁ niyamenāpekṣate, tad vaktavyam. svādhyāyānantaryaṁ tu samānam;

B.S.Bh., I-i-1, pp.49-51.

629 ucyate - nityānitya vastu vivekaḥ, ihāmutrāthabhoga virāgaḥ, śama damādi sādhana saṁpat mumukṣutvaṁ ca. teṣu hi satsu prāg api dharma jijñāsāyā ūrdhvaṁ ca śakyate brahma jijñāsituṁ jñātuṁ ca, na viparyaye;

B.S.Bh.., I-i-1, pp.71-3.

630 taṭa sthitā bodhayanti guravaḥ śrutayo yathā

prajñayaiva tared vidvānīśvarānugṛhītayā;

Viv.Cd., v.476, p.177.

631 girām āhur devīṁ druhiṇa gṛhiṇīm āgamavido

hareḥ patnīṁ padmāṁ hara sahacarīm adri tanayām,

turīyā kāpi tvaṁ duradhigama niḥsīma mahimā

mahāmāyā viśvaṁ bhramayasi para brahma mahiṣi;

S.L., v.97, p.II-277a;

also,

avidyāvasthāyāṁ kārya karaṇa saṁghātāviveka darśino jivasyāvidyā timirāndhasya sataḥ parasmād ātmanaḥ karmādhyakṣāt sarva bhūtādhivāsāt sākṣiṇaś cetayitur īśvarāt tad anujñayā kartṛtva bhoktṛtva lakṣaṇasya saṁsārasya siddhiḥ, tad anugraha hetuken aiva ca vijñānena mokṣa siddhir bhavitum arhati. kutaḥ? tac chruteḥ. yadyapi doṣa prayuktaḥ sāmagrī saṁpannaś ca jīvaḥ, yadyapi ca loke kṛṣy ādiṣu karmasu neśvara kāraṇatvaṁ prasiddham; tathāpi sarvāsveva pravṛttiṣvīśvaro hetu karteti śruter avasīyate. tathāhi śrutir bhavati - 'eṣa hy eva sādhu karma kārayati taṁ yamebhyo lokebhya un ninīṣate. eṣa hy evāsādhu karma kārayati taṁ yam adho ninīṣate' (Kauṣī. 3-8) iti 'ya ātmani tiṣṭ hannātmānam antaro yamayati' iti caivaṁjātīyakā;

B.S.Bh., II-iii-41, p.620.

[632] Surendranath Bhattacharya, 'The Philosophy of Śaṅkara' in The Cultural Heritage of India, vol. III, p.241.

[633] P.K. Sundaram, Advaita Epistemology, p.308.

[634] bhavāni tvaṁ dāse mayi vitara dṛṣṭiṁ sakaruṇāṁ

iti stotuṁ vāñchan kathayati bhavāni tvam iti yaḥ,

tadaiva tvaṁ tasmai diśasi nija sāyujya padavīṁ

mukunda brahmendra sphuṭa makuṭa nīrājita padām;

S.L., v.22, p.I-209a;

also,

dṛśā drāghīyasyā dara dalita nīlotpala rucā ....

vane vā harmye vā sama kara nipāto hima karaḥ;

ibid., v.57, p.II-79a.

[635] japo jalpaḥ śilpaṁ sakalam api mudrā viracanā

gatiḥ prādakṣiṇya kramaṇam aśanādy āhuti vidhiḥ

praṇāmas saṁveśas sukham akhilam ātmārpaṇa dṛśā

saparyā paryāyas tava bhavatu yan me vilasitam;

ibid., v.27, p.I-236a.

[636] manas tvaṁ vyoma tvaṁ marud asi marut sārathir asi

tvam āpas tvaṁ bhūmis tvayi pariṇatāyāṁ na hi param,

tvam eva svātmānaṁ pariṇamayituṁ viśva vapuṣā

cid ānandākāraṁ śiva yuvati bhāvena bibhṛṣe;

ibid., v.35, p.I-314a;

also,

bhavāni tvaṁ dāse mayi vitara dṛṣṭiṁ sakaruṇāṁ

iti stotuṁ vāñchan kathayati bhavāni tvam iti yaḥ,

tadaiva tvaṁ tasmai diśasi nija sāyujya padavīṁ

mukunda brahmendra sphuṭa makuṭa nīrājita padām;

ibid., v.22, p.I-209a;

also,

sva dehodbhūtābhir ghṛṇibhir aṇimādyābhir abhitoḥ

niṣevye nitye tvām aham iti sadā bhāvayati yaḥ,

kim āścaryaṁ tasya trinayana samṛdhiṁ tṛṇayataḥ

mahā saṁvartāgnir viracayati nīrājana vidhim;

ibid., v.30, p.I-253a.

637 Vinoba Bhave, Gītā Pravacana, p.100.

638 bhavāni tvaṁ dāse mayi vitara dṛṣṭiṁ sakaruṇāṁ

iti stotuṁ vāñchan kathayati bhavāni tvam iti yaḥ,

tadaiva tvaṁ tasmai diśasi nija sāyujya padavīṁ

mukunda brahmendra sphuṭa makuṭa nīrājita padām;

S.L., v.22, p.I-209a;

also,

avidyāvasthāyāṁ kārya karaṇa saṁghātāviveka darśino jivasyāvidyā timirāndhasya sataḥ parasmād ātmanaḥ karmādhyakṣāt sarva bhūtādhivāsāt sākṣiṇaś cetayitur īśvarāt tad anujñayā kartṛtva bhoktṛtva lakṣaṇasya saṁsārasya siddhiḥ, tad anugraha hetuken aiva ca vijñānena mokṣa siddhir bhavitum arhati. kutaḥ? tac chruteḥ. yadyapi doṣa prayuktaḥ sāmagrī saṁpannaś ca jīvaḥ, yadyapi ca loke kṛṣy ādiṣu karmasu neśvara kāraṇatvaṁ prasiddham; tathāpi sarvāsveva pravṛttiṣv īśvaro hetu karteti śruter avasīyate. tathāhi śrutir bhavati - 'eṣa hy eva sādhu karma kārayati taṁ yamebhyo lokebhya un ninīṣate. eṣa hy evāsādhu karma kārayati taṁ yam adho ninīṣate' (Kauṣī. 3-8) iti 'ya ātmani tiṣṭ hannātmānam antaro yamayati' iti caivaṁjātīyakā;

B.S.Bh., II-iii-41, p.620;

also,

taṭa sthitā bodhayanti guravaḥ śrutayo yathā

prajñayaiva tared vidvānīśvarānugṛhītayā;

Viv.Cd., v.476, p.177.

[639] sarasvatyā lakṣmyā vidhi hari sapatno viharate
rateḥ pātivratyaṁ śithilayati ramyeṇa vapuṣā,
ciraṁ jīvann eva kṣapita paśu pāśa vyatikaraḥ
parānandābhikhyaṁ rasayati rasaṁ tvad bhajanvān;
S.L., v.99, p.II-290a.

[640] japo jalpaḥ śilpaṁ sakalam api mudrā viracanā
gatiḥ prādakṣiṇya kramaṇam aśanādy āhuti vidhiḥ
praṇāmas saṁveśas sukham akhilam ātmārpaṇa dṛśā
saparyā paryāyas tava bhavatu yan me vilasitam;
ibid., v.27, p.I-236a.

[641] bhavāni tvaṁ dāse mayi vitara dṛṣṭiṁ sakaruṇāṁ
iti stotuṁ vāñchan kathayati bhavāni tvam iti yaḥ,
tadaiva tvaṁ tasmai diśasi nija sāyujya padavīṁ
mukunda brahmendra sphuṭa makuṭa nīrājita padām;
S.L., v.22, p.I-209a.

[642] ...sahasrāre padme subhaga subhagodeti subhage,
paraṁ saubhāgyaṁ yat tad iha tava sāyujya padavī;
Subh., v.51, p.300.

[643] japo jalpaḥ śilpaṁ sakalam api mudrā viracanā
gatiḥ prādakṣiṇya kramaṇam aśanādy āhuti vidhiḥ
praṇāmas saṁveśas sukham akhilam ātmārpaṇa dṛśā
saparyā paryāyas tava bhavatu yan me vilasitam;
S.L., v.27, p.I-236a;
also,
sarasvatyā lakṣmyā vidhi hari sapatno viharate

rateḥ pātivratyaṁ śithilayati ramyeṇa vapuṣā,
ciraṁ jīvann eva kṣapita paśu pāśa vyatikaraḥ
parānandābhikhyaṁ rasayati rasaṁ tvad bhajanvān;
ibid., v.99, p.II-290a;
also,
...sahasrāre padme subhaga subhagodeti subhage,
paraṁ saubhāgyaṁ yat tad iha tava sāyujya padavī;
Subh., v.51, p.300;
also,
ato'syāḥ saṁsiddhau subhaga subhagākhyā guru kṛpā
kaṭākṣavyāsaṅgāt sravad amṛtaniṣyanda sulabhā,
tayā viddho yogī vicarati niśāyām api divā
divā bhānū rātrau vidhur iva kṛtārthī kṛta matiḥ;
ibid., v.52, p.306.

644 jñānodayāt purārabdhaṁ karma jñānān na naśyati,
adatvā sva phalaṁ lakṣyam uddiśyot sṛṣṭa bāṇavat;
Viv.Cd., v.451, p.169.

645 saṁsiddhasya phalaṁ tvetaj jīvanmuktasya yoginaḥ,
bahir antaḥ sadānanda rasāsvādanam ātmani;
ibid., v.418, p.158;
also,
ato'syāḥ saṁsiddhau subhaga subhagākhyā guru kṛpā
kaṭākṣavyāsaṅgāt sravad amṛtaniṣyanda sulabhā,
tayā viddho yogī vicarati niśāyām api divā
divā bhānū rātrau vidhur iva kṛtārthī kṛta matiḥ;

Subh., v.52, p.306;

also,

sarasvatyā lakṣmyā vidhi hari sapatno viharate

rateḥ pātivratyaṁ śithilayati ramyeṇa vapuṣā,

ciraṁ jīvann eva kṣapita paśu pāśa vyatikaraḥ

parānandābhikhyaṁ rasayati rasaṁ tvad bhajanvān;

S.L., v.99, p.II-290a.

646 H.S. Prasad, 'Dreamless Sleep and Soul: a controversy between Vedānta and

Buddhism' in Asian Philosophy, vol. 10, p.72.

647 "The inhibition holds steady for a time, and that time is experienced as progressively longer, increasing with each repitition. From that experience of the lengthening time of the steadiness of the inhibition, it is inferred that there is a *saṅskāra* produced by mind in the state of inhibiton."

Y.S.V., aph. I-51, pp.171f;

also,

"When that *samādhi* called Raincloud of *Dharma*, corresponding with the maturing of right vision, comes about, *has been attained, Ignorance and other tatints are annihilated with their roots,* completely dissolved along with the *saṅskāra*-groups............ When that illusion has faded away, no one is ever known to be (re-)born anywhere."

ibid., aph. IV-30, p.411.

648 prārabdhaṁ balavattaraṁ khalu vidāṁ bhogena tasya kṣayaḥ

samyag jñāna hutāśanena vilayaḥ prāk saṁcit āgāminām,

brahmātmaikyam avekṣya tanmayatayā sarvadā saṁsthitās

teṣāṁ tat tritayaṁ na hi kvacid api brahmaiva te nirguṇam;

Viv.Cd., v.453, p.169.

[649] taṭillekhā tanvīṁ tapana śaśi vaiśvānaramayīṁ

niṣaṇṇāṁ ṣaṇṇām apy upari kamalānāṁ tava kalām,

mahā padmāṭavyāṁ mṛdita mala māyena manasā

mahāntaḥ paśyanto dadhati paramāhlāda laharīm;

S.L., v.21, p.I-204a.

[650] girām āhur devīṁ druhiṇa gṛhiṇīm āgamavido

hareḥ patnīṁ padmāṁ hara sahacarīm adri tanayām,

turīyā kāpi tvaṁ duradhigama niḥsīma mahimā

mahāmāyā viśvaṁ bhramayasi para brahma mahiṣi;

ibid., v.97, p.II-277a.

[651] pṛthivyāpas tejaḥ pavana gagane tat prakṛtayaḥ

sthitās tanmātrāstā viṣaya daśakaṁ mānasam iti,

tathā māyā vidyā tadanu ca maheśaḥ śiva itaḥ

paraṁ tattvātītaṁ milita vapur indoḥ para kalā;

Subh., v.5, p.28;

also,

vadanty eke santaḥ para śiva pade tattva milite

tatas tvaṁ ṣaḍviṅśā bhavasi śivayor melana vapuḥ;

ibid., v.35, p.206.

[652] girām āhur devīṁ druhiṇa gṛhiṇīm āgamavido

hareḥ patnīṁ padmāṁ hara sahacarīm adri tanayām,

turīyā kāpi tvaṁ duradhigama niḥsīma mahimā

mahāmāyā viśvaṁ bhramayasi para brahma mahiṣi;

S.L., v.97, p.II-277a.

[653] Rajesh Kumar Jha, 'Advaitism as Revealed in the Saundarya-laharī of Śaṅkara' in

Philosophy, Grammar and Indology, p.215.

[654] japo jalpaḥ śilpaṁ sakalam api mudrā viracanā

gatiḥ prādakṣiṇya kramaṇam aśanādy āhuti vidhiḥ

praṇāmas saṁveśas sukham akhilam ātmārpaṇa dṛśā

saparyā paryāyas tava bhavatu yan me vilasitam;

S.L., v.27, p.I-236a.

[655] ...sahasrāre padme subhaga subhagodeti subhage,

paraṁ saubhāgyaṁ yat tad iha tava sāyujya padavī;

Subh., v.51, p.300.

[656] teṣāṁ caturṇāṁ madhye jñānī tattvavit tattvavittvān nitya yukto bhavaty eka bhaktiś cānyasya bhajanīyasyādarśanād ataḥ sa eka bhaktir viśiṣyate viśeṣam ādhikyam āpadyate'tiricyata ity arthaḥ;

Bh.G.Bh., VII-17, pp.115f.

[657] avidyām antas timira mihira dvīpa nagarī

jaḍānāṁ caitanya stabaka makaranda sruti jharī,

daridrāṇāṁ cintāmaṇi guṇanikā janma jaladhau

nimagnānāṁ daṁṣṭrā mura ripu varāhasya bhavati;

S.L., v.3, p.I-58a;

also,

girām āhur devīṁ druhiṇa gṛhiṇīm āgamavido

hareḥ patnīṁ padmāṁ hara sahacarīm adri tanayām,

turīyā kāpi tvaṁ duradhigama niḥsīma mahimā

mahāmāyā viśvaṁ bhramayasi para brahma mahiṣi;

ibid., v.97, p.II-277a.

[658] K.H. Potter, Encyclopedia of Indian Philosophies, pp.77f.

[659] Śaṅkara has also authored *Śivānanda-laharī* and a *bhāṣya* on the *Viṣṇu sahasra nāma stotram*.

[660] ato'syāḥ saṁsiddhau subhaga subhagākhyā guru kṛpā

kaṭākṣavyāsaṁgāt sravad amṛtaniṣyanda sulabhā,

tayā viddho yogī vicarati niśāyām api divā

divā bhānū rātrau vidhur iva kṛtārthī kṛta matiḥ; Subh., v.52, p.306.

Bibliography

Primary Sources

A Thousand Teachings (The Upadeśasāhasrī of Śaṅkara), tr. Sengaku Mayeda, Univ. of Tokyo Press, Tokyo, 1979.

Bhagavadgītā (with bhāṣya of Śaṅkara), tr. Swāmī Gambhīrānanda, Advaita Ashrama, Pithoragarh, first ed., 1984.

Brahma-Sūtra-Bhāṣya of Śrī Śaṅkarācārya, tr. Swāmī Gambhīrānanda, Advaita Ashrama, Pithoragarh, fourth ed., 1983.

Brahma Sūtra Śāṅkara Bhāṣyam, ed. Śrī Anantakrishna Śāstrī, Chowkhamba Sanskrit Series Office, Varanasi, 1982.

Chāndogya Upaniṣad (with bhāṣya of Śaṅkara), tr. Swāmī Gambhīrānanda, Advaita Ashrama, Pithoragarh, second ed., 1992.

Eight Upaniṣads, vol. I (Īśā, Kena, Kaṭha and Taittirīya, with bhāṣya of Śaṅkara), tr. Swāmī Gambhīrānanda, Advaita Ashrama, Pithoragarh, second ed., 1991, (first ed. 1957).

Eight Upaniṣads, vol. II (Aitareya, Muṇḍaka, Māṇḍūkya & Kārikā,and Praśna, with bhāṣya of Śaṅkara), tr. Swāmī Gambhīrānanda, Advaita Ashrama, Pithoragarh, 1992.

Īśādinavopaniṣadaḥ (Īśā, Kena, Kaṭha, Praśna, Muṇḍaka, Māṇḍūkya, Taittirīya, Aitareya and Chāndogya, with bhāṣya of Śaṅkara), ed. Pt. Hari Raghunath Bhagvat, Chaukhamba Sanskrit Pratishthan, Delhi, first ed., 1991.

Kṛṣṇa-yajurvedīya Śvetāśvataropaniṣac chāṅkara bhāṣyopetā (Śvetāśvatara Upaniṣad with bhāṣya of Śaṅkara), Ananda Ashrama, Pune, 1982.

Pañcīkaraṇam of Śaṅkara, Advaita Ashrama, Pithoragarh, 1992.

Prapañcasāra Tantra of Śaṅkara, ed. Aṭalānanda Sarasvatī, Motilal Banarsidass, Delhi, 1989, (first ed. 1935).

Śaṅkara on the Yoga Sūtra-s, tr. Trevor Leggett, Motilal Banarsidass Publishers Private Limited, Delhi, first ed., 1992.

Saundarya-Laharī of Śaṅkara, tr. and commentary by Pandit S. Subrahmanya Sastri and T.R. Srinivasa Ayyangar, The Theosophical Publishing House, Adyar, 1985, (first ed. 1937).

Saundarya-Laharī of Śaṅkara (with the bhāṣya-s Lakṣmīdharā, Saubhāgyavardhanī, Aruṇāmodinī, Ānandagirīyā, Tāparyadīpinī, Padārthacandrikā, Ḍiṇḍimabhāṣya, Gopālasundarī, Ānandalaharī and Kaivalyavardhanī), ed., tr. and notes by A. Kuppuswami, Nag Publishers, Delhi, 1991.

Śrīmadbhagavadgītā (with bhāṣya of Śaṅkara), ed. Pt. Gaṇeśaśāstrī Jośī, Ananda Ashrama, Pune, 1981.

Śrī Rājarājeśvarī-Tripurasundarī Nityārādhana-Stotrāṇi, (containing Lalitā-Sahasranāma-Stotram), compiled by Sadānanda Brahmacārī, Published by Sri Arjun Bhai Modhavadiya, Dvarka, first ed., 1995.

Śrīvidyā-Ratna-Sūtram of Gauḍapāda (with bhāṣya of Śaṅkarāraṇya), Śrī Pītāmbarā Saṅskṛta Pariṣad, Datia (M.P.), 1979.

Subhagodaya-stotram of Gauḍapāda (with 'Amṛta-jharikānvayārtha-bodhinī' commentary of Swāmī Kāśikānanda Giri), Śrī Swāmī Kāśikānandaji Trust, Bombay, 1986.

Śvetāśvatara Upaniṣad (with bhāṣya of Śaṅkara), tr. Swāmī Gambhīrānanda, Advaita Ashrama, Pithoragarh, first ed., 1986.

The Bṛhadāraṇyaka Upaniṣad (with bhāṣya of Śaṅkara), tr. Swāmī Mādhavānanda, Advaita Ashrama, Pithoragarh, sixth ed., (first ed. 1934).

The Bṛhadāraṇyakopaniṣad (Upaniṣadbhāṣyam - vol. 3) (with bhāṣya of Śaṅkara), ed. Shri S. Subrahmanya Shastri, Mahesh Research Institute, Varanasi, first ed., 1986.

Vedāntaparibhāṣā of Dharmarāja Adhvarin, ed. and tr. S.S. Suryanarayana Sastri, The Theosophical Society, Adyar, 1984, (first ed. 1942).

Vivekacuḍāmaṇi of Śaṅkara, tr. Swāmī Mādhavānanda, Advaita Ashrama, Pithoragarh, 1992.

Secondary Sources

Bannerjee, N.V., *The Spirit of Indian Philosophy,* Arnold-Heinemann Publishers, New Delhi, first ed., 1974.

Bhattacharya, K.C., 'Studies in Vedāntism', *Studies in Philosophy,* ed. Gopinath Bhattacharya, Motilal Banarsidass, Delhi, second ed., 1983.

Bhattacharya, Surendranath, 'The Philosophy of Śaṅkara', *The Cultural Heritage of India,* vol. III, ed. Haridas Bhattacharya, The Ramakrishna Mission Institute of Culture, Calcutta, 1983, (first ed. 1953).

Bhave, Vinoba, *Gītā Pravacana,* Sarva-sevā-saṅgha Prakāśana, Varanasi, 1983.

Carr, Brian, 'Śaṅkarācārya', *Companion Encyclopedia of Asian Philosophy,* ed. Brian Carr and Indira Mahalingam, Routledge, London, 1997.

Dasgupta, S.N., *A History of Indian Philosophy,* vol. I, Motilal Banarsidass, Delhi, 1975, (first ed. 1922).

Dutta, D.M., *The Six Ways of Knowing,* University of Calcutta, Calcutta, 1972, (first ed. 1932).

Devaraja, N.K., 'Self and Freedom: The Vedāntic and Phenomenological
Perspectives', *Philosophy, Grammar and Indology,* ed. H.S. Prasad, Sri Satguru Publications, Delhi, 1992.

Gupta, Bina, *Perceiving in Advaita Vedānta,* Motilal Banarsidass, Delhi, 1995.

Hiriyanna, M., *Outlines of Indian Philosophy,* Blackie & Son Publishers Pvt. Ltd., Delhi, 1983, (first ed. 1932).

Jha, Rajesh Kumar, 'Advaitism as Revealed in the Saundarya-laharī of Śaṅkara', *Philosophy, Grammar and Indology,* ed. H.S. Prasad, Sri Satguru Publications, Delhi, 1992.

Jha, Rajesh Kumar, 'Post-modrnism and Advaitic Spirituality', *Reason, Dialectic and Postmodern Philosophy,* ed. Dr. Raghvendra Pratap Singh, Om Publications, Faridabad, 2001.

Mahadevan, T.M.P., *The Philosophy of Advaita,* Ganesh & Co., Madras, 1957.

Manju, *Advaitavāda aura Śūnyavāda,* Eastern Book Linkers, Delhi, 1986.

Manju, *Bhāratīya Darśana me Parivartan kā Svarūpa,* Eastern Book Linkers, Delhi, 1985.

Matilal, B.K., *Logic, Language and Reality,* Motilal Banarsidass, Delhi, 1985.

Murti, T.R.V., *The Central Philosophy of Buddhism,* George Allen & Unwin, London, 1980, (first ed. 1955).

Pandeya, R.C. and Manju, 'Pūrva Mīmāṁsā and Vedānta', *Companion Encyclopedia of Asian Philosophy,* ed. Brian Carr and Indira Mahalingam, Routledge, London, 1997.

Potter, K.H., *Encyclopedia of Indian Philosophies,* ed. K.H. Potter, Motilal Banarsidass, Delhi, 1981.

Prasad, H.S., 'Dreamless Sleep and Soul: a controversy between Vedānta and Buddhism', *Asian Philosophy,* vol. 10, 1, 2000.

Raju, P.T., *Stuctural Depths of Indian Thought,* South Asian Publishers, New Delhi, 1985.

Raman, N.S.S., *Methodological Studies in the History of Religions,* Indian Institute of Advanced Studies, Shimla, 1998.

Sarasvatī Śrī Hariharānanda (Śrī Karapātrī Swāmī), *Śrīvidyā-Ratnākaraḥ,* ed. Śrī Sitārāma Kavirāja, Śrīvidyā Sādhanā Pīṭham, Varanasi, second ed., 1987.

Sharma, C.D., *A Critical Survey of Indian Philosophy,* Motilal Banarsidass, Delhi, 1987, (first ed. 1960).

Sundaram, P.K., *Advaita Epistemology,* ed. T.M.P. Mahadevan, University of Madras, Madras, 1984, (first ed. 1968).

Tripathi, Ramakant, *Brahmasūtra Śāṅkara-bhāṣya (catuḥsūtrī),* Uttar Pradesh Hindi Granth Academy, Lucknow, 1975.

Tripathi, Ramakant, *Spinoza in the Light of the Vedānta,* Bhargava Bhushan Press, Varanasi, 1957.

Winternitz, Maurice, *History of Indian Literature,* vol. I, Motilal Banarsidass, Delhi, 1981.

www.ingramcontent.com/pod-product-compliance
Ingram Content Group UK Ltd.
Pitfield, Milton Keynes, MK11 3LW, UK
UKHW022214230426
12048UKWH00016BA/833

9 789356 681125